Fish Communities in Tropical Freshwaters

Fish Communities in Tropical Freshwaters

Their distribution, ecology and evolution

R. H. Lowe-McConnell, DSc.

Longman
London and New York

LONGMAN GROUP LIMITED
London

Associated companies, branches and representatives throughout the world

Published in the United States of America by
Longman Inc., New York.

First published 1975

Library of Congress Cataloging in Publication Data
Lowe-McConnell, R H
Fish communities in tropical freshwaters
Bibliography: p. 284
Including indexes.
1. Fishes, Fresh-water—Topics. 2. Fishes—Ecology. I. Title.
QL637.5.L68. 597'.05'26360913 74-75103
ISBN 0-582-44348-2

Filmset by Keyspools Limited, Golborne, Lancashire
and printed in Great Britain by
Whitstable Litho Limited, Whitstable, Kent

Dedication
To the many without whom this book would never have been written

Preface

This book is based on field studies over a long series of years in many parts of the tropics, born of the delight of watching fishes in their natural environments, for these waters are often large natural aquaria in which the interactions of many species may be observed. In such a book it is unfortunately not possible to describe fully the sounds and smells, the warmth and the colour, the interest of the local fishermen, the bird calls along the rivers, the glancing light – all the many-splendoured facets that make up the environmental whole. Yet often it is just the glancing light that gives a fish away, a ripple on the water surface, a shadow on the stream floor, leading predator to prey and woven into the overall pattern.

Freshwater fishes form a vital part of the diets of people throughout the tropics. The fact that the human population is increasing so alarmingly rapidly, lays emphasis on the urgent need to develop these resources fully, and to do this we need to understand the factors governing fish production. The aim of this book is to draw together material from widely scattered sources on various aspects of fish ecology, to make the findings more readily available, and to point to gaps in our knowledge. The need for further research is immense but time and resources to do it are limited.

The tropical fish fauna is a very rich one. The names of fishes, and even of their families (listed in Appendix 2), will be unfamiliar to most students in temperate regions. Students need not try to memorize these names (many of which may have to be changed as more is known about the relationship of the fishes), and may like to skip through Chapter 2 dealing with the fish fauna, returning to this after they have read later chapters. Reference to the outline drawings of the fishes characteristic of each continent, to Appendix 2, and the use of the index where the principal information about a fish is indicated, should help.

The bibliography, which draws attention to little-known publications (often difficult to obtain), is designed primarily for the specialist reader; publications readily available and helpful to the general reader are marked with an asterisk. The following books complement this book by dealing with certain aspects in more detail and have full bibliographies: *Methods for the assessment of fish production in freshwaters*, IBP Handbook no. 3, ed. W. E. Ricker, second edition 1971; *Tropical inland fisheries*, C. F. Hickling, 1961; *Fish Culture*, C. F. Hickling, second edition 1971; *The Cichlid Fishes of the Great Lakes of Africa: their biology and evolution*, G. Fryer and T. D. Iles, 1972; *The Inland waters of Tropical Africa: an introduction to tropical limnology*, L. C. Beadle, 1974. *The Nile: biological portrait of an ancient river*, ed. J. Rzoska, is in preparation.

Acknowledgements

'No man is an island' and this book, the product of field experience mainly in Africa and South America over more than a quarter of a century, owes its being to so many helpful people that it is impossible to mention them all by name. My especial thanks go to Dr E. B. Worthington who first made it possible for me to work in Africa; to Dr E. Trewavas who taught me what fishes I should find there and who has throughout all the years been a constant source of helpful information; to Dr P. H. Greenwood, a colleague first on the staff of the East African Fisheries Research Organization and later at the British Museum (Natural History) for stimulating discussions throughout; also to Mr R. S. A. Beauchamp, Director of EAFRO and to other colleagues on the staff of EAFRO; to colleagues and visitors at the British Museum (Natural History), and those involved in the International Biological Programme study on Lake George, Uganda. To Dr C. F. Hickling, Fisheries Adviser, and to the many who made the five years in Guyana (South America) so fruitful, particularly Mr E. McTurk, Mr W. H. L. Allsopp, Mrs M. Orella. To many members of the Tropical Ecology Group of the British Ecological Society, and Dr Dan Janzen, who broadened my ecological ideas and stimulated the desire to make data from tropical fish ecology available to a wider circle of ecologists. A very great deal, too, has been learnt from the fishermen of the lakes and rivers, from those observant people living on the shores of Lake Malawi (where I first worked) to the silently watching Amerindians hunting with bow and arrow the fishes in the natural aquaria of the forest streams of South America.

I am most grateful to the Trustees of the British Museum (Natural History) for working space on my return from the tropics and for the use of their splendid library facilities; to the Linnean Society of London for Appleyard Bequest funds to assist with travel expenses; to the Royal Society for the opportunity to work in the Mato Grosso and to attend International Biological Programme regional meetings in Argentina and Southeast Asia, where I learnt so much from those working over a very wide area.

Mr Gordan Howes has very kindly redrawn the fish figures (and also read an early draft of the script), and I would like to thank Mr P. B. Bayley for letting me use unpublished photographs of fishes. For permission to use previously published illustrations I am indebted to many authors, and to the following: the Zoological Society of London; the Linnean Society of London; The International Association for Theoretical and Applied Limnology; the Regents of the University of California; Dr W. Junk, b.v.; Oliver and Boyd; Her Majesty's Stationery Office; the Food and Agriculture Organization of the United Nations; the National Aeronautical and Space Agency, U.S.A.: and to the publishers of *Revue de Zoologie et de Botanique Africaines*; *Revista Brasiliera de Biologia*; *Physis Buenos Aires*; *Atas do Simpósio sôbre a Biota Amazónica* (Conselho Nacional de Pesquisas Brazil); *Biotropica*; *Annales Musée Royal de l'Afrique Centrale*.

To Dr M. E. Varley (Peggy Brown) I owe a special debt of gratitude for spurring me on to complete this book and for reading various incomprehensible drafts of it and making many helpful suggestions; also to Professor L. C. Beadle for his helpful criticisms of an early draft; and not least to my forbearing husband Richard who has 'lived with this book for so long'.

Cover photographs

top: An Amazon tributary, Mato Grosso (photo: Douglas Botting)
centre: Fisherman in the Malagarasi swamps, Tanzania (photo: R. H. Lowe-McConnell)
bottom: Tilapia from Lake Malawi, important food fishes (photo: Professor H. Peters)

Contents

Figures

Tables

1

Introduction

Why study tropical fish communities? Their significance for world food requirements

The brilliant colours, bizarre shapes and curious habits of many small tropical fishes are well known to aquarists, and throughout the tropics freshwater fishes are of immense importance in providing protein food for humans, especially in areas far from the sea and where cattle cannot be reared. The demand for such protein is rising exponentially with the rapidly accelerating increase in human population and attempts to raise living standards. Assessments of world protein requirements indicate that a fifteen to twenty-fold increase in fish production is needed in the next three decades, and that inland waters where control can be exercised over the factors governing production will have to bear the brunt of this increasing demand (Holt, 1967). There is thus an urgent need to understand the factors involved in fish production.

Fishes in tropical waters are also of the greatest interest to students of evolution, for the explosive speciations that have occurred, for instance among the cichlid fishes of the Great Lakes of Africa and among catfishes and characoids in South American rivers, have much to tell us about how new species evolve and how communities change with time. In aquaria tropical fishes are also being used for behaviour studies, and for these background information is much needed on how fishes behave under natural conditions.

Although the study of ecological processes is of fundamental importance for man's continued existence and wellbeing, tropical studies are still in their infancy, and theories about tropical communities are based on few hard data, many of them culled from the behaviour of bird or insect populations. Fishes have been investigated more than any other vertebrate group in the tropics (except man), as they are so important as food throughout the region, but the results have generally been published in specialist reports not readily available to the general ecologist and a wider public. This book aims to draw attention to such material, to make the findings more readily available, and to point to gaps in our knowledge. Tropical ecosystems are now being changed so fast by man, as he clears the forest, introduces new agricultural systems, and creates new lakes for hydroelectric power, that it is of paramount importance to study the complex web of interrelationships in order to avoid irreparable damage to the environment and its faunas.

Tropical communities are noted for the high diversity of flora and fauna and this certainly applies to the fishes. The Amazon system has over 1300 known species of fish, and the Zaïre (Congo) nearly as many, compared with but 192 fish species for the whole of Europe, or 250 from the Mississippi system in North America. Three of the African Great Lakes each have about 200 fish species, most of them endemic, species which have evolved in that particular lake and whose natural distribution is restricted to it. The Amazon and Zaïre drainages are vast, and the question arises as to whether the high numbers of species result from the many tributaries each carrying different species, or from many species actually sharing a habitat. Evidence reviewed in this book shows that each of these alternatives is in some respects true; it is not at all uncommon to catch up to fifty species of fish from one small pool in many parts of the tropics. The fish communities within one habitat are thus very complex, much more so than in temperate habitats, and questions then arise as to how so many species manage to coexist, and why so many species have evolved. For this we need to study the ecology of the fishes.

Ecology is the study of the relationships between an organism and its surroundings (in its oikos or home). Organisms cannot live as isolated units and the activities which comprise their lives are dependent upon, and closely controlled by, external circumstances, the physical and chemical conditions in which they live, and the populations of other organisms with which they interact. This complex entity of interacting inorganic and biotic elements is known as an *ecosystem*. Each aquatic ecosystem contains a number of interacting communities, for instance a lake has communities of littoral (inshore-dwelling), demersal or benthic (bottom-living), and pelagic (openwater-living) species. Throughout life fishes, like nearly all other creatures, need oxygen and food for their maintenance and growth, and shelter or some way of escaping from their enemies. The fishes themselves affect their surroundings, altering them in various ways. Ecosystems also evolve as the communities within them change and become more complex.

All living processes involve energy changes. The photosynthetic activities of plants transform energy from solar radiation into chemical energy of organic compounds, which is then transferred through the ecosystem by means of food chains or webs. The organic waste materials are decomposed by bacteria and fungi making inorganic salts available for recirculation in further plant and animal biomass. The ecosystem is thus a working, changing and evolving sequence of operations, powered by solar energy. The intake of energy to the system is balanced by energy loss as heat.

Communities and whole faunas are continually changing with time, though the scale and speed of change varies very much with the ecological conditions and with the faunas involved. On the geological time scale geomorphological changes (changes in land form and levels) and river captures bring new faunal elements into the system. The formation of a new lake behind a river blockage or dam leads to the riverine communities gradually becoming lacustrine ones, a process which it has recently been possible to study as experimental situations are provided by the formation of new manmade lakes. The history and geography of the area dictate the basic stocks of fish which gain access to it. Whether the fish then manage to persist there depends on whether suitable ecological conditions are present for all stages of the life history, for fishes are very mobile creatures, searching out different habitats to suit the particular requirements of the eggs, the young fish, juveniles or adults. Their social requirements change too, many fishes living in shoals when young, but in pairs or solitarily when adult. Thus the composition of the fish communities, the group of interacting populations within a particular habitat, may be changing continually.

The result of the interplay between fish and environment is that in certain places communities are very stable throughout the year and from year to year, and probably over long periods of time, while in other places community membership is changing radically all the time, often with seasonal regularity. The evolutionary effects of these different types of community are explored in a later chapter. Some fish species are eurytopic, that is to say they can withstand a great range of environmental conditions, such as changing temperatures or salinities, and they can eat diverse types of food, while other species are stenotopic, tolerating only a very narrow range of conditions.

The diversity of fish life

Fishes, cold-blooded vertebrates with gills and fins, are the oldest group of vertebrates and the most numerous. About 20 000 fish species are known (compared with about 4500 mammals, 8600 birds, and 8500 reptiles and amphibia). During the long course of their evolution fishes have become adapted for life in many kinds of aquatic environment, from the depths of the seas to high mountain streams, from the tropics to polar regions, even penetrating into hot springs and soda lakes, or living in the gill cavities of larger fishes. They range in size from a few centimetres to over 5 metres long. Forms and colours vary with the way of life: slender, swift silvery piscivores living in open water, deep-bodied vertically striped browzers in quiet water among water plants, armoured catfishes lurking beneath stones in swift rivers, long-snouted fishes probing bottom sediments for food organisms. Many fishes live in shoals, swimming and turning as though one organism: many of the more highly evolved species live solitary lives, guarding territories, using flashes of colour or sound, or electric signals, or scents, to signal to other members of the community. Most fishes lay eggs, casting abundant spawn into the water, where eggs may float, but more usually in freshwater sink to the bottom, or the fish may strew their eggs amongst water plants; many of the more highly evolved species make nests wherein they guard their less numerous young. Fishes thus present a wide variety of form and habit, and nowhere is this greater than in tropical waters, providing rich material for ecological studies.

Living fishes fall into three classes:

1. *Agnatha*, jawless lampreys and hagfishes not represented in tropical freshwaters;
2. *Chondrichthyes*, jawed fishes with cartilaginous skeletons, including the Elasmobranchii (sharks, rays etc), some of which have penetrated tropical rivers from the sea;
3. *Osteichthyes*, bony fishes, which include both (*a*) a few very ancient forms such as the lungfishes (Dipnoi) and lobefinned bichirs (Polyteridae), both found only in tropical freshwaters, and (*b*) the majority of living fishes, the rayfinned Actinopterygii. The fossil record suggests that some of the sharks and the lungfishes have changed little through the 350 million years (m.y.) since they first evolved in Devonian times, and the lobefins are also very old (Table 2.1). The Actinopterygii first appeared in the Jurassic less than 180 m.y. ago and have diverged to produce a multitude of new forms in the 100 m.y. since the early Cretaceous.

Species change through geological time, some only very gradually, others very rapidly. A *species* is a group of similar individuals having a common origin and a continuous breeding system. It thus represents a natural unit, though in practice it is divided by environmental factors into smaller interbreeding populations. Fishes in distinct geographical areas may be recognisable as subspecies. Species are grouped together as *genera*, hypothetical assemblages of species populations having a number of characters in common. These genera are in turn grouped into families, and they in their turn into suborders and orders, in each case sharing certain characters. Thus by knowing the systematic position of any fish, we also know a good deal about its characteristics and its relationships with other fishes.

Of the 20 000 recent fish species known to science, over 40 per cent live in freshwaters, and the majority of these live in waters lying within the tropics (i.e. between latitudes 23½° N to 23½° S). There are about 6650 species of primary freshwater fishes, belonging to families totally restricted to freshwater, and about 6200 of these belong to the Superorder group known as the Ostariophysi; there are another 1625 species of secondary freshwater fishes (freshwater representatives of marine groups), plus 115 diadromous species, which move between freshwater and the sea. This astonishingly high number of species of freshwater fishes reflects the degree of isolation possible in freshwater environments (Cohen, 1970).

The scientific names used for fishes express generic relationships and often some characteristic of the species, or where it lives, or who first collected it. Local names may cover a number of species, but once a species has been described and named, International Rules of Nomenclature govern any change of scientific name. If later study shows that a species has been named more than once the earliest name has priority. Or further study may show that two species previously grouped together in one genus are sufficiently distinct to warrant separate generic names: for example the mormyrid fishes of Africa have just been extensively revised, which entails the use of many new generic names (Taverne, 1972). As new nations emerge many names of countries and geographical features have also been changed (for example the Congo is now Zaïre).

Tropical regions and their characteristics

The tropical belt includes four main landmasses with their enclosed freshwaters (Fig. 1.1): South and Central America; Africa; tropical Asia and islands on the continental shelf; and northern Australia. These are known respectively as the Neotropical, Ethiopian, Oriental and Australian zoogeographical regions.

Africa, the largest landmass, is bisected by the equator into comparable areas of freshwater to the north and south of it. South America also lies across the equator, but here most of the landmass is in the southern hemisphere. Central America lies within the tropics too; for historical reasons the fish fauna here is a mixture of attenuated South American and North American faunas, with active speciation in some groups. The Asian division of the tropics includes the subcontinent of *India* lying well to the north of the equator, *mainland Southeast Asia* reaching down into equatorial regions, with the islands of the continental shelf straddling the equator. *Australia* lacks primary freshwater fishes except a lungfish and osteoglossid. This book is concerned mainly with studies in African and South American waters, where the author has had most field experience.

Tropical regions are characterised by high temperatures, except where these are modified by altitude, and by relatively little seasonal variation in temperature or daylength compared with temperate regions. In equatorial regions the daylength is practically constant at twelve hours throughout the year; even at 10° N and 10° S annual variations in day length are less than one hour. Seasonal variations do, however, exist in most parts of the tropics, caused primarily by fluctuations in rainfall, which lead to regular flooding of immense tracts of country, expanding the aquatic environments seasonally on a scale quite unknown outside the tropics.

As tropical rains fall mainly when the sun is overhead, rainfall maxima occur mainly around May to July north of the equator and November to January south of it. The rainy seasons are, however, modified by the shape of the continent, the presence of mountain masses, and the wind systems. Equatorial regions have two rainfall peaks a year centred on the March and September equinoxes as the sun passes overhead. In Kenya such rains cause the rivers to flood twice each year, though which peak causes the main flood may vary from year to year.

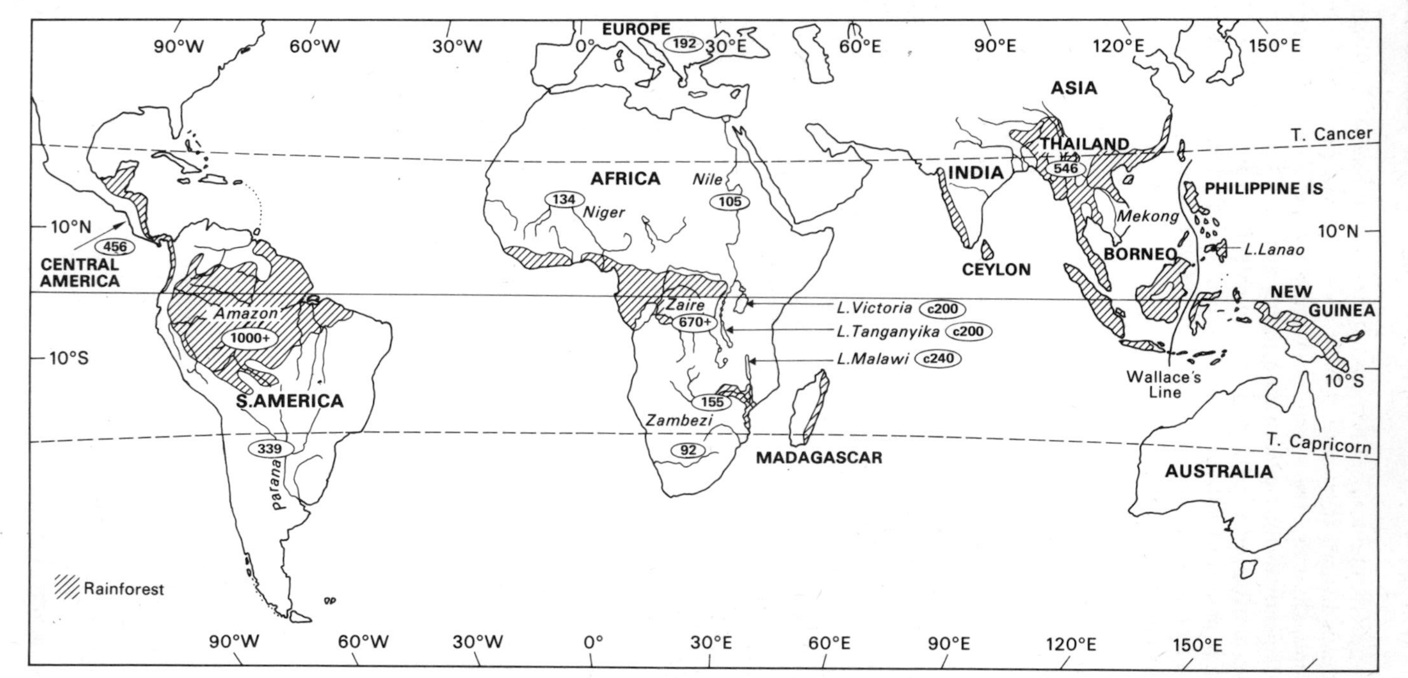
90°W
60°W
30°W
0°
30°E
60°E
90°E
120°E
150°E
EUROPE
192
ASIA
T. Cancer
THAILAND
546
INDIA
PHILIPPINE IS
AFRICA
Nile
105
134
Niger
10°N
456
CENTRAL AMERICA
Mekong
BORNEO
L.Lanao
CEYLON
NEW GUINEA
Zaire
670+
Amazon
1000+
L.Victoria c200
L.Tanganyika c200
L.Malawi c240
10°S
Wallace's Line
S.AMERICA
155
Zambezi
T. Capricorn
339
92
MADAGASCAR
AUSTRALIA
Parana
Rainforest

The equatorial regions have the heaviest rainfall (over 1500 mm per annum) and the rain is well distributed throughout the year. The seasonality of the climate, including rainfall and flooding, increases northwards and southwards with increasing latitude. The zones of heaviest rainfall carry dense forest (except where this has been cleared by man) through which large permanent rivers flow; this forest slows the runoff from the land. Bush, passing to wooded savanna, savanna, then desert succeed each other progressively in areas of lower rainfall, and the rivers diminish in volume and persistence, drying into seasonal pools. The mirror image effect of decreasing rainfall with increasing latitude to north and south of the equator can best be seen in Africa, though the most arid regions within the African tropics are slewed to northeast and southwest. The largest river systems, the immense drainages of the Amazon and Zaïre, flowing mainly through dense forest, receive tributaries from both sides of the equator; these flood at opposite times of year, causing a bimodal flood or a prolonged highwater season in the lower reaches. The more seasonal rivers at higher latitudes inundate enormous tracts of country during the highwater seasons, flooding into seasonal swamps and over surrounding savanna. Floodwater which takes a long time to travel downstream may arrive after local floods have subsided, causing a second flood. The fishes respond to a rise in water level rather than to local rains; near Lake Chad in Africa, for example, the Chari/Logone and Yobe river systems reach peak levels at least two months after the scanty local rains have ceased, giving rise to vast areas of rich aquatic habitat on an otherwise arid plain.

The high temperatures throughout the year speed up development and growth processes. Aquatic plants may continue to grow throughout the year giving cover both to the fishes and to the aquatic invertebrates so important as fish food, and very varied food sources are generally available throughout the year compared with temperate zone habitats. The large amount of plant material decomposing in the water leads to rapid depletion of oxygen. As oxygen becomes less soluble in water as the temperature rises, deoxygenation is more of a problem in static waters at tropical temperatures than it is in temperate regions. Many tropical fishes have special respiratory adaptations enabling them to use atmospheric air. Enormous areas of swamp may dry out completely, either annually or during dry phases of climatic cycles, and certain fishes have evolved mechanisms which overcome this desiccation.

The latitude within the tropics determines the seasonality of the flood regime which has such profound effects on the biology of the fishes. Tropical conditions grade gradually into subtropical and temperate ones. Certain lakes technically within the tropics, such as L. Chad and L. Kariba, are at

Fig 1.1 The tropical regions indicating the provisional numbers of freshwater fish species found in various drainages. Note the high numbers of species in the equatorial rainforest rivers and in the Great Lakes of East Africa, compared with but 192 species for the whole of Europe.

high enough latitudes for seasonal changes in temperature and illumination to affect fish behaviour and growth. The lower temperatures at higher altitudes also affect fish biology.

In tropical lakes a seasonality may also be imposed by wind action bringing nutrient-rich bottom water into circulation; the southeast trade winds which blow from April to September up the great lakes Tanganyika and Malawi appear particularly important in this respect.

Types of aquatic environment

Aquatic environments are divided broadly into two groups: running-water (lotic environments) such as streams, and rivers; and standing-waters (lentic or lenitic environments) such as lakes, ponds and swamps. River systems pre-date lakes, which are formed when rivers are dammed. Many of the tropical river systems are immense and have a very long history, though their form may have changed radically during this time; parts of both Zaïre and Amazon for example have been large lakes at intervals in their long history. Tectonic changes have led to great changes in river level, falls and rapids forming barriers isolating fish populations, while river captures have introduced new elements into the local faunas.

The smaller 'classical' temperate rivers are typically divided into three regions: (1) torrential upper reaches with a steep profile and a swift current, flowing over rocky or stony bottoms; (2) the profile flattening as the river emerges from foothills, depositing its silt load; and (3) the river broadening out and gaining organic matter from plant and plankton-production in the slower flowing meandering lower reaches. Such temperate rivers are inhabited by a succession of fish communities, often trout in the upper reaches and 'coarse' fish such as cyprinids in the lower reaches. But the picture is much more complex in the large tropical rivers, as changes in land levels have led to rivers originating in swampy regions, while falls and rapids at widely spaced intervals along their courses allow an alternation of swift-water and calm-water species. Such alternations help to explain the high numbers of species in these tropical rivers. Classifications of types of running-water have been discussed by Hynes (1970) and Pennak (1971).

As in temperate rivers, conditions in headwater streams depend very much on the *slope*, which dictates both the current speed and the nature of the bottom deposits. Whether a stream flows through dense forest or is open to the sunlight affects the sources of fish food. Where sunlight penetrates to the water surface, algal growth or floating meadows of aquatic plants are often important sources of fish food, but where light is cut off by the overhanging forest, the fishes are very dependent on allochthonous (exogenous) foods, such as plant debris and aerial insects produced in the forest. Gallery forest persists along the streams far into savanna areas, and the width of the stream thus affects light penetration.

A feature of these large tropical rivers is the very extensive lateral flooding in the highwater season, due either to local rains or to floods arriving downstream from higher in the catchment. This lateral flooding leads to temporarily lacustrine conditions over vast areas annually, and it is hard to draw distinctions between riverine and lacustrine fishes as many fishes lead a lotic existence at low water when they retreat to the river bed, and a lentic existence in the flooded areas with their interconnected pools and swamps, in the highwater season. Conversely some fishes adapted for life in rushing waters in flooded streams have to withstand conditions in stagnant pools in the dry season. Some fishes may be trapped in ponds throughout the year in years of low rainfall. The rivers themselves, with their anastomosing channels and quiet backwaters and islands that block the current, also provide some lentic biotopes. Lotic and lentic conditions may exist side by side on river bends, where the current is less than 20 cm/sec on the inner bank but exceeds this on the opposite 'bounce' bank.

These laterally flooded areas are mainly flooded forest shaded from the sun in equatorial regions, or savanna open to the sun at higher latitudes. The forest waters remain cool and lack light for photosynthesis, and the penetration of light is often further reduced as the waters are darkly stained with humic acids. The areas of flooded savanna on the other hand heat up rapidly in the sun and there is abundant light for plant growth. Decomposing tree debris makes the flooded forest waters very acid and deoxygenated, and the trees protect the river surface from wind mixing. On the flooded savannas the oxygen falls sharply as the water rises and submerged vegetation rots, but the oxygen supply is replenished with the aid of wind mixing, diurnal temperature changes, and photosynthesis. These flood plains carry important fisheries in many parts of the tropics.

Many physical and chemical changes accompany flooding. The violent increase in water velocity may be accompanied by a drop in temperature and rise in turbidity together with changes in water chemistry. Where these effects fluctuate seasonally they are generally non-catastrophic and the aquatic life is adapted to take advantage of the flood conditions, particularly for breeding. In the smaller rivers and streams the dominant factor may be desiccation, partial or complete, which leads to spatial contraction, isolation, rise in temperature and deoxygenation. These are limiting factors to which some fishes have become adapted, but which the majority of fishes avoid by active migration when conditions become intolerable. Small streams in the tropics often rise overnight but cease to flow shortly after the rains and are then reduced to interconnected pools and swampy depressions.

The fishes respond to the changing conditions in rivers by moving about a very great deal, seemingly in a rather haphazard way (as far as we at present know) in the equatorial forest rivers, but often making very long and well-defined migrations up and down the more seasonally fluctuating rivers. Some of the fishes living in lakes may continue to make such movements up inflowing rivers to spawn, but many lake fishes appear much less influenced by seasonal changes, making more stable communities.

Large swamps are characteristic of all three tropical regions. In these the limiting factor is generally deoxygenation or desiccation in the dry season, restricting the fish fauna to species which have structural or behavioural adaptations that enable them to live through the difficult periods. Conditions in the immense swamps of Africa are discussed by Beadle (1974) and Rzoska (1974), and comparable areas in South America (for example, the Gran Chaco) and Asia present the same basic problems to the fishes even though different faunas are involved.

The immense river systems such as the Zaïre and Amazon receive tributaries which pass through both forested and open country, and through many degrees of latitude. In the forest rivers conditions are relatively stable (as in the equatorial forest itself), compared with the more seasonal conditions in the savanna rivers (and on the savannas).

Many tropical rivers have very long estuarine reaches, especially in Asia and South America, where the land surface is lower than in most of Africa. Above the brackish water zone the freshwater may be backed up by the tides for long distances (over 160 km in some Guyana rivers in South America). The fresh/salt water interface moves long distances up and down river seasonally (over 200 km up and down the Amazon).

Tropical lakes vary enormously in size from mere ponds to the 68 635 km^2 Lake Victoria in East Africa which is nearly as large as the Republic of Ireland. The ratio of inflow to storage volume also varies greatly. Certain storage reservoirs on the Nile, and probably many 'varzea' lakes on the Amazon, are flushed through with river water many times each year, whereas in Lake Tanganyika the inflow is only 1 : 1500 of the volume of water stored in the lake. In the flushed lakes new nutrients are brought in with the river water, in amounts and proportions depending very much on the geological formation over which the river flows. In lakes lacking a regular influx of nutrients, production is governed by recycling processes within the lake.

The enlargement of the pelagic zone with calm water suitable for plankton growth is a feature of lakes compared with rivers. In tropical lakes the water temperature and available light energy are generally high throughout the year, and the availability of nutrient salts for plankton growth often limits production. Tropical lakes stratify (as do temperate lakes in summer); the surface water (epilimnion), the euphotic zone inhabited by the plankton, is separated from the deeper nutrient-rich but generally deoxygenated hypolimnion water by a relatively steep temperature gradient or discontinuity (thermocline). At the higher temperatures prevailing in the tropics water has a greater density difference per degree of temperature change, and in tropical lakes stability may be maintained despite very small temperature differences between surface and bottom water. In temperate lakes winter cooling of the surface water leads to an 'overturn' bringing nutrient-rich bottom water into the euphotic zone. Most tropical lakes lack this winter cooling, and very deep lakes such as L. Tanganyika and L. Malawi, may remain more or less permanently stratified. Some nutrients are, however, mixed into the epilimnion by wind induced currents (as discussed by Beadle,

1974). These winds are often seasonal, but in shallow equatorial lakes (e.g. L. George; see p. 166) winds throughout the year lead to a daily exchange of nutrients from the bottom mud to the lake water.

The Great Lakes of East and Central Africa have been much studied, as they have valuable commercial fisheries; they also have spectacular faunas of endemic fishes, mainly cichlids, of great interest to students of evolution, as reviewed by Fryer and Iles (1972). The study of endemic species in small crater lakes in Cameroon has helped to illuminate ways in which fish communities have evolved in the Great Lakes, and the new manmade lakes have provided large-scale field experiments in which to study the changes that occur when a riverine community becomes converted into a lacustrine one.

Studies on smaller lakes include intensive work by a team on the equatorial Lake George in Uganda in an attempt to determine why this lake appears to be so productive. Lack of space precludes discussion in this book of numerous other studies in smaller lakes, many of which in Africa are considered by Beadle (1974). These include some extreme environments for fishes, such as Lake Magadi, a soda lake (pH 10·5) in the Kenya Rift Valley, with hot springs and a salinity of 40 per cent, where the small endemic *Tilapia grahami* lives in water up to 39° C, only two degrees below its lethal temperature (Coe, 1966).

South America has no comparable great lakes at the present time, but the trumpet-shaped mouths of Amazon tributary rivers have many lake-like features, and innumerable small lakes become cut off temporarily from the anastomozing river channels when the water level is low. The world's highest lakes occur in the Andes, the largest being Lake Titicaca (*c*. 7600 km^2 at 3800 m). In Southeast Asia the Great Lake of the Tonlé Sap of the Khmer Republic (formerly known as the Grand Lac of Cambodia), a lateral lake of the Mekong river system, used to support one of the world's largest freshwater fisheries, and many new lakes are now being created in the Mekong system. In India most of the lakes and 'tanks' which support fisheries are manmade. Southeast Asia has a very long tradition of pond fish culture.

2

Freshwater Fish Faunas of Tropical Regions and their Distributions

All these tropical regions have very complex freshwater fish faunas, each with several thousand species, the names of which, and even of their families, will be unfamiliar to most temperate zone readers. These families are listed in Appendix 2 for reference, and the general appearance of some characteristic fishes is shown in Figs. 2.2, 2.5 and 2.8.

Freshwater fish faunas include:

1. *primary freshwater fishes*, groups which have evolved in freshwaters since the early teleosts moved into them, are confined to them and cannot tolerate seawater (for example, the Ostariophysi, Dipnoi, Osteoglossidae, Mormyridae);
2. *secondary freshwater fishes*, of families now confined to freshwater but of marine origin and relatively tolerant of seawater at least for short periods (for example, the Cichlidae and Cyprinodontidae);
3. *freshwater representatives of marine families* (for example some clupeids, sciaenids, tetraodont puffers);
4. *diadromous fishes* making regular migrations from salt to freshwater or vice versa at different stages of the life history (for example, some anadromous clupeids and catadromous anguillid eels);
5. *occasional sporadic visitors*, euryhaline members of marine families (such as some snappers, sharks, grey mullets).

Continental freshwater faunas consist mainly of primary and secondary freshwater fishes, and only when these are scarce (as in Australia and New Guinea) do complementary species, often diadromous, dominate in freshwater (Myers, 1949). Fossil records show that families of primary freshwater fishes go back to Eocene times, but morphological evidence suggests that many groups are very much older; Myers (1967) considered that characoids evolved in freshwater in a southern continent in Jurassic or even Triassic times (Table 2.1), and have retained their physiological intolerance of seawater ever since. The distribution of primary freshwater fishes (such as Ostariophysi) thus indicates the former connections of the landmasses, as is discussed further below (p. 17), for to these fishes the sea presents an impenetrable barrier. Secondary freshwater fishes (such as cichlids) may be able to cross short stretches of sea. Freshwater representatives of marine families have probably in most cases immigrated into, or evolved within, each continental landmass independently.

Freshwater fish faunas in the tropics, as elsewhere, are dominated by the Ostariophysi (well known as carps, minnows and catfishes). These are physostome fishes (that is the swim bladder when present is connected with the alimentary canal by an open duct), characterised by the presence of Weberian ossicles, modifications of parts of the first four vertebrae which connect the swim bladder with the inner ear. Many of these ostariophysian fishes produce sounds, and some such apparatus may help with the location of sound. It has also been suggested that it may help with detection of pressure (and hence depth) changes (Alexander, 1962).

The ostariophysian fishes fall into three groups, now considered to be suborders of the Order Cypriniformes (Roberts, 1973*b*):

1. Cyprinoidei or carps,
2. Characoidei, characoids or characins (found only in South America and Africa),
3. Siluroidei or catfishes of many families.

On morphological grounds the characoids are believed to be the most primitive (Greenwood *et al*., 1966). The siluroid offshoot probably appeared very soon after the characoids (in Gondwanaland freshwaters probably in the Jurassic or Triassic, Table 2.1). Myers (1967) considered that the cyprinoid fishes probably evolved in Asia from some toothless proto-cyprinid characoid which got across the Tethys Sea from Africa, then blossomed in Eurasia into the largest family group of the Ostariophysi, and invaded Africa across the greatly shrunken Tethys in the Tertiary (when they also invaded North America via a Bering landbridge).

The cyprinids dominate the freshwater faunas of tropical Asia, as they do in the temperate zone (Fig. 2.1). They are well represented in Africa too, but entirely lacking from South America. Cyprinids lack jaw teeth but the pharyngeal teeth are well developed, and the body form is rather uniform. In South America the characoid fishes flourish and fill niches occupied by cyprinids in the other two continents. The characoids have well-developed jaw teeth which have undergone evolutionary changes in relation to the food consumed, and these fishes show much greater variation in body form than do the cyprinids. The characoids are, together with the catfishes, the dominant fishes in South American waters; other species of characoid live in Africa (no species or genera are shared), but characoids occur nowhere else in the world – none are found in Asia.

The Siluroidei includes about thirty families of catfishes from tropical waters. Two of these, the Ariidae and Plotosidae, have become secondarily marine (about the only ostariophysian fishes to do so) and are widely distributed, the former in all tropical regions including Australia, the latter in countries bordering the Indo–Pacific. There are fourteen endemic families of truly freshwater siluroids in South America, eight in Asia and three in Africa, and in addition to these the Bagridae, Schilbeidae and Clariidae occur in both Asia and Africa.

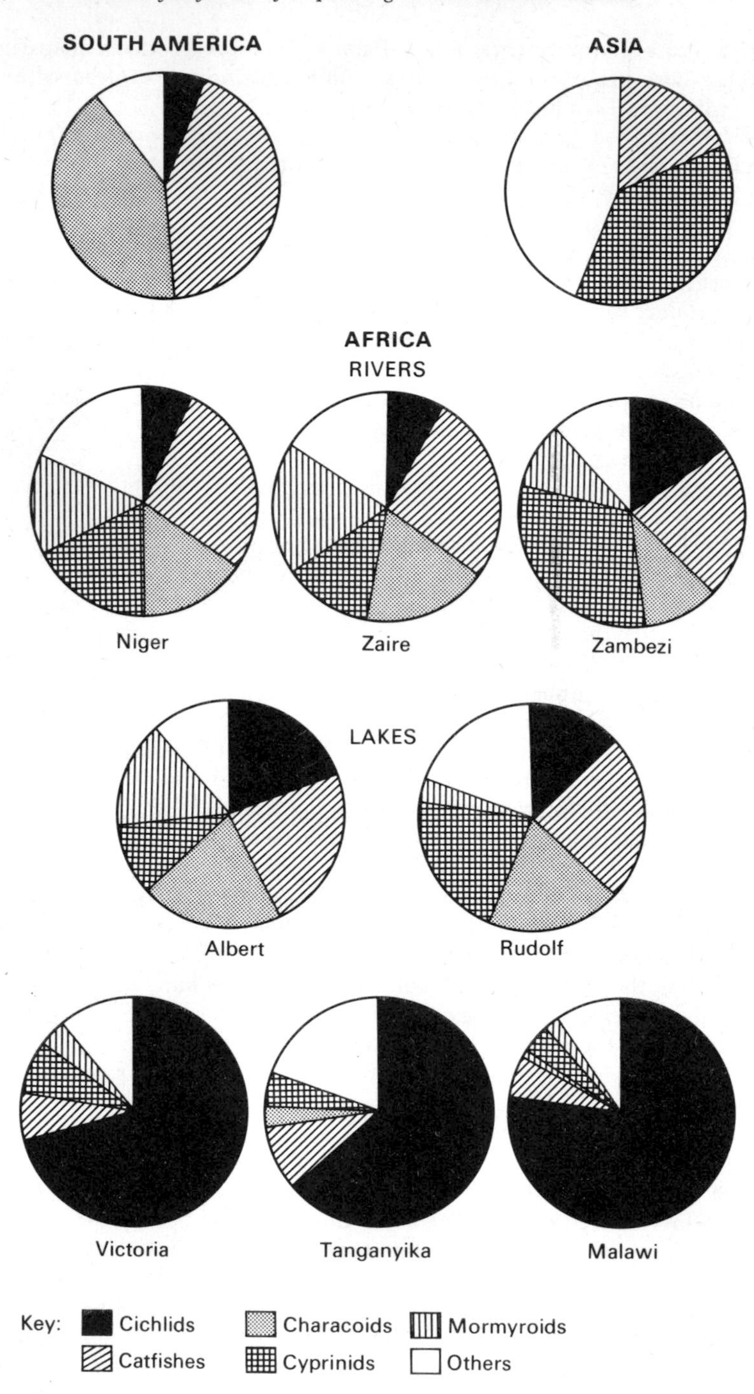
SOUTH AMERICA
ASIA
AFRICA
RIVERS
Niger
Zaire
Zambezi
LAKES
Albert
Rudolf
Victoria
Tanganyika
Malawi
Key:
Cichlids
Catfishes
Characoids
Cyprinids
Mormyroids
Others

The perchlike cichlid fishes have a natural distribution restricted to South America and Africa apart from a few species in Madagascar, Ceylon and southern India, but some tilapias are now circumtropical pond fishes. The cichlids have undergone spectacular adaptive radiations in the Great Lakes of Africa and parallel radiations in South and Central America. The genus *Cichlasoma* has evolved over seventy species in the waters of Central America (Miller, 1966). As cichlids are tolerant of seawater they may have spread from South to Central America before the Pleistocene landbridge was formed (Myers, 1966).

Relict species of certain archaic groups of primary freshwater fishes are widely distributed. The living Dipnoi comprise *Lepidosiren paradoxa* in South America, four species of *Protopterus* in Africa, and *Neoceratodus forsteri* in Queensland, Australia. The Osteoglossidae include *Arapaima gigas* and two species of *Osteoglossum* in South America, *Heterotis niloticus* in Africa, two species of *Scleropages* in Southeast Asia and Queensland in Australia.

The small family Nandidae is represented in all three tropical areas. Nandids are most numerous and include larger species such as *Nandus nandus* and *Pristolepis fasciatus* in Asia, where they also go into brackish water. Two genera of small but voracious nandids (*Monocirrhus* and *Polycentrus*) occur in South America, and another two (*Polycentropsis* and *Afronandus*) in Africa; the leaflike appearance of these fishes enables them to drift near to unsuspecting small fishes on which they prey, as is well known to aquarists.

The Cyprinodontidae, small oviparous secondary freshwater fishes, the toothed carps or killifishes of aquarists, occur in all tropical regions except Australia. In South and Central America most of the cyprinodontoids are live-bearing poeciliids.

The Notopteridae, Mastacembelidae, Anabantidae and Channidae (= Ophiocephalidae), which all occur in both Asia and Africa, are more conspicuous members of the faunas in Asia, suggesting that they probably originated there (or in India when India was closer to Asia than to Africa).

In addition to these families, there are in Africa an unparalleled assemblage of archaic primary freshwater families known only from this continent: Polypteridae, Denticipitidae, Pantodontidae, Mormyridae, Gymnarchidae, Kneriidae, Phractolaemidae. Another unique feature of the African fauna is the great flowering of osteoglossiform mormyroid electric fishes.

The proportion of freshwater fishes of marine origin is much higher in Southeast Asia and South America, where low-lying land has permitted sea fishes to move far up river, than in Africa where much of the continental

Fig. 2.1 The proportional composition of the freshwater fish faunas of *South America* (Brazil), *Asia* (Thailand), *African rivers* and *African Great Lakes*. Numbers of species expressed as a percentage of the known fauna (1 per cent = 3·6°). Note relative importance of Cichlidae in lakes and cypriniform fishes (Characoidei and Cyprinidae) in rivers (after Lowe–McConnell, 1969*b*).

landmass is high and falls or rapids near the coast obstruct the passage of fishes, as for example in the Zaïre River.

Body form is closely related to habitat, and the similarity of conditions in the three tropical areas has led to beautiful examples of parallel evolution and convergence (as can be seen by comparing Figs. 2.2, 2.5 and 2.8). Much can be learnt of the way of life of a fish from its general shape, the position of the mouth and fins, etc. Functional design in fishes, which is not specifically a tropical problem, has been discussed by Alexander (1970).

Many surface-dwelling fishes are small species, with an upturned mouth well adapted to feed on particles caught in the surface film or to take well oxygenated water from just below the surface. The habit of emerging from the water to escape from predators has been developed independently in the gasteropelecid characoids in South America (which skitter along the river surface) and in the osteoglossomorph *Pantodon* in Africa (which leaps vertically from the water). Midwater-dwellers in full current are strongly swimming fishes with fusiform bodies; these fishes often live in schools and have dark humeral and caudal spots. Fishes living in calm water amongst macrophytes generally have laterally flattened deep bodies, as do the characoid *Metynnis* in South America and *Citharinus* in Africa. Bottom dwellers such as many catfishes in all three areas are often dorsoventrally flattened, with upward-turned eyes. Crevice dwellers are often anguilliform in shape: many are nocturnal fishes with reduced eyes and other sense organs well developed. Crevices in the tree litter in forest streams provide substitutes for rock crevices.

The most outstanding example of convergence is in the electric fishes, the osteoglossomorph mormyroids in Africa with the completely unrelated gymnotoids (cypriniforms) in South America. In these, convergences in body form (Fig. 9.8) are matched by convergences in methods of producing electric signals (p. 233), and in ways of life: they are all nocturnal fishes, many hiding in crevices by day, mainly insectivorous, the larger species piscivorous. No such electric fishes are known from Asian freshwaters.

Remarkable convergences are also shown by armoured catfishes of unrelated families which occur in the stony streams of all three continents: loricariids in South America, certain amphiliid genera in Africa, and *Sisor rhabdophorus* in India (p. 253). These armoured fishes when young all live in rushing stony streams where the rapid flow might damage naked skins against the rocks. Possibly the armour by its weight helps these dorsoventrally flattened fishes to adhere to the flat rock surface when water flow is fast; the swim bladder has been lost in both *Sisor* and in the loricariids.

Adaptations for life in fast flowing water include dorsoventrally flattened bodies, enlarged horizontal paired fins, and suctorial devices enabling the fishes to adhere to rock surfaces (modified pelvic fins in some Indian fishes, suctorial mouths in others) as discussed by Hora (1930). Special modifications to enable the fish to respire are needed when the mouth adheres to the substratum. In a number of hillstream fishes the body is very elongated with a whiplash tail which propels the fish forward in rapid jerks.

Freshwater fish distribution in relation to continental movements

The affinities of African freshwater fishes have long suggested that there have been land connections between Africa and South America, and between Africa and Asia (Regan, 1929). Evidence from some fish parasites also supports this view (Manter, 1963). Recent geophysical and other evidence makes it virtually certain that a southern continent, Gondwanaland, fragmented to give rise to Africa, South America, Australia, India, Madagascar and Antarctica. The separation of Africa from South America probably began in the early Cretaceous about 100 m.y. ago, but McKenzie and Sclater (1973) now estimate that the main period of drift which produced the Atlantic Ocean dates from the late Cretaceous, *c.* 75 m.y.b.p. (before present) (Table 2.1). The characid freshwater fishes provide the strongest evidence of the former connection of Africa and South America; the generalised African genus *Alestes* and the South American genus *Brycon* appear to be the most closely related, though the smaller *Petersius* of Africa is very similar to *Astyanax* of South America (Eigenmann, 1917; Myers, 1958; Weitzman, 1962). African bagrid catfishes greatly resemble the South American pimelodids, suggesting descent from a common ancestor. The South American doradid catfishes also somewhat resemble the mochokids of Africa, but their skeletal structures are quite different, and this resemblance is apparently due to convergence (Regan, 1929).

The cyprinids, absent from South America, appear to have entered Africa from Asia long after the separation of Africa from South America. Africa was broadly connected with Arabia over a long period of time, including the Miocene (25 m.y.b.p.), but when this whole landmass was connected with Eurasia is still uncertain. The possession of the same genera of fish in the African and Asian faunas (the cyprinids *Labeo*, *Garra* and *Barilius*, also *Clarias* and *Mastacembelus*) indicates that these faunas have been in contact relatively recently. Banister (1973), reviewing relationships among the large *Barbus* of Africa and the Middle East, pointed out that there is as yet no fossil evidence to show which way these *Barbus* moved, and movements may well have been complex. Dates of possible contacts are still very uncertain. Dietz and Holden (1970, fig. 5.19) indicated a contact between Africa and Eurasia at the end of the Cretaceous (*c.* 65 m.y.b.p., long prior to the contact of India and Asia) which could have allowed a protocyprinid characoid access to Eurasia (as required by Myers, 1967, see p. 13), though Gass (1973) since suggested tentatively that the African–Arabian plate impacted Eurasia only 10 m.y.b.p. (Upper Miocene). The main Asian–African faunal exchange was probably post-Miocene.

Recent geophysical evidence suggests that India and Madagascar separated together from Africa in the Lower Jurassic (perhaps 150 m.y.b.p., Flores, 1970), too long ago for India to have taken other than ancient fishes (such as Dipnoi and osteoglossids) with it to Asia. McKenzie and Sclater (1973) suggested that the Indian plate collided with the Asian plate *c.* 45

Table 2.1 Geological time scale and events affecting freshwater fish distribution in present tropical areas (based on current interpretations of continental movements; time scales after Holmes, 1960).

TIME SCALE		Million years ago (m.y.a.)	FISH EVOLUTION	EVENTS AFFECTING FRESHWATER FISH DISTRIBUTION			
				South America	Africa	India	S.E. Asia
CAENOZOIC Quaternary	Recent		Adaptive radiations of cichlids in African Great Lakes	Manmade lakes; fish transfers by man and escapes			
	Pleistocene			Lowered sea levels during glaciations; pluvials			
				Mixing of Amazon tributary fishes	Formation of Great Lakes	Faunal exchanges with Africa	Large islands connected with mainland
		2–3					
Tertiary	Pliocene		Adaptive radiations of fish groups		L. Malawi, L. Tanganyika originate	Receives fishes from Asia	
		11					
	Miocene			Continent isolated Reversal of Amazon drainage	Africa-Arabia plate contacts Eurasia (Upper Miocene)		
		25					
	Oligocene			Andes starts to rise		Himalayas start to rise as India contacts Asia (*c.* 45 m.y.a.)	
		40					
	Eocene						
		60					
	Palaeocene				*		
		70					
MESOZOIC	Cretaceous		Many modern fish groups appear	*c.* 75 m.y.a. separation of continents as Atlantic opens			

Table 2.1 – *continued*

TIME SCALE	Million years ago (m.y.a.)	FISH EVOLUTION	EVENTS AFFECTING FRESHWATER FISH DISTRIBUTION			
			South America	Africa	India	S.E. Asia
	135				*c.* 150 m.y.a. India + Madagascar separate from Gondwanaland	
Jurassic			GONDWANALAND			
	180					
Triassic		Teleosts appear				
	225					
PALAEOZOIC						
Permian						
	270					
Carboniferous						
	350					
Devonian		Dipnoi appear				

↑ arrows denote faunal movements. Fish groups present in both South America and Africa are of Gondwanaland stock, but India and Madagascar broke away from Gondwanaland too early to take any except ancient fish groups with it to Asia. The asterisk (*) denotes a possible end-Cretaceous or early Tertiary contact between Africa and Eurasia (indicated by Dietz and Holden, 1970) which could have permitted a protocyprinid characoid access to Eurasia (as suggested by Myers, 1967, see text); the main Asia-Africa faunal exchange was probably post-Miocene, facilitated by Pleistocene lakes and sea level changes in the Middle East.

m.y.b.p. (Eocene times). Madagascar lacks characoid fishes and has none of the characteristic freshwater fishes of Africa except a few cichlids, fishes able to cross short stretches of sea. From this Regan (1929) concluded that the separation of Madagascar from Africa must be very ancient, a conclusion now supported by geophysical studies.

The endemic Madagascan cichlids (nine species) differ greatly from African ones (Trewavas, pers. comm). One genus, *Paratilapia*, is thought to be derived from African stock, and another, *Paretroplus*, to be closely related to the Indian genus *Etroplus* (Kiener and Mauge, 1966). Of Madagascar's 43 endemic fish species (32 freshwater fishes and 11 euryhaline), the freshwater species are mainly members of marine families such as Atherinidae and Gobiidae (Kiener and Richard-Vindard, 1972). The island does have three endemic catfishes but these are ariids (not bagrids as stated by Kiener), a family of catfishes which can make sea crossings. The five species of *Tilapia* and carp cultured in ponds are all introduced species.

The Indian freshwater fish fauna has many Malayan and South Chinese elements. Hora (1937) concluded that this fauna originated mainly in South China and spread westwards, aided by river captures and marshy conditions along the whole of northern India, some forms continuing westwards to Africa. Many freshwater fish fossils are known from India: (1) the lungfish *Ceratodus* from Upper Triassic deposits 170 m.y. old; (2) Upper Jurassic and Cretaceous ganoid fishes (like the *Ceratodus* these are now extinct in India); (3) Lower Eocene teleosts in peninsular India (Madhya Pradesh) of the families Osteoglossidae, Nandidae, Anabantidae and Cyprinidae; then a long gap till (4) Pliocene fossils of various catfishes and of *Channa* (Menon, 1955). Menon thought that *Ceratodus* and the ganoids entered India from the north 'probably along the corridor that stretched across the Tethys Sea through present-day Assam until the Middle Eocene'. However, the recent evidence on continental drift (summarised in Table 2.1) suggests that *Ceratodus* must have travelled with India from Gondwana, and that some (if not all) of the teleost families found fossilised in Lower Eocene deposits in peninsular India did so too (e.g. Osteoglossidae and Nandidae both shared with South America, but less likely the Anabantidae and Cyprinidae neither shared with South America). The presence of cyprinid fossils in India at this early date would suggest that the Indian–Asian contact must have occurred very early in the Eocene. Is it possible that an ancestral catfish travelled to Asia with India too?

All the fish genera common to India and Africa are also found in Asia east of India. At present India has about 89 genera of primary freshwater fishes; of these 66 also live in countries east of India, 19 both to the east and to the west, while only 1 genus occurs only to the west; the 23 endemic Indian genera are all closely related to forms found further east (Menon, 1955). None of these endemic Indian genera also occurs in Ceylon (Jayaram, 1974). The Himalayan upheaval during the Pliocene seems to have created suitable conditions for marsh-loving fishes to travel along the base of the Himalayas; fishes of the clear-flowing rivers were probably later (Pleistocene) migrants.

During glacial epochs when the sea level was 100 m or so lower, and Himalayan glaciers descended below 1500 m, conditions in Indian rivers would have been very different from those prevailing there today. Both the lowered sea levels and the formation of large lakes in the Middle East during pluvial periods could have facilitated Pleistocene exchanges between Asian and African faunas.

Hora (1937) assumed that India had been connected with the Far East 'at least from the Cretaceous onwards', whereas Indian Ocean studies now suggest that India travelled northwards relatively rapidly as an island continent until it contacted Asia in Eocene times. Hora's (1949, 1950) 'Satpura hypothesis' suggested that hillstream fishes somehow crossed the Bengal (Garo–Rajmahal) gap (through which the Ganges and Brahmaputra now reach the sea) to the Satpura trend of hills leading to the Western Ghats and thence into peninsular India. This hypothesis stimulated much biogeographical discussion (Hora *et al.*, 1949; Menon, 1951, 1955, 1973; Jayaram, 1974), but is considered unrealistic in the context of geomorphological changes and biogeographical evolution of the biota as a whole by Mani (1974). Mani suggests that possible convergences and parallel evolution of hillstream fishes from a formerly much more widely distributed common stock need to be considered – that multiple origins of species and genera may be more frequent than we realise.

Mani (1974) considered that the ancient Gondwana-derived fauna of India was a humid forest one. (The Indian amphibia are evidently almost all derivatives of Gondwana stock, as are some of the fishes and invertebrates.) On contact with Asia the Assam gateway allowed a two-way and continuous exchange between the ancient Indian fauna and that of Euro–Asiatic intruders into India; Ethiopian elements may have entered India later, and Palaearctic species later still in Pleistocene times. Mani stresses the dynamic nature of biogeographical distribution patterns, continually affected by geomorphological and climatic changes, as well as by evolution within the communities themselves. The fauna of peninsular India has been much impoverished. The influence of Pleistocene glaciations in the Himalayas extended almost to the south of the peninsula and the Himalayan uplift affected the climate, so that the ecology of nearly the whole of India is now dominated by the rhythm of the monsoon rainfall climate. Such changes, together with irreversible changes brought about by man in clearing forest and destroying habitats over almost the whole of India, can account for the present discontinuous distribution of many Indian species.

The only primary freshwater fishes in Australia are the lungfish *Neoceratodus* and the osteoglossid *Scleropages leichardti*. Australia lacks Ostariophysi except species of the secondarily marine siluroid Ariidae and Plotosidae. Thus evidence from fishes suggests that Australia has been separated for a very long time from Africa and South America (as also from Asia, p. 50). Australia is now thought by some geophysicists to have remained connected with Antarctica until the Eocene (45 to 55 m.y.b.p.) and it has been suggested that a connection between the southern tip of South America and Antarctica until Eocene times would have enabled marsupials to cross between South America and Australia via Antarctica (Jardine and McKenzie, 1972). If this occurred it is strange that no modern fishes appear to have crossed by this route. Or were any that did so destroyed by desiccation or cold?

Africa

The African freshwater fish fauna

There are in Africa about forty families with *c.* 280 genera and over 2500 species of freshwater fishes (Appendix 3), representatives of which are illustrated in Fig. 2.2. Poll (1973) has listed the numbers of genera and species at present known in each family. The spectacular adaptive radiations of the perchlike cichlid fishes in the Great Lakes have attracted most study, and most communities in these lakes are dominated by these fishes. In the rivers the ostariophysi predominate, though not as completely as in the South

Table 2.2 The fish faunas of the African Great Lakes (data from sources as summarized by Greenwood (1974) and updated by him; excluding affluent rivers)

	VICTORIA	MALAWI	TANGANYIKA	ALBERT	RUDOLF	GEORGE & EDWARD	NABUGABO
Families	11	8+2?	13	13	14	7	9
Non-cichlid genera							
Total	20	19	29	21	22	10	11
Endemic	1	0	7	0	0	1	0
Cichlid genera							
Total	8	23	37	2	3	4	4
Endemic	4	20	33	0	0	0	0
Non-cichlid species							
Total	38	42	67	36	32	17	14
Endemic	16	26	47	3	5	2	0
Cichlid species							
Total	c 150–170	c 200	126	10	7	c 35–40	10
Endemic	all but 3	all but 4	126	4	2	all but 5	5
Haplochromis species							
Total	all but 8	120+	2	6	2	all but 4	6
Endemic	all but 1	all but 1	2	4	2	all but 1	5

American rivers (*c*. 54 per cent of the number of species in the Zaïre basin compared with *c*. 85 per cent of the Amazon fauna), and there are numerous endemic mormyrid species. Communities in certain areas may also include a few species belonging to smaller endemic families, together with relics of archaic families, of families shared with Asia, and of marine families. The numbers of species in the various families in representative rivers and lakes are given in Appendix 3.

Cichlids spawn in still water so were preadapted to colonise lakes. There are about twenty-two cichlid genera in the rivers of Africa and lakes other than Tanganyika and Malawi; in these two lakes their spectacular adaptive radiations have produced numerous endemic genera, thirty-three in Lake Tanganyika and twenty in Malawi (Table 2.2), the former with 126 species, all endemic, the latter with 200+ species, over 100 of them belonging to one genus *Haplochromis*. This genus is also particularly well represented in Lake Victoria. The family cichlidae includes the important food fish *Tilapia*, endemic to Africa though a few species are now circumtropical pond fish. There are about seventy known species of *Tilapia*; they are all basically herbivorous or plankton feeders when adult (though some include bottom debris in the diet), and not more than six indigenous species ever occur together in one lake (in contrast with the *Haplochromis* which have undergone adaptive radiations to use all kinds of food enabling many species to live together in one lake). *Tilapia* fall into two groups: (1) herbivorous species with few gill rakers, substratum spawners in which both parents guard their young, the *T. zillii* and *T. rendalli* ('*T. melanopleura*') group of the genus *Tilapia*; and (2) phytoplankton-feeding or bottom-feeding microphagous species with more numerous gill rakers which practise oral incubation; this group includes the majority of tilapias, the *Sarotherodon* group.*

Another Percomorph family, the marine family Centropomidae, is represented in African freshwaters by the large predatory *Lates niloticus*, the Nile or Niger perch which grows to over 120 kg. This is widely distributed from West Africa to the Nile and the Zaïre, including Lake Chad. It also lives in Lake Albert (Mobutu Sese Seko), where it has given rise to an endemic species offshore (*L. macrophthalmus*), while a subspecies of *L. niloticus* (or full species *L. rudolfianus*) in Lake Rudolf has also developed an offshore form (*L. longispinis*), and in Lake Tanganyika a species flock of three endemic *Lates* and two *Luciolates* has evolved, all large predatory species. *L. niloticus* has been introduced into many other lakes, including Lake Victoria.

The Ostariophysi in Africa include eighteen genera and very numerous (*c*. 560) species of cyprinids; these are mostly omnivorous feeders on benthic insects and vegetable debris. The immense genus *Barbus* includes some very

* Since this manuscript was prepared these two groups of *Tilapia* formerly regarded as distinct groups (Thys, 1968) have been designated genera (Trewavas, 1973), so the majority of *Tilapia* (the microphagous species with numerous gill rakers which mouthbrood their young) should now be called *Sarotherodon* (see Index of Fish Names for synonyms).

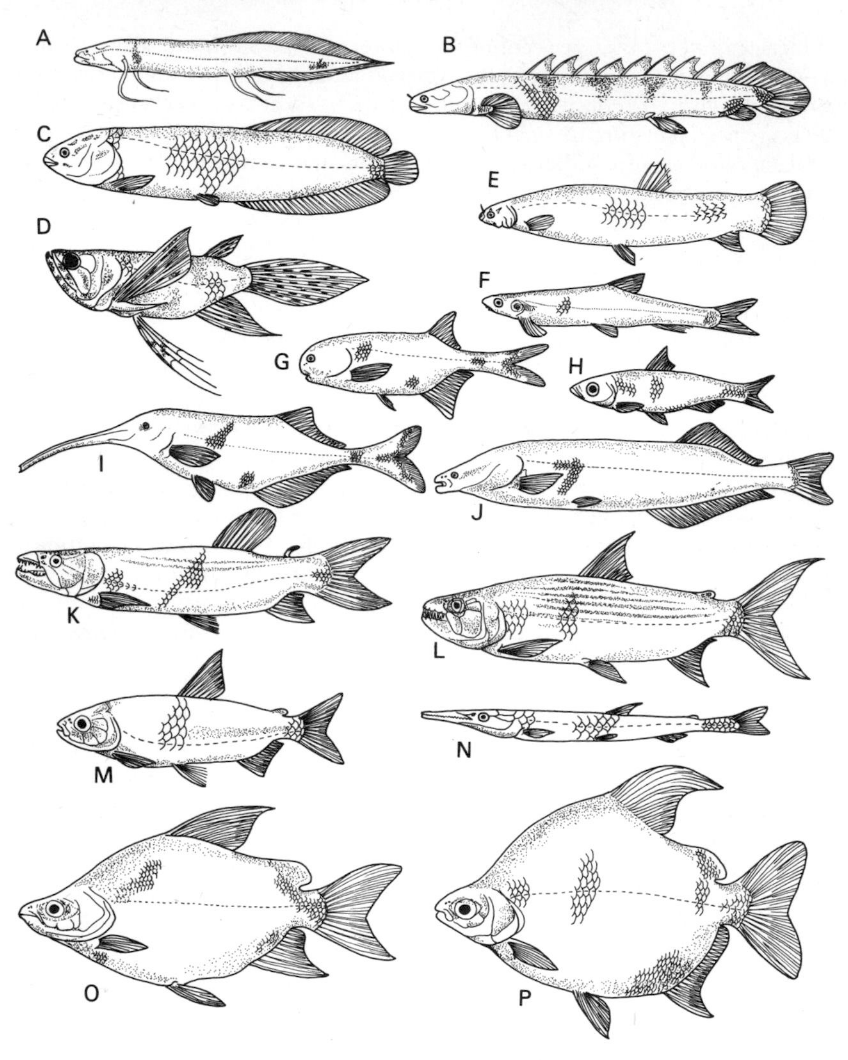

Fig. 2.2a Representative African freshwater fishes I. (Numbers in parentheses are total lengths commonly encountered.)
A. *Protopterus* Lungfish (100 cm, Dipnoi); B. *Polypterus* (40 cm, Polypteridae); C. *Heterotis* (50 cm, Osteoglossidae); D. *Pantodon* (6 cm, Pantodontidae); E. *Phractolaemus* (6 cm, Phractolaemidae); F. *Kneria* (6 cm, Kneriidae); G. *Petrocephalus* (15 cm, Mormyridae); H. *Pellonula* (14 cm, Clupeidae); I. *Campylomormyrus* (12 cm, Mormyridae); J. *Mormyrops* (100 cm, Mormyridae); K. *Hepsetus* (30 cm, Hepsetidae); L. *Hydrocynus* (50 cm, Characidae); M. *Alestes* (12 cm, Characidae), N. *Belonophago* (12 cm, Ichthyoboridae); O. *Distichodus* (50 cm, Distichodontidae); P. *Citharinus* (70 cm, Citharinidae).

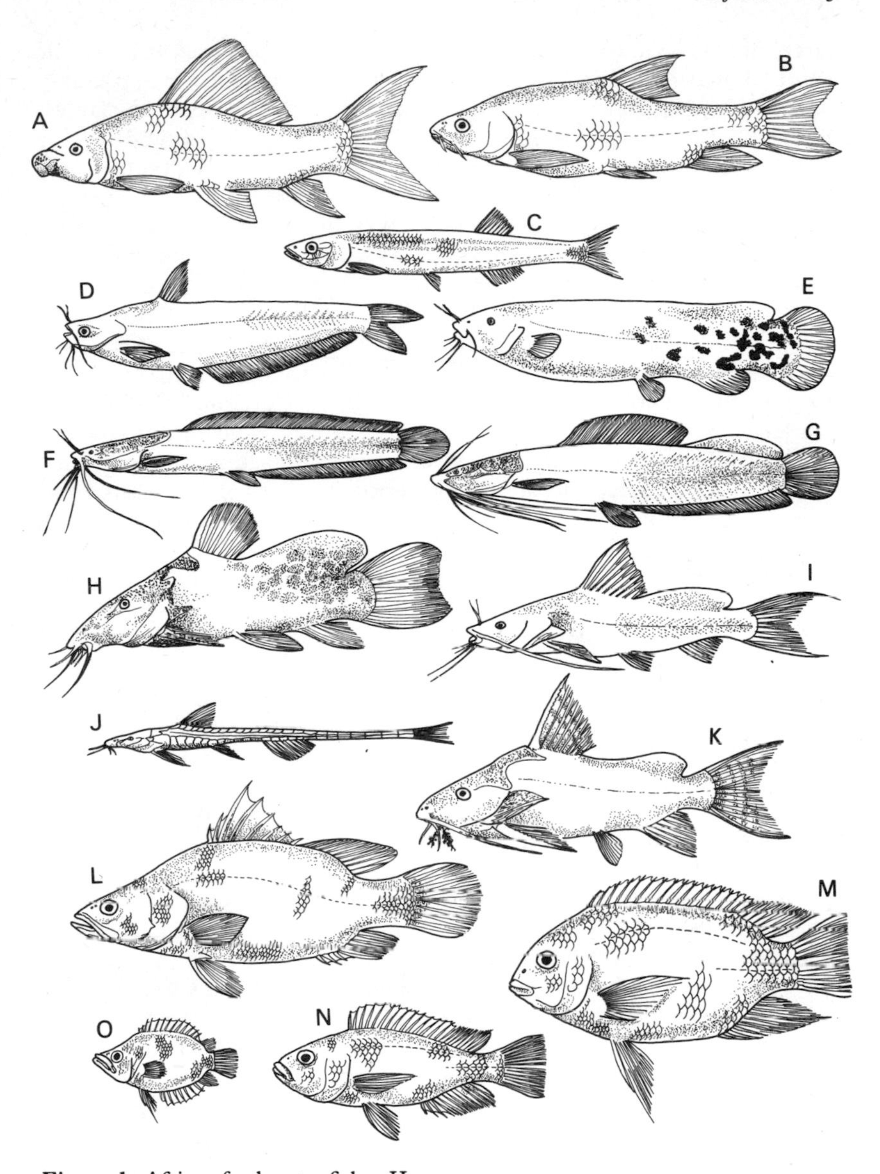

Fig. 2.2b African freshwater fishes II.
A. *Labeo* (50 cm, Cyprinidae); B. *Barbus* (50 cm, Cyprinidae); C. *Engraulicypris* (10 cm, Cyprinidae); D. *Schilbe* (20 cm, Schilbeidae); E. *Malapterurus* Electric catfish (25 cm, Malapteruridae); F. *Clarias* (50 cm, Clariidae); G. *Heterobranchus* (120 cm, Clariidae); H. *Auchenoglanis* (80 cm, Bagridae); I. *Bagrus* (100 cm, Bagridae); J. *Belonoglanis* (8 cm, Amphiliidae); K. *Synodontis* (50 cm, Mochokidae); L. *Lates* Nile Perch (100 cm, Centropomidae); M. *Tilapia* (30 cm, Cichlidae); N. *Haplochromis* (12 cm, Cichlidae); O. *Polycentropsis* (6 cm, Nandidae).

large species (up to 90 cm long) used as food fishes, some of which provide sport for anglers, and innumerable small species very similar in appearance and hard to identify, often endemic to a particular river system. The far less numerous *Varicorhinus* resemble *Barbus*. The genus *Labeo* of mud-feeding fishes with suctorial mouthes, some growing to 80 cm long, supports several important fisheries. *Labeo* were in many cases caught mainly as they migrated upriver to spawn, and several of these fisheries have been severely damaged by this practice; the runs of *L. altivelis* up the Luapula from Lake Mweru virtually ceased in the early 1950s (de Kimpe, 1964), those of *L. victorianus* from Lake Victoria have been much reduced (Cadwalladr, 1965), while those for *L. mesops* from Lake Malawi could be so affected. In Lake Malawi two endemic species of large *Barilius* were also fished on spawning migrations upriver (Lowe, 1952). *Engraulicypris* are small (less than 10 cm long) silver pelagic cyprinids, abundant in certain lakes, and amongst the relatively few freshwater fishes in which the adults feed on zooplankton.

The African Characoidei are now grouped into five families: the Characidae (22 genera, *c.* 120 species in Africa and also present in South America), and three endemic families, the Hepsetidae (monospecific), Citharinidae, Distichodontidae, Ichthyoboridae. *Hepsetus odoe*, thought to be the most primitive characoid in Africa (Roberts, 1973*b*), is widely distributed from West Africa to the Zambezi, living mainly in shallow backwaters. The Characidae include large piscivorous *Hydrocynus* species all with well-developed canine teeth, the chief predatory fishes in many river communities, and considered excellent sport fish by anglers. There are four common species of these tiger fish, *H. vittatus* the main predatory species of the Zambezi system, the smaller *H. forskahlii* common in Lake Albert and West Africa, *H. brevis* a large species common in Lake Chad, and *H. goliath* a giant species of the Zaïre basin which has pushed up into Lake Tanganyika. Their respective sizes range from up to about 58 cm 860 g in *H. forskahlii*, 70 cm 3 kg in *H. vittatus*, 90 cm 8 kg in *H. brevis*, to 1·3 m 38 kg in *H. goliath*. *H. vittatus* has the widest distribution, from the Limpopo, Zambezi, Katanga, Zaïre basin, Nile to West Africa (where it was formerly known as *H. lineatus*) and in Lakes Tanganyika, Rudolf, Albert and Chad. In Lake Albert it is less common than the smaller *H. forskahlii*, a species which in this lake turns from feeding on fishes to a diet of *Caridina* prawns as it grows (Holden, 1970). *H. forskahlii* ranges right across West Africa to the Nile system and L. Rudolf, and *H. brevis* from West Africa to the Nile.

Non-piscivorous characids large enough to support important fisheries include various *Alestes*, such as *A. baremose* and *A. dentex*, both widely distributed across West Africa to the Nile system; these migrate up rivers to spawn and may change their diet seasonally. The numerous small characid species (over fifty species of fourteen genera: Poll, 1967) fill some of the niches that the tetragonopterine characids fill in South American streams; but there are not so many kinds of small characoids in Africa as in South America, and in Africa their roles are shared by small cyprinid species (absent from South America).

Citharinidae and Distichodontidae include deep-bodied fishes, mud-feeding *Citharinus* and *Distichodus* which strip leaves from macrophytes, both with many species in the Zaïre basin and West Africa. These fishes resemble the vegetarian serrasalmines in South American rivers; no comparable flesh-tearing species have evolved in Africa, though Hopson reports that female *Hydrocynus brevis* in Lake Chad may bite pieces out of other fishes. The Ichthyoboridae (10 gen., 19 sp.) are long slender characoids, found mainly in Zaïre, with tightly adhesive scales, elongate jaws and teeth able to rasp scales or fins of other fishes (Matthes, 1961*b*).

The seven families of siluroid fishes in Africa include four also present in Asia (Ariidae, Bagridae, Schilbeidae, Clariidae) and three endemic ones Mochokidae, Amphiliidae and Malapteruridae. *Arias gigas*, which lives over muddy bottoms in the River Niger, is the only truly freshwater ariid in Africa. The Bagridae (16 gen., 102 sp.) includes very large species of *Chrysichthys* in the rivers of West Africa and Zaïre, and a *Chrysichthys* species flock has evolved in Lake Tanganyika. *Bagrus* is one of the main predators in rivers over a wide area and in some of the Great Lakes, where *Bagrus docmac* in Lake Victoria and *B. meridionalis* in Lake Malawi are important food fishes. *Auchenoglanis* species are particularly abundant in equatorial West Africa, but the omnivorous *A. occidentalis* has a very wide distribution from the Gambia to the Nile and south to Zambia. In the Zaïre River small endemic bagrids live over sandy bottoms in swift water. The Schilbeidae (8 gen., 42 sp.), open water catfishes with about eight genera in Africa, include small, almost transparent, laterally compressed species in the Zaïre basin and West Africa, while the more robust and predatory *Schilbe mystus* and *Eutropius depressirostris* are very widely distributed. In these latter two species the females grow larger than the males, as in many of these ostariophysian fishes.

The family Clariidae (12 gen., 102 sp.), of elongated catfishes with long dorsal and anal fins and no fin spines, includes two ancient and widely distributed genera *Clarias* and *Heterobranchus* (known from Lower Pliocene deposits in India and thought to have moved westwards into Africa: Menon, 1951). Africa has numerous *Clarias* (over fifty living species, compared with but about twelve in Asia), fishes with a dorsoventrally flattened head, wide mouth and long barbels. Most of them live over muddy bottoms where they are rather omnivorous bottom scroungers; *Clarias* are valuable food fishes, especially those which penetrate into rather dry areas where few other fishes are found. An arborescent respiratory organ in a cavity behind the gills enable *Clarias* to live in very deoxygenated water, and to wriggle overland through wet grass, which helps to explain their wide distribution. *Clarias* run up small streams to spawn in temporarily flooded areas. In the open waters of the Great Lakes and in turbulent well-oxygenated rivers clariids may lose these accessory respiratory devices, as have *Xenoclarias*, *Dinotopterus* and '*Bathyclarias*' endemic to the lakes, and *Gymnallabes* in the rapids of the Lower Zaïre river. African clariids have diverged to produce a number of anguilliform genera (such as *Clariallabes* of numerous species in rivers, and the ditypic *Gymnallabes*, the monotypic *Channallabes* and *Dolichallabes* in Zaïre) in which reduction of the bony headshield and of the eyes, confluence of the dorsal, caudal and anal fins, and reduction or absence of pelvic fins (and pectorals too in *Channallabes*) appear to be adaptations to burrowing habits. A monotypic albino clariid lacking eyes (*Uegitglanis*) lives in subterranean waters in Somalia. *Bathyclarias*, of which there is a species flock in Lake Malawi, belongs to the *Heterobranchus* group; there are about nine species of *Heterobranchus* living in Africa of which the large *H. lonifilis* is very widely distributed and an important food fish (growing to 170 cm long).

The endemic family Mochokidae (9 gen., 155 sp.) includes over eighty species of *Synodontis*, their heads protected by bony armour, and with formidable dorsal and pectoral spines. Most are bottom dwellers, exploring the soft deposits with the ventral mouth and ramified mandibular barbels. *Hemisynodontis membranaceous* floats down the rivers ventral side uppermost feeding on micro-organisms at the surface (Poll, 1971, and personal observation), and like *Synodontis nigriventris* has reversed countershading (which may become 'normal' when fish live dorsalside uppermost in aquaria). Many *Synodontis* species are distinctively spotted or coloured. In the Niger at Kainji eighteen species of *Synodontis* were taken from between the two coffer dams (p. 98). This family also includes another eight genera of smaller mochokids which live mainly in streams, of which the multispecific *Chiloglanis* is widely distributed, but the other genera are most restricted in distribution, several of them found only in the Zaïre basin, and have relatively few species.

The Amphiliidae (6 gen., 45 sp.) is an endemic family of stream catfishes. The eight genera include the multispecific and widely distributed *Amphilius* species, and some armoured forms, such as *Belonoglanis* and *Phractura*, which provide examples of convergence with armoured catfishes in South American and Asian waters. These all live over hard bottoms, generally in swift streams, many of them having elongated, slender bodies. The Electric catfish (*Malapterurus electricus*: Malapteruridae 1 gen., 2 sp.) is widely distributed in rivers and is common in Lakes Tanganyika and Kariba. The dermal electric organ, with which it can give a formidable shock (personal experience) is wrapped around the body, giving the fish a characteristic pudgy appearance. Young of 15–20 cm long already give appreciable shocks. *M. electricus* feeds on invertebrates of many kinds. Pairs of ripe fish are caught from holes at the start of the floods (Poll and Gosse, 1969).

Of the endemic families, the Mormyridae has the most numerous genera (sixteen) and over 200 species (Taverne, 1972), and these are especially abundant in the Zaïre and West Africa. Mormyrids all have electric organs. The mormyroid *Gymnarchus niloticus*, an electric fish growing to over a metre long, moves by undulations of the long dorsal fin. This edible species makes a floating nest in the swamps. Another endemic osteoglossoid, *Pantodon*, is a short compressed fish known to aquarists; it has very large pectoral fins and distinctive elongated filamentous pelvics. Found from Zaïre to the lower Niger, *Pantodon* lives close to the water surface, feeding on insects, and can leap out of water; it makes a floating nest for its large eggs.

The Kneriidae (1 gen., 20 sp.) and Phractolaemidae (1 gen., 1 sp.) are endemic families of small species, the latter probably derived from the former. Like the cyprinids when damaged they produce 'alarm substances' which warn other members of the shoal to take avoiding action. The many *Kneria* species live in swift mountain streams in Angola, West Africa and Cameroon, feeding mainly on *aufwuchs* (the algae on rocks with contained microorganisms); the males have a curious opercular apparatus of unknown function, but probably to assist mating. The microphagous *Phractolaemus* lives in swampy regions in the lower Niger and Zaïre, and has an epibranchial accessory respiratory organ. *Cromeria* (1 sp. *C. nilotica*) and *Grasseichthys* (1 sp. *G. gabonensis*) are included in the family Kneriidae by Greenwood *et al.*, 1966.

The endemic Polypteridae, with two genera, the monospecific *Calamoichthys* an elongated form in West Africa, and about ten species of *Polypterus* living in West Africa and the Zaïre (and one eastwards to the Nile), are ancient fishes with brachypterous paired fins and hard shiny ganoid scales. Voracious carnivores, they do not guard their young (Arnoult, 1966) and do not aestivate. The adults respire partly by gills and partly by a swim-bladder lung; the young have external gills.

Of the non-endemic families the Osteoglossidae includes one African species, *Heterotis niloticus*, a large-scaled fish growing fast to over 78 cm long (5+ kg) which can be cultured in fish ponds; a microphagous species with an accessory respiratory organ on the fourth branchial arch. Distributed across West Africa to the Nile, *Heterotis* lives in shallow swampy areas, where the parents make a nest among aquatic plants during the wet season and guard their young. The archaic fishes also include the dipnoan *Protopterus* (four species), well known for their ability to breathe air and to aestivate in a mucous cocoon in the mud in the dry season. Carnivorous fishes with strong crushing jaws, their diet includes molluscs. A nest is made in the swamps; the tadpole-like young have four pairs of external gills which regress as they grow.

Of families present both in Africa and Asia, the Anabantidae, a very important family of food fishes in Asia, is represented in Africa by a few (*c.* 29) small species of *Ctenopoma* (very close to *Anabas* of Asia) and *Sandelia*. As in their Asian relatives, these have a labyrinthine accessory respiratory organ in a suprabranchial cavity which enables them to live in deoxygenated water. The eggs of *Ctenopoma* are laid in a bubble nest at the water surface. The Notopteridae includes elongate and laterally flattened fishes propelled by undulations of the long anal fin; Africa has two species, *Papyrocranus afer* (which resembles the Asian *Notopterus*) and *Xenomystus nigri*. These live on the bottom among plants, feeding nocturnally on insects and small fish; they have an epibranchial accessory respiratory organ. The Channidae (= Ophiocephalidae) (1 gen., 2 sp.), long cylindrical predatory fishes with accessory respiratory organs, common in Asia, have one genus with two species in Africa, of which *Parophiocephalus obscurus* is widely distributed in marshy places in tropical Africa. Of the Mastacembelidae (2 gen., 44 sp.), the main genus in Africa, *Mastacembelus*, also occurs in Asia. These are elongated fishes with a series of dorsal spines and a long snout supporting tubular anterior nostrils; they live among rocks in rivers, some partly buried. A *Mastacembelus* species flock has evolved in Lake Tanganyika, and an eyeless species, *Caecomastacembelus brichardi*, lives amongst rocks in the Zaïre rapids below Pool Malebo (Poll, 1959*b*). It is interesting that most of the fishes present in both Africa and Asia have accessory respiratory organs. This indicates the value of such organs in the achievement of a wide distribution, and may even suggest that the fishes have had to cross swampy regions or otherwise deoxygenated waters in their passage from one continent to the other.

Of the marine families the Clupeidae (herrings) (taken to include Congothrissidae, 1 gen., 1 sp., and Dussumieriidae, 3 gen., 3 sp., by Greenwood *et al.*, 1966) are represented by about eleven genera of freshwater species (*c.* 19 sp.) in Africa, mostly small species living in the rivers, but Lake Tanganyika has two pelagic endemic species which support an important fishery. Lake Mweru has three clupeid species, and another two have colonised the new Volta lake. Clupeids from Lake Tanganyika have been introduced to the new Kariba Lake to crop the zooplankton. Synbranchidae (2 gen., 2 sp.), long eel-like fishes, are represented by one genus and species (*Synbranchus afer*) in West Africa. True eels, *Anguilla* (family Anguilliidae) of several species run up the rivers of eastern Africa from the sea, and occur in Lake Kariba and Lake Malawi. *Eleotris* and a few other gobies have colonised freshwaters, but not nearly as many as have done so in Asian waters. About five species of puffer fish (Tetraodontidae (2 gen., 8 sp.)) live in Zaïre, and a freshwater flat fish (the sole *Dagetichthys*) and a freshwater stingray (*Potamotrygon garouensis*) are both found in the Benué River far from the sea.

The distribution of fishes within Africa

Much of present-day tropical Africa is drained by four great river systems, the Niger, the Nile, the Zaïre, and the Zambezi, together with smaller rivers flowing to east and west coasts (Fig. 2.3). There are also several inland drainage areas, such as Lake Chad, which lies between the Niger and the Nile, Lake Rudolf to the east of the Nile, and the Okavango swamps and Makarikari depression in Botswana.

The African fish fauna is richest and most varied in equatorial West Africa and the Zaïre. In Gondwanaland times this would have been the centre of the area connected with South America, a region once probably drained by rivers tributary to the proto-Amazon in Cretaceous times. The rivers of eastern Africa, on the other hand, have numerous types of fish such as cyprinids which appear to have entered Africa from Asia in the north at a relatively late date and worked their way southwards down the east side of the continent. Much of this land is higher, with cooler waters, which suit cyprinids well. Cyprinids also reached West Africa, where *Labeo* species are

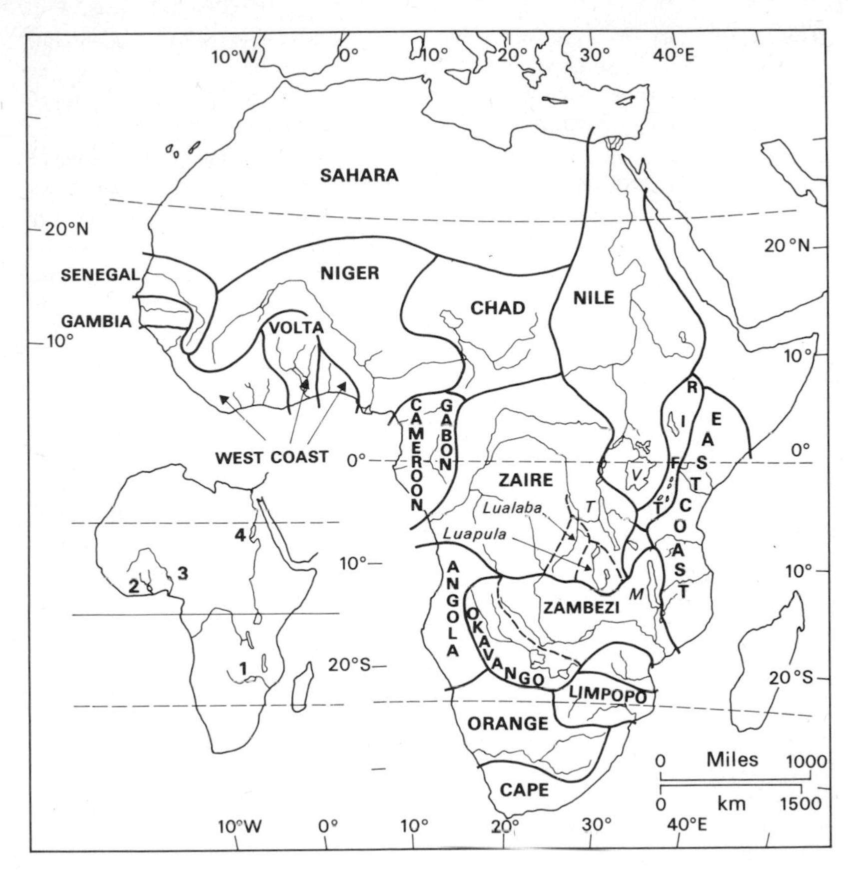

Fig. 2.3 The major river basins of the African continent.
Fish faunal regions in most instances coincide with drainage basins but the East African Great Lakes Victoria (V), Tanganyika (T), and Malawi (M), each have their own distinctive endemic faunas. The inset map indicates the sites of the large new manmade lakes considered in the text: 1. L. Kariba, 2. Volta Lake, 3. L. Kainji, 4. L. Nasser.

now common, which would have been easier to do when the Sahara region was better watered.

The Zaïre basin has the richest fish fauna, a very high proportion of it (probably well over 80 per cent) endemic to the region. Poll (1959*b*) considered that there are probably nearly 1000 fish species (representing 25 families and at least 164 known genera) within the Zaïre system (excluding Lake Tanganyika); at the present state of knowledge Poll (1973) says there are 669 species of which 548 (80 per cent) in 42 genera are endemic in the Zaïre basin (excluding Lake Tanganyika). Each expedition produces numerous new species. In addition to the Ostariophysi which dominate the

Zaïre fauna (23 per cent siluroids, 15 per cent characoids, 16 per cent cyprinids) this Zaïre basin has a spectacular number of mormyrids (75 species, 18 per cent of the fauna) (Appendix 3). The siluroids include 36 mochokid species, 27 bagrids and 23 clariids, many of them belonging to endemic genera. The 32 cichlids also include endemic genera. The ancient polypterids are here represented by 7 species and *Protopterus* by 2 species (*P. dolloi* and *P. annectens*). The numerous endemic genera include the mormyrid *Genyamyrus*, the characid *Clupeopetersius*, the citharinids *Mesoborus*, *Phagoborus*, *Belonophago* and *Eugnathichthys*, the cyprinid *Leptocypris*, the bagrid *Gnathobagrus*, the clariid *Channallabes*, and the cichlids *Teleogramma*, *Heterochromis* and *Steatocranus*. The separate regions of the Zaïre system are considered later (p. 34).

The west-flowing rivers of Cameroon and Gabon contain both west African and Zaïre elements, and the fauna is a very rich one (Holly, 1930). Biotopes of the Ivindo basin in Gabon and their fishes were described by Gery (1965).

Of the subequatorial regions lying either side of Zaïre, the 'Soudanian' region to the north has a much more diverse fish fauna than the Zambezi system to the south. This soudanian region includes the savanna rivers south of the Sahara from Senegal on the West Coast to the Nile, and the Lake Chad area. The subequatorial Niger and Nile have many species in common: the osteoglossid *Heterotis*, the mormyroid *Gymnarchus niloticus*, *Cromeria*, and identical species (in some cases subspecifically distinct) of the mormyrid *Hyperopisus* and of the catfishes *Siluranodon*, *Clarotes* and *Mochocus*. However, West Africa has on the whole a much richer fauna than the Nile; Poll (1957) considered that the differentiation between Niger and Nile faunas is almost as great as between Niger and Zaïre. Fish common to the Zaïre and Niger but not found in the Nile include *Phractolaemus*, *Pantodon*, the characids *Hepsetus* and *Bryconaethiops*, the cyprinid *Garra* and certain *Polypterus* species.

Although the soudanian region has far fewer fish species than the Zaïre, it still has a very diverse fauna made up primarily of Ostariophysi (39 siluroid species, 24 characoids, and 23 cyprinids in the Middle Niger: Daget, 1954). In addition to families found in the Zaïre, West Africa has an osteoglossid, a nandid and a denticipid, and a second genus of polypterid (the elongated *Calamoichthys*). This soudanian fauna is probably a very ancient one, formerly even more widely distributed than at present, a suggestion supported by the presence in Tanzania of a fossil denticipid (Greenwood, 1960) and a fossil osteoglossid (Greenwood and Patterson, 1967), both families now restricted to West Africa.

In West Africa Daget distinguished between 'soudanian' fish species living in the waters of the extensive savanna-covered peneplain, and 'guinean' species in forested streams. Ecological replacement species are well marked in some genera (for example in the clariids, anabantids and cyprinodonts). Daget commented that the complexities of the river systems, with frequent river captures and variations in climates over long geological periods, have resulted in the soudanian and guinean species occurring within the same river system, separated neither by watersheds nor by waterfall barriers. However, ecological conditions, particularly presence or absence of forest, would appear to account for their continued coexistence within one river system, though it may be more difficult for a species to extend its range when the river system already contains a closely related species.

Guinean species are found in the upper reaches of Niger tributaries and in the higher more dissected country in Guinea, but in the Ivory Coast the situation is reversed as they occur in the lower reaches of the rivers which are here forested, while the open country to the north carries soudanian species. This suggested that the over-riding factor is shade or food from the forest, guinean species loving forest waters while soudanian species prefer open water. The Dahomey Gap, where a belt of savanna comes south to the coast, breaks the guinean forest zone into distinct western and eastern sectors, affecting the distribution of certain forest-water species (Fig. 4.3, p. 96).

The soudanian savanna species, which often grow larger than their guinean counterparts, tend to be widely distributed right across Africa south of the Sahara from the Atlantic to the Indian Ocean. The savanna rivers of this wide area have an annual cycle of flooding caused by summer rains when they inundate huge tracts of country. Many of the fishes here undergo extensive longitudinal migrations up and down river and lateral migrations out over the flooded country, so it is not surprising that these species are so widely dispersed. In some species subspecific differences have been noted in the widely separated parts of their range, in the Niger and Nile, sometimes with intermediate subspecies in the Lake Chad area. The Gambia and Senegal have many of the same species as the Niger, which is explicable as the Upper Niger flowed westwards into the sea off Senegal in the early Pleistocene, until this westward flow was blocked by sand dunes in a dry epoch; the Upper Niger then drained into a large closed basin west of Timbuktu until it connected with the lower Niger only 5000 to 6000 years ago (according to evidence summarised by Beadle, 1974, p. 125).

In West Africa coastal lagoons and estuarine reaches carry many species of marine families, some of them visiting brackish water sporadically or seasonally or for some stage of the life history. Above the brackish zone, where the coastal plain is wide and the land is flat, long stretches of river are affected by the tidal rise and fall as this backs up the freshwater (compare similar conditions in northeast South America and in Asia). This is particularly so in Gambia, where the freshwater swamps reflect tidal rhythms (Johnels, 1954).

The Zambezi is much less rich in the families well represented in West Africa and the Zaïre (such as characoids, polypterids and mormyrids), but the numbers of cyprinids and cichlid species are high, and the kneriids are at home here (Appendix 3). The Zambezi is divided into three zoogeographical regions: the *Lower Zambezi* from the delta to the Cabora Bassa rapids; the *Middle Zambezi* from Cabora Bassa to the Victoria Falls, including the Luangwa River and the new man-made Lake Kariba; and the

Upper Zambezi above the Victoria Falls, where the fish fauna is richer than in the Middle Zambezi, probably for ecological reasons as the many swamps provide cover round the year for the fishes whereas the Middle Zambezi shrinks into pools in the dry season. The tributary Kafue River flows into the Middle Zambezi below Lake Kariba, but the fish fauna here is more like that of the Upper Zambezi with certain Zaïre elements (Jackson, 1961*a*).

Fish faunas are continually receiving or losing species from other systems, as the establishment of the Upper Zambezi species *Alestes lateralis* in Lake Kariba demonstrated (p. 178). Bell-Cross (1965*a*) recorded the movement of fishes from the Zaïre to the Zambezi system in the Mwinilunga District of Zambia. The watershed is here a low flat plain, dotted with many small shallow depressions which become pools in the rains. Six species of fish (*Barbus puellus*, *Clarias theodorae*, *Aplocheilichthys johnstoni*, *Tilapia sparrmanii*, *Ctenopoma ctenotis* and *C. multispinis*) invaded these pools; the fish moved freely up the gentle slope of the Zaïre tributary on to the watershed plain, but it seemed unlikely that a similar movement occurred up the more steeply sloping Zambezi tributary. Towards the end of the rains the fishes moved back into the tributary streams on both sides of the watershed.

The history of the fish fauna of Angola, which has five zoogeographical regions, is of movements from Zaïre and Zambezi to other waters and retreats during dry periods (Poll, 1966).

The rivers of southern Africa, such as the Limpopo, the many smaller rivers flowing east, and the Orange River flowing west, have increasingly attenuated faunas from north to south, but faunas in which the cyprinids continue to be particularly important. Because of the warm sea currents in the Indian Ocean along the east coast, in contrast with cold Atlantic currents moving north along the west coast, the climate is milder in the east, and tropical species come further south in the east-flowing rivers. Tropical fishes such as *Tilapia* tend to be restricted to lower altitudes further south, presumably a temperature effect. In the extreme south, the Cape region, the fauna is reduced to endemic galaxiids (two species), freshwater representatives of marine families (one goby, one *Anguilla*, and one clupeid), and three freshwater families (cyprinids with nineteen species; bagrids and anabantids each with two species).

The east-flowing rivers of East Africa also have somewhat attenuated faunas, with some nilotic elements such as the clariid *Clarotes laticeps*, but more are conspicuous by their absence (Whitehead, 1962; Bailey, 1969). As in southern Africa, cyprinids and cichlids are important, many families present in the Zaïre are absent, and others have here fewer species.

The Zaïre system (Fig. 2.4) is divided into the following regions (Poll, 1957):

1. the Lower Zaïre (below Boma), which has many euryhaline species (pristids, elopids, sphyraenids, mugilids), freshwater representatives of marine families (clupeids, gobies, *Periophthalmus*, tetraodonts), and secondary freshwater fishes (cichlids, cyprinodonts);
2. a stretch with 32 falls and rapids in the 350 km between Matadi and Pool

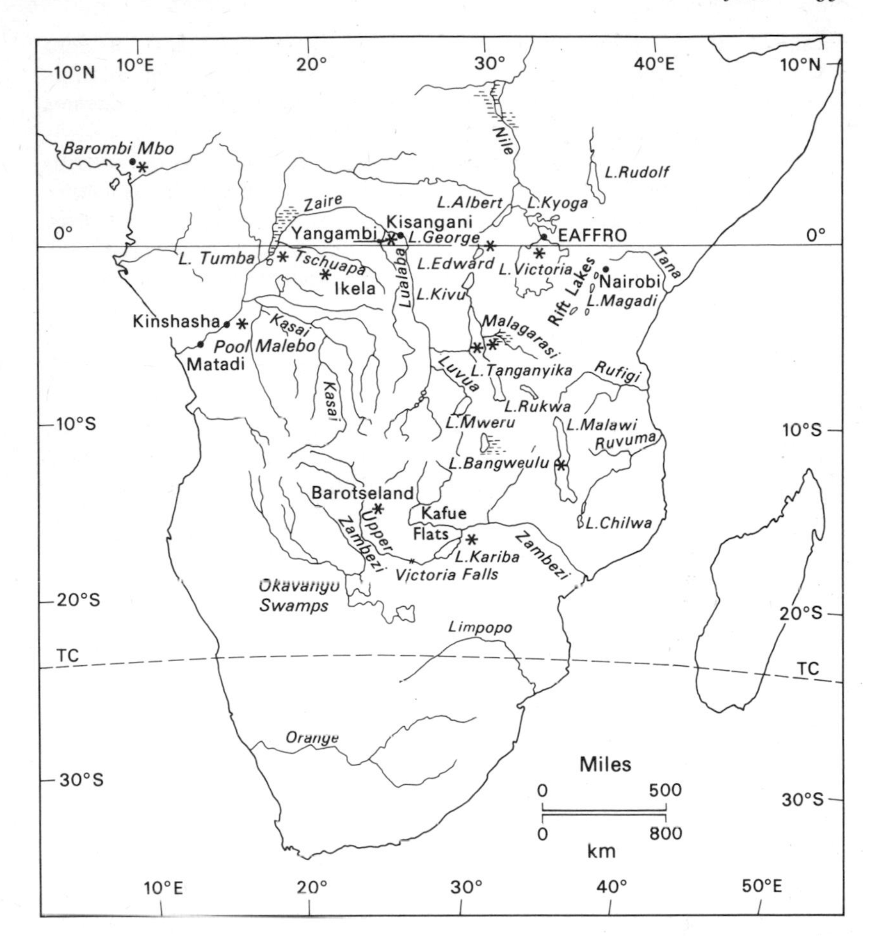

Fig. 2.4 Central, East and Southern Africa indicating places mentioned in the text. The main studies were at sites marked with an asterisk.

Malebo (= Stanley Pool), one of the most extensive stretches of such rapid water in the tropical world; this bars access to marine fishes, and here live many species adapted to fast-flowing water (cyprinids *Garra* and *Labeo*, catfishes *Atopochilus*, *Euchilichthys*, *Chiloglanis*, *Gymnallabes*, and cichlids *Steatocranus*, *Teleogramma*, *Leptotilapia*);

3. Pool Malebo;
4. the great central basin of the Zaïre, with increased numbers of genera (see Appendix 3) plus Notopteridae and *Phractolaemus*;
5. the Upper Zaïre basin or Lualaba above Stanley Falls near Kisangani, where species with 'nilotic affinities' are encountered.

Pool Malebo has five species showing feeble endemism (really little different from more widely distributed species), and Lake Tumba in the central basin has another three feeble endemics. (Lake Fwa, which is a limestone sinkhole lake, has more distinctive endemics.) Most of the central basin complex of waters lies in forest, but some tributaries flow through savanna country; the cyprinodont genera *Aphyosemion* and *Epiplatys* are found mainly in the forest waters, and *Aplocheilichthys* and *Hypsopanchax* in savanna areas. The Kasai tributary of the Zaïre has evidently captured Upper Zambezi fishes at some time (Poll, 1957). Each new expedition brings back numerous new species and many more must remain to be discovered.

The Lualaba in Shaba (= Katanga) has a number of species known from the Nile (some subspecifically distinct from the Nile ones) but not found in the rest of the Zaïre, for example, *Protopterus aethiopicus congicus, Polypterus bichir katangae, P. senegalus meridionalis, Ichthyoborus besse, Ctenopoma muriei*). The capture of the proto-Lualaba by the Zaïre river probably occurred at the Portes d'Enfer, an event possibly associated with volcanic activity and uplift in the Kivu area about the end of the Pliocene (Poll, 1963). After this capture some upper Lualaba fishes spread downstream as far as the Stanley Falls near Kisangani (Stanleyville), and certain Zaïre river fishes pushed upstream as far as the falls near Bukama. Above these falls, in the many lakes on the Kamolondo Plain in the Upemba National Park, some species with 'nilotic affinities' (probably relics of an ancient widespread fauna) are present (8 'nilotic' ones, together with 28 with Zambezi affinities, 26 endemic, and 113 from the Zaïre basin). Many Zaïre basin species which might be thought to fare well in the swamps of this region are lacking, presumably because they have not been able to withstand conditions in the rapids which bar access to these lakes.

The Luapula–Mweru–Bangweulu area now drains into the Zaïre but it contains many Zambezi species, such as the cichlids *Serranochromis*, *Tilapia macrochir*, *Pseudocrenilabris philander* and *Haplochromis mellandi*. The mormyrid–characid–citharinid fauna is reduced compared with the Zaïre, and the cyprinids and cichlids are important as in the Zambezi. The rapids on the Luvua River connecting Lake Mweru to the Lualaba prevent Zaïre river species entering Lake Mweru (Jackson, 1961*c*), and there are two barriers on the Luapula (the Johnson Falls and the Mumbatala Falls) which divide this area into the lower or Mweru region, richer because of the presence of some Zaïre species, and the upper or Bangweulu region.

The three largest of the Great Lakes of East and Central Africa lie each in a different drainage system, Victoria flowing into the Nile, Tanganyika into the Zaïre, and Malawi (formerly known as L. Nyasa) into the Zambezi (Fig. 2.4). Lakes Tanganyika and Malawi are very deep lakes lying in the rift valleys whereas Lake Victoria is a relatively shallow saucer-shaped lake filling a depression where the ground has sagged between the two East African rift valleys. Initially fishes from the rivers must have colonised these Great Lakes, but as the lakes developed, new species evolved within them in response to the changed conditions. In all three lakes the cichlid fishes preadapted for lacustrine life underwent the most extensive adaptive radiations, and are now dominant elements of the faunas (Table 2.2). In L. Tanganyika

126 of the 193 lake species (64 per cent) are cichlids, all of which are endemic; in L. Malawi the total of 245+ described species includes over 200 cichlids, most of them endemic, and in L. Victoria 80 per cent of the 200 described species are cichlids, all but three of them endemic. Among the non-cichlids the proportion of endemic species is not so high, but is nevertheless striking: 47 of the 67 non-cichlids in L. Tanganyika, 26 of the 42 species in L. Malawi, and 16 of the 38 species in L. Victoria. Such figures are only provisional as almost every new collection yields undescribed species.

These Great Lakes arose primarily from post-Miocene tectonic events associated with the formation of the present East African rift valleys which led to great drainage changes in East and Central Africa. Their histories have been summarised by Fryer and Iles (1972) and Beadle (1974). There is reason to believe that the relative proportions of endemic species reflect the ages of these lakes: Tanganyika may be between 6 and 15 m.y. old, Malawi perhaps 2 m.y. old, and Victoria only *c.* 750 000 years old.

Lake Tanganyika has evidently been connected with rivers flowing into the Zaïre basin from early in its history, for the Malagarasi River flowing westwards into this lake contains Zaïre riverine species none of which are found within the lake (*Polypterus ornatipinnis*, *Labeo weeksii*, *Tetraodon mbu*, and *Serranochromis janus* which is endemic but very close to a Zaïre species; Poll, 1951). Lake Tanganyika probably had no outflow for a few million years and was an inland drainage area for long enough for the water to develop its characteristic high concentration of salts. Being a very deep lake (over a mile deep) it is unlikely to have dried out during its history, but there is evidence that it developed as two distinct basins for part of the time. When the Virunga volcanoes arose (perhaps 35,000 years ago) blocking the western rift valley and the drainage from the Lake Kivu region to the Nile, Lake Kivu formed behind this dam, rising until it found an outlet down the Ruzizi River to Lake Tanganyika. Kivu has an impoverished Nile fauna, and the rapids on the Ruzizi River have evidently prevented the Lake Tanganyika fish, with the exception of *Barilius moori*, from moving up into Kivu.

Greenwood (1973*a*, 1974) has discussed recent ideas on the formation of Lake Victoria. Fossil *Lates* are known from near the Kavirondo Gulf showing that the Victoria basin once had a nilotic fauna, but this was wiped out and the developing lake region was isolated from other drainage systems for long enough to develop its own 'Victorian' fauna before being reconnected with the Nile. The Murchison Falls on the White Nile prevented the return of *Lates* into Lakes Kyoga and Victoria, which both lacked this species until it was stocked there recently. It is now thought that Lake Victoria originated during the mid-Pleistocene, about 750 000 y.b.p. following the ponding back of rivers that flowed westwards across its present basin to the western rift system (i.e. to the proto Lakes Edward–George–Albert area (Greenwood, 1973*c*)). Uplift near the western rift valley led to the development of extensive swamps spread along the watershed, and probably to strings of small lakes lying in what is now the Victoria lake basin. Thus the faunas of Lakes Victoria, Edward and George probably evolved in parallel from the same basic stocks of fish (Greenwood, 1973*a*).

Of the other great lakes in East Africa, Lakes Edward (Idi Amin Dada) and George flowing to the Nile also have a large endemic fauna of cichlids, whereas Lakes Albert and Rudolf, which also have nilotic faunas, both have very few cichlid species. The suggestion that this was due to the presence of large predatory *Lates* and *Hydrocynus* in these latter lakes led to much discussion, analysed at length by Fryer and Iles (1972). Lakes Albert and Rudolf appear to have received fully differentiated riverine faunas, leaving little opportunity for cichlids to radiate. Lake Chad also lacks an endemic cichlid fauna, which is less surprising as this lake almost dries out at intervals.

Much has been written about the relative effects on African lakes of geomorphological changes, and of pluvials and interpluvials thought by some authorities to have been contemporaneous with the glacials and interglacials of the temperate zone; these aspects are discussed by Beadle (1974). The existence of wet and dry cycles, which must have greatly affected fish distribution, is well established. The Kalahari sands, mainly Miocene in origin, extended widely during later dry intervals, desiccating much of the Central Zaïre basin 50 000 years ago, and in another cycle they extended as far as the mouth of the Zaïre River as recently as 12 000 years ago, a time of desiccation in the Lake Chad area too. Radiocarbon dating indicates that there was a vast lake in the Chad basin 22 000 years ago and again about 8000 years ago, with fluctuating levels in between times, shrinking in a dry period 12 000 years ago. To achieve this mega-Chad, the region lying between the Niger and the Nile systems, must have been much wetter than it is today. The present desertic conditions in the Sahara appear to have started about 8000 years ago.

South America

Freshwater fish fauna

South America has few basic groups of freshwater fishes compared with Africa, yet it now has the largest number of species in its freshwater fish fauna of any zoogeographical region. The present very diverse fauna is the product of extensive adaptive radiations within these groups, initiated during the long isolation of the continent during the Tertiary. Although many rivers are not yet explored, over 2400 Neotropical freshwater fish species are known. Numerically, both in numbers of species and in numbers of individuals, the fauna is now dominated by characoid and siluroid fishes. These include the most conservative living forms and also some of the most specialised, with teeth and body form greatly modified according to the fish's diet and way of life.

Morphologically the characoid fishes are one of the most diverse groups of living vertebrates, and their marvellous adaptive radiations to fill all kinds of ecological niche rival those of the cichlid fishes in the Great Lakes of Africa (Fig. 2.5*a*). About 250 genera of characoid fishes are known from South America, with 1000 to 2000 species, far outnumbering the African chara-

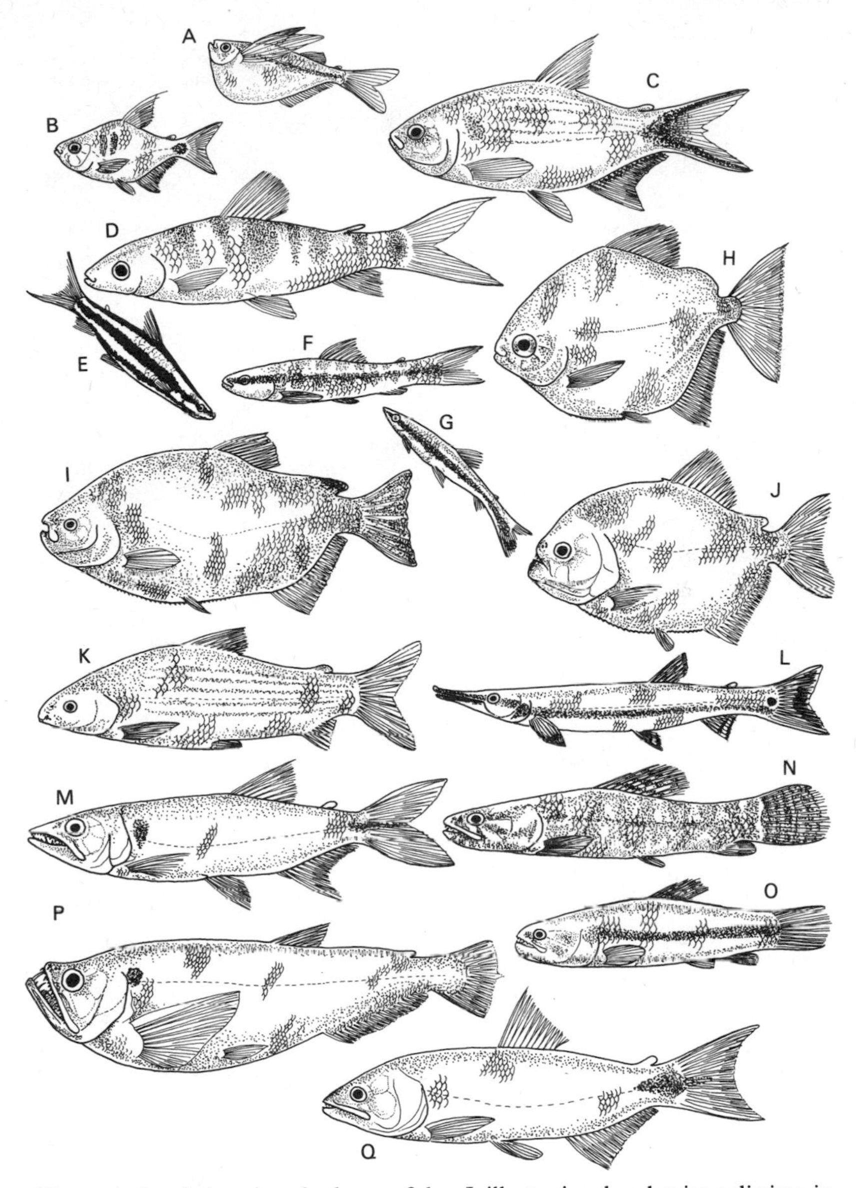

Fig. 2.5a South American freshwater fishes I, illustrating the adaptive radiations in characoid fishes.
A. *Gasteropelecus* (6 cm); B. *Tetragonopterus* (12 cm); C. *Brycon* (50 cm); D. *Leporinus* (30 cm); E. *Anostomus* (12 cm); F. *Characidium* (4 cm); G. *Poecilobrycon* (4 cm); H. *Metynnis* (12 cm); I. *Colossoma* (50 cm); J. *Serrasalmus* (30 cm); K. *Prochilodus* (40 cm); L. *Boulengerella* (45 cm); M. *Acestrorhynchus* (20 cm); N. *Hoplias* (30 cm); O. *Hoploerythrinus* (25 cm); P. *Hydrolicus* (60 cm); Q. *Salminus* (50 cm).

A
B
C
D
E
F
G
H
I
J
K
L
M
N
O
P
Q

coids. There is as yet no complete agreement about their family groupings; Greenwood *et al.* (1966) recognise twelve families (Appendix 2), and this is supported by osteological studies (Roberts, 1969).

These characoid fishes include the huge complex of tetragonopterine genera (family Characidae s.s.), mostly smallish species, many of them so similar that they 'mimic' one another when living together. A number of the smaller colourful species are well known to aquarists (e.g. characins and tetras, *Hyphessobrycon* and *Hemigrammus* species; pencil fish, *Nannostomus* species; hatchet fish, *Gasteropelecus*, *Carnegiella*). This family also includes the deep-bodied, laterally flattened, serrasalmine fishes, a group which diverged to produce large vegetarian species with nutcracker teeth, such as the pacu *Colossoma* and *Myleus*, and the notorious carnivorous piranha *Serrasalmus* species which have shearing teeth used to bite pieces from their prey. The characoids also include at least four independent lines of piscivorous fishes which swallow their prey whole: the pikelike *Acestrorhynchus* species (Characidae), the widely distributed *Hoplias malabaricus* (Erythrinidae), *Boulengerella* (Ctenoluciidae), and the Cynodontidae of which the best known species *Hydrolicus scomberoides* has two enormously elongated canines in the lower jaw. The gasteropelecid characoids or freshwater 'flying fishes' live near to the river surface. In the anostomids the mouth is vertical and the teeth are complex; many of these feed head downwards grazing food from rocks or plants. The *Leporinus* species have forceps-like teeth, but some are known to eat plants. The chilodontids and hemiodontids are highly selective in removing food items from the substrate. The Prochilodontidae include about thirty species of large migratory mud-feeders which support important fisheries in many parts of the continent: in these fishes the teeth are reduced to minute lip teeth on the enlarged fleshy lips which can be everted into a broad rasping sucking disc. Although many characoid fishes are kept in aquaria, we are only just beginning to study their foods and behaviour in natural waters and they present an exciting field for further study.

The Gymnotoidei are considered to be an offshoot of primitive characoid stock; they all have electric organs and about 35 species belonging to 18 genera are known. These are now put into four families, the Electrophoridae with one species, the well-known 'electric eel' *Electrophorus electricus*, the Gymnotidae with one genera of few species, predatory, widely distributed

Fig. 2.5b South American freshwater fishes II.
A. *Potamotrygon* Stingray (30 cm, Elasmobranch); B. *Lepidosiren* Lungfish (50 cm, Dipnoi); C. *Anableps* Foureyes (15 cm, Anablepidae); D. *Osteoglossum* (50 cm, Osteoglossidae); E. *Electrophorus* Electric eel (60 cm, Electrophoridae); F. *Colomesus* Puffer (5 cm, Tetraodontidae); G. *Cichlasoma* (10 cm, Cichlidae); H. *Cichla* (40 cm, Cichlidae); I. *Crenicichla* (25 cm, Cichlidae); J. *Hoplosternum* (15 cm, Callichthyidae); K. *Ancistrus* (15 cm, Loricariidae); L. *Megalodoras* (70 cm, Doradidae); M. *Hypostomus* (15 cm, Loricariidae); N. *Pimelodus* (30 cm, Pimelodidae); O. *Arapaima* (150 cm, Osteoglossidae); P. *Pseudoplatystoma* (120 cm, Pimelodidae); Q. *Vandellia* (4 cm, Trichomycteridae).

fishes, and like all the gymnotoids nocturnal in habit. The Apteronotidae (or Sternarchidae) and Rhamphichthyidae are represented by about nine and seven genera respectively; the former includes crevice-dwelling territorial species; the latter includes a species which burrows into the sand when young. Very little is known about the biology of many of these gymnotoids; for none of them, not even the electric eel, are the breeding habits yet described. The larger ones are piscivorous, the smaller ones mostly insectivorous. In many of the gymnotoids the body is very elongated, the anus very far forward, and the posterior part pointed, elongate, with or without a small caudal fin, and capable of great regeneration if damaged. The anal fin is generally very long, the rippling movement enabling the fish to swim backwards and forwards with equal ease while the body is held rigid, which is important for the proper functioning of the electric impulse-emitting and receiving systems (Fig. 9.8). Gymnotoids hide away in crevices or other sheltered places by day, and may be very territorial.

The South American siluroids also provide splendid examples of adaptive radiation. These range in size from the giant *Brachyplatystoma* species, reputedly growing to over 3 m long, which move up and down the main rivers, to minute trichomycterids living in the gill cavities of other catfishes. The naked bodied 'skinfish' are widely distributed and include a huge number of species. The Hypophthalmidae has but one species *Hypophthalmus edentatus*, a plankton-feeder with long sievelike gillrakers. Many small catfishes such as auchenipterids live in crevices. There are three armoured families: the doradids, many of which have hooked dermal plates along their sides, live in the rivers and lagoons, the callichthyids live in forest streams, hunting their insect food, such as Ephemeroptera nymphs, amongst the leaf debris, and the loricariids live mainly in stony places often in streams which become torrential seasonally, where they suck algae off rock surfaces. Bottom-living fishes all of these, their dermal armour may assist them to keep close to the bottom undamaged by abrasion in fast water. The armour may also assist them to withstand desiccation when pools dry up. *Callichthys* and some small doradids can move through damp leaf litter or grass from pool to pool, using their pectoral fin spines and flexures of the body; in the Mato Grosso *Callichthys* were seen to move many metres over dry ground in this way, and to be able to withstand great changes of temperature (personal observation). The armour may also deter predators.

The Loricariidae is the largest family of South American catfishes, with over 400 species (*c.* 50 gen.), distributed from La Plata to Panama. Their bodies covered in bony scutes, they are beautifully adapted for bottom-living, with a suctorial ventral mouth and the long coiled intestine of an algal or detritus feeder. They live amongst stones or roots mainly in small streams, working themselves forward by clinging to these objects. Some penetrate into the torrents and cataracts of the Andes. Unlike most catfishes with sombre colours for nocturnal life, hypostomine (= plecostomine) loricariids carry very vivid distinctive markings, often with light or dark spots (see p. 232). Male *Ancistrus* carry branched tentacles of unknown function on the snout, and the males of *Pseudancistrus* have particularly well-developed bristles on the sides of the head, also of unknown function. Loricariids are also unique in having an iris lobe, a peg-shaped process which expands over the pupil in the light; these algal-grazers (*Hypostomus* species) feed by night, but hide under rocks by day in clear streams where the light is very bright. Secondarily naked catfishes of the related Astroblepidae (1 gen., 40 sp.) live in the torrents of the northern Andes to Panama; when climbing falls these use the mouth as a sucker, having respiratory modifications to enable them to breathe at the same time (Hora, 1930).

The Doradidae is also a large family (*c.* 30 gen., 75 sp.), living mainly in the Amazonian region, but with representatives south to La Plata and north to Venezuela. Mainly riverine fishes feeding on bottom deposits, some grow to several kilograms in weight. The third armoured family, the Callichthyidae, includes about 8 genera, many monotypic, hardy widely distributed species of bottom-living fishes which penetrate to the headwaters of forest streams, where they, like so many other catfishes, are active by night. The little *Corydoras* which make such delightful aquarium fishes are exceptional in being active by day.

Fishes of the largest family of naked (unarmoured) catfishes in South America, the Pimelodidae, greatly resemble those of the Bagridae in Africa and Asia, a family considered to be near the basic stock from which many other catfish families are derived (Hora, 1937). About 250 species (55 gen.) of pimelodids are known. Many are very common omnivorous bottom-scroungers, belonging to large genera such as *Pimelodus* and *Pimelodella* (badly in need of revision). The vividly marked piscivorous *Pseudoplatystoma* (Sorubi) (Fig. 2.5*b*) grows to over 2 m long and is valued as a food fish in many parts of the continent. *Brachyplatysoma* species grow even larger (over 3 m), and are dreaded by fishermen in frail canoes. The common genus *Rhamdia* is represented as far north as Central Mexico. Species of the family Ageneiosidae (2 gen., 30 sp.) which have only two pairs of barbels, grow to 50 cm long. The Auchenipteridae (*c.* 16 gen., 60 sp.) are mostly less than 15 cm long; they include the widely distributed nocturnal *Trachycorystes* which wedge themselves into crevices in sunken logs by day, erecting their stout dorsal and pectoral spines when attempts are made to dislodge them; these too have a wide distribution from La Plata to Panama. The Trichomycteridae (25–30 gen., *c.* 280 sp.) include free-living species in Andean torrents, and parasitic species living in the gill cavities of larger fishes, often other catfishes; some species can be caught by suspending a piece of cow's lung in the river, and one species, the candiru (*Vandellia cirrhosa*), is reputedly attracted to urine and widely believed to enter the orifices of unwary bathers. The Cetopsidae (4 gen., *c.* 14 sp.) also includes some parasitic species, independently evolved (Roberts, 1972). The small families of catfish include the Aspredinidae, 4 genera of short-bodied aspredines found mostly in Guyana, and the more widely distributed bunocephalines, dorsoventrally flattened species, known as 'banjoman' for the loud noises that they produce, and in which the eggs are carried on the belly of the female.

The family Cichlidae includes about 20 genera with 100–150 species in South America, perciform fishes which guard their eggs and young and thrive in still water. Many are well known as aquarium fishes, such as the angel fish *Pterophyllum*, the discus *Symphysodon*, the oscar *Astronotus*, the *Cichlasoma* dempseys and various dwarf cichlids. Of the genus *Cichlasoma* which has speciated so abundantly in Central America very little is yet on record about the ecology of the individual species.

In South America cichlids are today riverine fishes, but abundant in areas of still water. Hardy species penetrate right up into headwater streams, where dwarf cichlids hide in the leaf litter. *Aequidens* and *Cichlasoma* of numerous species (mostly fishes up to 15 cm total length) live in small groups and feed mainly on invertebrates and vegetable debris. Larger species, such as those of the genus *Crenicichla* (pike cichlids) which has many species, and of *Cichla*, which has only about three, are piscivorous and live more solitary lives. The widely distributed *Cichla ocellaris* is the largest cichlid, growing to over 8 kilo in weight, a good food and sport fish. Some weed-frequenting species, such as *Symphysodon*, have very deep bodies. *Chaetobranchus* has the long gill rakers of a plankton feeder. The South American cichlids have thus, like the African cichlids, undergone adaptive radiations, but evidently long enough ago for their food habits to be fairly uniform within the present genera, in contrast with the very diverse food habits within an African genus such as *Haplochromis*.

The Osteoglossidae include *Arapaima gigas*, one of the world's largest freshwater fishes, which grows to over 3 m long and over 100 kg. Earlier reports of 5 m long, 170 kg are perhaps exaggerated according to Allsopp (1958); Rupununi specimens now rarely exceed 2·5 m long and 70 kg, but Bard (1973) describing the culture of *Arapaima* in ponds, gives 5 m and 200 kg as attainable. Carnivores, they feed on loricariids amongst other fishes, sucking them into the large mouth where the bony toothed tongue can crush them. *Osteoglossum*, which are much smaller fish (*c*. 64 cm long), are also carnivores; they cruise along just below the river surface, cirrhi outstretched, and include even little river bats in their diet; unlike *Arapaima*, *Osteoglossum* practises oral incubation, though which sex broods the young is not yet on record.

The neotropical cyprinodontoid fishes, all small, include the livebearing Poeciliidae, Jenynsiidae, Goodeidae and Anablepidae, and the oviparous Cyprinodontidae. Of the live bearers the poeciliids, e.g. the guppy *Poecilia* ('*Lebistes*') *reticulata* are the most widely distributed and most numerous in South America (11 gen., *c*. 15 sp.); the family Jenynsiidae comprises only two or three species restricted to the La Plata, and the Goodeidae occur only in Central America and Mexico. The Anablepidae, larger fishes (to *c*. 23 cm total length (TL)) are found in both Central and South America. The Neotropical Cyprinodontidae are divided into two subfamilies: the Rivulinae (9 gen., 40+ sp.), some of which are annual fishes spending the dry season as resting eggs (p. 226), and the Orestiinae, which are restricted to Lake Titicaca and other high lakes in the Andes, and which radiated in L.

Titicaca to form a species flock of *c.* 18 endemic species. The Anablepidae are unusual in living in estuaries and at the edge of the sea in Guyana, where small shoals of them bob about at the water surface, their turret eyes looking like bubbles. Each eye is divided horizontally and has two lenses, the upper for aerial vision, the lower for vision under water, though in Guyana the water in which they live is so turbid with mud that underwater vision would appear to be of very little use to them. Here their aerial vision appeared useful for avoiding predation by the many piscivorous birds feeding along the edge of the tide (terns and herons and the skimmer *Rynchops*). Guyana has two species of *Anableps*; *A. anableps* which lives mainly in the estuaries and *A. microlepsis* found on the open coast. They both appeared to be detritus or mudfeeders, *A. anableps* lying like sausages in the channels in the wet mud in estuaries as the tide went down, straining the outflowing water. These Guyana species were never seen to use their aerial vision to catch insects, as *Anableps* are said to do in textbooks.

South America has many fishes of marine origin; these include stingrays (*Potamotrygon*) which produce live young far up the rivers; *P. hystrix* in the Rupununi produced two young at a time born at the start of the rains. The Amazon has about 50 freshwater representatives of predominantly marine families, many of them (about half?) endemic (Roberts, 1972). These include two elasmobranchs (a shark *Carcharinus leucas* found right up in the Rio Ucayali according to Thorson, 1972, and a *Pristis* sawfish), and bony fishes of the following families: Clupeidae (herrings), 5 species; Engraulidae (anchovies), about 12 species, half of them endemic; Sciaenidae (drums), about 10 species, several endemic; Achiridae (flatfish), 9 species, most endemic; Belonidae (needle fish), 3 species; Eleotridae, 2 species; and single species of Hemirhamphidae (half-beak), Mugilidae (grey mullet), Tetraodontidae (Puffer), Batrachoididae (toadfish), Synbranchidae. The wide zone of brackish water in the estuary and its seasonal displacement must assist such invasions. In the lower reaches of the Amazon (Para) many other marine fishes come in on the rising tide to feed in the flooded areas (including species of Centropomidae, Mugilidae, Belonidae, Sciaenidae, Pomadasyidae, Lutjanidae, Carangidae, Clupeidae, Engraulidae, Dasyatidae). These flooded grasslands are some of the most productive areas of the whole Amazon system as the sea salts enrich plant growth, and the tidally inundated land provides plenty of fish food, which is less subject to seasonal variation than that in the flooded lands further up river.

The distribution of fishes within South America

Gery (1969) recognised eight faunal regions in South America as shown in Fig. 2.6; (1) the *Guianean–Amazonian* region (which appears to have had two main centres of evolution) with interconnections to (2) the *Orinoco–Venezuelan* region to the north, and (3) *Paranean* to the south; (4) *Magdalenean* and (5) *Trans-Andean* in the northwest; (6) *Andean* and (7) *Patagonian*, south of this with (8) the *East-Brazilian* in rivers flowing to the

Atlantic coast. The main pattern of fish distribution is of central richness (despite poverty of ancestral stocks) greatest in the Amazon, somewhat less in adjacent drainages north and south, less in the isolated Magdalena, and moderately poor in the western drainages of Colombia and Ecuador; progressively poor starting in southeast Brazil but interrupted by the south-flowing Paraná–Paraguai system; the Andes with a poor fauna mainly of specialised torrent fishes and a radiation of certain cyprinodontoids in the high lakes; in the far south transition to a completely different fauna of antarctic peripheral fishes.

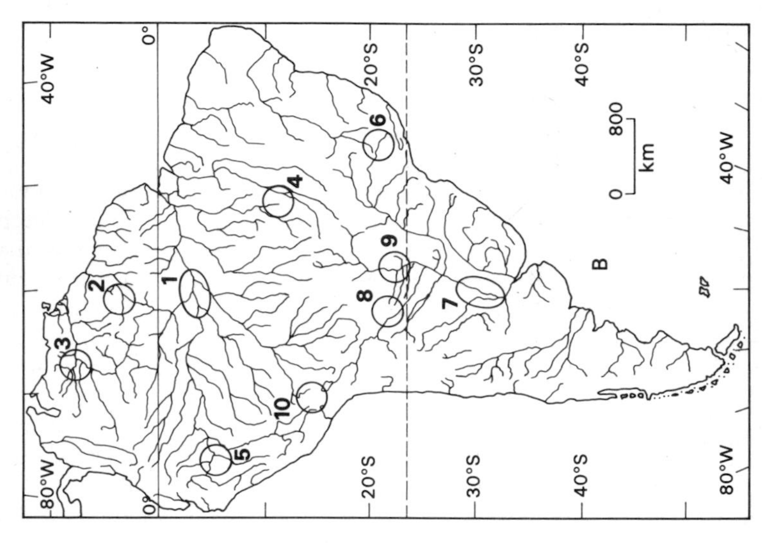

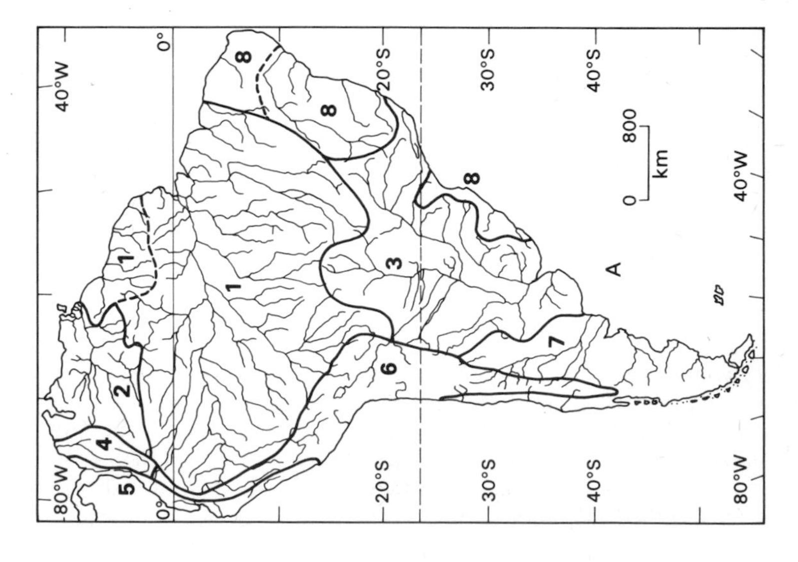

The numbers of species so far recorded in the various countries indicate the relative richness of the regions, though figures are only very provisional as great areas are not yet explored: Brazil (mostly Amazonas) 1334 species; Peru 503; Venezuela 494; Paraguai 447; Colombia 397; Guianas 364; Argentina 339 (including subspecies); Bolivia (mostly Amazonas) 277; Uruguay 105; Chile 23.

Of these faunal regions the *Guianean–Amazonian* is by far the richest. The Amazon basin has the richest freshwater fish fauna in the world, probably more than 1300 species, 85 per cent of them Ostariophysi, with representatives of almost all South American groups (including *Lepidosiren* which is not found in Guiana, Osteoglossidae and Nandidae). The peripheral areas, such as the upper and middle courses of the Amazon, Orinoco tributaries, and the Guianas, show greater similarities amongst themselves than with the fauna of the central Amazon basin. The Peruvian Amazon has more than 100 species in common with the remote Guianas, and there are many species shared by the Upper Tocantins–Araguaia–Xingu in Brazil and upper Rio Meto in Colombia, whereas the fauna is quite different in the centre of the basin. This suggests that a primitive fauna spread around the Amazon basin (then possibly a marine gulf, and later large lakes), and that the rich fauna of the Amazon proper diversified later.

At the present time the main Amazon river presents an ecological barrier to many fish species, while ecological conditions in certain peripheral streams are much alike. The fishes of the Araguaia tributaries far to the south of the Amazon mainstream show closer affinities with those of the Guianas far to the north of the Amazon than either of these do with fishes in Andean tributary waters away to the west, which suggests that these fishes may have moved across what is now the delta region of the Amazon. How much these distributions are accounted for by ecological conditions, and how much by the geological history of the area, is not yet clear. Myers (1972) has considered the effects of the Pleistocene changes in sea level on the rivers of this region (p. 73).

Many Amazonian fishes penetrate south to the great *Paranean* region which comprises the La Plata–Uruguay–Paraná–Paraguai system, the second largest drainage system in South America (3 200 000 km^2). Amazon tributaries such as the Guaporé may have been migration paths, as during wet years their headwaters contact those of the Paraguaian tributary Jauru around 15° S and 59° W (Fig. 3.1). The Upper Paraná and Uruguay River

Fig. 2.6
A. The fish faunal regions of South America (after Gery, 1969):
1. Guianean-Amazonian; 2. Orinoco-Venezuelan; 3. Paranean; 4. Magdalenean; 5. Trans-Andean; 6. Andean; 7. Patagonian; 8. East Brazilian.
B. Sites of studies discussed in text:
1. Central Amazon (Brazil); 2. Rupununi District (Guyana); 3. Orinoco tributaries (Venezuela); 4. Mato Grosso streams (Brazil); 5. Andean Amazon tributaries (Peru); 6. Rio Mogi Guassu (Brazil); 7. Middle Paraná (Argentina); 8. R. Pilcomayo (Bolivian waters); 9. Paraguaian Chaco (Paraguai); 10. L. Titicaca.

have a rather different biota from the Paraná–Paraguai; there is a remarkable decrease in species and biomass, and the flora and fauna show close relationships with those of the rivers of the Atlantic slope of Brazil and the São Francisco basin; this is possibly due to contacts in other paleogeographical conditions, or a remarkable ecological parallellism, or a combination of both (Bonetto and Drago, 1968). Looking at a relief map it is clear that the Upper Paraná has been captured from the Uruguay River.

Still further south, the *Patagonian* region lies well outside the tropics. The impoverished fauna here is characterised by a few Andean endemic Ostariophysi, mostly primitive, which have been pushed into this cold area by more recently radiating groups.

The *Andean* fauna includes the cyprinodont genus *Orestias*, the ancestors of which are thought to have been present before the mountains were formed and to have risen with the mountain chain. These speciated into *c.* 18 species in Lake Titicaca (3800 m), some species growing to 20 cm long. Limnological conditions in this lake were described by Gilson (1964). This endemic species flock was of the greatest scientific interest and a valuable source of food for the local Indian population, but these fishes have almost disappeared since the introduction of salmonids into Andean streams. A sporozoan parasite introduced with rainbow trout spread to *Orestias* and contributed to their decline (Villwock, 1972). This region also has a specialised fauna of torrent-living catfishes, mainly trichomycterids, and of characoids; these show an impoverishment in species, even in the equatorial zone, from 1000 m to 4200 m altitude. *Pygidium* and *Orestias* are found up to 4200–4500 m, altitude; *Astroblepus* to 4000 m, *Hemibrycon* to 3500 m, *Ancistrus* and *Acrobrycon* to 2400 or 2700 m (Eigenmann and Allen, 1942).

The *Trans-Andean* fauna is part of the general South American fauna cut off since the elevation of the Andes formed an effective barrier. Eigenmann (1921) found here about 390 species representing 108 genera, of which 60 per cent was also found on the Atlantic slopes and about 26 per cent endemic (the derivation in many cases quite evident and direct), while of the remainder 9 per cent was of Central American immigrants or their derivatives, and 5 per cent was of modified immigrants from the sea. There is a marked impoverishment from north to south as the country dries out to semidesert in the south.

The isolated *Magdalenean* fauna, derived mostly from that of the Upper Orinoco, has, in its 150 species, about 65 characoids and gymnotoids, some 65 catfishes and 10 or so cyprinodonts and cichlids, the rest being fishes of marine origin (Miles, 1947).

The *Orinoco–Venezuelan* region with about 494 species was divided by Mago (1970*b*), into seven faunal districts corresponding to drainage areas: (i) the Maracaibo basin, with a fauna related to the Magdalena as well as of the Orinoco; (ii) the Orinoco, comprising most of the country and with great affinities with the Guianas and the Amazon (with which it is connected via the Casiquiare canal (Fig. 3.1), with two smaller drainage areas (iii) to the Rio Negro in the south, and (iv) to the Cuyuni in the east; (v) the coastal

Caribbean, with a small enclave (vi) in and around Lake Valencia, and another small distinct area (vii) in the Gulf of Paria. Off this Gulf lies the large island of Trinidad, originally part of the mainland, with 74 species, only 36 of them genuinely freshwater fishes, of which five are endemic (Boeseman, 1960).

In the *East-Brazilian* region, some of the small coastal rivers show a high rate of endemicity. In the Rio Ribeiro half the fauna is endemic and Gery (1969) reported that the characids here show remarkable resemblances with those of the most remote region, Trans-Andean Colombia and Ecuador, almost down to species level (in *Salminus*, *Byconamericus*, *Pseudochalceus* and *Astyanax* groups); the reason for this is not at all clear. Both regions lack piranhas (*Serrasalmus* species). *Serrasalmus* and gymnotoids are both absent from northern Brazil; here the impoverished fauna, which is otherwise rather similar to that of the lower Amazon, may be related to the dry and unpredictable climate. The Rio São Francisco has a fauna distantly related to the Amazonian one but lacking many groups (such as *Lepidosiren*, osteoglossids, bunocephalid catfishes) and with some endemic species (for example among the serrasalmines).

Asia

The freshwater fish faunas of tropical Asia and their distribution

Fish communities in tropical Asia are not discussed in any detail in this book, but certain points are made for comparison with the other two tropical areas.

Geographically the Asian tropics may be divided into three regions (Fig. 2.7): the subcontinent of India; mainland Southeast Asia; and the islands. The islands lying on the 'Sunda' continental shelf, Borneo, Sumatra, Java, and certain others, were connected with the mainland at intervals during the Pleistocene glaciations when the general sea level was much lower (*c.* 100 m lower when water was locked up in the icecaps). An extinct river system, the bed of which is now covered by the sea, flows into the China Sea between the present day coastlines of Borneo and the Asian mainland. The rivers of East Sumatra, western Borneo (and according to Vaas, 1952, even some from India, Thailand and Indochina), were tributaries of this vast river system, which accounts for many similarities in fish fauna between the islands and the mainland. North Borneo rivers did not join this system, and the fauna is here somewhat impoverished. Islands lying off this Sunda shelf have completely different freshwater fish faunas, mostly of marine immigrants.

Myers (1951) referred to the section of Wallace's line down the Makassa Straits between Borneo and Celebes as the most spectacular zoogeographical boundary to be found among the world's freshwater faunas. To the west Borneo teems with 300 or more species of primary freshwater fishes (17 families); only 140 km to the east, Celebes has but two species of primary

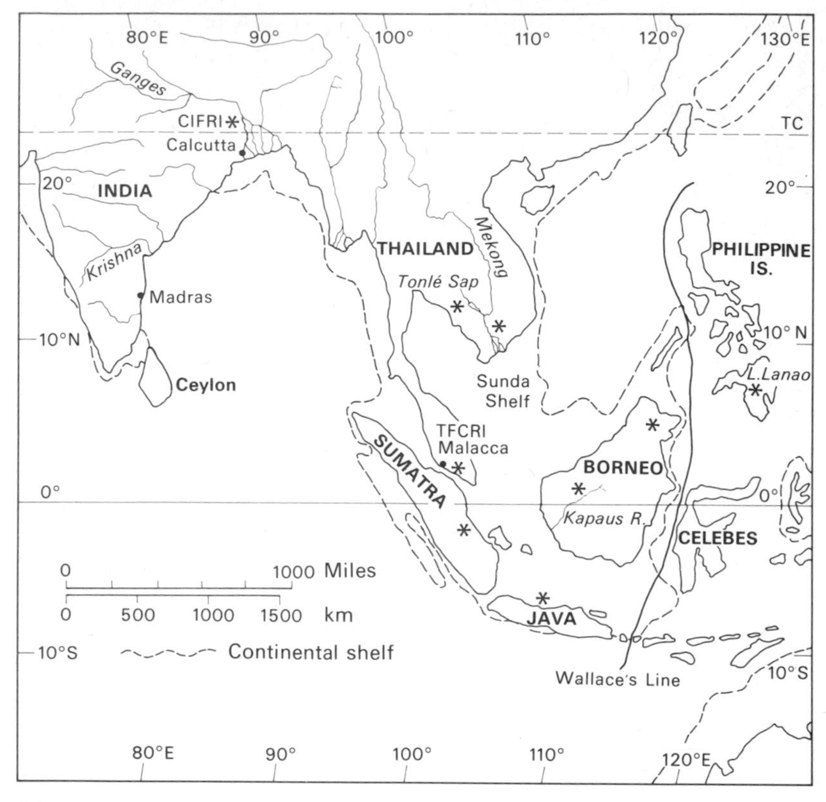

Fig. 2.7 The Asian tropics and sites mentioned in the text. Note the continental shelf; the sea level fell to about this level during Pleistocene glaciations and many of the large islands were then united with the mainland (Sundaland).

freshwater fishes, *Anabas testudineus* and *Channa striatus*, both probably introduced by man. Celebes, like Borneo, also has a few secondary freshwater fishes (cyprinodonts, a synbranchid and vicarious atherinids). Wallace's line, which separates the Oriental and Australian zoogeographical regions, continues south between Java and Lombok, where differences are not quite so spectacular, as the freshwater fish fauna of Java is much less rich than that of Borneo. But Java still has nearly 100 species of primary freshwater fishes (12 families), compared with 5 species (3 of them probably carried by man as food fish) of 4 families in Lombok.

According to Myers (1951) the freshwater fish evidence very strongly supports the conclusion that there has been no dryland connection whatsoever between the islands of the Asiatic continental shelf (Sundaland) with Celebes or Lombok or any island east of this during the entire Cainozoic. It further suggests that even in the Mesozoic there was never any dry land connection between Asia and Australia. Only three relicts of the Mesozoic fish fauna remain in this area today, one osteoglossid (*Scleropages formosus*) in Sundaland, another (*S. leichardti*) in Queensland (and possibly in New Guinea which connects with the Australian continental shelf), and the Queensland lungfish *Neoceratodus forsteri*. The rest of the New Guinea and Australian freshwater fish fauna is of marine origin.

The relationship of Indian fishes to those in neighbouring countries was considered above (p. 20). The present drainage systems of India described by Mani (1974) fall into two major groups: (1) *peninsular rivers* fed entirely by monsoon rains and which more or less dry up every year, and (2) *extra-peninsular rivers* fed by melting snow from the Himalayas which never dry up completely. The peninsular rivers include over six hundred short coastal streams on the west coast, and both west- and east-flowing inland rivers, the east-flowing ones with wide fan-shaped catchments and often large deltas. Of the extra-peninsular rivers those draining the northern slopes of the Himalayas, such as the Brahmaputra, are antecedent rivers older than the Himalayas, which have kept their channels open by faster erosion as the mountains rose; rivers draining the southern slopes, as does the Ganges, are consequent rivers which assumed their present form in the Pliocene or Pleistocene and now wander as slow streams over the plains of northern India. These extra-peninsular rivers have extensive deltas.

This tropical Asian fish fauna is dominated by cyprinids. Siluroids are also very abundant, and there are very many species of marine origin. To take the freshwater fish fauna of Thailand as an example (Smith, 1945), the total of 549 species (48 families) is made up of: 214 cyprinid species (39 per cent); 99 siluroids (18 per cent); 80 gobioids (15 per cent); 71 species of other marine families (13 per cent); 18 anabantoids (3 per cent); and 67 species of other freshwater families (12 per cent). The gobioids and other species of marine origin together make a marine component of 28 per cent.

The siluroid families of Asia include Ariidae, Bagridae, Schilbeidae, Clariidae (all found in Africa) and 9 endemic families (Appendix 2). The Schilbeidae includes *Pangasianodon gigas* of the Mekong, one of the world's largest freshwater fish, growing to over 2 m long, a strict vegetarian, lacking teeth in the adult. The Indian catfishes include *Heteropneustes fossilis* (Heteropneustidae) which has very long air sacs as accessory respiratory structures, and *Sisor rhapdophorus* with dermal armour.

The cyprinids are all non-piscivorous fishes which forage for plant and invertebrate food. In most tropical communities the number of predators is very high, and in Asian waters the predators include various siluroids (such as *Wallago*), also species of *Channa* and *Notopterus*, many of them large fishes.

Archer fishes, *Toxotes* (Toxotidae), are engaging Asian fishes common in sea level swamps, where they shoot down their prey, aerial insects, using a jet of water from the mouth to do so; there are several species of which *T. jaculatrix*, a fish growing to about 23 cm long, has been most studied.

Fish culture is very important throughout tropical Asia and some of the

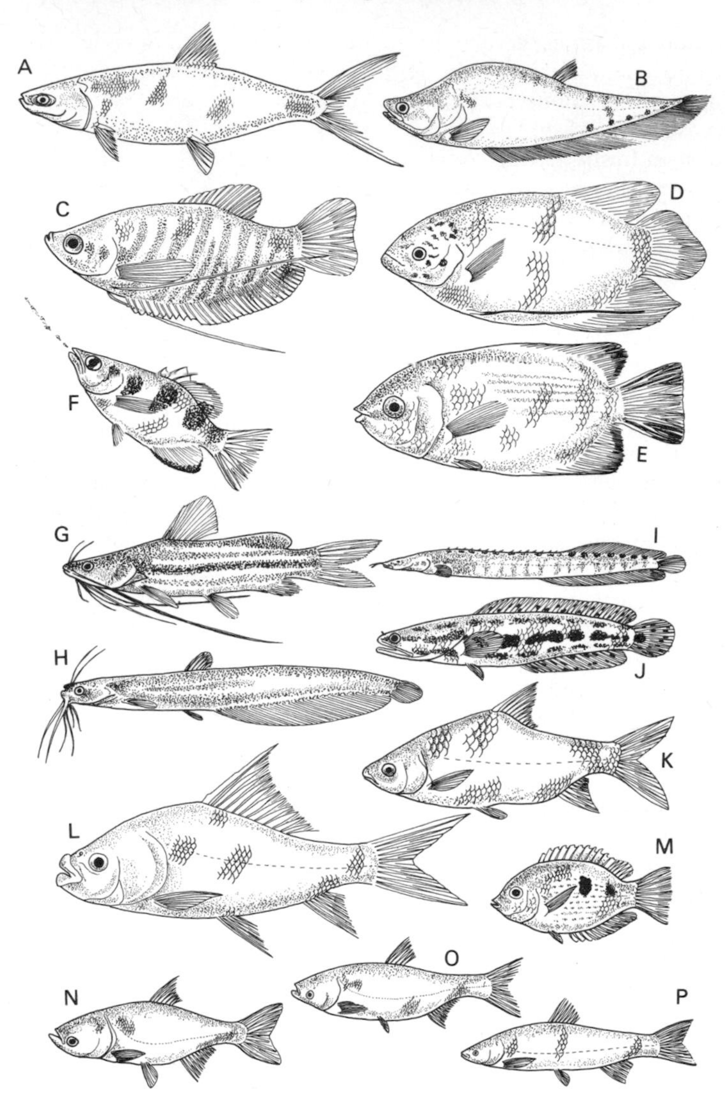

Fig. 2.8 Representative Asian freshwater fishes cultured or used as food.
A. *Chanos chanos* Milfish (150 cm, Chanidae); B. *Notopterus* Featherback (75 cm, Notopteridae); C. *Trichopterus pectoralis* (25 cm, Anabantidae); D. *Osphronemus goramy* (65 cm, Osphronemidae); E. *Helostoma temminckii* (30 cm, Helostomatidae); F. *Toxotes* Archer fish (20 cm, Toxotidae); G. *Mystus* (50 cm, Bagridae); H. *Heteropneustes* (30 cm, Heteropneustidae); I. *Mastacembelus* (40 cm, Mastacembelidae); J. *Channa* (90 cm, Channidae); K. *Barbus* ('*Puntius*') (50 cm, Cyprinidae); L. *Catla catla* (180 cm, Cyprinidae); M. *Etroplus* (30 cm, Cichlidae); N, O, P, Chinese carps (Cyprinidae): N. *Aristichthys nobilis* Bighead (60 cm); O. *Hypophthalmichthys molitrix* Silver carp (60 cm); P. *Ctenopharyngodon idella* Grasscarp (120 cm).

cultured species are shown in Fig. 2.8. The history of Asian fish culture goes back 4000 years. In Indonesia these cultured fishes include anabantids, plankton-feeding or vegetarian species which live in very weedy places, and which, like many of these Asian fishes, have accessory respiratory organs (labyrinths) to cope with life in deoxygenated water. The milkfish *Chanos chanos* (Chanidae) is a very important cultivated fish in brackish ponds in the Philippines. In Java fish have been introduced and cultured for so long that it is difficult to know how much of the present fauna is indigenous (Vaas and Schuurman, 1949). Manmade lakes in Java produce very high yields for large water bodies; for example 500–600 kg/ha/yr from a 25 km^2 lake in West Java, mostly of *Cyprinus carpio*, *Puntius javanicus* and the *Helostoma temmincki* (Vaas and Sachlan, 1952).

The extensive freshwater fish research in India centres around the biology of species used to stock dams and lakes, rather than on natural fish communities, but life history studies have been made of most of the main commercial species (bibliography by Tripathi *et al.*, 1962). In India the 'major carps' *Catla catla*, *Labeo rohita*, *L. fimbriatus* and *Cirrhina mrigala* are the main cultured fishes (see p. 189). Carp spawning places in the rivers of India have been mapped (David, 1959) as carp fry are much in demand for stocking tanks and other water bodies. Most of these carp spawn in the wet season, July to September (Qasim and Qayyum, 1961). Should the rains fail, the fish may not spawn that year; Khanna (1958) reported a failure of carps to spawn three out of eight years due to insufficient flooding. Methods have now been developed of inducing these fishes to spawn in ponds by means of pituitary hormone injections. Chinese carp (the grass carp *Ctenopharyngodon idella*, silver carp *Hypophthalmichthys molitrix* and bighead *Aristichthys nobilis*) are also now much used for fish culture in tropical Asia, where they grow much faster and mature earlier than in their home territory further north outside the tropics (Amur River and other waters). In India life history studies include those of *Mystus* catfishes found in all the principal rivers, where they support fisheries second in importance only to those for the clupeid *Hilsa ilisha* and the carp *Cirrhina mrigala*. The male *Mystus seenghala* guards its nest until the young are 45 mm long and they are said to subsist on a secretion exuded by him (Saigal and Motwani, 1961).

Tidal influences are felt over 50 km up some Indian rivers and the fish communities have many species of marine origin. Anadromous clupeids such as *Hilsa ilisha* support important fisheries; in the Hooghly river flowing past Calcutta these fishes ascend twice a year, the main run being in the monsoon season (Pillay, 1958). The construction of dams has affected some of these fisheries (Ganapati, 1973).

Sri Lanka (Ceylon) remained geographically part of the Indian mainland until quite recent times, with intermittent connections from the Miocene until 10 000 years ago or later (Jacob, in Hora *et al.*, 1949). This large island has no natural lakes but it has 103 rivers and over 10 000 lakes created by man over 1500 years, mostly small (less than 300 ha) in the low country and dry zone, plus fifty-one larger lakes more recently created for hydroelectric power. The 54 indigenous fishes are essentially stream and marsh-living forms; about 17 of these are of some economic importance, 8 of them (3 carps, 3 catfishes, *Channa* and the cichlid *Etroplus suratensis*) occurring in numbers large enough to support regular fisheries in low-country reservoirs (Indrasena, 1970). But the main economic production is of introduced *Tilapia* (Fernando, 1973); the 65 ha Beira lake enriched by heavy pollution yielded 2230 kg/ha/yr of *Tilapia mossambica. Osphronemus goramy*, *Trichogaster pectoralis* and *Cyprinus carpio* have also been introduced, and there is pressure to make further introductions for high country reservoirs. Unlike other tropical Asian countries Sri Lanka has no history of fish culture.

In Malaya, which has 250 species of freshwater fishes (less than 100 of them common), Johnson (1967) found distinctive fish associations in black waters, 'tree-country' streams, and ricelands. In tree-country streams fish faunas are very diversified; in black waters and ricelands they are restricted by low pH and low oxygen respectively. Faunas contain both specialists and generally tolerant species, the latter more important in the more extreme habitats. Cyprinids, particularly *Rasbora* species, are the predominant fishes in the acid and unproductive forest streams and blackwaters (less so in riceland habitats); a contrast with European waters where cyprinids generally live in the more productive waters. The riceland fish fauna in Malaya is depauperate compared with that in neighbouring countries; of the 14 more frequent species, 9 were air-breathers, 3 surface swimming, and two come to the surface when oxygen is low, as it is at night. *Anabas testudineus* and *Trichogaster trichopterus* are common riceland species.

In the Philippines certain islands on the Sunda shelf have Bornean primary freshwater fishes, and 3 genera have reached Mindanao along the Sula chain (Myers, 1951). The fishes of Lake Lanao on Mindanao are of major evolutionary interest, as this lake has a species flock of cyprinids, about 20 species of the genus *Barbus* (*Puntius* of some authors), plus 5 species so peculiar that they have been placed in 4 endemic genera. Myers (1960*a*) concluded that these had all evolved from a single ancestral species, *Barbus binotatus*, still found in most of the lowland streams and forming local races throughout its range. Lake Lanao was then thought to be only 10 000 years old. However, other evidence suggests that the lake is much older than this, possibly even deriving from the late Tertiary (Frey, 1969), and that there may have been several divergent populations of the species in the streams before the lake was formed (Kosswig and Villwock, 1965). These endemic Lanao genera have evolved some extreme specialisations, such as the lower jaw modifications in *Mandibularca*, unique in the family Cyprinidae, transcending the morphological limits of all non-Lanao cyprinids: features termed by Myers (1960*a*) 'supralimital specialisations' and which may be of great importance for the evolution of new lines of fish (p. 262).

These endemic cyprinids evolved in the absence of any serious fish predators, since Lake Lanao is cut off by falls over 50 m high which have prevented any piscivorous marine species, such as gobies, from entering the lake. About 1962–4, however, the white goby (*Glossogobius giurus*) was accidentally introduced (presumably with milkfish fry). This erupted into a large population which by 1969 had made serious inroads into the populations of some of the endemic cyprinids (as well as of the palaemonid shrimps), threatening some of the species with extinction. Other species have also been introduced into the lake, which now contains *Clarias batrachus*, the anabantids *Anabas testudineus* and *Trichogaster pectoralis*, the anguillid *Anguilla mauritiana*, the ophiocephalid *Ophiocephalus striatus*, the cyprinid *Cyprinus carpio*, the cichlid *Tilapia mossambica*, the centrachid *Micropterus salmoides*, the chanid *Chanos chanos*, as well as *Glossogobius giurus*, a mixture of species from many geographical areas (Frey, 1969). Already it may be too late to study the ecology of the endemic cyprinid species flock which would have been of the greatest scientific importance and about which virtually nothing is yet known.

3

Equatorial Forest Rivers: Ecological Conditions and Fish Communities

Africa: the Zaïre River system

Geography and history of the Zaïre basin

The Zaïre (formerly known as the Congo) system is divisible into about five distinct regions (p. 34). We are here concerned with the vast central basin, the main equatorial forest stretch cut off from the estuarine reaches by a long stretch of rapids, and separated from the Lualaba by the falls just above Kisangani (Stanley Falls), over 1500 km up river and almost on the equator. Within this central basin many fish species are widely distributed and this can be regarded as one faunal unit.

In Pliocene times the Zaïre basin contained a great lake or lakes which drained westwards when a coastal river broke through its western rim. The lower courses of streams flowing into this lake then extended across the lake floor to form the present Zaïre system. The main Zaïre river and most of its tributary rivers now flow in an anticlockwise direction; the affluent streams of the left bank cross the low-lying central basin and enter the river through swampy zones, whereas the right bank tributaries come from higher ground and have a different fauna of stream fishes above the 500 m contour.

In this central basin the middle Zaïre River falls only from 450 to 30 m in the 1500 km from Kisangani to Pool Malebo (Stanley Pool), on which Kinshasa is situated. For much of its course the 6–12 km wide Zaïre River flows around many islands in a 75 km wide belt of recent alluvia, much of which is inundated at high water. Swampy pools remain long after the water subsides. This alluvial tract ends at latitude 2° 36′ N where the river enters a 220 km long reach confined by low hills to a single channel; this stretch, where the water is relatively deep (23 to 30 m) and the current swift, receives the Kasai tributary from the south, and ends in Pool Malebo. Immediately below this cataracts and rapids ensue, the river falling 300 m in 340 km to Matadi, 136 km from the sea, which is entered at 6° S through a mangrove-fringed estuary.

This great river system straddles the equator where rain falls throughout the year. Tributaries stretching far north of the equator flood from August to

November, those far to the south of it from May to June, bringing their waters into the lower reaches in a bimodal peak. At Yangambi near Kisangani there is a short fall in river level between January and March, a longer fall between May and October. The 'dry seasons' here do not affect the fishes as profoundly as do those at higher latitudes, but many of the fishes do have peaks of breeding activity at high water. Much of this central Zaïre basin is cloaked in equatorial rain forest and the flooded river spills out and inundates huge areas of forest many kilometres from the main river.

Further details of the physical features of the Zaïre system are given by Marlier (1973) when comparing the limnology of the Zaïre and Amazon rivers. Marlier pointed out that although lowland equatorial environments have given these two rivers a general aspect and many features in common, these similarities must not obscure significant differences between them in altitude and relief, in water chemistry, and in accessibility to marine fishes. The Zaïre basin is smaller in area and only 34 per cent of it is covered by forest (compared with 80 per cent of the Amazon basin). The Zaïre has a highly variable slope, the watersheds a succession of plateaux separated by abrupt changes of elevation resulting in the formation of rapids, some steep enough to isolate elements of the biota (whereas the central Amazon has a very gentle slope and is at a low enough altitude to receive many marine immigrants). The Zaïre is a much shallower river, with only small fluctuations in level (*c*. 3 m compared with 15+ m at Manaus), the lakes and swampy depressions in the upper courses absorbing the heavy rain. Geological differences affect the water chemistry (the main Amazon being turbid with continually shifting sediments from the Andes). The lakes in the Zaïre system, particularly the tectonic L. Tanganyika, are much more distinct from the river than are any Amazonian lakes, showing a high degree of endemism unmatched by any region of the Amazon.

The ecology of Zaïre basin fishes has been studied at four widely separated points: (1) in and around Pool Malebo (Poll, 1959*a*); (2) around Yangambi near Kisangani *c*. 1500 km up-river (Gosse, 1963); (3) on the large tributary Tschuapa River in the Ikela district; and (4) in Lake Tumba, a lateral lake below the Tschuapa/Zaïre confluence (Matthes, 1964).

The main biotopes of the Zaïre basin

Specific associations of fishes characterise the *main river*, the *marginal waters* along the shores and islands and in the bays and creeks, the *inundated forest zone*, which lead back into *swamps* ± permanent pools, and *affluent rivers* and *streams* of various sizes. But most fishes change their habitat, and thus their association, as they grow, also with their sexual activity and with the season. Fishes of many species move into the inundated forest at high water to breed and feed, and back to the low-water channels as the level falls. Some fishes, especially the young, may stay behind in pools which become isolated as the level falls, and fishes with special adaptations to withstand deoxygenated conditions may remain in the swamps.

The shallow marginal waters along the banks and islands (and over them when the river level is high) carry far more fishes than do the open waters. Gosse (1963) used a 'bank coefficient' (the number of times the length of a stretch of river is multiplied by the length of banks within it, including around the contained islands) as an index to the richness of a stretch for fishes. Young fishes of numerous species abound in the shallow marginal waters where luxuriant vegetation supports a rich fauna of invertebrate fish food and provides cover from predators. The open waters are turbid in shallow stretches.

Of the fishes in the families listed in Appendix 4, the clupeids are found only in the main rivers. The mormyrids are principally fluviatile, though several species of each genus occur in streams and swamps. Among the characids, citharinids and cyprinids the large species are fluviatile, while small species frequent streams, and none live in swamps. Of the catfishes the bagrids and mochokids live mainly in the large rivers, but some species occur in streams. The schilbeids are typically open water catfishes, all living in rivers except for one species specialised for life in forest streams in each of the two principal genera *Schilbe* and *Eutropius*, the convergence between these two species being remarkable. The behaviour of the Clariidae allows them to colonise all three biotopes, river, stream and swamp, but in each of these they frequent calm muddy bottoms. The Amphiliidae, on the other hand, are current-loving fishes of forest streams and river rapids. Cichlids in the rivers include various *Tilapia* species, *Tylochromis* and *Lamprologus* mocquardi, while other species are confined to small streams. The cyprinodonts are specially adapted for life in streams and small bodies of water. The anabantids occur only in the swamps.

The Yangambi area, which lacks rocks and rapids, has none of the current-loving and rock-frequenting species found in the rapids below Kinshasa, but is rich in forest-loving mormyrids, characids, bagrids and cyprinids absent from Pool Malebo. Some of these forest water species also occur in Cameroon and Gabon.

The rapids below Kinshasa, the longest stretch of such rapid water in Africa, have a fish fauna specialised for life in very fast turbulent water, highly oxygenated, over rocks, and with poor visibility. Fishes are well-shaped for adhering to the rocks or with anguilliform bodies for living in crevices between them. Both the accessory respiratory organs and the eyes are much reduced in the catfish *Gymnallabes* living here, and the eyes are no longer functional in the endemic *Caecomastacembelus*. Species of several families show convergent adaptations for a sedentary life with reduced vision. Poll (1959*a*, *b*) pointed out that the endemic fishes here are representatives of lowland families (cyprinids, mochokids, cichlids), not of families (such as Kneriidae) typical of headeater streams in Africa.

The swamps are either permanent, carrying a very specialised fauna adapted for life in deoxygenated waters, or temporary, part of the inundation zone, carrying a much more varied fish fauna seasonally. The swamp water is very acid (pH 3·8–5·0), the water shallow (a few centimetres to 3 or

4 m) often over a leaf-carpeted bottom of organic mud. Many of the fish are very dark in colour. Apart from the omnivorous piscivorous species, almost all the fishes feed on insects; primary production is very low. A few species living here, such as the cyprinodonts and *Hepsetus odoe* take the better aerated water from just below the water surface, but most of the other species have accessory respiratory organs: lungs in *Polypterus* and *Protopterus*, epibranchial organs in *Papyrocranus* ('*Notopterus*') and *Phractolaemus*, arborescent organs in clariids, labyrinthine organs in anabantids, pharyngeal diverticula in *Parophiocephalus*.

Residual pools from the wet season, shallow swampy places where *Protopterus dolloi* nest amidst rotting vegetation, have very acid water (pH 4·8) with only traces of dissolved oxygen. Only fishes with accessory respiratory organs live here, 17 species in all, namely: *Protopterus* (*P. dolloi* and *P. aethiopicus*); *Polypterus palmas*; *Xenomystus nigri*; *Pantodon buchholzi*; 6 clariids (4 *Clarias* species, *Chanallabes apus* and *Clariallabes melas*); 2 *Ctenopoma* species; *Parophiocephalus obscurus*; and the cichlids *Hemichromis bimaculatus* and *Pelmatochromis ocellifer*. *Phractolaemus ansorgei* and *Ctenopoma fasciolatum* were found in the nests of *Protopterus dolloi* where analyses revealed virtually no dissolved oxygen. The anguilliform clariids *Clariallabes* and *Channallabes* have reduced paired fins and burrow in the rotting vegetation. *Protopterus dolloi* breeds here when the water is low, the male guarding the young in a mud burrow which has a mud chimney to the surface air (Brien, Poll and Bouillon, 1959). This behaviour in these swamps which do not dry out contrasts with that of *P. annectens* in West Africa and *P. aethiopicus* in East Africa, which both aestivate when seasonal swamps dry up and breed when the water level rises (Johnels and Svensson, 1954; Greenwood, 1958).

In and around Pool Malebo Poll (1959*a*) differentiated between the faunas of the main Pool and those of the marginal waters with their inflowing streams and swamps, the muddy places where *Protopterus dolloi* nests were found, and the rapids below the Pool (Appendix 4). The Pool itself is a 500 km^2 enlargement of the river, rarely more than 10 m deep, which contains a large island and an archipelago of smaller ones and sandbanks. The level here varies about 3 m during the year, falling in February/March and for longer periods between July and October. The water is turbid, the bottom mainly sandy, the water temperature around 27° C, pH 6·5.

Of the 20 families of fishes found in Pool Malebo the Mormyridae includes by far the most species, 38, of which 26 are common (*Petrocephalus* and *Stomatorhinus* species the most common). Many of these mormyrids live in the open water, in large schools near to the bottom, their orientation within the school perhaps assisted by the signals emitted from electric organs in the caudal peduncle (p. 235). Their gregarious behaviour, conducive to the formation of local populations, may help to explain the presence of numerous species within the Pool (Poll, 1959*b*). In the open water four small species of pelagic clupeids are very abundant, preyed on by piscivorous characids. Large species of *Alestes*, *Bryconaethiops*, *Hydrocynus* and *Hepsetus* are found in the Pool, while the large *Citharinus* and *Distichodus* live mainly in the marginal waters where their foods, detritus, plankton and plants, are more abundant. The siluroid catfishes inhabiting open water include some almost transparent forms. The bagrid catfishes are characteristic of mobile sand bottoms; common ones living here are *Chrysichthys cranchii*, two *Gephyroglanis* species, and endemic dwarf (< 10 cm) species of *Leptoglanis*, transparent bagrids with upturned eyes. Mochokid catfishes are also common in the river, especially *Synodontis alberti* (with very long maxillary barbels) and *S. nummifer*. Two species of cyprinid and some cichlids are also abundant in the pool: *Lamprologus*, *Nannochromis* and two tilapias, *T. tholloni*, a herbivore and *T. galilaea* ('*T. boulengeri*') a plankton-feeder.

Vast swampy regions border the shores of Pool Malebo and the mouths of the affluent streams. These streams are shallow with sandbanks and swampy shores (with *Papyrus* and palms), their channels connecting through to the open waters of very large pools in the swamps. These stillwater pools with water lilies (*Nymphaea*) may be cut off from Pool Malebo by barriers of floating water hyacinth (*Eichhornia*), a South American waterplant which has invaded the Zaïre and Nile systems blocking many channels. These pools have a temperature around 26° C, pH 8·5, and 7·3 mg/l dissolved oxygen. These marginal pools, streams and creeks provide habitats for most of the small fishes endemic to the region, species not found in fast-flowing water (Characidae, Citharinidae, Cyprinodontidae, Tetraodontidae, Mochokidae, Anabantidae, Eleotridae). *Protopterus* and *Polypterus* (*P. palmas*) are here abundant, also notopterids, *Pantodon* and *Phractolaemus*, but relatively few mormyrids (only 7 out of 38 species).

Further up the river the fish communities in the various biotopes of the Yangambi area 1500 km above Pool Malebo, and of the intermediate Ikela District and L. Tumba regions, are discussed by Gosse (1963) and Matthes (1964) respectively. The faunas are so complex that it is impossible here to more than outline their findings.

Both authors distinguish between biotopes of open waters; marginal waters; swamps; and streams. In the main rivers the biotopes are much more numerous and diversified than in the streams and swamps, the number of species is much higher, the fish associations are more numerous and less well defined. The rivers more than 50 m wide, exposed to sun and wind, have higher temperatures (25·5–33° C) than the streams.

The open waters have pelagic and benthic zones. In the pelagic zone live immense shoals of plankton-feeding fishes, small clupeids (*Microthrissa*) which migrate up and down river seasonally, *Clupeopetersius* (Characidae) and small *Barbus* (Cyprinidae), followed by predators such as *Hydrocynus vittatus*. In the Ikela District large characoids and cyprinids also live in the open water in shoals, feeding mainly on aerial insects stranded on the water surface, and themselves preyed on by large *Hydrocynus* and *Lates*. At Yangambi, Gosse commented that the current-loving fishes in the main river, living at the surface, midwater, or on the bottom, are less well known than marginal species, as they are more difficult to catch. The associations of species living near the river surface along the banks depend largely on allochthonous food.

The true benthic fauna is light-shy and hides away in holes among the submerged branches, or on rocky or muddy bottoms. These fishes prefer still water with its numerous retreats along shaded banks and in the bays and channels, holes behind sandbanks, etc.; they are mainly nocturnal mormyrids and siluroids, but in the Ikela district citharinids (*Distichodus* and *Citharinus*), cyprinids (*Labeo*) and cichlids such as *Tylochromis* live here too. The benthic fishes are mainly bottom insect-feeders, such as many mormyrids, *Chrysichthys* and *Synodontis*, *Tylochromis* and *Barbus*, but they also include the mud-eating *Citharinus*, detritus-feeding *Chrysichthys*, some omnivores, and piscivorous *Polypterus*, *Mormyrops*, *Chrysichthys* and *Parophiocephalus*. Rocky bottoms are rare in the Zaïre basin but the litter of fallen trees provides hiding places equivalent to those offered by rocks, and these are frequented by nocturnal species, mormyrids and siluroids. Rocky biotopes where they exist are poor in food, lacking any flora, and most of the fishes associated with them are carnivores feeding mainly on bottom insects.

Sand banks in the main river have shallows with rapidly flowing water upstream of them, while downstream the shore is steep forming mud-bottomed holes 3 to 5 m deep where there is no current. Near Yangambi these holes are frequented by *Citharinus*, *Tilapia* and *Polypterus*, the adults living where the water is deepest, accompanied by *Lates niloticus* and large siluroids (*Clarias* and *Heterobranchus*). Many mormyrids are caught here at night, which by day live in schools in the current alongside these muddy bottoms, while bagrids are equally abundant on the mud beds by day and by night. The juvenile fishes live in less deep holes, as do small fishes fond of muddy bottoms, *Tylochromis*, *Schilbe* and *Barbus*. *Tilapia* and *Tylochromis* fry live in the warm shallow pools on the sand banks, preyed on by fish-eating birds. Sand or gravel beaches along the shore of the islands form different biotopes according to current speed. The unstable bottoms have poor faunas, mainly current-loving small characoids and cyprinids, which feed on surface insects, and some bottom-living *Labeo* and *Tetraodon*.

The marginal waters present a diversified series of biotopes, very important to the fishes, many of which reproduce and spend much of their lives here. These are transitional waters between the open water and the inundated forest zone. The water here has little current and the temperature is high (25–35° C) although the banks are usually shaded. The bottoms may be rich in vegetable debris, sand, mud or occasionally stony or rocky. These waters are rarely more than 3 m deep (occasionally up to 10 m in some channels). Relatively stable habitats, they are nevertheless subject to greater seasonal variations than the open waters.

Matthes recognised separate fish associations in

1. the littoral zone, further subdivided into that with (*a*) rocky shores (wave-washed laterite cliffs), (*b*) sandy or stony beaches, (*c*) marshy shores,

shaded, with sandy or muddy bottoms littered with vegetable debris.
2. Channels, creeks and dead arms (oxbows), the pools and bays shaded, calm, with little or no current, bottoms muddy or sandy, rich in vegetable debris.
3. Floating meadows, along the shaded banks and in heads of bays.
4. Inundation zones, inundated forest and pools adjacent to the rivers, unstable habitats rich in vegetation and fish foods.

The ecological factors shared by all these marginal waters are the still water, shallow depth, generally dense vegetation, abundant fish food, and bottoms littered with debris, often over organic mud. The aquatic flora is well developed and the invertebrate fauna is particularly rich and diversified. The fish fauna is immensely varied, almost all species spending part of their lives in such waters, though most only come here periodically, some in the floods to reproduce, others in the dry season when the inundation forest is dry. The young fishes find here shelter from predators and current as well as abundant food.

In the Yangambi area the inundation zones carry juvenile fishes of many species: entomostracans and insect larvae are here abundant, also rich bottom deposits for young *Citharinus* which become mud-feeders when about 3 cm long. At times of low water the young fish move from this zone into the floating meadows or marginal macrophytes, where an intensive basket fishery catches many species of mormyrid, the characoids *Hydrocynus*, *Distichodus*, and *Citharinus*, siluroids *Clarias*, *Synodontis*, *Schilbe* and also *Tilapia*. Large predators such as *Hydrocynus* frequent the margins of the vegetation, while *Distichodus* live in it, feeding on macrophytes.

The streams near Yangambi flow from the plateau. They are shaded, with very small variations in microclimate, the bottoms of mobile sand. The upper reaches are colonised by an association of insectivorous fishes. In a rotenone sample of 670 individuals representing 16 fish species, 84 per cent had been feeding almost exclusively on terrestial insects (compare Amazonian streams, p. 82, and Bornean streams, p. 85; aquatic insect larvae, shrimps and fish formed the other foods (Gosse, 1963).

The edges of the streams and their lateral extensions are occupied by a series of species which though present in all the streams do not form typical stream associations. These lateral extensions often communicate with the swamps and are colonised by swamp-loving species, such as the anabantid *Ctenopoma* and cyprinodonts which take insects from the water surface, and the cichlid predators (*Hemichromis*) which accompany them.

The open water of the streams presents a succession of biotopes, the extent of each governed mainly by the depth and current speed. The shallow zones less than 50 cm deep, with mobile bottom deposits, have few fishes, though some *Mastacembelus*, *Amphilius* and *Auchenoglanis* hide in the little piles of branches in the sand. The stillwater zone along the bank is inhabited by young individuals of the marginal species, exploiting insects which fall into the water and organic debris from the water surface. Where the water is deeper (1+ m) the current is stronger and the stream physiognomy changes completely; often the deeper sections are littered with tree debris. Fishes here tend to be omnivores staying near to the bottom, with predators such as *Hepsetus odoe* and *Mesoborus crocodilus* lurking in holes in the banks, while light-shy siluroids hide by day in the tangle of submerged branches.

The lower stretches of the streams carry the same associations along their margins and in open water, but as the stream widens and the current slows down the bottom omnivores become more prominent. The numbers of species, the size of the individual fish, and the length of the section they colonise, depend on many factors, such as the breadth and depth, types of bank and water levels. Many riverine species move into streams at certain times, *Hydrocynus vittatus* and *Distichodus* only into the larger streams. The young stages of *Citharinus*, *Alestes* and *Distichodus* move upstream in the floods and out into the inundated forest where they make their first growth.

The fish fauna of these streams is thus a well characterised association with the admixture of swamp and river species. The succession in these associations is governed principally by current speed. The upper reaches carry mainly insect-feeding fishes living on aerial insects, and as the current slows bottom omnivores appear. The absence of plankton-feeders reflects the absence of plankton in flowing water.

The Zaïre system carries several large lateral lakes. The best studied of these, Lake Tumba a 765 km^2 extent of water near the equator, is not a true lake but a permanent zone of river inundation, most organisms living here dependent on materials brought in by the inflowing streams (Marlier, 1960; Matthes, 1964). The maximum depth ranges from 6 to 10 m (mean depth 3–5 m). The banks are covered with forest which is inundated at high water twice each year, a little flood in May/June and a larger one in September to January. The water is brown with humic acids (pH 4·5–4·9), very reducing and notoriously poor in dissolved salts (conductivity k^6 24–32). Dissolved oxygen is however present all year throughout the water mass, as this is shallow open water, stirred by violent winds. Temperatures range from 27 to 33° C. The lake bottom is of kaolin mud with finely divided organic debris. The plankton is sparse, though enriched at the heads of bays and close to inflowing streams with some Cladocera. Insects dominate the invertebrate fauna, their types and abundance linked with the presence of vegetable debris. The ephemeropteran *Povilla adusta*, the nymphs of which burrow in dead wood, is abundant, also some Trichoptera, with chironomids in the floating meadows and swampy coves. Large prawns (*Palaemon*) live near the shores feeding on leaves. Sponges colonise objects which are periodically submerged. Molluscs are absent (as from most very acid waters).

Lake Tumba has a rich fish fauna with numerous mormyrids, characoids, bagrids, clariids and cichlids, with a small endemic species of pelagic characoid *Clupeopetersius*. A local fishery takes mainly *Citharinus* (especially *C. macrolepis*) 76 per cent by weight; *Hydrocynus* (*H. goliath* and *H. vittatus*) 6 per cent; *Distichodus* 4 per cent; *Auchenoglanis* 3 per cent; also *Mormyrops deliciosus*, *Microthrissa parva*, *Chrysichthys* and *Alestes* species and others (Marlier, 1960). Most species breed in August–September at the start of the main flood when the fish move into the inundated forest. The fish return to the lake as the water level falls.

The richness of the Lake Tumba fish fauna, despite the chemical poverty of the water, appears to be due to a combination of the very extensive shoreline, with its rich littoral fauna and flora and exogenous material (insects and vegetable debris) contributing to the food supply, and the floods allowing the fishes to find food far from the lake in the inundated forest. Should the banks be cleared and the fish denied access to the forest, the fishery would cease to be productive (compare the Grand Lac of the Mekong system, p. 123).

The ecology of Zaïre fishes

Trophic groups Fishes in the Zaïre waters have to adapt themselves to the seasonal foods; the main feeding time is at high water, when foods are most abundant and most varied, whereas many fishes are restricted to using bottom debris when the water is low (compare the Rupununi, p. 105). The foods eaten also change with the size and age of the fish. Many piscivorous fishes often eat invertebrates when young. The amount of food ingested also varies with the gonad state, sexually active fishes eating less than at other times.

From analyses of stomach contents Matthes (1964) drew up a complex table listing the species of fish in the different trophic groups in the various habitats in the Ikela and Lake Tumba regions. These trophic categories, indicated in Table 3.1, include: *mud-feeders* taking in micro-organisms and organic matter with fine mud; *detritus feeders*, utilising bottom debris, mainly vegetable and insect debris and human refuse (many species turn to this at low water); *herbivores*, both algal and macrophyte feeders; *plankton feeders*, which are not very abundant as the river has so little plankton; *omnivores*, each family and almost every genus having a representative which uses all forms of food (and which often becomes the most widely dispersed species); and *carnivores*.

The carnivores include those taking medium-sized prey, mainly insects from the surface or benthic insect stages. The river margin carnivores also feed mainly on aquatic insects and Crustacea. Carnivores taking large prey include those using a mixed diet of fishes and large invertebrates (shrimps and Odonata), piscivores swallowing whole fishes, and finbiters specialised to tweak pieces from the fins of living fishes.

Matthes listed the species representing each of these trophic groups in each of the main habitats in the regions investigated, showing both the preferred habitat of the species and other habitats where it may also be found. His table is too detailed for reproduction here, but the summary of it in Table 3.1 indicates the preferred biotopes of the various genera of fishes. Most of these genera are represented by a number of species each preferring a different biotope. Certain species occur in several habitats; and a biotope may have several species (in some cases of the same genus) occupying a particular trophic niche. For instance, two macrophyte-feeding *Distichodus* (*D. noboli* and *D. fasciolatus*) occur in bays and pools, and another two omnivorous species (*D. sexfasciatus* and *D. atroventralis*) both live in the littoral zone.

Within each habitat as broadly defined here Matthes recognised that there are clearly a multitude of ecological niches differing in detail, and that there are also continuous changes in the course of time, particularly with seasonal changes in water level, food available, and with the numbers of particular species present. Such an unstable medium is dynamic and resilient, and the diversity of niches in a relatively small stretch of water permits the existence of numerous closely related species with apparently identical ecology, as is the case for certain mormyrids, characids, citharinids, siluroids. The seasonal instability explains the absence of very highly specialised trophic forms (as found in the Great Lakes of Africa) but there is not as much seasonal variation in food abundance as in seasonal rivers such as the Niger. Zaïre species which are apparently specialised can really adapt themselves to diverse conditions; for example, the long rostral probe in *Campylomormyrus tamandua* can seek insects in the bottom mud or sand, or in organic debris or among rocks. Predators which specialise by biting fins of other fishes can live in any biotope where suitable prey fish are present. Under normal conditions most of the Zaïre fish species showed a marked preference for one particular biotope, for which they are probably slightly better adapted, but if conditions change suddenly they can survive. These Zaïre species are also eurythermic, able to withstand temperature changes of the order of 5° to 10° C (Matthes, 1964).

Breeding seasons Cichlids appear to breed more or less throughout the year in equatorial waters, but most of the Zaïre basin fishes spawn at the start of the highwater season, September–October (continuing until December for some species in Lake Tumba), with another breeding season of less general importance during the high water in April–June (Matthes, 1964). The relative importance of the two seasons may vary in different parts of the Zaïre basin and from year to year. Away to the south in the more seasonal Lualaba, and in the Luapula-Mweru tributary system, the principal breeding season for most species is at high water in January to March, with a secondary peak for cichlids in September–October (Poll and Renson, 1948, and de Kimpe, 1964, respectively).

Most species migrate upstream as the waters start to rise, then laterally into the inundated forest. Around Lake Tumba fishes penetrate many tens of kilometres into the flooded forest to spawn and feed on the abundant and varied foods (Matthes, 1964). Exceptions to this include certain pelagic species, clupeids, cyprinids and schilbeids, and some benthic bagrids and mochokids tied to habitats in large rivers or lakes.

Fish eggs hatch very quickly, within several hours or two days at the most, and growth is fast in the inundated zone. The larger young leave this zone at the same time as the adults when the water starts to fall. But many

Table 3.1 The preferred biotopes of fish genera representing various trophic groups in equatorial forestwaters of Central Zaïre (data abridged from Matthes, 1964, who listed the particular species and indicates all the biotopes where each occurs).

HABITATS	OPEN WATERS		MARGINAL WATERS			SWAMPS	FOREST STREAMS
TROPHIC GROUPS	Pelagic zone	Benthic zone	Littoral	Bays, pools, creeks, dead arms, channels	Floating prairies	Pools seasonal *permanent	
Mud-feeders		*Citharinus* *Labeo*	*Synodontis*			*Phractolaemus*	
Detritus-feeders	*Alestes*	*Gnathonemus* *Chrysichthys* *Auchenoglanis*	*Petrocephalus*	*Auchenoglanis* *Synodontis*		*Stomatorhinus* *Clarias* **Clariallabes* *Channallabes*	*Clarias*
Omnivores	*Bryconaethiops* *Barbus*	*Gnathonemus* *Chrysichthys*	*Gnathonemus* *Petrocephalus* *Alestes* *Micralestes* *Petersius* *Bathyaethiops* *Distichodus* *Parauchenoglanis*	*Alestes* *Phenacogrammus* *Xenocharax* *Clarias*	*Distichodus* *Barbus*	*Stomatorhinus* **Ctenopoma*	*Alestes* *Bryconaethiops* *Phenacogrammus* *Congocharax* *Neolebias* *Barbus* *Nannochromis* *Ctenopoma*
Herbivores							
algal-feeders				*Hemigrammopetersius* *Pelmatochromis*	*Neolebias*		
macrophyte-feeders			*Eutropius*	*Distichodus* *Tilapia*	*Distichodus* *Synodontis*		
Plankton-feeders	*Microthrissa* *Clupeopetersius*		*Barbus*		*Aplocheilichthys*		

Carnivores using allochthonous material (surface insects)	*Petersius* *Barilius*		*Micralestes* *Barilius*	*Phenacogrammus* *Bathyaethiops*		*Pantodon* **Ctenopoma*	*Micralestes* *Phenacogrammus* *Epiplatys* *Aphyosemion* *Hypsopanchax*
Bottom† insect-feeders		*Gnathonemus* *Barbus* *Gephyroglanis* *Synodontis*	*Petrocephalus* *Marcusenius* *Gnathonemus* *Chrysichthys* *Tylochromis*	*Polypterus* *Petrocephalus* *Gnathonemus* *Parauchenoglanis* *Microsynodontis*		*Polypterus* *Stomatorhinus* *Clarias* *Kribia* **Ctenopoma*	*Barbus* *Auchenoglanis* *Clarias* *Eutropius* *Chiloglanis* *Amphilius* *Mastacembelus*
River margin carnivores			*Mormyrops* *Microstomatichthyoborus* *Eutropius*	*Polypterus*	*Xenomystus* *Nannocharax* *Hemistichodus* *Heterochromis* *Ctenopoma*		*Phractura* *Nannocharax* *Trachyglanis* *Hemichromis*
Mixed carnivores	*Mesoborus*	*Mormyrops* *Chrysichthys*	*Polypterus* *Mormyrops* *Schilbe* *Eutropius* *Malapterurus*	*Protopterus* *Clarias* *Pelmatochromis*	*Ctenopoma*	*Clarias*	*Hemichromis* *Ctenopoma*
Piscivores	*Odaxothrissa* *Hydrocynus* *Lates*		*Phagoborus*	*Parophiocephalus*			*Hepsetus*
Fin-biters	*Eugnathichthys*		*Phago*	*Belonophago*			*Phago*

* Genera found in permanent swamps.
† Over rocky bottoms or amongst tree debris genera include: *Gnathonemus, Chrysichthys, Dolichallabes, Synodontis, Nannochromis, Lamprologus, Mastacembelus.*

juveniles remain behind in the numerous creeks, bays and ponds. Some species are well adapted for life in these stillwaters; others are merely trapped here and many of these perish in the shrinking pools. We know virtually nothing as yet about the breeding behaviour of many of the species of economic importance.

Growth rates Hardly anything is yet known about the rates of growth of the Zaïre fishes. The sizes of juveniles taken in August–September suggested that sexual maturity is generally attained towards the age of two years in the large species, while certain small species are annual (Matthes, 1964). The two periods of highwater during which the fish grow well complicate age determination from marks on skeletal structures (p. 201). In residual pools and swamps fishes often mature at a smaller size than they do in the main river (nanism).

South America: the Amazon system

Geography and history

The Amazon system, which has an even richer fish fauna than the Zaïre, drains 6·5 million km^2 and is without rival in the area of its drainage and volume of freshwater carried to the sea. Its water mass is four times that of the Zaïre and eight times that of the Mississippi; 400 km wide near its mouth, the muddy freshwater discharging into the Atlantic is detectable to *c.* 100 km offshore.

In the Amazon basin over 2·5 million km^2 are less than 200 m above sea level, mostly covered by dense rainforest. Here many large tributary rivers join the main stream (Figs. 3.1 and 3.2). These inland waters include a huge system of anastomosing channels, creeks and streams, sidearms and mouth-lakes, lagoons in the floodplain (*varzea*) and lakes on slightly higher ground (*terra firma*), flooded forest both on the flood plain and islands and in the inundation zone (*igapo*) along the water courses, swampy valleys, and in places periodically flooded grassland (*campo*). The cross section of the lower Amazon valley Fig. 3.3, shows the relationships of these various types of water (Sioli, 1964).

The tributaries, many of them large rivers over 2500 km long, fall into four groups:

1. *Andean headstreams*, such as the Ucayali, Huallaga and Marañon, all tributaries of the Solimões (Upper Amazon) which drain the eastern side and much of the interior of the Cordilleras between latitude 3° N and 20° S. Plentifully supplied with water by a rainy season lasting most of the year (September–June), and melting snow water, these rivers carry vast loads of sediments from the mountains to the plain, and are known as 'whitewaters'. This sediment is deposited alongside the main river,

forming the varzea floodplain of relatively fertile soil allochthonous to the central Amazon region (Fittkau, 1969).

2. *Right bank tributaries*, such as the Tapajós and Xingú, 'clearwaters' that drain much of the Brazilian plateau. With headwaters south of 10° S these reach high water in March or April; they drain such a vast area that they have a predominant, though delayed, influence on the main Amazon, which at Obidos is highest in May, but because of the northern contribution stays high until July.
3. *Left bank tributaries*, such as the Rio Negro, 'blackwaters' which rise in the uplands of Guyana and Colombia well north of the equator. These have high water in June, reflecting the northern hemisphere rain regime.
4. *Rainforest rivers*, such as the Purus and Juruá, which rise on the floor of the basin itself and meander in large loops and where we as yet know little of the fish ecology (Fig. 3.2).

Throughout most of the Central basin the rainfall ($\pm$3000 mm) is well distributed around the year and supports dense forest. However, between

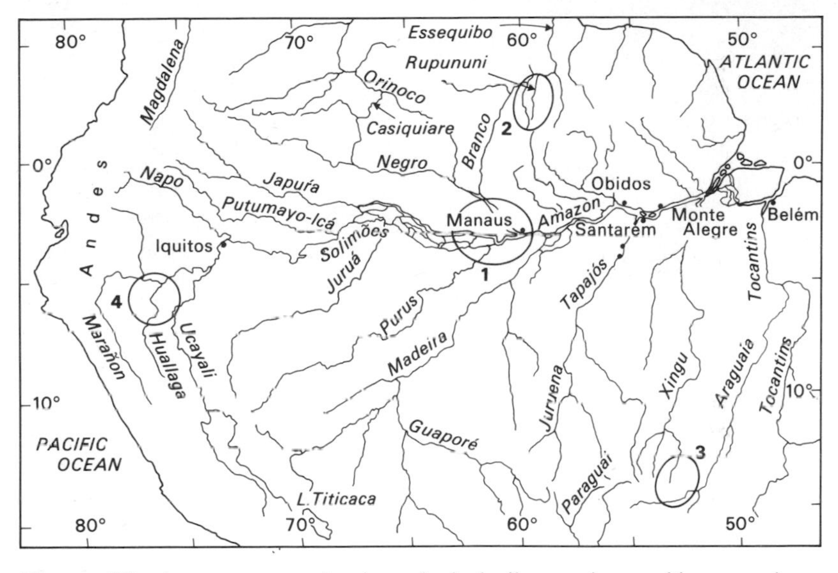

Fig. 3.1 The Amazon system showing principal tributary rivers: white water rivers (e.g. Marañon) flowing from the Andes, blackwater rivers (e.g. Rio Negro) from forests to the north, clear rivers (e.g. Tapajós and Xingú) from crystalline shield areas to the south, and meandering forest rivers (e.g. Juruá) arising in the basin itself. Note connection to Orinoco via the Casiquiare canal, and proximity of Guaporé to a Paraguai tributary. Studies considered here were made mainly: (1) in the Solimôes, Rio Negro and streams and lakes around Manaus; (2) in the Rupununi District of Guyana (where a tributary of the Rio Branco connects intermittently with the Rupununi River, tributary to the Essequibo); (3) in Mato Grosso headwater streams flowing both to the Xingú and to the Araguaia; (4) in Andean tributaries of the Huallaga and Ucayali.

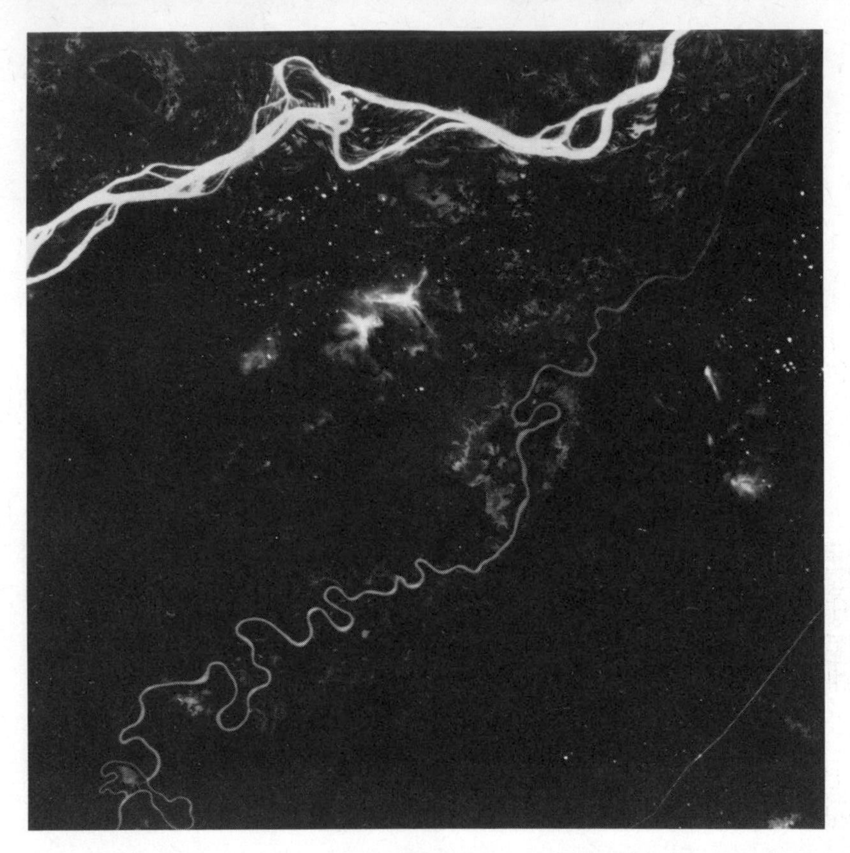

Fig. 3.2 Multispectral scanner satellite photographs of the Purus and Solimões Amazon west of Manaus. **Fig. 3.2a** (Band 5 red) brings out the highly silty white water in the main Amazon (Solimões).

the Xingú and Rio Negro there is sometimes little rainfall in the 'dry season', the second half of the year, and here forest tends to give way to savanna.

In the Upper and Middle Amazon the huge rainfall causes a large annual variation in the water flow leading to extensive lateral flooding of forest and savanna. The seasonal flood rises about 6 m at Iquitos, 15 m at Manaus, 12 m at Obidos and 4 m at Belem. Below the Rio Negro confluence the current at low water flows at 2 to 3 knots (*c.* 1·7 m/sec) increasing to 5 knots (2·5 m/sec) in some places at highwater. The river here averages 25 to 30 m deep, but is much deeper (nearly 70 m) where it contracts into a narrow channel below Obidos. The floodplain, extensively inundated at highwater, averages 48 km wide, but is much wider in places. The lowest parts of many tributaries are lakelike 'mouthlakes', that of the Tapajós 110 km long. The estuary has many large islands, and the northern shore has a notable bore (the pororóca). The effects of tides backing up the freshwater are felt as far upstream as

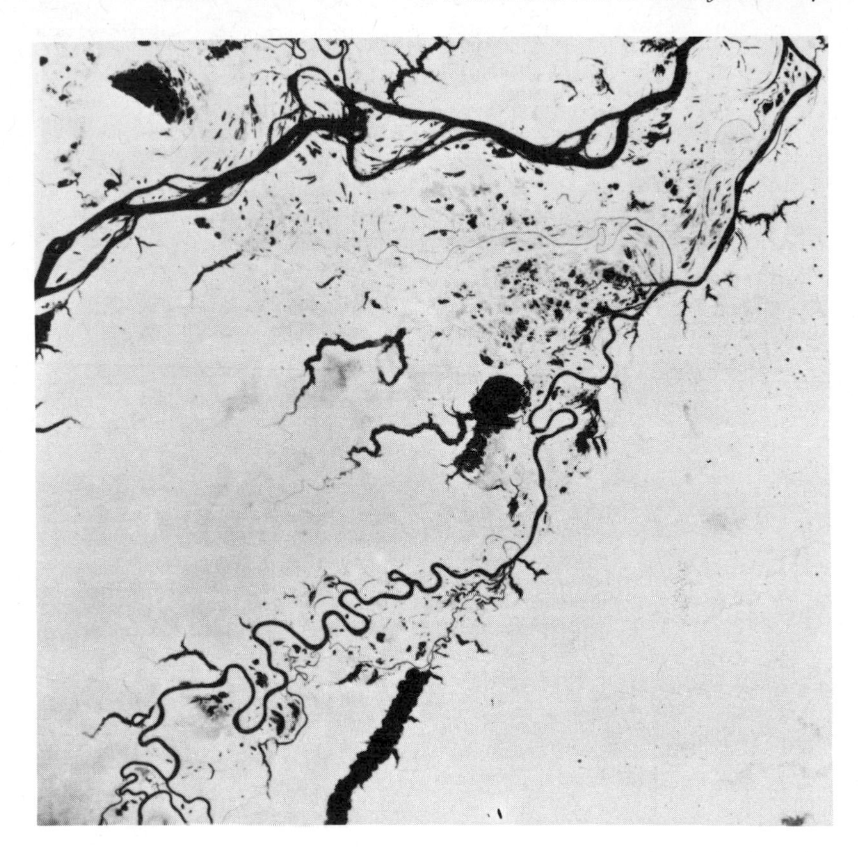

Fig. 3.2b (Band 7 infrared) shows the clear and blackwater lakes and tributaries. (ERTS water quality photographs by courtesy of the National Aeronautics and Space Administration (NASA), U.S.A.)

Obidos; the mixed zone of salt and freshwater may move 200 km up- and down-river according to the river flow. In the estuary much of Marajó Island is covered by 2 m of water from January to May; when the rains subside in May, the island slowly dries up, mostly by evaporation, and the biota becomes restricted to a few shallow lakes and interconnecting rivers. The largest lake becomes a highly concentrated brine solution. This island lies only just south of the equator, yet a seasonality is imposed on its ecology by events outside the area, by floods which come to it from regions of higher latitude, a seasonality which is reflected in the fish breeding seasons (Schwassmann, 1971).

The most spectacular anastomoses of channels (*furos*) occur between the Solimões and Rio Japurá. These facilitate the dispersal of the fishes into the forest at high water. Many channels have a two-way flow depending on the relative heights in different parts of the drainage system at the time. This is

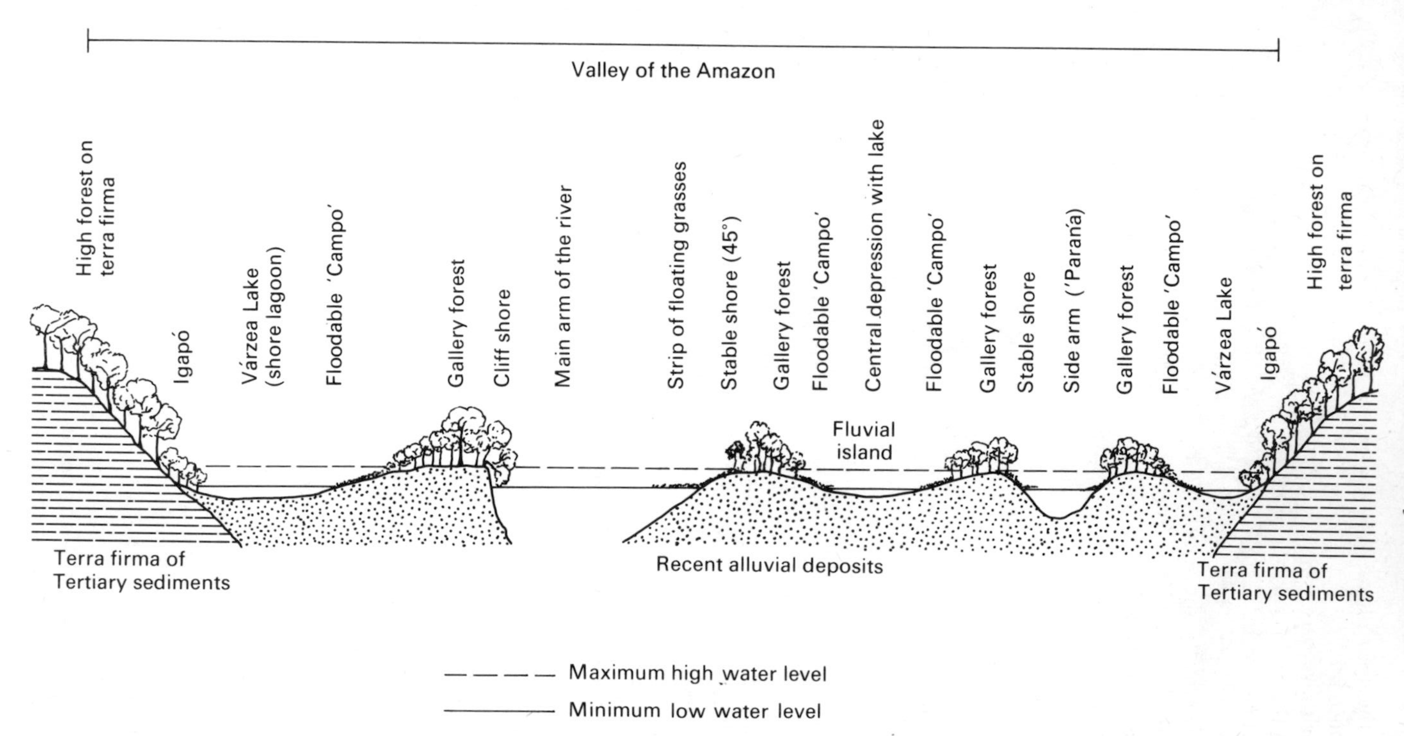
Valley of the Amazon
High forest on terra firma
Igapó
Várzea Lake (shore lagoon)
Floodable 'Campo'
Gallery forest
Cliff shore
Main arm of the river
Strip of floating grasses
Stable shore (45°)
Gallery forest
Floodable 'Campo'
Central depression with lake
Floodable 'Campo'
Gallery forest
Stable shore
Side arm ('Paraná)
Gallery forest
Floodable 'Campo'
Várzea Lake
Igapó
High forest on terra firma
Fluvial island
Terra firma of Tertiary sediments
Recent alluvial deposits
Terra firma of Tertiary sediments
Maximum high water level
Minimum low water level

also the situation in the Casiquiare canal which joins the Amazon to the Orinoco system; at one time of year the flow is from Amazon to Orinoco, at other times from Orinoco to Amazon.

In the main river the water temperature fluctuates no more than 1° C on either side of 29° C. In small and shaded forest streams temperatures may be as low as 23·4° C, in wide stagnant pools as high as 33·9° C (Sioli, 1964).

Historically the Amazon area once drained westwards to the Pacific, before the rise of the Andes reversed the drainage probably in Miocene times. The waters were then evidently dammed to form a huge lake, or lakes, before they broke through to the Atlantic in the Pleistocene (Sioli, 1964). During the Pleistocene glacial phases when the sea level was lowered the rivers would have run in deep valleys, but in the warm interglacials the sea level, up to 100 m higher than at present, would have ponded back these lakes, and Myers (1972) suggested that the hills at the Monte Alegre bottleneck may have prevented the incursion of saline water above this point, and that such fluctuations in conditions would have led to a great mixing of fish populations in this central basin at perhaps 10, 20, 50 and 100 000 year intervals. Today most of the Amazon lakes except the mouthlakes are shallow and young, even transitory, and the fishes in them move in and out of the rivers, so that there is little distinction between lacustrine and riverine fish populations, and there appear to be no great areas of endemism (as in the great lakes in the river systems of Africa). Conditions as the fishes evolved may have been quite different from those prevailing today (compare the Pliocene lake(s) in Zaïre p. 56, and see also p. 262).

Much of the Amazon system is still not yet explored, and studies of fish ecology have only been made at the relatively few places where facilities for such work exist. Many of them have been made around Manaus, where the blackwaters of the Rio Negro join the whitewaters of the Solomões (upper Amazon) to form the Amazon proper (papers by Sioli, Marlier, Fittkau, Knöppel, Junk, Geisler, etc.). Fishes have also been studied in various tributary rivers, in Peru, in Guyana, and in the Mato Grosso, but these waters are more seasonal so they are considered in a later chapter (p. 102).

To study the ecology of fishes in such a vast, remote and little explored area is a daunting task, and it is further complicated by the presence of so many fish species, many of them greatly resembling one another, making their correct identification very difficult. Many of the Amazon fishes are, however, widely distributed in South America, and the ecology of some of them has been studied where they are more readily accessible (e.g. in Guyana and Argentina). The osteoglossid *Arapiama gigas*, the cichlids *Cichla ocellaris* and *Astronotus ocellatus*, and the characoid *Prochilodus*, are among species cultured as food fish especially in the dry northeast of Brazil, where their breeding biology and growth has been studied in ponds (paper by Azevedo, Fontenele, Braga).

Fig. 3.3 Cross section through the lower Amazon valley; height exaggerated (after Sioli, 1964).

Fish fauna and main biotopes of the Amazon basin

The Amazon system includes numerous representatives of nearly all the families of South American fishes already described (p. 38). Central Amazon fish markets frequently display as many as a 100 different species at a time (Myers, 1947). A list of 195 indigenous names is used for market statistics and from these the 20 kinds most frequently recorded at Manaus are listed in Table 3.2.

Table 3.2 The principal fish species in Manaus (Amazon) fish markets in order of their frequency in market statistics according to Meschkat (1960). Over 700 fish species occur within 20 km of Manaus and markets may display over 100 species. Local names may cover a number of species, and may be used for different species in other areas. For synonyms see Index of fish names.

LOCAL NAME	GROUP	
1. Pirarucú	(osteoglossid)	*Arapaima gigas*
2. Tambaquí	(characoid)	*Myletes bidens*
3. Jaraquí	(characoid)	*Prochilodus sp.*
4. Pescada	(sciaenid)	*Plagioscion surinamensis*
5. Acari	(siluroid)	*Plecostomus spp.*
6. Pirapitinga	(characoid)	*Brycon pirapitinga* (? *Brycon orbignyanus*)
7. Pacu	(characoid)	*Myletes 'edulis'* and others
8. Sardinhas	(clupeids)	*Rhinosardinia* and *Neosteus spp.*
9. Curimbatá	(characoid)	*Prochilodus corimbata*
10. Aracú	(characoid)	*Leporinus* and *Schizodon spp.*
11. Branquinha	(characoid)	unidentified (? *Curimatus latior*)
12. Dourado	(siluroid)	*Brachyplatystoma flavicans*
13. Matrinchã	(characoid)	*Brycon hilarii*
14. Paraíba	(siluroid)	*Brachyplatystoma filamentosum*
15. Cuijuba	(siluroid)	*Oxydoras kneri* (? *Oxydoras niger*)
16. Aruaná	(osteoglossid)	*Osteoglossum bicirrhosum*
17. Tucunaré	(cichlid)	*Cichla ocellaris*
18. Mapará	(siluroid)	*Hypophthalmus edentatus*
19. Sorubim	(siluroid)	*Pseudoplatystoma fasciatum*
20. Acará	(cichlid)	*Astronotus ocellatus*

Fish stocks are poor in the main river but the density increases near to banks and beaches. Large catfishes such as *Brachyplatystoma* and *Pseudoplatystoma* are taken from the main riverbed on lines. Accumulations of fishes occur where rivers meet and at the entrance to side channels, and populations are larger in the numerous side arms where there is less current. The slower the current, the more the fish communities acquire the character of lacustrine ones, with a high proportion of characoids and cichlids, and fewer large or armoured catfishes. The plankton-feeding mapará catfish *Hypophthalmus edentatus* lives in schools in the deep clear water of the mouth lakes of the big southern affluents, Xingú and Tapajos, where phytoplankton blooms occur; these fishes may undergo vertical migrations, coming to the surface and inshore at night (Meschkat, 1960). They are found in the Tocantins throughout the year.

Most Amazon fishes appear to move about a great deal, between varzea lakes and the river, and from rivers to flooded forest at highwater to feed and reproduce, retreating to the river as the water falls, so fish communities are very unstable. Fish predators are numerous, not only the very many kinds of piscivorous fishes, but also mammals, birds and reptiles. Despite the high number of predators, many of the larger fishes give the impression of being old fishes; this is a characteristic of little-fished populations. The fishing seasons vary with the rhythm of the inundations, occurring at low water only, and so mainly from June to February in the middle Amazon.

The main food fish at Manaus, the osteoglossid *Arapaima gigas*, a piscivorous fish, lives in shallow lagoons alongside the rivers, surfacing every ten minutes or so (more frequently when small) to take air into the swim bladder which is used as a lung. They breed during the rains when both sexes scoop a hole in the bottom, where the eggs are laid; the eggs hatch in five days, and the larval fishes swim around the head of the male near the water surface, attracted to the parent fish by a chemical secretion (pheromone) exuded from pores in the adult's head (Lüling, 1964); they stay with the parent for forty days, by which time they are 8 to 10 cm long (Bard, 1973). In northeast Brazil, where *Arapaima* are grown in fish ponds, they mature when four or five years old.

Fish migrations coincide with floods, the characoid *Prochilodus* and *Brycon*, for example, moving upstream at the start of the flood season. Certain Amazon characoids are known to have two migration periods and two spawning seasons a year (Meschkat, 1960), but it is not known if the same individual spawns twice a year. The fishermen follow the migrating *Prochilodus* guided by the sounds emitted by these fish. Species which do not spawn in the river migrate to lakes and overflow areas.

The constantly changing conditions as the waters rise and fall drastically alter the faunal composition. At any one time many of the species at one site are likely to have recently arrived there, or to be moving away from habitats that have become unfavourable. In side channels of the Rio Solimões Roberts (1972) found that a rotenone collection might include 70 to 80 fish species, but only a third of these were common, and it frequently happened that a dozen or so species were represented by a single specimen. These solitary fishes must have come from populations established elsewhere, their presence in the collecting area was largely due to chance, and they would soon disappear unless joined by additional individuals. Roberts suggested that the brilliant colours of many of these small forest water species (for instance in the *Hyphessobrycon* characins such as *H. innesi* known to aquarists as the neon tetra) may help the fishes to find one another and so to build up viable breeding populations.

In the Amazon basin it is not possible to make a clear distinction between riverine and lacustrine fishes, for the slow-flowing tributaries have much the same fauna as the varzea lakes. The lake fishes may have to retreat to the rivers at times of low water, as lack of dissolved oxygen, removed from the water by the abundant decaying vegetation, may drive from the lakes those fishes which do not have some respiratory device enabling the fish to use atmospheric air.

The white water varzea lakes have a somewhat different fish fauna from the clear or blackwater terra firma lakes. A comparative study throughout the year of two such waters near Manaus, the whitewater varzea Lake Redondo and the blackwater terra firma Rio Prêto da Eva, less than 100 km apart, stressed the influence of water chemistry on the ecology of the fishes (Marlier, 1967, 1968). Of the 47 fish species taken from L. Redondo (mainly by gillnets) and 49 species from R. Prêto da Eva, only six were common to both places (*Osteoglossum bicirrhosum*, *Serrasalmus rhombeus*, and three cichlids, *Cichla ocellaris*, *Geophagus surinamensis* and *Cichlasoma festivum*, all species widely distributed in South America). The foods consumed by the fishes in L. Redondo are discussed later (p. 80).

Chemically the Amazon system includes both dark and clearwaters comparable with those in the Zaïre, but the whitewater brought down by Andean tributaries is loaded with silt and richer in nutrients than the other types of water. These whitewaters, with their high content of suspended materials throughout the year (transparency of only 10 to 50 cm, pH 6·2 to 7·2) form an effective barrier to some species; no submerged flora nor lamellibranchs can live in them, nor can phyto- or zooplankton develop. Fishes living in them feed mainly on foods of terrestrial origin or are piscivores; they include fishes in which senses other than sight are well developed, large numbers of siluroids, and the characoid 'pacu' (*Colossoma*) which can crush hard nuts such as those falling in from rubber trees. The sediment load has by annual flooding built up around the river bed a huge alluvial plain, the varzea, which is up to 100 km wide in the Amazon–Madeira valley. Depressions in the plain form lagoons or lakes in which the sediment settles leaving clearer water, rich in nutrients which are replenished when the lake is flushed with river water in flood seasons. The floating meadows which develop in the whitewater varzea lakes form one of the most productive biotopes in the Amazon system.

These floating meadows, formed mainly of the grasses *Paspalum repens* and *Echinochloa polystachya*, which cover many square kilometres in the middle Amazon support immense numbers of individuals and species of animals which use them partly as substratum and partly as food (Junk, 1973). Experiments with synthetic materials showed that phytoplankton and detritus trapped in the roots are important sources of food, particularly in the clearer sedimented water. In dense floating islands which are several years old, the oxygen content can be limiting for some animals. Junk recognised three types of floating meadows: (1) those in the flowing whitewaters developed seasonally (February to November in the middle Amazon) where the roots trap predominantly inorganic suspended matter (these had faunal biomasses up to 0·3 to 4·2 g/m^2 dry, 20 g/m^2 wet, weight); (2) and (3) in standing water, clearer as the silt had sedimented, of which type (2) persists only for about a year, has well-oxygenated water and is very productive (faunal biomass up to 11·6 g/m^2 dry, 62 g/m^2 wet, weight), while (3) is perennial and heavily colonised by terrestrial vegetation, in which the central zones of the stands tend to be anoxic and to lack fauna (biomass of 0 to 0·3 g/m^2 dry, 0 to 1·8 g/m^2 wet, weight). The fauna varies with the type of meadow.

Fishes characteristic of the floating meadow biotopes include many species widely distributed in South America: small *Hemigrammus* and *Hyphessobrycon* characoids, the cichlids *Cichlasoma severum* and *C. festivum*, *Gymnotus carapo*, *Synbranchus marmoratus* and a small eleotrid. These fishes remain largely in the peripheral areas where there is more available oxygen, except for the eel-like *Synbranchus*, well adapted to wind its way among the dense plant masses and able to use atmospheric air. Species also found here by Junk included the predatory characoids *Hoplias malabaricus*, *Serrasalmus* species, *Mylossoma* a deep-bodied vegetarian, *Leporinus fasciatus*, small *Cheirodon* and *Pyrrhulina*, the gymnotoids *Eigenmannia* and *Sternopygus*, the siluroids *Hoplosternum* and *Anadoras*, the cichlids *Cichlasoma bimaculatum*, *Acaronia nassa* and *Apistogramma*, and the cyprinodont *Rivulus*. As an indication of the numbers of fishes under a floating island, where oxygen conditions permit, Junk quoted Geisler (personal communication) who took from under a 25 m^2 island in the Amazon near Manaus: 1090 charoids (including 650 *Abramites microcephalus* and 40 *Leporinus* sp.), 5 *Astronotus*, 1 *Electrophus electricus* and 32 *Farlowella*, though the netmesh size was too large for the sample to be considered quantitative.

Clearwater rivers, such as the Xingú and Tapajos, carry only small amounts of suspended matter, the transparency of their greenish water ranging from about $\pm$0·6 to 4 m in rainy and dry seasons, pH 4·5 to 7·8. These rivers have a stable upper course between terra firma shores, then as the river bed widens on reaching the soft sediments deposited by the lake(s) present here in Tertiary times the current slows down and any sediments are deposited (Fig. 3.4). This sedimentation zone is characterised by elongated islands, generally forest-covered, behind which the shallow water is more or less stagnant. Below this zone the river is very clear (transparency $\pm$2 or 4 m throughout the year, limited mainly by phytoplankton growth). The drowned river mouth forms an enormous trumpet-shaped open water surface extending to the main river. The current is here slowed to a few cm/sec. Limnologically these river mouths resemble lakes rather than rivers, with clear, bright, sandy beaches and some deposits of very soft mud. Such river-lakes (mouth lakes) are characteristic of the lower and middle Amazon. Phytoplankton blooms develop in some of them (Xingú and Tapajos) despite the apparent paucity of nutrients in the clear waters, and shoals of the plankton-feeding catfish *Hypophthalmus edentatus*, are caught off the mouths of these clearwater rivers.

The blackwater rivers, with very acid (pH 3·8 to 4·9) dark waters, extremely poor in inorganic ions ('almost distilled water') lack primary production, as neither plankton nor floating meadows develop in them. They

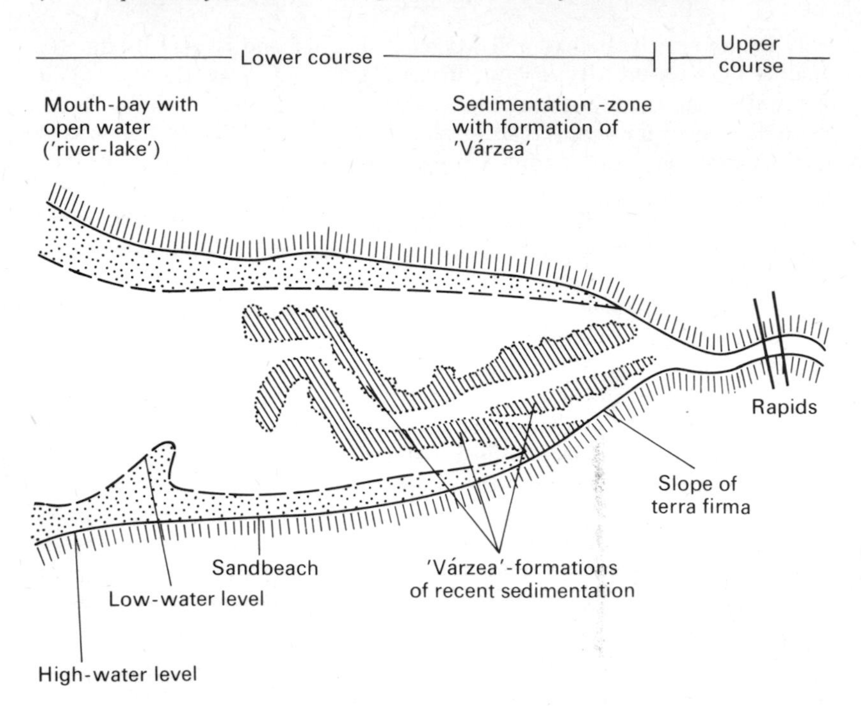

Fig. 3.4 Sedimentation in the lower courses of Amazon affluents ('mouth lakes') (after Sioli, 1967).

also lack aquatic insects.* Only certain fish species can live in these waters, and they have to depend largely on allochthonous forest foods. Decomposing vegetation reduces the oxygen content of the water. In the Rio Negro fish kills occur when cold winds blow in May, and these kills were found to be due to the upwelling of water with little or no oxygen in slow-flowing stretches (Geisler, 1969). The Rio Negro has a multitude of islands, which normally increase the fish fauna, but here the high shoreline-coefficient does not make up for the unproductive nature of its dark and acid waters, the least productive in the Amazon region.

The small streams in the rainforest of central Amazonia present extreme biotopes for the fishes as the trees closing over the stream prevent light from reaching the water surface, also nutrient salts are scarce. Aquatic plant life is virtually non-existent, and food webs are dependent on allochthonous forest debris raining onto the stream, pollen, flowers, fruits, leaves, insects and spiders (compare streams in Zaïre, p. 62, and Borneo, p. 85). Fishes, mainly small species, are, however, often surprisingly abundant; from 30 to 50 species may be taken from one stream, mainly Characidae, with siluroids, gymnotoids, cichlids and in muddy sections cyprinodontids.

The streams have three sections (Fig. 3.5): an upper source and erosion

* See Janzen (1974).

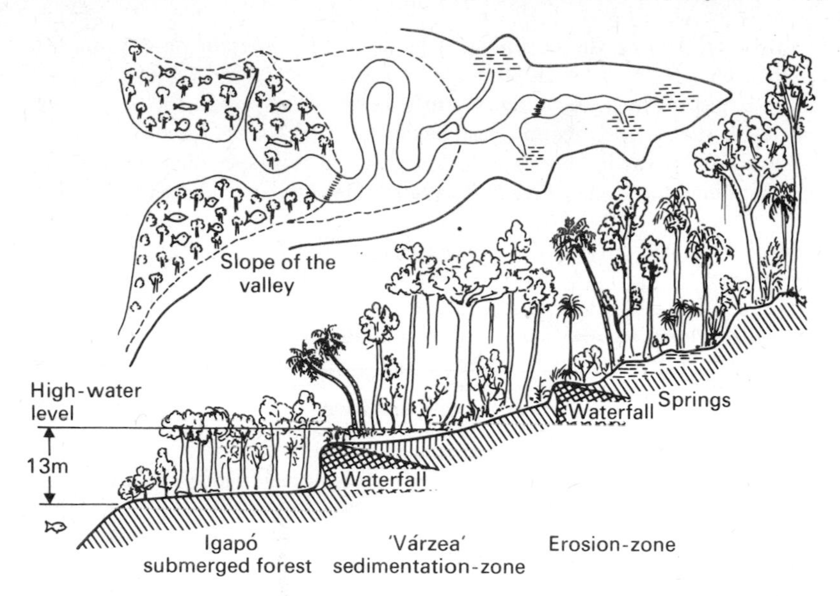

Fig. 3.5 Ecological regions of a Central Amazon rainforest stream (after Fittkau, 1967).

zone where the gradient is steep, fast-flowing stretches over rock alternating with sandy-bottomed pools; a middle sedimentation zone, with meanders over a sandy bed; and the 'igapo' zone, where seasonal variations in the water level of the main river back up the stream water so that it ceases to flow for much of the year. In the upper and middle courses the fauna changes with the current velocity, current-loving species living where the flow exceeds 20 cm/sec. At lower speeds organic materials sediment. Piles of drifted leaves provide cover on the bottom, alternating with bare sandy or rocky stretches. Tree and epiphyte roots, and the debris of fallen trees lying in the water also provide cover for the invertebrates on which the fishes feed, and daytime hiding places for the nocturnal fishes.

The ecology of Amazon fishes

Trophic groups Foods used have been studied in fishes (1) from the varzea Lake Redondo and some neighbouring lakes (Marlier, 1967, 1968), and (2) from small streams near Manaus (Knöppel, 1970, 1972).

The L. Redondo studies showed that food webs are very complex even in such a small lake (35 ha and 3·5 m deep). In this varzea lake the littoral floating meadows provide the main source of substances at the base of the food chains. Marlier commented that before the banks were cleared of forest, floating meadows were probably less extensive, and the allochthonous fruits and leaves from trees would have been a main food. Marlier distinguished between fish species which take only either plant or animal food (stenophages) and those which combined these in their diet (euryphages)

(Table 3.3). Among the euryphages he recognised certain predominantly carnivorous species, such as *Osteoglossum* and *Serrasalmus rhombeus*, and a rather larger number of predominantly vegetarian species. Of those with restricted diets, one group was basically carnivorous, another group vegetarian. The carnivores include a number of non-specialists taking any kind of animal food according to its availability, and specialists using either

Table 3.3 Trophic categories of Amazon Fishes from Lake Redondo (data from Marlier, 1968).

I. STENOPHAGES	**Carnivores**	**Herbivores**
Non-specialists	*Geophagus surinamensis*	*Cichlasoma bimaculatum* (filt. algae+ plants)
	Plagioscion squamosissimus	*Cichlasoma festivum* (epiphytic diatoms, seeds)
	Eigenmannia virescens	*Anodus laticeps* (phytoplankton, epiphytic diatoms)
	Colomesus asellus	
	Serrasalmus nattereri	
	Serrasalmus elongatus	
	Pimelodella cristata	
	Apistogramma taeniatum	
Specialists	**Piscivores**	*Colossoma bidens* (fruit)
		Ctenobrycon hauxwellianus (grass seeds)
	Cichla ocellaris	*Metynnis hypsauchen* (plants)
	Arapaima gigas	*Leporinus maculatus* (plants)
	Boulengerella cuvieri	*Poecilobrycon trifasciatus* } (algae and
	Ageneiosus ucayalensis	*Poecilobrycon unifasciatus* } aufwuchs)
	?*Synbranchus marmoratus*	
		Mud-eaters (bacteria in bottom mud)
	Insectivores	
		Curimatus sp.
	Triportheus elongatus	*Potamorhina pristigaster*
	Oxydoras niger (burrows)	*Prochilodus* sp.
		Pterygoplichthys multiradiatus
	Zooplankton feeders	
	Astyanax fasciatus	
	Hypophthalmus edentatus	

II. EURYPHAGES	**Predominantly carnivorous**	**Predominantly vegetarian**
	Osteoglossum bicirrhosum	*Acarichthys heckelii* (seeds, molluscs)
	Serrasalmus rhombeus	*Pterophyllum scalāre* (littoral zooplankton and plants)
		Metynnis lippincottianus (algae, plants, and Cladocera)
		Corydoras sp. (aufwuchs)
		Pyrrhulina brevis
		Cheirodon piaba
		Hyphessobrycon 3 spp.
		Anchoviella brevirostris

other fishes (piscivores such as *Cichla ocellaris* and *Arapaima gigas*), or insects (such as some doradid catfishes), or zooplankton (such as the catfish *Hypophthalmus edentatus*). Stenophagic plant-eaters included mud-feeders, which get their nourishment from bacteria and other small organisms in the mud, as do the *Prochilodus* which are of major importance in the lower reaches of many rivers (see p. 113), as well as non-specialists having a mixed diet of higher plants and algae, and specialists taking higher plants. Phytoplankton was too sparse in these lakes to support any phytoplankton-feeding specialists.

Knöppel (1970) examined the stomach contents of over 11 000 fishes collected by Fittkau and others by chemofishing three types of stream near Manaus:

1. the 'Igarape Taruma', a 2–3 m wide blackwater stream in high forest, above 15–20 m falls, which yielded six species of fish (2 characoids, 1 gymnotoid, 1 siluroid, 1 cyprinodont, 1 cichlid);
2. the 'Igarape Barro Branco', a 1 m wide clearwater sandy-bottomed stream, which yielded 17 species (5 characoids, 5 gymnotoids, 4 siluroids, 3 cichlids);
3. the 'Lago Calado', a clearwater rivulet and varzea lake, sunlit, with Solimões water, where 41 species were taken (18 characoids, 3 gymnotoids, 4 siluroids, 16 cichlids).

Fishes were collected from all three streams in the 'dry season' (October–November, 1965), when the water level was falling, and further samples were taken from (2) and (3) in May and July 1967. In these streams the daily rainfall influences the water levels more than do the seasonal oscillations of the main rivers. Collecting the fishes proved extremely difficult as the creek floors were littered with fallen trees and branches.

Fishes were abundant, despite the low primary production in all but the Lago Calado open to the sun. The five collections at three localities produced more than 32 000 fish of 53 species: 22 characoid species, 6 gymnotoids, 7 siluroids, 17 percoids (mainly cichlids), 1 cyprinodont. Of the 11 000 stomachs examined 94 per cent were at least half full. Foods were listed in twenty-four categories, and both main stomach contents and particular food items were recorded.

The major surprise was that so few of the fishes appeared to specialise on any particular food (despite the very specialised teeth of many of the characoids). Most species ingested many different items, and the lists of stomach contents for the main families were relatively uniform. Nor was there spatial or temporal separation, as foods from the surface and from the bottom were often found in the same individual, suggesting that the fish obtained its food from the whole living space, even in fishes which appeared to be adapted for living in a certain zone in the stream. Also, the stomach contents of one species collected at different times of year were generally similar.

The main food items in the fish stomachs were:

1. young stages of *aquatic insects*, found in 27 species and the main food in

9 species, though no fish showed a clear preference for any particular kind of insect prey;

2. *terrestrial insects*, especially ants (Formicoidea) which occurred in 13 species, together with some Isoptera (termites), Coleoptera and Diptera;
3. *plant remains*, coarse litter, fruits and flowers of allochthonous origin, in 26 species;
4. *algae*, found only in small quantities and only in fishes from the lake open to the sun;
5. *detritus*, in 19 species, certain small species making it their main food;
6. *fine sandy mud*, which filled the intestines of the characoids *Prochilodus*, *Chilodus* and *Curimatus*;
7. Crustacea, including Copepoda, Ostracoda, Cladocera and palaemonid prawns, in 21 species: only *Hoploerythrinus* contained a high percentage of decapods;
8. *fishes*, found in 20 species, but all of these, even the characoid *Hoplias malabaricus* and the predatory *Crenicichla* species, contained some other food as well as fish.

The great contribution of allochthonous foods from the forest could account for the large numbers of fishes present despite the lack of primary production. Many kinds of fish ingest these forest products directly and the role of fishes in recycling them needs further investigation.

If food has little selective influence in these streams, then what factors do control fish numbers and diversity? The numbers and types of piscivorous fishes did not seem to be very high in these streams, compared with the usual high numbers in most tropical waters, nor were there marked fluctuations in size of habitat. It seems likely, however (from evidence in Mato Grosso streams, p. 107, and elsewhere), that only euryphagous fishes are able to penetrate into these headwater streams; most of the species found here are widely distributed in South American waters, and their tooth specialisations may be of greater use to them in other parts of their range.

A high proportion of predatory species is noticeable in most tropical faunas, for example amongst birds. Fittkau (1967) commented on the large variety of predators among the invertebrates in these Amazon streams, not only among the normally carnivorous Odonta nymphs, here abundant, but also among the nymphs and larvae of the usually non-carnivorous Plecoptera, Ephemeroptera and Lepidoptera. In the Amazon generally (as in the Zaïre and Southeast Asian waters) the proportion of piscivorous fishes is also very high.

The Amazon has over 40 species of primarily or exclusively piscivorous characoids, as well as piscivorous cichlids (*Cichla* and *Crenicichla* species), large siluroids, large gymnotoids, sciaenids, *Arapaima* and *Osteoglossum*. Certain *Serrasalmus* bite chunks out of larger fishes; serrasalmines of milder disposition are often found with these species and may benefit from this association (Gery, 1963). Some piscivorous species are very widely distributed, such as *Hoplias malabaricus* (the ecological equivalent of *Hydrocynus* in African waters). This species penetrates to the headwaters of tributary streams and can live in savanna ponds and swamps where there is little oxygen by keeping near to the water surface (Carter and Beadle, 1931); it is a voracious fish which swallows its prey whole and takes a wide variety of small fishes. We do not as yet know how many of the characoid tooth specialisations are used, for example, the two spectacularly long canines in the lower jaw of *Hydrolycus scomberoides*.

Four genera and about ten species of Amazon fishes feed mainly on the scales of other fishes, having specialised dentitions to do so and often a projecting lower jaw (Roberts, 1970). About 30 species of Amazon fishes belonging to two unrelated families of catfishes, Trichomycteridae and Cetopsidae, actually parasitize other fishes. Some of these remove circular chunks of fish flesh from their prey, others live in the gill cavities of the large catfishes such as *Brachyplatystoma*, and of *Arapaima*. The adaptive responses of other fishes to avoid being preyed upon are discussed below (p. 252).

Biomass and production Marlier's comparative studies in various lakes indicated that biomass and production are higher in white than in black and clear waters, where food cycles depend very much on allochthonous forest products and most of the nutrients are locked up in the bodies of the fauna. The numbers of animals present is important for production; these both store nutrients which would otherwise be lost to the effluents of the

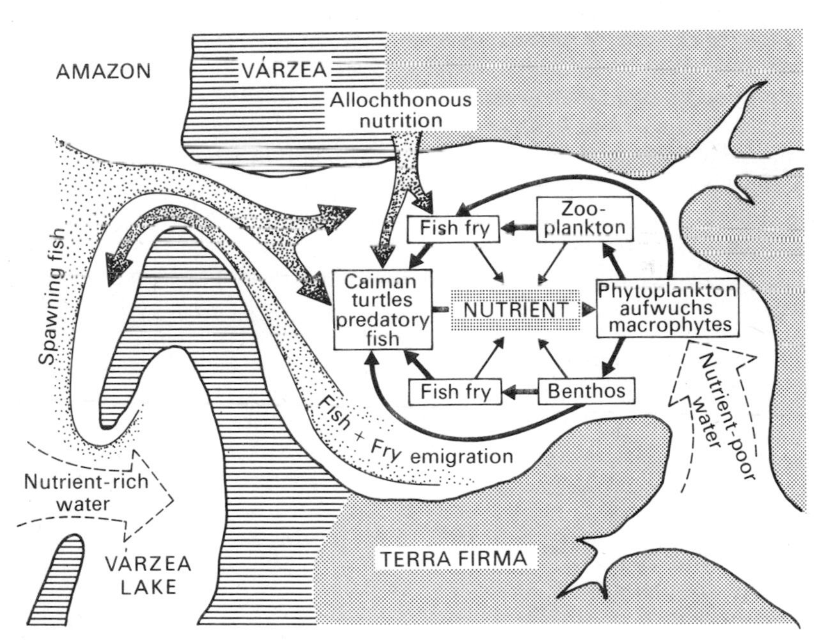

Fig. 3.6 The nutrient cycle in a mouthlake of an Amazon affluent (after Fittkau, 1970).

lakes (a density dependent process) and secondly these increase the speed of mineralisation of littoral plant material which falls into the water (a density and diversity dependent process). Herbivores such as the Sirenian manatee or seacow, *Trichechus inunguis*, which used to be fairly common in the Amazon, have a beneficial role on production as these feed on water meadows and excrete into the water, thus converting these plants into nutrients available for plankton growth; herbivorous fishes have a comparable role (Marlier, 1967, and compare the role of *Tilapia* in African lakes, p. 244).

Predatory species may also make important contributions to the nutrient salts. Fittkau (1970, 1973) noted that when caimans disappeared from the mouthlakes of Amazon tributaries, following intensive hunting for their skins, the populations of all kinds of fish diminished markedly. He postulated that this was due to fishes originating in the nutrient rich waters of the Amazon river and its varzea lakes migrating into the lower reaches of the affluent rivers to spawn, where they were preyed on by caiman, turtles, and piscivorous fishes, and part of this allochthonous food being immediately transformed into nutrient salts by the rapid metabolism of these predators (Fig. 3.6). These nutrients would then support a limited production of plankton for the rising generation of fishes. Measurement of salts (N, P, Ca, Mg, Na and K) excreted by captive caiman (medium-sized *Caiman crocodilus*) over fifteen months suggested that caimans daily add quantities of these salts (mostly of allochthonous origin) to the water. The caiman's ability to undergo long periods of starvation, during which it continues to excrete salts, makes it well adapted to the extreme environment of the mouthlake (Fittkau, 1973). Beadle, however, questions whether these particular salts are limiting in these waters (personal communication).

In waters where most of the nutrients are bound up in the fauna the mass removal of fishes or other creatures is likely to lead to rapid impoverishment of the whole ecosystem. This has to be kept in mind when planning fishery development in these waters. The whitewater rivers in which some nutrients are replaced with each flood are the most productive, but Marlier (1969) stressed that the myth of the economic richness of Brazilian equatorial waters must be seriously reconsidered.

The diversity of the Amazon fish fauna The high diversity of the Amazon fish fauna has been attributed to many factors: (1) the age and size of the drainage basin, (2) the succession of habitats offered by the meandering rivers with certain habitats such as high gradient streams separated by long distances, (3) the diverse niches in the lowland rivers and their adjacent lakes, and (4) the high proportion of the basin at low levels with comparatively stable conditions and capable of supporting large numbers of individuals; also (5) river captures and faunal exchanges (Roberts, 1972, Marlier, 1973, Patrick, 1964).

The Orinoco Basin and the Guianas have been independent areas of species diversification and river captures by Amazon tributaries have undoubtedly enriched the faunas of all three areas. For example, the Amazonian species *Arapaima gigas* has moved via the Takutu River in the Rupununi savanna district into the Essequibo system (Lowe-McConnell, 1964). There are reputed links between the Amazon and Magdalena systems, and from the Tocantins to the São Francisco, as well as with the Paraguai system by the Tapajos and Guaporé. Some links may only be open in very wet years, and long-term wet or dry cycles will have had profound effects on fish distribution and ecology.

Many species are represented by widely separated populations over the entire Amazon basin and adjacent basins; this probably contributes to the evolution and maintenance of species diversity, and furthermore such conditions provide the geographical isolation for allopatric speciation. Although local extinctions must occur frequently, rapid total extinctions of whole species are unlikely in species which are so widely dispersed.

Southeast Asian forest rivers and their fishes

In Southeast Asia fish communities have been studied in forested rivers on the large equatorial island of Borneo (7° N–4° S), in North Borneo by Inger (1955) and Inger and Chin (1962), and in the west-flowing Kapuas River and adjacent waters by Vaas (1952). Vaas *et al.* (1953) also examined the fishes in southeast Sumatra where much of the forest has been cleared. These large islands have much the same fauna as the mainland. More recently a comprehensive study has been made of the limnology of the Gombak River in Malaya (Bishop, 1973).

In North Borneo heavy rainstorms are often very localised, and there are wide fluctuations in heavy rainfall from year to year at any one place. The mountainous west coast has swift clear streams over gravel and rock while rivers running to the mangrove swamps on the flatter east coast are slower and turbid over silt bottoms. During Inger and Chin's survey, streams 1 to 10 m wide flowing largely through untouched forest were fished with rotenone, and the larger rivers were fished with lines, nets and traps. Among the 77 species collected (representing 21 fish families) cyprinoids predominated (*c.* 17 genera), with siluroids of 8 families; there were 5 anabantids, 3 mastacembelids, and most of the rest were freshwater representatives of marine families (especially gobies). Insect larvae and nymphs were abundant in every stream, Plectoptera, Neuroptera, Trichoptera and Diptera most numerous in fish stomachs. Many fishes contained terrestrial invertebrates, especially ants, spiders, and Orthoptera, which are washed into the water by the heavy rain. Decapod crustacea were also important fish food. As many fish species fed mainly on terrestrial insects as those feeding on aquatic insects.

Studies on the vertical zonation of these fishes by Inger and Chin showed that most of the clear forest streams had 1 or 2 surface-dwelling species, 1 or 2 living just below the surface, 3 to 5 midwater species, 2 to 4 living just above the bottom, and 3 to 10 living on or in the bottom. Within a drainage system the nature of the bottom and the current speed dictated the numbers of fish species present; the number was smaller (both absolutely and relatively) when the bottom was of silt or sand than when it was of large rocks. Close to the sources of small streams the fish communities became impoverished in a way that affected the strata differently. As the stream becomes smaller and also shallower, the layers occupied by surface and benthic species remain, but the middle layers are compressed. The relative importance of surface and benthic species remain constant or increase, whereas that of the midwater species decreases. The stratification of species in the major rivers is virtually unknown. Some of the differences in faunas between drainages in Borneo result from geographical impoverishment.

The food habits of fishes from the westward flowing River Kapuas and its adjacent lakes and sidearms in Borneo, and from rivers in southeast Sumatra and nearby *lebaks*, areas inundated by high water and gradually drying out, were studied by Vaas (1952) and Vaas *et al.* (1953). These data, summarised in Table 3.4, showed many species to be omnivorous, sharing a wide variety of animal and vegetable foods, or of various kinds of animal food. In the forested waters of Borneo inundated vegetation was an important source of food, more so than in neighbouring Sumatra where much of the land had been cleared for rice cultivation. In Borneo waters predatory fishes were very abundant. Although vegetable-eating cyprinids and the anabantoid *Helostoma* were caught in great numbers, the bulk of the catch was of predatory (piscivorous) siluroids, *Channa* and *Notopterus*, particularly in pits retaining fishes in the dry season. Many of these piscivorous fishes in the little fished Kupuas river system appeared to be large, old, fishes; in Sumatra where fishing had been more extensive, the accumulation of large predators, which are caught for food by the local population, was not so marked. Vaas quoted a Borneo pit which on poisoning was found to contain 7 species of predators to 10 species of vegetarian and omnivorous fishes, and the predators numbered 177 fishes (50 kg weight) compared with only 38 fishes (16 kg) of non-predators.

The longitudinal zonation of fishes in the Gombak River, Malaya, which joins the Klang River in Kuala Lumpur, was studied by Bishop (1973) as part of the most comprehensive study of the limnology of a small tropical river yet attempted anywhere. The primary object was to define hydrobiological conditions in a small unaltered river not subject to seasonal change, and physical, chemical, floral and faunal analyses were made at five stations over two years. Quantitative studies included measurements of the input of allochthonous material.

The Gombak River drains a forested hill area, 22 km long by 5·5 km wide, from a steepsided mountain range (altitude 1443 m) through more gently sloping foothills to an alluvial plain. In Malaya major drainages have been topographically isolated since the Pleistocene, and stream captures are infrequent. This river lies between the relatively poor acid black water streams of low latitude country in southern Malaya and the richer 'tree country' streams of the north, and it carries mainly eurytopic species (rather

Table 3.4 Food habits of fishes in Asian equatorial freshwaters. The numbers of species and types of fish sharing the various food sources.
A. Western Borneo: R. Kapuas, adjacent lakes and river arms (data from Vaas, 1952).
B. South-eastern Sumatra: R. Oran and R. Komering, lebaks and other waters (data summarized from Vaas, Saachlan and Wiraatmadja, 1953).
C. Malaya: The Gombak River (data from Bishop, 1973).

	BORNEO		SUMATRA		MALAYA	
FEEDING REGIME	**No. spp.**	**Types of fish**	**No. spp.**	**Types of fish**	**No. spp.**	**Types of fish**
Plankton feeders	5	4 cyprinids 1 anabantid	7	5 cyprinids 2 anabantoids		
Herbivores						
(*a*) small plant parts, periphyton, plankton, algae, detritus	5	5 cyprinids	5	1 siluroid 3 anabantoids 1 pristolepid	1	1 cyprinid (detritivore)
(*b*) large plants, seeds, fruits (aquatics and inundated land plants in Borneo)	8	6 cyprinids 1 anabantid 1 pristolepid	1	1 cyprinid		
Omnivores						
(*a*) herbivore dominant (plant parts, zoo-plankton and insects)	5	5 cyprinids	17	17 cyprinids	5	5 cyprinids
(*b*) predator dominant						1 cyprinid 2 bagrids 2 clariids 2 anabantids 1 flutid
(*c*) bottom feeders	5	1 cyprinid 2 siluroids 2 mastacembelids	3	1 cyprinid 2 siluroids		
Carnivores						
(*a*) exogenous arthropods (surface and aerial insects)	2	1 cyprinid 1 toxotid	2	1 anabantoid 1 toxotid	5	1 siluroid 1 anabantid 2 hemiramphids 1 sole
(*b*) endogenous arthropods (aquatic) insects, prawns + small fish	18	3 cyprinids 10 siluroids 2 mastacembelids 2 clupeids 1 lobotid	17	3 cyprinids 9 siluroids 1 anabantid 3 channids 1 mastacembelid	3	2 mastacembelids 1 poeciliid
(*c*) large predators (fish, decapod Crustacea)	7	2 siluroids 4 channids 1 notopterid	5	3 siluroids 2 notopterids	6	1 cyprinid 1 siluroid 4 channids

than specialists from either area). Fish populations were estimated by electrofishing, and the fishery yield by riparian fishermen was assessed by questionnaires backed by sampling. In the upper zone the river flows through forest, in the lower zones through cleared land where there is some pollution. Light and temperature conditions were governed mainly by presence or absence of forest (the upper two stations were in forest, the lower three fully exposed). River temperature variations were small, the means varying only 1° – 2° C seasonally; the daily temperature ranges were also small (means 23° C ± 1·7° C at the top station, 26·8° C ± 2·3° C at the bottom station), showing a greater range downstream, particularly in the maxima which periodically exceeded 33° C at the unshaded lower site. Considerable rain occurred in all months, and river discharges were highly variable, characterised by rapidly rising and falling flood peaks with each intense storm.

The Gombak River has 28 fish species representing 21 genera and 12 families, the cyprinids predominating (30 per cent), followed by Channidae and Anabantidae. The various species of *Channa* (4), *Clarias* (2) and *Mastacembelus* (2) were found to be segregated according to altitude or stream size, but apart from these geographical replacements the longitudinal zonation is characterised by the addition of species downstream where physical and chemical conditions are more stable and spatial and feeding niches are more complex. The diversity of species increased linearly with stream order, generally where the channel order changes (where tributaries join one another), and with the associated changes in stream size, gradient, substrate, and sometimes temperature. Some niches are also lost or reduced at these points (such as fast water or riffles from lower stretches).

A large part of the ichthyofauna examined was indiscriminately euryphagous, deriving much of its food from allochthonous sources (fruits, flowers, leaves, terrestrial insects), but also taking endogenous benthos as available. The specialised feeders constituted only a minor part of the community. Few of the fishes were strictly carnivorous, and none were cited as piscivorous. The catfish *Macrones* was present in all streams of sufficient size to support a mixed predator often together with a predatory *Channa* or *Clarias* species. The only dependent herbivore, the detritus-feeding deep-bodied cyprinid *Osteochilus*, was only common in the lower zone where adequate decomposing detritus was available. In the upper zone terrestrial insects, especially ants, were important food. In the very small channels not all of the allochthonous food was consumed, possibly because the water surface is too disturbed here to allow any species to specialise on using this food source in this zone, but it was gradually swept downstream with the current and utilised in the lower reaches.

Electrofishing produced 35, 11 and 9 fish per hour in the upper, middle and lower zones respectively, but the biomass was *c.* 250 g/h in all zones. The mean catch of 0·2 fish/m^2 was equivalent to *c.* 3·6 g/m^2 of fish flesh. This was probably a considerable underestimate for the standing crop of fish, many fish escaping the electric shocker. The fishery questionnaire suggested that an annual crop of 30 tonnes was taken from a water surface of around one-third of a square kilometre, representing a yield of 87 g/m^2 (very much more than the standing crop estimates from electrofishing). The ability of the fish population to support this fishing pressure was debated, but such a high yield was considered possible with the high temperatures, continuous recruitment, and the surfeit of most foods.

Thus, as in South American and African forest streams, studies in Southeast Asia have stressed the role of allochthonous forest products, tree debris and arthropods, in headwaters, whereas detritus becomes increasingly important as fish food lower down the river. Fishes in headwater streams are euryphagous, taking whatever food drops into the water, and feeding at different levels, rather than just taking it from the surface. Lower down the river bottom omnivores become more abundant. Apart from a few ecological replacement species, successional changes are mainly additional, diversity increasing with stream order and size, reflecting the greater complexity of niches in lower zones.

4

Seasonal Rivers in the Tropics: Ecological Conditions and Fish Communities

Within the tropics the rainfall becomes increasingly seasonal with increasing latitude, leading to annual flooding of the rivers. The amount of rainfall also diminishes with increasing latitude on either side of the equatorial forest supporting only savanna grassland over which the rivers spill in the dry season. In both Africa and South America where much of the land is very old flat peneplain, the rivers inundate immense areas, on a scale unknown in temperate regions. Submerged seasonally and drying out for part of each year, these floodplains are interspersed with creeks, pools and swamps, some of which retain water throughout the year. The percentage of permanent water to that covered at the height of the floods on nine African floodplains

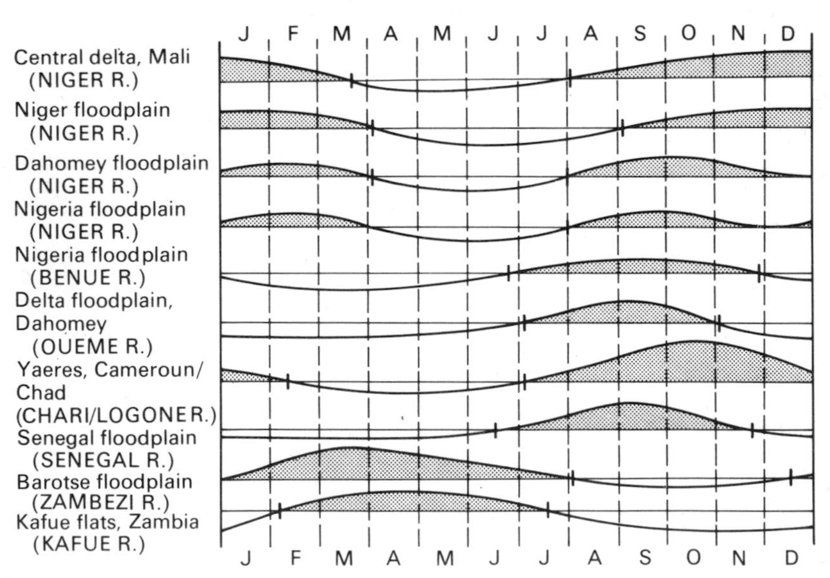

Fig. 4.1 Hydrological regimes of African floodplains (after Welcomme, 1972). (Stippled area denotes flooding.)

has been estimated to vary between 4 per cent and 30 per cent, with a mean of 13 per cent (Welcomme, 1972*a*). The hydrological regimes of these floodplain rivers are indicated in Fig. 4.1. The extent of flooding at any one place varies considerably from year to year, variations which have important effects on fish growth and survival.

In the lower reaches of large rivers (such as the Middle Paraná in Argentina) the flood regime is complicated by contributions from various tributaries: the relative volumes of their inflows may also vary from year to year as the heavy rains of tropical regions are often very local in effect.

A good deal of information is now available about the annual cycle of events and fish communities in seasonal rivers from which a general picture can be drawn. In West Africa many studies have been made of the ecology of Niger fishes: in the Middle Niger 'delta', in the region of the new Lake Kainji, and on the tributary Sokoto and Benué Rivers; also from rivers around Lake Chad and many other rivers. In Central Africa the ecology of Zambezi fishes has been investigated in the Upper Zambezi, on the Barotse floodplain, in the region of the new Lake Kariba and on the flats of the tributary Kafue. In South America studies of fish ecology in seasonal rivers include those north of the equator in Guyana and Venezuela, south of the equator in the headwater streams of Amazonian tributaries, and in the Parana system mainly at three points: the Mogi Guassu in Brazil, the Middle Parana in Argentina, the Pilcomayo in Bolivia. Fish tagging experiments in the Parana have given very good returns, illuminating fish movements and growth rates. In the Asian tropics the rivers in peninsular India are very seasonal and there is a large literature on many aspects of the ecology of fishes used as food. Many studies have also been made in the Mekong system which supports some of the world's most important freshwater fisheries. These and other studies are here examined in the light of my own field experience in South America over five years on the seasonal rivers in Guyana and later in the Mato Grosso, and over many years in various parts of Africa.

The annual cycle of events in seasonal floodplain rivers

The annual cycle of events in these floodplain rivers is summarised in Fig. 4.2. Rains occur in summer months (after day lengths and temperatures have been increasing), but in most of the rivers the peak flood occurs well after the rains have started, and in some cases several months after the local rains have ceased; the delay depends on the origin of the main floodwater and how long it takes to travel downstream to the floodplain. The time of peak flood may vary slightly from year to year, for example from March to May at Kafue.

Local rains may flood some savanna ponds into the river, but more often the rising river runs first up the channels and creeks on to the floodplain connecting with ponds and swampy areas isolated in the dry season and releasing the fishes imprisoned in them. As the river continues to rise, the

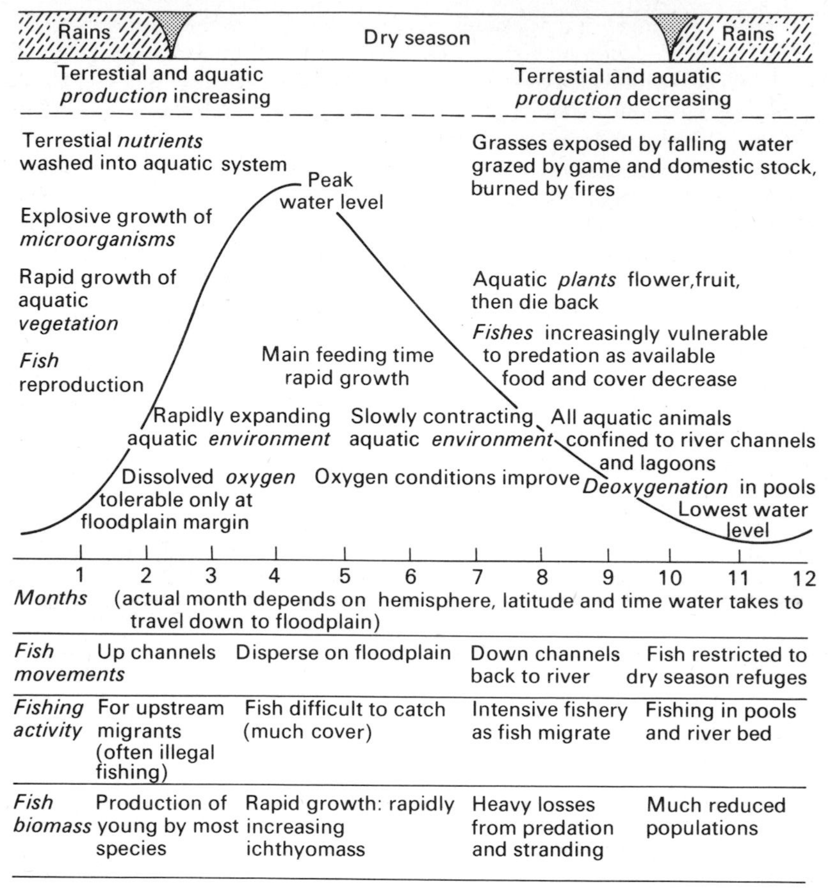

Fig. 4.2 The seasonal cycle of events in a floodplain river.

water floods over any banks which may delineate the river and its channels from the floodplain, making a vast sheet of water.

As the savanna floods, the water is greatly enriched in nutrient salts from the breakdown of organic matter, decaying vegetation and the droppings of animals which grazed on the dry plain, calcined by sun and fire. This leads to an explosive growth of bacteria, algae and zooplankton, which in turn supports a rich fauna of aquatic insects and other invertebrates. The aquatic vegetation, both rooted and floating, grows very rapidly. These plants flower and fruit while the water is high, dying back as the plain dries up. There is thus an extremely rapid increase in the production and biomass of all kinds of fish foods of both plant and animal origin, and the fishes grow very fast at this time. Most floodplains have a rich and varied fish fauna. The rapid decomposition of decaying terrestrial vegetation leads to deoxygenated conditions, except at the margins of the floodplain, as the water rises.

In the dry season fishes are confined either to the bed of the river, which may be broken into pools, or trapped in small lakes, ponds or swamps isolated on the floodplain. These waters often become very deoxygenated and only fishes adapted to withstand such conditions can survive in them through the dry season.

Many fishes migrate up-river as the water rises, then make lateral movements out onto the flooded plain when conditions permit. Their reactions to water flow are thus complex and have as yet been little investigated; the fish move against the flow going upstream, and generally with the flow on to the savanna, though in some years local rains may cause savanna ponds to flood down towards the river. Among fishes which make such movements are many Ostariophysi (cyprinids, characoids and catfishes), also some mormyrids.

The majority of these ostariophysian fishes are 'total spawners' (p. 216) in which all the eggs ripen at one time each year. These spawn early in the flood season either in the main river, as at Kainji (p. 98), or in the channels as the fish move out onto the floodplain, or on the floodplain. The eggs hatch fast (within about two days), and the young fishes are thus born at a time when food is plentiful, and plant growth provides cover from predators. Species which guard their young (cichlids and some catfishes) produce smaller batches of young at frequent intervals and often have their first batch at low water before the floods, or on the first sign of rising water. Certain zooplankton-feeders such as the African clupeids (*Pellonula* and *Microthrissa*) and small *Barilius niloticus*, are unusual in spawning at low water; zooplankton develops best in still water pools as the waters are subsiding.

The highwater time is the main feeding, growing and fattening season for nearly all species. The abundance of most foods is then greatest, though the young fish are more readily available to predators as the floods subside and in the dry season pools. A wider spectrum of foods is available during the rains; larvae, nymphs, insects and adults are then most abundant, and there are numerous other invertebrates, prawns and molluscs in some waters, also the fruits and seeds of aquatic plants. Fish growth is extremely rapid and fat stores are laid down as ribbons along the alimentary canal in many species. This rapid growth, like the diminished growth in the dry season, is recorded on the skeletal structures (scales and bones) of many of these fishes, enabling their ages and growth rates to be determined.

As nutrients are depleted and the water level falls, the vegetation dies back and the fishes move back to the main river. The large predators move down first and lurk around the mouths of the channels down which the abundant young-of-the-year pass back to the main stream, where the predatory fishes feed heavily on them. This is also the main fishing season for other predators such as birds (many of which have also produced their young during the rainy season) and man. Many fishes remain stranded in the rapidly diminishing pools, and fish mortality is particularly high at this time.

Mortality must also be very high in dry season refuges where there is little cover. Many kinds of fish feed little in the dry season, when there are few types of food available (except zooplankton and fish) and food is not abundant.

Many fishes in these seasonal tropical environments mature by the next flood season, or at the most the one after that, in contrast with fishes in large tropical lakes which may take three years to mature (and those in temperate waters which may take even longer).

Fishes in these seasonal rivers may make very long migrations between feeding and spawning areas; tagging experiments showed movements of 600–700 km up-river (a 1200 km round trip) in the Parana in South America (p. 117). In West Africa some Lake Chad fish may run many hundred kilometres up the Chari system to spawn, and Daget concluded that in the middle Niger *Alestes leuciscus* may move 125 to 400 km up-river, while fish move up to 50 km from the main river to the edge of the floodplain. Few tagging experiments appear to have been carried out in Africa, but in Nigeria at least one *Alestes baremose* was recaptured 80 km up the Yobe river from where it was marked near Lake Chad (Hopson, personal communication). In Asia various fishes are reputed to make long migrations up and down the Mekong, but tagging experiments are needed.

Many mysteries remain about these fish movements. Some species move up-river as the floods subside; for example, *Labeo senegalensis* and *Alestes* species at the Markala barrage just above the Central Niger 'delta' which are fed upon by following predatory fishes. Fishes may respond to local conditions, for example in the Maiduguri River in Nigeria such an up-river movement brought the fishes retreating from the drying floodplain to a small permanent lake, L. Aloe (Hopson, personal communication).

The various species of fish move up or downstream in a definite order, often moving only at a certain time of day, or at a particular water level, and sometimes only at one phase of the moon. Siluroids in all three continents move mainly by night, mormyrids in Africa by night, cyprinids and some characoids by day. Further details are given for Guyana fishes by Lowe-McConnell (1964), for Chad basin fishes by Durand (1970), for Benué fish by Stauch (1966), and for Mekong fishes by Blache and Goossens (1954). Daget pointed out that differences in times of movements of closely related species will help to keep them distinct: for example at the Markala barrage on the Niger the movements of successive shoals of *Alestes leusicus* depended on the phase of the moon, whereas the closely related *A. nurse* did not show a lunar rhythm.

From this summary of the annual sequence of events in seasonal rivers the following points emerge:

1. The general sequence of events on floodplains is the same throughout the tropics, in Africa, South America, and parts of Southeast Asia and India, and both north and south of the equator, though floods come at different times of year, and different fish faunas are involved.
2. The size of the whole aquatic environment fluctuates seasonally, and may vary considerably from year to year.
3. The production and biomass of most fish foods (except zooplankton)

increases with rising water level, and high water is the main feeding and growing time for most fishes. Zooplankton becomes abundant in still-water pools and piscivorous fishes feed heavily as water levels subside.

4. Fish populations are geared to this expansion of the environment and resources, as most fish spawn as the water rises, the eggs hatch fast and the young are produced at a time when food supplies are abundant and aquatic vegetation provides cover from predators. Changing conditions and the large numbers of piscivorous species provide strong selection pressures for very rapid development and growth of young.
5. Many of the fishes are known to be very sensitive to small changes in water level, and such changes rather than the local rains appear to trigger the fish movements and spawning; experimental studies are needed and different species of fish may respond to different factors.
6. As most fish species mature in one or two years on tropical floodplains and life cycles are short, the turnover of populations is very fast, and the results of 'good' or 'bad' spawning years are reflected very rapidly in the catches. Spawning success is affected by factors such as: (*a*) the extent of flooding and whether fishes stay trapped in ponds or are released into the river system, (*b*) by physical and chemical conditions just after the eggs are laid (deoxygenation if the water rises too fast, or stranding if it drops again temporarily – as it often does – before they hatch); (*c*) biotic factors such as the numbers of predators present (which is itself influenced by their spawning success in the previous year(s), as the variations in abundance of *Serrasalmus* in the Rupununi ponds (p. 103) demonstrated). These floodplain fish populations are characterised by very high proportions of young-of-the-year. Thus a dynamic system of interacting variables results in great fluctuations in fish numbers, both seasonally and from year to year.
7. Fish mortality appears to be greatest when the water is falling at the end of the rains; many fishes are then stranded in drying pools and predator pressure is also at a maximum. Many of the predators also spawn as the water rises and large numbers of them lie in wait for the young as they leave the cover in drying lakes and move back down channels to the main river. Mortality is also very heavy in dry season pools and in the river bed where there is little cover. Deoxygenation and desiccation also cause heavy mortalities in the dry season.
8. Selection pressures, both abiotic and biotic, fluctuate seasonally, and they appear to be at a maximum when the food resources are shrinking. An attempt to express these relationships is made in Fig. 9.4, and their possible effects on fish evolution are discussed in a later chapter (p. 214).
9. Most riverine fishes move around a great deal and young fishes and adults of the same species often live in different biotopes and form part of different communities. Only when fishes are in dry season retreats in pools cut off from the river is the composition of the community static; in the dry season bed of the river it is still affected by upstream and downstream movements of the fishes.

Seasonal rivers of Africa

The African seasonal floodplain rivers fall into two groups: those north of the equator across the sudanian region, the savanna zone south of the Sahara from the Senegal to the Nile; and south of the equator in the Zambezi and its tributary systems.

West Africa

The ecology of soudanian fishes in rivers has been studied in the Central Niger 'delta' (Daget, 1954, 1957*a*) in the Benué (Daget and Stauch, 1963), in the Ivory Coast (Daget and Iltis, 1965) and in rivers flowing into Lake Chad (Blache and Miton, 1962, 1964; Durand, 1970) (Fig. 4.3). The Central

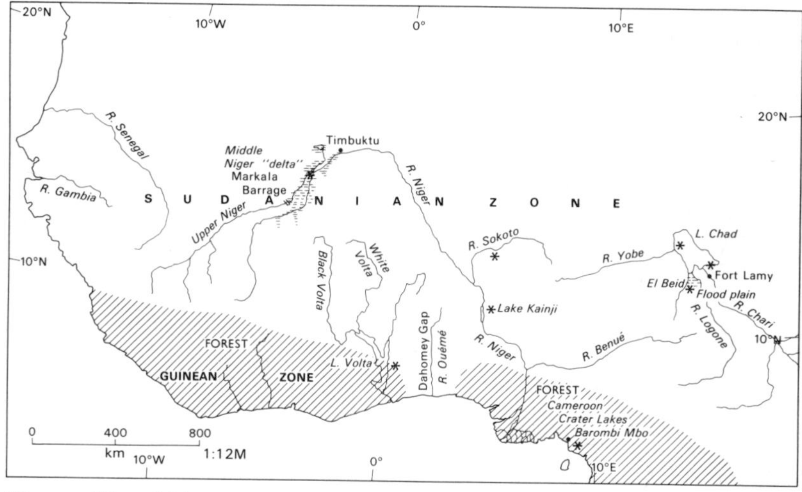

Fig. 4.3 West African sites mentioned in the text.

Niger 'delta' floods from rains in the Upper Niger basin; there is a timelag as the water travels down river and the river starts to rise in mid-July. By October the country is covered with a 17 000 km² sheet of water (30 000 km² including land flooded along affluent rivers); in May the main river is only 6 m wide, reduced in volume twenty-five times. From this area 40 000 tonnes of fresh fish were taken each year, although the Niger waters are said to be poor in nutrients. Traps in the Markala barrage, just above the Central Niger 'delta' have produced a good deal of information about fish movements.

In West Africa Daget has made special studies of the ecology of species of *Alestes*, *Citharinus*, *Heterotis* and *Tilapia*. *Alestes* change their food seasonally, feeding heavily on the floodplain on seeds and insects but subsisting on zooplankton in dry season pools, losing weight and fat content while doing so (Daget, 1952). Within the genus *Citharinus*, all deep-bodied mud-feeding characoids, Daget (1962*a*) found that three species coexist in the Logone-

Chari and Benué (*C. citharus*, *C. latus*, *C. distichodoides*), and another three in the Zaïre basin (*C. congicus*, *C. gibbosus*, *C. macrolepis*). In the first case the three species are known to share the same food, to have the same breeding season and comparable early growth rates, and the young live together; the three species in the Zaïre are also often caught together. As Daget commented, these appear to provide exceptions to the competitive exclusion principle (p. 255), but they only coexist in regions where the biotopes suitable for *Citharinus* are vast and permit ample migratory movement; in these ecosystems the three species are able to occupy the same ecological niche, but smaller river systems each have only one species (*C. citharus* in the Gambia, *C. latus* in South Dahomey for example).

In the Chad basin 90 000 km^2 of floodplain (known in Cameroun as 'yaérés') are flooded in 'normal' years, from which fisheries in 1964 took between 60 000 and 80 000 tonnes of fresh fish; a catch representing only 12 to 15 kg/ha as the area is so vast. (The main species caught are listed in Table 8.2.) More recently droughts must have led to a decline in the fisheries. The great migrations of the fishes from Lake Chad into the extensive inundation zone of the Chari–Logone (Fig. 4.3) take the fishes many hundreds of kilometres up from the lake (Blache and Miton, 1962). Many fish move across the inundation zone and back to L. Chad down the El Beid River. These rivers all flow into L. Chad from the south. The fishes migrate up river as the waters rise in July, August, September, they are dispersed in the inundation zone during the high water in October; the level then falls and the fishes return to the lake in December, January, February, remaining there during the low water period from March to June. Durand (1970) listed 74 species from the El Beid River of which 95 per cent of the total catch (by number and by weight) returning downstream were young fishes in the first year of growth; the catches decrease and the species composition changes as the river level falls; different species run by day and by night. The biology of these fishes in L. Chad is considered in a later chapter (p. 170).

The main biotopes of this vast soudanian area were described by Daget (1954) and Blache *et al.* (1964): large rivers with rocky, sandy, or mud-bottomed stretches, temporary streams down which water floods and subsides seasonally, plains inundated at high water, the residual pools on the plains, some permanent, many temporary, lakes larger pools and swamps.

In the Central Niger 'delta' the latitude is here high enough for the water to cool during the winter months, December to February (January has a minimum water surface temperature of 20° C compared with 29° C in June), which affects fish growth. The wet season is also the warm season, so eggs and young fish spawned as the water rises develop when temperatures are high which speeds their development. Chemically the Middle Niger water is pH 6–7 and not very rich in nutrients, and throughout the area the inundation zones are the main feeding grounds for the fishes. These also provide the right conditions for species which make nests amongst water plants (such as *Heterotis* and *Gymnarchus*) and for these spawning starts earliest downstream, where fishes have access to the inundation zones sooner.

The riverine fish faunas vary with the type of bottom and speed of flow. Rocky stretches with rapids and falls occur mainly in the upper reaches where they shelter a specialised fauna, species such as the cyprinid *Garra waterloti* which has an adhesive buccal disc, and the elongated cichlid *Gobiocichla wonderi*. In the lower stretches sandy bottoms are most frequent. Moving sands are rather barren, though frequented by small cyprinids (*Barilius* and *Barbus*). Where the sand is fine and hard it is colonised in the wet season with filamentous algae and a rich fauna of aquatic insects, particularly Odonata, Hemiptera and Coleoptera. Such places are frequented by *Alestes* species, and predatory *Hydrocynus*, also by *Labeo*, *Barbus* and *Tilapia*. Where the bottom is muddy with aquatic plants in the shallows live many mormyrid and *Synodontis* species, the osteoglossid *Heterotis*, large catfishes such as *Auchenoglanis* and *Heterobranchus*, and *Tilapia*. In the Chad delta the bivalve oyster *Aetheria* forms reefs which provide a substitute for sand bottoms, allowing sand-frequenting species to live in the mud zones (Blache *et al.*, 1964).

A unique opportunity to census the fishes in a stretch of the R. Niger was provided during the construction of the Kainji dam (Motwani and Kanwai, 1970). Half the river, which is here divided by an island, was enclosed between two coffer dams in mid-May 1966, and the water was pumped out in July. This enclosed area formed a lake 1·7 km long (180 000 m^2), with steep walls of rock over a rocky bottom covered with coarse sand, a channel lacking aquatic vegetation. From this channel 90 species of fish were taken (Table 4.1). Fifty species had mature or ripe gonads; spawning activity had already

Table 4.1 Fish species caught from the coffer-dammed channel of the River Niger (data summarized from Motwani and Kanwai, 1970).

FAMILY	Total no. species	No. species mature or ripe	Individuals caught		Total weight	
			No.	Per cent	(kg)	Per cent
Mormyridae	19	13	1198	20·7	219	19·5
Characidae	8	6	2103	36·3	136	12·1
Citharinidae	5	5	354	6·1	212	18·9
Cyprinidae	6	2	192	3·3	48·3	4·3
Schilbeidae	3	2	463	8·0	40·6	3·6
Bagridae	7	7	422	7·2	204·2	18·2
Mochokidae	18	11	1044	18·0	209·5	18·7
TOTALS	82*	50*	5776(+)		1069 kg(+)	

* Plus some specimens of *Polypterus endlicheri*, *Heterotis niloticus*, *Malapterurus electricus*, *Lates niloticus*, *Tilapia nilotica*, *Tilapia zillii*, *Tetraodon fahaka strigosa*, *Microthrissa miri*.

commenced in the coffer-dammed area, as was evident from the gonad states of some fish and from the many fry and young fishes which were collected from the delivery end of the water pumps. This channel appeared to be an inhospitable home for fish; it was probably used as a low water refuge, and some fishes may have been moving up or down-river when they were trapped between the coffer dams. The water level here normally starts to rise in August, but the local rains at Kainji start in April/May and are at a maximum in July.

The residual pools, depressions in the West African plains where the water is deeper than over most of the inundation area, have clay, or sometimes mud, bottoms. The turbidity varies very much from pool to pool, being affected by the fishes present, for fish such as *Clarias* which burrow in the bottom stir up the mud. Many pools lack vegetation, others have *Nymphaea* (water lilies) and *Utricularia* (bladderwort). Fish faunas vary very much from pool to pool; pools tend to keep the same types of fish from year to year, but conditions change as pools silt up, and new pools are formed as the rivers change course. As the water level falls the fish population from a wide area becomes concentrated in these pools, and spectacular catches can be made from them (8 tonnes from a 0·2 ha pool is quoted by Blache *et al.*, 1964). In Dahomey special trenches are dug on the floodplains to act as residual pools to retain water and fishes well into, or through, the dry season, a form of fishery which could well be introduced on other floodplains (Welcomme, 1972*b*).

The pools become stagnant and fishes living in them must be able to withstand deoxygenated conditions. Adaptations to cope with drying out include encystment in a mucous cocoon in the mud in the lungfish *Protopterus*, burrowing in the mud in *Clarias* (which can also wriggle overland from pool to pool through damp vegetation) and drought-resistant eggs in certain small cyprinodonts.

In the Sokoto River in Northern Nigeria tagging experiments were carried out by Holden (1963) on 14 of the 27 fish species common in residual pools (pools of 0·07–4·7 ha, cut off from the river for about four months of each year). These experiments showed that: (1) pools with a sandy or sandy-mud bottom had a higher biomass of fish than had mud-bottomed pools (Table 8.3); the latter appeared to be used as nursery pools and had few large fish. There was a direct relationship between fish size and pool size. (2) The biomass of fish in a particular pool depended both on the species present and on the area drained by the pool and varied considerably from year to year. (Unlike a fish pond of fixed size, the quantity of fish did not depend on primary production within the pool.) Some species were represented by only one- or two-year classes. The ratio of herbivores to carnivores in these pools was 80 per cent by numbers and 74 per cent by weight; the herbivores included a high proportion of *Tilapia*. The mean biomass was 415 kg/ha for the dry season area of the pools, but as these occupied only 3 to 4 per cent of the floodplain, this crop was estimated to represent only about 12 to 17 kg/ha from the floodplain. Tagging showed that the same individuals of *Hydrocynus vittatus* and *Lates niloticus* were found in a particular pool from one year to the next, *Tilapia nilotica*, *T. galilaea*, *Hemichromis fasciatus* and *Schilbe mystus* in the pools did not appear to be migratory. Some species, such as *Distichodus rostratus*, *Parophiocephalus obscurus*, *Alestes leusicus*, and

Hepsetus odoe were only caught in the pools in certain years. Good year classes appeared to be due to an early rise in river level.

Africa south of the equator: the Zambezi system

In the Zambezi system south of the equator the main biotopes and the seasonal cycle of events are very similar to those of the Sudanian area, though the floods come at the opposite times of year, and the fish fauna is somewhat different. Fewer families of fishes are represented (see Appendix 3), and cyprinids and cichlids (which here include predatory *Serranochromis* species) form a higher proportion of the fish fauna and of the commercial catch. The Zambezi is far enough south for seasonal changes in daylength and water temperature as well as the flood cycle to affect the fishes.

In Central Africa Jackson (1961*a*; 1963) distinguished between rivers flowing out of a reservoir (a lake or extensive swamp) and 'sandbank' rivers. The reservoir buffers the effect of the rains, releasing water gradually so that the floodplain is inundated for a longer period and there is a margin of aquatic vegetation all year. A sandbank river such as the Middle Zambezi, on the other hand, rises very abruptly to a great height during or shortly after the rains, then dwindles rapidly, often drying out into a series of pools, and the steep banks lack aquatic vegetation.

The Upper Zambezi flows 1125 km from its origin in northwest Zambia until it plunges over the Victoria Falls, flowing mostly through sandy or rocky country, its banks lined with *Phragmites* reeds, but with little other aquatic vegetation except in lagoons and backwaters, where *Potamogeton*, *Nymphaea* and *Utricularia* grow. The river rises and floods the surrounding plain with the onset of the rains in December, and starts to fall again in April or May. The main fishery is on the Central Barotse flood plain, 240 km long (Kelly, 1968; Duerre, 1969). Here most of the adult fishes are widely dispersed in the flood season, withdrawing to the main river as the water starts to fall in April or May; the great migration of the young-of-the-year back to the river follows in May and June. All the fish spawn before the height of the flood in late March, and do not start again until the water begins to rise again in December, with the exception of the cichlid *Serranochromis macrocephalus* which starts in October at the first sign of any rise in level. Most of the young fish hatch during the flood season when there is almost no zooplankton, and grow to around 10 cm long before a significant amount of this becomes available; they appear to feed largely on periphyton from submerged grass and bushes, so most of the primary production originates in, or is dependent on, the terrestrial vegetation (Kelly, 1968). Fish growth reflects the pattern of inundation, and scale rings have enabled growth rates to be calculated for the cichlid species (Fig. 9.1).

In the Middle Zambezi ecological studies were made in the river prior to the formation of Lake Kariba. This region had bimodal floods due to local rains in November/December and the Barotse floods later in the year (with a peak around May) when Upper Zambezi water arrived. At the end of the dry season the river was here reduced to a small flow between deep clear pools or shallow shingle-bottomed ones, with sandbanks and rocks exposed everywhere and hardly any aquatic vegetation. The fishes here moved out of the main river into adjacent flooded areas, low-lying land, oxbows, creeks and estuaries of tributary rivers, at highwater, but had to retreat to the river bed, to reduced and open water lacking vegetation as cover, in the dry season (Jackson, 1961*a*). Most of the fishes here spawned during the flood period, and growth was very rapid while the water was high. In April–May fishes of all ages, very sparse in the main river, were very abundant in the flooded tributaries, and a very large proportion of the population was of fishes in their first year of life (especially of the more abundant species such as *Hydrocynus vittatus*, *Labeo altivelis* and *L. congoro*). The larger-growing species (adults > 18 cm) in this region are indicated in Table 8.2 p. 188.

The influence of the large piscivorous *Hydrocynus vittatus* on the ecology of the other fishes in the Zambezi was stressed by Jackson (1961*b*), and Bell-Cross (1968) concluded that in the Upper Zambezi the open water is comparatively free of other fishes except those in some way fitted to escape its predation. Attributes which they considered help fishes to escape this predation included: large size (above about 20 cm long in cichlids and siluroids), or very small size and specialised habits (as in the catfishes *Chiloglanis* and *Leptoglanis*), or morphological features such as stout fin spines (as in *Synodontis*) or with behaviour patterns such as migration away from the area to spawn (as in *Labeo*).

These *Hydrocynus* live in size shoals; length frequency data suggested that they grow to about 18 cm their first year and 25 cm their second year. Preliminary tagging experiments showed movements of up to 21 km downstream. In neighbouring rivers where *Hydrocynus* were absent three other predatory species were common, but in the Upper Zambezi these three occupied rather different biotopes, thus competition with *Hydrocynus* appeared to be limited: *Hydrocynus* keeps to the main river channels whereas *Hepsetus odoe* is restricted to lagoons and backwaters, *Serranochromis angusticeps* to swampy areas, and *S. thumbergi* is rare.

The ways in which the Zambezi fauna has changed in the Kariba area since the formation of the new lake is discussed in a later chapter (p. 177). Plans to construct another lake on the Kafue River, a tributary of the Zambezi which enters the Middle Zambezi below Kariba, stimulated pre-impoundment surveys on the Kafue Flats in Zambia (Carey, 1971; Chapman *et al.*, 1971; Lagler *et al.*, 1971; Williams, 1971; Kapetsky, 1974).

The Kafue River, a tributary of the Zambezi entering it below the new Lake Kariba (Fig. 2.4), lacks a number of Zambezi species, including *Hydrocynus*. The flats, a plain 1240 km long by 10 km wide flooded with water for about six months of the year, lie at an altitude of over 1000 m. Although well within the tropics (16° S) the air temperature falls to below 10° C (50° F) in the dry season. Very distinct growth checks are shown on the scales of *Tilapia* and other fishes here enabling ages and growth rates to be determined (Chapman *et al.*, 1971). These data showed that the growth of young *Tilapia* is better in high flood years, which may be related to better feeding conditions in a more expanded environment; and that *Tilapia* survival rates are better in high flood years, which is perhaps related to better cover and the fact that fish are more difficult to catch when spread over a wide area.

On these flats *Hepsetus odoe* is the main piscivorous species, taking a variety of prey fishes including mormyrids, *Syndontis*, *Alestes*, *Barbus*, cichlids and *Ctenopoma*. The catfish *Schilbe mystus* eats many of the same species, but also ingests insects, Crustacea, and plant fragments, as do the two species of *Clarias* and two of *Serranochromis* living here (Carey, 1968, 1971).

The fish communities were also sampled by chemofishing to get a total count of fish by netting off an area 0·25 ha in extent and using 75 per cent emulsifiable toxaphene (Lagler *et al.*, 1971). Chemofishing has revolutionised attempts to determine community structure and the relative numbers and biomasses of species present. Care is, however, needed in the interpretation of results (as discussed on p. 194). As only small areas can be treated, there is much variation in figures obtained in slightly different biotopes and at different water levels, and results are then often extrapolated for huge areas, so that sampling differences are enormously magnified. In nine such operations on the Kafue flats a total of 2·25 ha was treated, and the area of lagoons on the flats was estimated to be around 141 700 ha. The biomasses of fish in each biotope, calculated as kg/ha, are indicated in Table 8.3; they ranged from 64 kg/ha in grass marsh to 2683 kg/ha amongst vegetation in a lagoon, compared with 337 kg/ha in a river channel; in the open lagoons biomasses were higher at low water. Subsequent calculations suggested that of a highwater total ichthyomass of around 96 000 tonnes, 40 per cent were lost between July and September due to fishing and natural mortality. As catch statistics indicated that only 3000 tonnes were taken by the fishery, this suggested that the natural mortality must be of the order of 35 000 tonnes, 36 per cent of the highwater ichthyomass, which does seem very high. The high mortality would be partly due to mass strandings of fishes as the water falls, and partly to intense predation by birds as well as by fishes.

Seasonal rivers of South America

The same pattern of events as in the floodplain rivers of Africa occurs in the savanna floodplain regions of South America. North of the equator the seasonal cycle was studied in the Rupununi savannas of Guyana (Lowe-McConnell, 1964), and in Venezuela by Mago (1970*a*), south of the equator in Argentina by Bonetto *et al.* (1969).

Fishes living under seasonally changing conditions in headwaters of Amazonian tributaries have been studied in the Mato Grosso of Brazil (personal observation) and in Peru by Luling. Fish movements in South

American rivers have been illuminated by tagging experiments in the Paraná–Paraguai system in both Brazil and Argentina.

The Rupununi district, Guyana

Unlike the coastal district of Guyana, the Rupununi savannas at 2° to 4° N (Fig. 2.6) have only one rainy season a year, May to August, during which the rivers flood the extensive savannas to a depth of 1 to 2 m, and the growth of water plants is exuberant. In wet years connection is made across the wide stretches of flooded savanna between the Essequibo drainage system, into which the Rupununi River flows, and the Amazon system to which the Takutu and Ireng rivers draining the western side of the savannas flow via the Rio Branco and the Rio Negro. After the rains the country dries up rapidly.

The Rupununi fish fauna includes numerous small (less than 5 cm) aquarium-sized fishes, and about 150 species of larger fishes, most of them used as food by local inhabitants: 61 characoid species (45 per cent), 35 siluroids (27 per cent), 19 cichlids (14 per cent), 9 gymnotoids (6 per cent), with a few representatives of about 9 other families, 3 sciaenids, 2 osteoglossids, 2 clupeids, and single species of flatfish *Achirus*, puffer *Colomesus*, *Synbranchus*, and stingray *Potamotrygon*. In the dry season, savanna pond communities include 60 to 70 of the larger species, many of them different from the species in the main river bed and river pools; for instance the red-bellied piranha *Serrasalmus nattereri*, of bad repute, was common in savanna ponds, while the larger but less feared black piranha *S. rhombeus* was only caught in the river. *S. nattereri* were extremely abundant in all the savanna ponds in certain years; they were noticeably scarce in other years; this appeared to be the result of good or bad spawning years in the previous year or two, largely determined by the way in which the savannas were flooded, inadequate floods failing to release fishes trapped in some of the ponds and fluctuating water levels stranding spawn.

As in the Sokoto River in Nigeria (p. 99) the larger pools carried larger-growing species, the small pools only small species; the size of the dry season refuge pools appears to be an important factor governing fish distribution in the Rupununi. Savanna pond species were in almost all cases found in both Essequibo and Amazon drainage systems; species which can withstand conditions in these ponds are well equipped to cross the divide. Among the riverine species, on the other hand, some were found only on the Amazon drainage side.

These Rupununi waters were mostly very clear natural aquaria, where the behaviour of the fishes could be observed. There was a marked change-over at dawn and dusk between the diurnal fishes (cichlids and most of the characoids) and the nocturnal catfishes and gymnotoids which hid in crevices by day. At night cichlids and characoids hide away, motionless, against the bank or among tree litter. The nocturnal species, often larger than the diurnal ones, hide by day in crevices in tree litter or rocks; these hiding places appear to be of particular significance for the development of a rich nocturnal fauna, the tree litter providing daytime shelter above the often deoxygenated bottom water. At one collecting station crevices in tree litter in the dry season yielded 17 fish species, 15 of them catfishes of six different families with auchenipterids (such as *Centromochlus*, Fig. 10.1) predominating, many of the fishes packed into the same crevice. Other small fishes hid in the leaf litter carpeting the pools at the end of the rains, while the elongated and transparent young of the gymnotid *Gymnorhamphthichthys hypostomus* (Fig. 9.8) burrowed and hid in the bottom sand with only the snout protruding.

When the rivers began to rise at the start of the rains, fish movements included upstream movement by large characoids, such as *Myleus pacu*, *Hydrolycus scomberoides* and *Boulengerella cuvieri*; and lateral movements along sidecreeks into the flooded savannas. Characoids including *Prochilodus* spawned as they moved into side creeks and onto the savannas. Other species making lateral movements, such as *Cichla ocellaris* and *Osteoglossum bicirrhosum*, often spawned before moving, and the lateral movement was probably associated with feeding. At the end of the rains there was a general return movement down creeks back to the main rivers. Many of the species caught while making such movements were those found in savanna ponds, showing that some individuals move downstream and others become imprisoned in the ponds. Trap catches showed that there is a particular order in which species move down river, and that different species travel at different times of day or night.

On the whole the principal breeding season for most of the species is in the main rains. This is particularly marked in characoids such as *Prochilodus* in which the eggs are shed at one time, and less marked in species which brood their eggs and produce fewer eggs at a time, often at more frequent intervals, such as the cichlids, *Osteoglossum*, and loricariid catfishes. The main spawning season was also in the rains for *Hoplias malabaricus*, a 'partial-spawning' characoid (see p. 216) whose biology has been studied in Brazil (Azevedo and Gomes, 1953), and *Arapaima gigas*, in which the ova do not all ripen at once. Sudden changes in water level present great dangers to eggs and small fishes, putting a premium on rapid development; eggs and alevins (yolked young) develop very fast. In many cichlids the males were larger than the associated females but in many characoids the females were larger.

This well-defined spawning season at the start of the rains enabled growth rates of young fish to be determined from length-frequency data (p. 202). The scales of many species showed growth checks in the 'physiological winter' of the dry season. These indicated that the sizes at which many of the cichlids and some of the characoids matured could be reached in one year's growth, though this might depend on the prevailing conditions and be delayed a year. In some other large species, such as *Osteoglossum*, size distributions suggested that these fishes are at least two years old before they spawn.

Foods are extremely limited in the dry season. The many species crowded together in small drying pools share whatever supplies there are, mainly bottom debris, so there is then much overlap in food eaten by different species, but competition is reduced as feeding levels are lowered, the fishes living off their fat and protein stores. In the wet season many more foods become available and the fishes develop fat ribbons along the intestine, showing that this is a rich feeding time. There is little information about how much the fishes specialise on different foods as they become widely scattered in the enlarged flooded environment, and are then most difficult to catch.

The fishes are subject to great seasonal changes in conditions. Species such as the armoured loricariid *Lithoxus*, beautifully flattened and able to adhere to rock surfaces when the water flow is very fast, have to be able to live in still, rather deoxygenated pools in the dry season. Many Guiana fish species have evolved accessory methods of respiration (studied by Carter 1934, 1935) often involving the use of part of the alimentary canal, which tends to be empty of food at this time of year (Appendix 5). The dry season exposes the fishes to intense crowding in areas of little food, intense predation, desiccation and deoxygenation. Stout, often sharp, dorsal and pectoral spines, and an armour of dermal bones in three catfish groups, may help to protect them from predators, and there were beautiful examples of protective resemblances to twigs (*Farlowella*) or gnarled pieces of wood (*Agmus*). The eggs and young of many species are guarded by the parent fishes, either by oral incubation (as in some *Geophagus* and *Osteoglossum*), or in other ways.

In the natural aquaria of the stream pools the importance of communications between fishes was obvious. In the diurnal characoids and cichlids specific recognition is helped by specific markings, often black and yellow or red, on the caudal fin, sides of the body, or on the adipose fin when present in characoids. The nocturnal gymnotoids produce specific electric signals, species living in fast-flowing water using higher frequencies than those in still water (p. 233). Many of the nocturnal siluroids produced characteristic sounds. Several of the characoids were also heard to produce specific noises, including *Prochilodus* on their spawning runs, and *Serrasalmus* of all sizes, as discussed later (p. 232).

Conditions in the Rupununi appeared very similar to those described for seasonally inundated areas of West Africa. In Guyana changes in water levels, resulting from river captures, drainage changes, and oscillating cycles of wet and dry years, would appear to have had major roles in the evolution of the very complex fish fauna. In these meandering rivers with their numerous side arms and lateral lakes, fish populations become split into separate units at times of low water, then recombined in highwater years, often providing opportunities for allopatric speciation.

Venezuelan savanna waters

In neighbouring Venezuela the ecology of fishes in lagoons and channels near the River Apuré, in the Orinoco drainage (7° to 9° N) described by Mago (1970*a*) is very like that in the Rupununi. Here too the annual rains, from

May to November, control the lives of the fishes and affect their evolution. Fishes adapted to special biotopes include:

1. species which partially bury themselves in the sandy bottoms, such as the stingrays (*Potamotrygon*), the gymnotoid *Gymnorhamphichthys*, the characoid *Xenagoniates*;
2. crevice dwellers, which include many nocturnal fishes, electric eels and other gymnotoids and catfishes;
3. fishes associated permanently or temporarily with the carpets of floating vegetation, including many cichlids such as *Aequidens* and *Apistogramma*, doradid and *Corydoras* catfish, small characids such as *Hyphessobrycon*;
4. fishes found in marginal vegetation of rivers, which included juveniles of many loricariids, gymnotoids and cichlids, with adult *Farlowella* living there permanently;
5. fishes seeking shelter in the semisubmerged trees and bushes at high water;
6. annual fishes, the cyprinodonts *Pterolebias* and *Austrofundulus*, which can withstand the dry period as resistant eggs. Among the special habits of the fishes living in the Orinoco drainage area were:
   (*a*) examples of mimicry, for instance young *Colossoma* resembling the predatory *Serrasalmus notatus*, and of young *Abramites hypselonotus* resembling *Leporinus fasciatus*;
   (*b*) the ability to move overland through wet vegetation, shown by both *Hoplias* and *Hoplyerythrinus*;
   (*c*) sound production by doradids and many others;
   (*d*) colour blotches important for sexual recognition and for shoaling.

As in Guyana the start of the rains (May–June) marked the start of the spawning season for many species: the characoids *Serrasalmus notatus*, *Salminus hilarii*, *Hydrolycus scomberoides*, *Hoplias malabaricus*; the catfishes *Pseudoplatystoma fasciatum*, *Sorubim lima*, *Pinirampus pirinampu*, *Ancistus hystrix*, *Hypostomus* sp., *Pterygoplichthys* sp.; the cichlid *Astronotus ocellatus*; the sciaenid *Plagioscion squamosissimus*. Mago thought that specialisations to get food were probably needed when food was short in the dry season, rather than in the rains (contrast Rupununi findings and see p. 214).

The lagoons formed alongside highways, where earth had been removed to build the roads, became naturally stocked with fish. Chemofishing one such lagoon (1225 m^2 in area) produced 25 species of fish, 25 000 individuals totalling over 120 kilo weight, equivalent to 100 g (fresh weight)/m^2, or 1000 kg/ha of fish (Table 8.3). The biomass of predatory species was very high (*c*. 75 per cent of the total biomass) and *Hoplias malabaricus* formed 47 per cent of the catch (compare lagoons from Argentina, Fig. 4.5).

Mato Grosso headwater streams

In the Mato Grosso streams far to the south of the Amazon (*c*. 12° S) many of the same fish species as present in the Rupununi or their ecological equivalents were encountered. These streams flow to the Amazon either via the

Rio das Mortes, Araguaia and Tocantins, or via the Suia-Missu to the Xingú. The rainy season here is from November to April. Gonad states, and the abundance and length frequencies of young fishes in March–May, showed that breeding is here very seasonal, the main spawning season for most species being early in the rains (possibly just before them in some species) as in Guyana. Many of the fishes had well-defined growth checks on their scales and by the end of the rains fishes of most species had large fat ribbons along the intestine, indicating that the rains are the main feeding time here too. Stomach contents stressed the importance of allochthonous foods (vegetable debris and aerial insects, such as flying ants) in fishes from the forest streams, and also of aquatic insects, particularly Ephemeroptera and Odonata nymphs (pers. obs.).

The fish fauna sampled at only one time of year and with inadequate gear included about 140 species, of which a surprisingly high proportion of the small characids proved new to science – perhaps 40 per cent of them (Gery, personal communication). This illustrates the difficulties of ecological studies when identification of the species presents such problems, and stresses the very provisional nature of estimates of species numbers when figures for different river systems are compared. Apart from this high rate of endemicity, the characoid fauna was here more like that of Guyana than of Central Amazonia, with many of the same species as in Guyana. About 60 per cent of the species were characoids, about 21 per cent siluroids of about eight families, 8 per cent cichlids, 4 per cent gymnotoids, together with individuals of eight other families (clupeids, puffer, garfish, cyprinodonts and poeciliids).

The numbers of species diminished towards the headwaters of the tributary streams. Here only about a dozen species were found, all hardy and ubiquitous ones, the nocturnal species larger than those active by day. In temporarily flooded areas the fast-growing young of *Hoplerythrinus* lived in small shoals of up to a dozen fishes, feeding largely on allochthonous matter, and dropping downstream as the water fell; the adults had already moved downstream. Further downstream and in pools open to the sunlight, the numbers of species were much greater.

The Andean tributary streams in Peru

The fish communities of meadow ditches, brooks and streams flowing into the Rio Huallaga, an Andean tributary of the Amazon in eastern Peru, near Tingo Maria (9° S, 75′ W, 670 m altitude, Fig. 3.1) were described by Lüling (1970, 1971*b*). Some of the same species as in Mato Grosso streams were present, including the very aggressive *Hoplias malabaricus* and the hardy catfish *Callichthys callichthys*, while alternative species of *Aequidens* and *Crenicichla* lived in the quieter waters, and numerous small characoids, such as *Astyanax* species, in the current. The fauna in Peruvian headwater streams is scanty compared with that in the white waters in the rainforest, the huge richness in species and numbers beginning below the 300 m contour. Data for numbers of fish and other species in four Peruvian headwater streams near Tingo Maria at 600 m summarised by Patrick (1964) showed that these streams had 31 species of fish or less, compared with 96 species from a section of the Amazon and 124 species from part of the River Nanay near Iquitos. Patrick attributed the richness of these latter sites to the many more niches possible on the Amazon floodplain with its ponds than in the smaller headwater rivers, also to other factors such as the age of the basin.

Lüling (1971*a*) studied the behaviour of the annual cyprinodont *Rivulus beniensis* in the meadow ditches. These fishes die after spawning and hard-shelled eggs remain viable through the dry period from June to late December. As the pools diminish in size in late May, the *Rivulus* jump repeatedly over the damp soil until they reach the deepest pools, behaviour which concentrates the breeding populations. Changes in water chemistry, particularly conductivity and increases in pH and alkalinity, were thought by Lüling to stimulate spawning. These temporary meadow ditches provide a habitat free from predatory fishes such as *Hoplias malabaricus* (see Fig. 9.6, p. 226).

Fish communities in the Paraná–Paraguai system

The ecology of the fishes in the immense Parana–Paraguai system (Fig. 4.4) has been investigated at various points:

1. in the Mogi Guassu and other tributaries of the Upper Parana in São Paulo State, Brazil (papers by von Ihering: Schubart; Godoy);
2. in the Middle Parana River, below the confluence of the Parana and Paraguai rivers (27° 3′ S), which although south of the tropics carries many of the same species as the Amazon, from Argentina's Institute Nacional de Limnologia at Santa Fé (Bonetto *et al.*, 1969);
3. fish migrations up the Pilcomayo, a 1500 km long tributary of the Rio Paraguai which rises in the Bolivian Andes, were studied by Bayley (1973);
4. the special problems of the Paraguayan Chaco swamps were studied by Carter and Beadle (1931).

From these studies we have a picture of the fish communities in dry season pools in the Middle Parana and of the fish-spawning migrations in Brazil, Argentina and the Pilcomayo in areas marked in Fig. 4.4.

Middle Paraná pool communities Parana River fluctuations are complicated by the water received from various tributaries but near Santa Fé the water level reaches its maximum in summer (February–March) and its minimum in August–September. During the flood the river overflows its dry season bed reaching the numerous ponds and lakes on the many islands, and fishes migrate between the river and the ponds. The shallow pools, dried up at the end of the low-water season, receive fingerlings and large quantities of fishes of various species and sizes. When the water level falls many fishes remain in oxbow lakes and pools alongside the rivers and swamps, and large numbers of fish stranded in the drying pools perish.

The riverside pools, channels and small depressions contain abundant diverse small characoids (*Astyanax*, *Characidium*, *Acestrorhynchus*, etc.) also the young of many larger-growing species, such as 7 to 12 cm long *Prochilodus* (as well as some 40 to 50 cm adults). The oxbow lakes, riverine in origin but lentic in conditions, lack rooted vegetation but have extensive covers of floating hydrophytes. One 190 000 m^2 lagoon ('Don Felipe') contained 52 species of fish (779 128 individuals, a mean of 6·2 individuals per cubic metre of water; Ringuelet *et al.*, 1967). However, only five large species were relatively abundant (the three characoids *Prochilodus platensis*, *Leporinus obtusidens* and *Schizodon fasciatum*, and two pimelodid catfishes), the remaining 47 species were small species or the juveniles of large species. The proportions of the different trophic types were:

		Per cent of total number of individuals
Mud-feeders	7 species	14
Detritus-feeders	5 species	8
Herbivores	12 species	12
Omnivores	12 species	3
Invertebrate feeders	12 species	62
Piscivores	11 species	0·5

The fish communities in various temporary oxbow and riverside lakes were studied near Santa Fé at low-water season (Bonetto *et al.*, 1969). The convolutions of the river typical of this huge whole region are shown in Fig. 4.5a, which gives the location of these temporary pools in islands in the Rio Coronda branch of the Middle Paraná River. From these six oxbow lakes on the Isla los Sapos and two lakes on the Isla El Vado came 41 species of fish, representing 37 genera, 13 families, 7 orders. Characiform fishes predominated in all of them and the numbers of individuals was very high. The mean biomass was high, over 1000 kg/ha of pool area. Numbers and biomasses varied very much from pool to pool, from 175 kg/ha to 6500 kg/ha for the two El Vado pools. As these pools contained fishes concentrated from a wide area this biomass was not produced in this area, as it would have been in a fish pond.

In the six Isla los Sapos Lakes (Fig. 4.5b) a large proportion of the biomass was made up of relatively few species and types of fish. Over 30 per cent of the total biomass was of one species, the mud-feeding *Prochilodus platensis*, a species also important in the riverside pools of Isla El Vado. The predator *Hoplias malabaricus* was present in all the pools and dominated the fauna in certain oxbow lakes, making up 25 per cent of the total biomass in the los Sapos lakes (Fig. 4.5). The innumerable small characids (such as *Astyanax*) and characoid curimatids also made up over 20 per cent of the total biomass. Cichlids (mainly *Aequidens*) were abundant in oxbows with abundant plant cover. Other species present in numbers included *Pimelodus clarias*, *Schizodon fasciatum*, *Leporinus obtusidens*, *Synbranchus marmoratus*, hypostomine and loricariid catfish, *Serrasalmus* and other small carnivores. Most

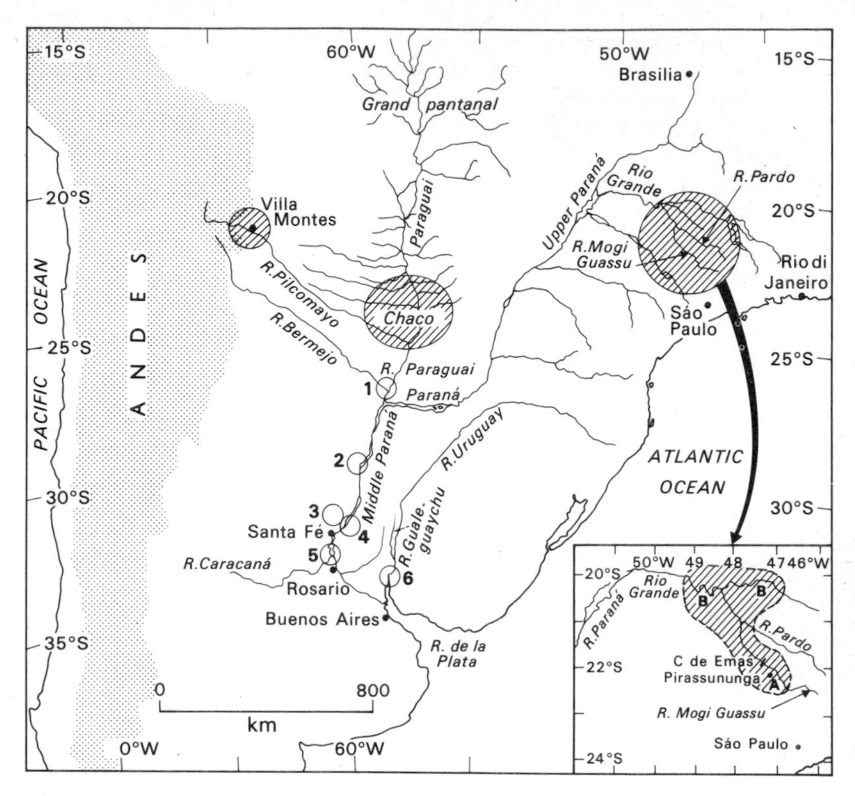

Fig. 4.4 The Parana–Paraguai river system with sites mentioned in the text. The numbers 1–6 on the Middle Parana denote fish-tagging stations (see Table 4.2). The inset map of the Rio Mogi Guassu shows the main tagging station at Cachoeira de Emas; spawning grounds of *Prochilodus scrofa* lie upstream of these at A, while their main feeding grounds are about 600 km downriver on the Rio Grande and Pardo at B (inset map after Godoy, 1967).

fishes were the young of lotic species, not yet sexually mature, though a few species, such as the piscivorous *Hoplias malabaricus* and the eel-like *Synbranchus*, are characteristically stillwater fishes.

The faunal composition in different pools (Fig. 4.5) suggested that there was no clear relationship between the predominant species and amount of plant cover, except for the cichlid *Aequidens* which was only common where there was abundant plant cover (pool A); *Prochilodus* were present in pools with or without it. The ratios of forage fishes (non-piscivorous species) to the piscivores ranged from 0·75 in a pool (D) which had only semi-aquatic *Ludwigia* plants on the margins, to 12·4 in a pool (G) which was totally covered with floating vegetation. This relationship between vegetation (which provided cover) and proportion of forage fishes did not, however, hold in all cases, as there was a high ratio of 6·8 in one pool (B) which lacked

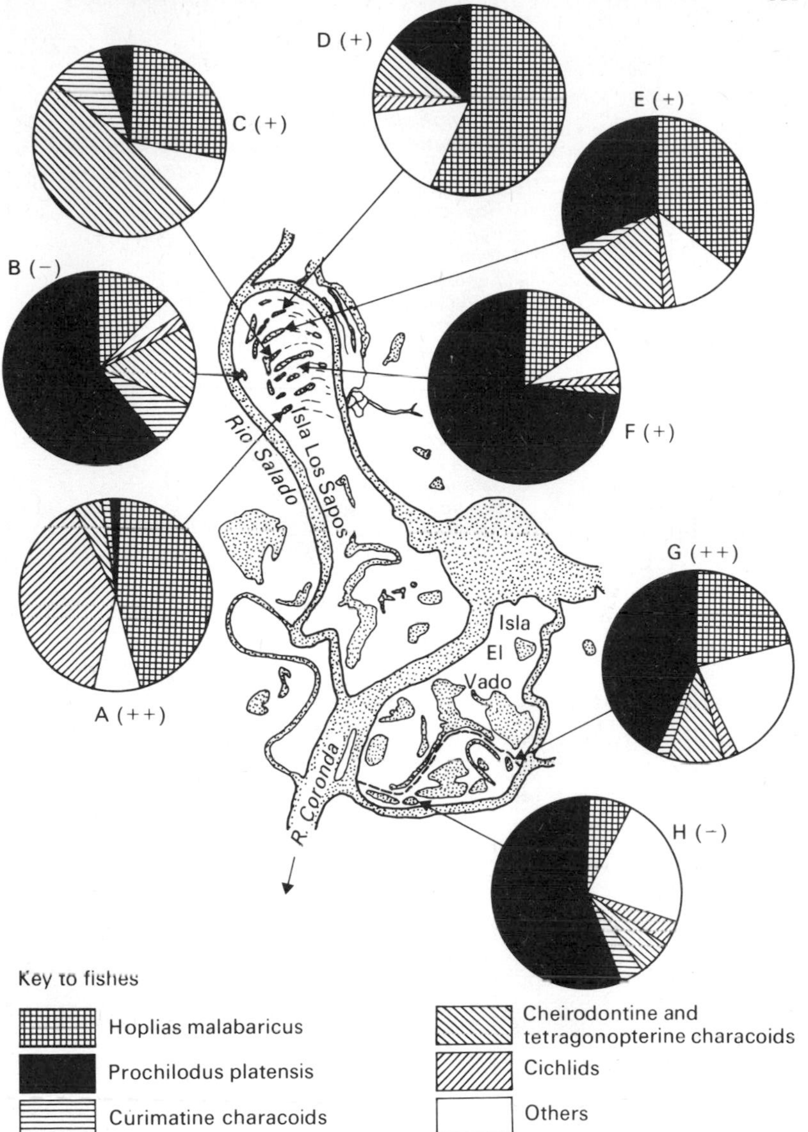

Fig. 4.5 The complexity of aquatic systems in the Middle Parana, and the fish populations in seasonal lakes (**a**, adapted from Bonetto *et al.*, 1969*a*; **b**, after Bonetto *et al.*, 1969*b*).

Fig. 4.5a The proportions of different types of fish taken by total fishing eight temporary lakes in two islands in a tributary near Santa Fé. (The abundance of plant cover, indicated in parentheses, ranged from pool A with abundant vegetation to pools B and H which lacked it; pool G was completely covered, and pool F half-covered, with floating vegetation; pool D had only semi-aquatic *Ludwigia* around it.)

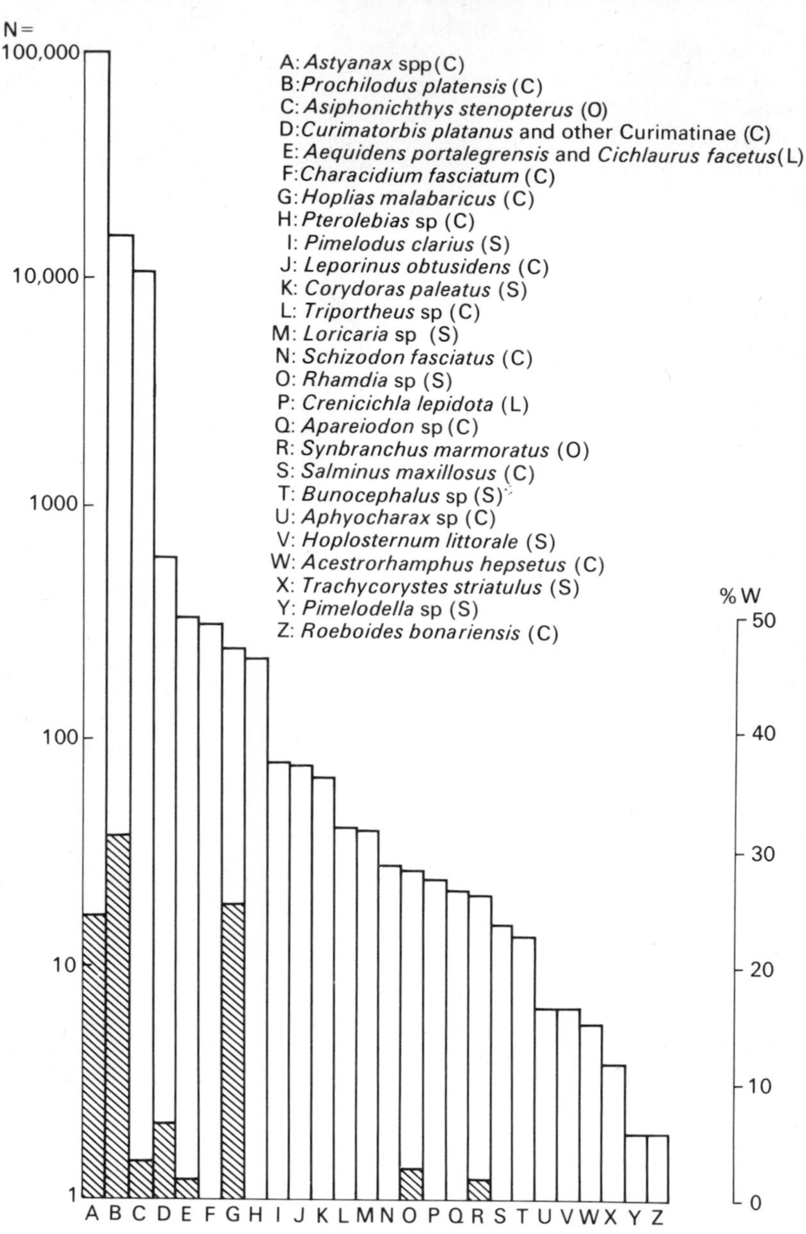

Fig. 4.5b The specific distribution of the fish populations obtained by total sampling the six Isla los Sapos island oxbow lakes ('madrejones').

(Log numbers and percentage weights (hatched) of species making up more than 1 per cent of total catch; family group indicated after specific name thus: characoid (C); siluroid (S); cichlid (L); other (O).)

hydrophytes. The shoaling habits of some of these fishes, which would lead to all or none being trapped in pools as the water fell, would affect such ratios.

Fish populations of four permanent pools were then examined using chemofishing and mark-recapture methods (Bonetto *et al.*, 1970). Here again *Prochilodus platensis* were predominant (61 per cent of the biomass) followed by loricariids (6 per cent), *Pimelodus clarias* (5 per cent), *Hoplias malabaricus* (4 per cent). The shallowest pool (semi-permanent) had most *Hoplias*. Certain species present in temporary pools were totally absent, while the young of some large species, such as dorado *Salminus maxillosus*, sorubi *Pseudoplatysoma coruscans*, and pacu *Colossoma mitrei* were found in permanent pools but not in the temporary ones. The biomass was again high, 1100 kg/ha of pool. Some species, such as *Hoplias malabaricus* were the same as in Venezuelan lagoons, others such as the *Prochilodus* species were ecological equivalents.

Over much of South America these *Prochilodus* are important for human food (Mago, 1972). They are all mud-feeders, for which they have many adaptations including a suctorial mouth and very long intestine. In the Rio de la Plata great gatherings, estimated at over 200 million *Prochilodus platensis* accumulate in the summer, but break up in February–March as the water gets colder (Ringuelet *et al.*, 1967). These consist of populations from various areas, showing some biometric differences but very variable. Some individuals go up the Rio Parana, appearing at the junction of the Lower Paraná and Paraná in April, May, June; others go up the River Uruguay. There are two main reproductive periods, one in spring (October–December), and another at the end of summer and in autumn (May–June). The fish movements are complex; in October, November, December, shoals in the river may be moving in opposite directions, those that have spawned moving to the estuary to feed, those that have still to spawn moving upriver. They are preyed on by large *Pseudoplatystoma* catfish (surubi) and by *Salminus maxillosus* (dorado) (Fig. 4.6).

The dorado, a large food and sport fish that is rather salmon-like in appearance, is found from the Rio de la Plata to Amazonas; it is a regular migrant in the lower and Middle Paraná river and in the Pilocmayo and upper Paraná. In October–November when the water level is rising it arrives in the Mogi Guassu River in Brazil where females spawn in the river, each accompanied by three to four males.

Fish spawning runs in Brazilian rivers The spawning runs of many South American river fishes, known locally as 'piracema' (fish swarms) are well known to the Brazilian fishermen and have been described by von Ihering (1930*b*), Schubart (1943, 1953, 1954), Godoy (1959) and others. They have been much studied in the Mogi Guassu River (São Paulo State) a 473 km river with many rapids which rises in springs at 1650 m altitude then flows westwards to join the upper Paraná (Fig. 4.4). At the Cachoeira de Emas (Emas rapids) where the river is 80 m wide and 2 to 3 m deep, a fish

Fig. 4.6a

Fig. 4.6b

Fig. 4.6c

ladder alongside a hydroelectric dam has enabled the fishes to be trapped easily, and here the movements of tagged fish have been observed for more than ten years. The fish runs occur with the start of the floods in September–November. The fishes moving up at this time are mostly large characoids: *Salminus maxillosus*, *Prochilodus*, *Brycon*, *Leporinus* species. The first fertilised eggs are found in early December. Wheeling circles of spawning fish known locally as 'rodada', occur on a rising flood between November and February. When in rodada the fishes are oblivious of any disturbance. Some species spawn in inundated prairies, others in the main river, often in special places out of the main current. Shoals of small fishes gorge themselves on the eggs, and eggs in shallow water perish if the level falls. Development is extremely rapid, the alevins appearing two or three days after fertilisation. In the river the floating fertile eggs are carried down to quiet stretches, where they develop fast in the warm shallows. The phase of the moon is important for the spawning of some species (Schubart 1943, 1954).

Spawning in *Prochilodus scrofa* (Curimbatá) has been observed and photographed in the Mogi Guassu (Godoy, 1954). The males move up river in the centre of the channel, emitting sounds as they do so. The females, slightly larger fish, move up near the banks and out into the centre of the river to spawn. Similar behaviour has been observed for *Prochilodus platensis* in the Pilcomayo (Fig. 4.7), though this species spawns by day, whereas *P. scrofa* spawns only at the end of the afternoon and at night. In the Rupununi male *Prochilodus* were seen and heard moving upstream out onto the savanna in a rising flood at the start of the rains.

Prochilodus scrofa migrate in schools: aggregations of 60 000 to 80 000 are reported in the Mogi Guassu, where both sexes appear in their thousands in the Emas rapids fish ladder at the end of August. During the up-stream migration they move both by day and night (unlike some other migrating fishes which only move at one time of day). The *Prochilodus* moving upstream here are a heterogeneous group of several age classes, including first-year class (20+ cm) fishes not yet mature. Growth data from scale rings determined by Godoy (1959), showed that the males mature when two years old (*c.* 25 cm), and are most abundant from three to seven years old in the upstream runs; the females mature when three years old (*c.* 31 cm), and are most abundant from four to eight years. Males rarely reach 58 cm total length (2720 g) and nine years old, whereas females grow to 68 cm (5800 g) and live to thirteen years old; the sex ratio was 1 female to 1·05 males.

Fig. 4.6a *Prochilodus platensis*, the sábalo, an important and numerous food fish in the Paraná system; this grows to *c.* 50 cm total length.

Fig. 4.6b *Salminus maxillosus*, the dorado, which preys on *Prochilodus* and is an important food and sport fish. This commonly grows to 75 cm and 6 kg, but specimens of over 1 m 15 kg are known.

Fig. 4.6c *Serrasalmus nattereri*, the red-bellied piranha, a widely-distributed and much feared fish in South America; this grows to *c.* 30 cm long. (Photographs by P. Bayley.)

Fig. 4.7a *Prochilodus platensis*, the sábalo of the Pilcomayo River (*c.* 40 cm long).

Fig. 4.7b *Prochilodus platensis* spawning in the Pilcomayo River. (Photographs by P. Bayley.)

Fish movements in the Paraná–Paraguai system Fish-tagging experiments carried out in the Mogi Guassu River, Brazil, and in the Middle Paraná, have given a surprisingly high percentage of returns, particularly considering the great distances involved and sparse human populations. This success is due partly to the co-operation of the fishermen, and also to recaptures of fishes in fish passes around hydroelectric dams. Of the 27 000 fishes tagged in Brazil between 1954 and 1964, 10·1 per cent were returned. In Argentina returns ranged from 0·2 per cent in a wetland area with a low human population, to 18·9 per cent on a tributary river with a pass round a dam. The distances ranged by the fish are spectacular.

Of the 95 fish species in the Mogi Guassu River, 12 are of commercial importance: ten characoids and two catfishes (*Prochilodus scrofa*, *Salminus maxillosus*, *Myloplus asterias*, *Leporinus elongatus*, *L. copelandii*, *L. octo-*

Fig. 4.8 *Prochilodus scrofa*, curimbatá, a 58 cm fish tagged at Cachoeira de Emas, Rio Mogi Guassu, on 6 November 1962 (14.30 hours), recaptured here 5 November 1963 (15.05 h.), marked a second time, released, and recaptured near here 16 October 1964 (15.00 h.), demonstrating the regularity of migration here in three consecutive years (from Godoy, 1967).

fasciatus, *Triurobrycon lundii*, *Leporellus vitatus*, *Salminus hilarii*, *Schizodon nasutus*, and the pimelodid catfishes *Pimelodus clarias* and *Paulicea lutkeni*).

Tagging experiments carried out over ten years in the Mogi Guassu, using a hydrostatic tag (a cylindrical tube with a message inside) fixed through the muscles at the base of the dorsal fin (Fig. 4.8), concentrated mainly on *Prochilodus scrofa* which forms 50 per cent of the commercial catch. These fish begin their upstream migration, together with other species, at the end of winter (August–September), and in spring (September–December) they become concentrated in shallow waters below dams and rapids. They arrive at the Emas rapids in September–November and spawn between December and February. After spawning they may continue to swim upstream for a short distance (for some unknown reason), then migrate downstream to the Rio Grande where they feed and remain almost sedentary till they start their upstream migration again. All over South America *Prochilodus* are noted for their ability to lay down fat reserves, which are used on their spawning migrations, when they feed little.

This ten-year study of tagged fish, mainly characoids and siluroids, has shown that some characoids and pimelodids in their migrations upstream to breed and downstream to feed, cover distances totalling 1200–1400 km/year, and involving three rivers of the upper basin of the Paraná River: the Mogi Guassu, Pardo and Rio Grande (Fig. 4.4). Breeding grounds for most of the migrant fishes are in the upper Mogi Guassu, while the feeding, growing and fattening areas are in the Middle Grande River, 600 to 700 km downstream (Godoy, 1967).

Returns of tagged fish showed that *Prochilodus scrofa* move upstream at a mean speed of 10 to 16 km/day, but much faster speeds are reported: up to 43·75 km/day over two days, 34·3 km in one day, 20·1 km/day over three days; 14·6 km/day over 6 days. *Salminus maxillosus* moved 10 to 12 km/day, and *Pimelodus clarias* also 10 to 12 km/day. Recaptures provided evidence that the migrations are remarkably regular. They also gave some data on growth rates (Godoy, 1967). Fifty-two fishes tagged at the Emas rapids were recaught here one or two years later, almost at the same hour of day. These recaptures thus suggested that predation is not too intense once the fish reach a certain size. Among these fishes Godoy reported:

(*a*) 1 *Salminus maxillosus* recaptured after 358 days, during which time the 61 cm fish had grown 3·5 cm.

(*b*) 1 *Pimelodus clarias*, recaptured after 371 days, a 28·5 cm fish when marked which then grew 3·0 cm.

(*c*) 50 *Prochilodus scrofa*, of which 40 were recaught one year (between 344 and 378 days) later, and 10 were recaught two years (between 709 and 744 days) later.

These *Prochilodus* were fishes between 31·5 and 63·5 cm when marked, the growth in those returned after one year ranged from − 1·0 to 4·5 cm, and for those recaptured after two years from 0·0 to 6·0 cm. The *Prochilodus scrofa* shown in Fig. 4.8 which was caught at Cachoeira de Emas in three consecutive years provided evidence of the seasonal regularity of the migration. First caught and tagged on 6 November 1962 at 14·30 hours, a 58·0 cm fish, it was recaptured at the same place on 5 November the following year at 15·05 hours, and again on 16 October 1964 at 15·00 hours, thus providing evidence that it had come here for three consecutive years.

Fishes often home to particular areas, but transplantation experiments with *Prochilodus scrofa*, moving marked fish from the Mogi Guassu down to the Rio Grande, suggested that the homing instinct can be upset, for they showed three types of behaviour: some remained at or near the place of release; others were recaught upstream in the Grande (i.e. having moved up a different river); and some moved from the Grande to the Pardo, to be recaught 3 km up from the Mogi Guassu River mouth.

In Argentina, 40 000 fishes of 25 species were tagged in a programme initiated in 1961 (Bonetto and Pignalberi, 1964). Most tagged fish were *Prochilodus platensis* (70 per cent), *Pimelodus clarias* and *Hoplias malabaricus* (10 per cent each), *Schizodon fasciatum* (1 per cent), various doradids (1·8 per cent), and smaller numbers of *Leporinus obtusidens*, *Pimelodus albicans*, *Luciopimelodus pati*, and *Salminus maxillosus*. From the estuary near Buenos Aires *Prochilodus* moved up both Parana and Uruguay rivers; from Santa Fé they moved down into the estuary, those tagged near the junction of the Paraná and Paraguai moved up both these rivers, while *Salminus maxillosus* tagged here were only recaptured downstream. Thus though recaptures showed that there appear to be reproductive movements up-river and trophic movements down-river, the situation is here a complicated one. Further tagging experiments were therefore planned.

In 1965–66, 11 288 fish were tagged from six centres as indicated in Fig. 4.4 (Bonetto *et al.*, 1971). Of these fishes 70 per cent were *Prochilodus platensis*, 18 per cent *Salminus maxillosus*, and the rest were of various other species. From north to south these centres were: (1) on the Rio Bermejo, above the upper Paraná inflow, where 89 per cent of the tagged fish were *Prochilodus*; (2) between here and Santa Fé, in wetlands where returns were poor as the human population is low; (3) and (4) at two sites near Santa Fé, a lagoon from where a very varied selection of species was marked, and the Rio Coronda, where 70 per cent were *Prochilodus*; (5) on the Rio Carcaraña, a right-bank tributary with a hydroelectric dam, from where returns of *Salminus maxillosus* were spectacular (18·8 per cent from January marked fish, 14·9 per cent from those marked in November); *Pimelodus albicans* were also recaptured here but few *Prochilodus* were tagged; (6) further south on the Rio Gualeguaychu, a tributary of the Uruguay River.

The movements of the recaptured fishes in these various areas, the maximum distances moved and the average speeds of movement are indicated in Table 4.2. The most spectacular movements were of *Prochilodus platensis* moving up to 700 km up the R. Bermejo, at speeds of up to 8·7 km/day, and of *Salminus maxillosus* up to 255 km up-river, at 6·0 km/day, and to 610 km down-river at 5 km/day. *Salminus* tagged on the Rio Carcaraña tributary moved both 555 km up the main Paraná River and 475 km down the Parana river; one *Salminus* moved 237 km in eleven days (21 km/day). Unfortunately the gonad states of the tagged fishes could not be specified.

Fish movements in the Pilcomayo tributary of the Paraguai In the Pilcomayo River studied by Bayley (1973) the main feeding grounds for most of the large fishes appear to be in the swamps of the Lower Chaco: it is not known whether these fishes move further downstream, but they migrate up into the Andean reaches of the river to spawn. The major ascents of most of the important food fish occur in the winter months. The first migrations are normally encountered in March or April at the Argentinian/Bolivian Border, and they reach Villa Montes, 120 km upstream near the Andean foothills, in May or June. Here the migration reaches maximum intensity in July/August, drops off in September–October, and most of the fish descend when the large floods come down in November–December. This applies to most of the *Prochilodus platensis*, *Leporinus obtusidens*, *Schizodon fasciatum*, *Colossoma mitrei*, and small- or medium-sized *Salminus maxillosus* and *Pseudoplatystoma coruscans*. The larger specimens of the two latter species were seen migrating in the summer months when the water is higher during the rains.

Bayley (1973) suggested that the migration may be initiated by the annual flooding in the summer months in the Lower Chaco, which would liberate the fishes from the lakes and oxbows, when these become connected with the rising river, and possibly by the fall in water temperature towards the end of

Table 4.2 Movements of tagged fishes in the Middle Parana. Tagging station number refers to number on map (Fig. 4.4). ↑ denotes upstream, ↓ downstream movement, S recaptured within 10 km from where tagged (data summarized from Bonetto *et al.*, 1971).

TAGGING STATION	NUMBER TAGGED	PER CENT RETURNED	MOVEMENT	RECAPTURES					
				Prochilodus platensis			Salminus maxillosus		
				No.	Max. distance km	Max. speed km/day	No.	Max. distance km	Max. speed km/day
1. R. Bermejo	1399*	1.9	↑	16	700	4·8–8·7	1	255	6·0
			↓	3	512	3·5	—	—	—
			S	1	—	—	—	—	—
2. San Javier lagoons	2264	0·2	↑	—			—	—	—
			↓	5	255	1·5–2·0	—	—	—
			S	—	—	—	—	—	—
3. Monte Vera lagoons Santa Fé	4293	2·9	↑	12	150	0·7–3·0	5	62	0·9–1·6
			↓	9	90	0·3	37	610	1·6–5·0
			S	—	—	—	18	—	—
4. Rio Coronda	1328	3·7	↑	26	100	0·3–0·5	1	250	0·8
			↓	9	570	0·5	3	600	0·8–3·0
			S	6	—	—	—	—	—
5. R. Carcarañá (hydroelectric barrage)	949	16·0	↑	—	—	—	15	555	2·4–6·0†
			↓	—	—	—	19	475	9·1
			S	—	—	—	82	—	—
6. R. Gualeguaychu	1055	1·7	↑	2	108	—	1	237	21·5
			↓	3	200	0·9	—	—	—
			S	—	—	—	—	—	—

* *Prochilodus* predominated at Stations 1–4 (89 per cent of tagged fish at Station 1, 84 per cent at 2) but relatively few were tagged at Station 5.
† 1 *Pimelodus albicans* was returned from 11·5 km upstream, and 14 were recaught less than 10 km from where tagged.

the wet season. These fish all move upstream to spawn, carrying quantities of fat. The gonads of both sexes mature during the migrations, and some immature fishes accompany them (as in Brazil). Bayley described the spawning behaviour of *Prochilodus platensis*, 25 km upstream of Villa Montes in November 1970, after the first flood of the rainy season had occurred. The water was turbid and fairly low, and the water temperature high (29·5° C); the fishes' behaviour was very much as described for *Prochilodus scrofa* in Brazil, except that *P. platensis* spawned by day, and at midday the whole pool was disturbed by threshing pairs or trios of fish (Fig. 4.7*b*).

Fishes of the Paraguayan Chaco swamps Over much of the vast swampy region of the Paraguayan Chaco, the physicochemical conditions restrict the fishes that can live here. The fauna of these swamps is considerable and varied but never rich. With open plains, so flat that the whole country is liable to be flooded with the sudden heavy storms, in many areas there is hardly any water which does not dry out during prolonged droughts, and even in normal years great areas become dry (Carter and Beadle, 1931). The swamps are mostly 1 to 1·5 m deep, over black mud and choked with floating and rooted plants. There is little phytoplankton in any of the swamp waters though the reason for this is not at all clear (Beadle, personal communication). The oxygen content of the water is very low, especially where the surface is protected from wind disturbance by the floating blanket of weeds or by clumps of plants, for the rapid decay at the high temperatures uses up most of the oxygen in the water. The premium here is on the ability to obtain enough oxygen for respiratory needs, and many of the fishes have special adaptations for this. Some of the fishes living here, such as the lungfish and *Synbranchus*, can aestivate.

Of the 20 species of fishes found in these swamps, 18 of them living here all year, 8 species belonging to 7 genera are able to breathe air and demonstrate six independent forms of air-breathing (Appendix 5): representatives of the characoid genus *Hoplerythrinus* and siluroid genera *Callichthys*, *Hoplosternum*, *Ancistrus*, the gymnotoid *Hypopomus*, and *Synbranchus* and *Lepidosiren*. These fishes are not confined to such swamps.

The oxygen available in the very shallow surface layer of water is used by the fishes without adaptations to breathe air. These fishes lie below the surface, drawing water from the surface over their gills often for many minutes at a time; these include many small fishes, such as *Tetragonopterus* and *Pyrrhulina*, but also larger *Aequidens*, and *Hoplias malabaricus* up to 30 cm in length. This last does not swallow air, but is drowned if it is prevented from reaching the surface in poorly oxygenated water.

Many of these swamp fishes can escape from drying pools by wriggling overland through very shallow water or damp vegetation; *Hoploerythrinus*, *Hoplias* and *Callichthys* are adept at this.

In the Chaco swamps the lungfish *Lepidosiren paradoxa* makes a burrow up to 1 m vertically downwards through the bottom mud and clay, in which it aestivates sometimes for many months while the whole country is dry, but in many years the deeper swamps do not dry out and the burrow is not then made. *Synbranchus* also aestivates in similar burrows (Carter and Beadle, 1930). Both species leave their burrows as soon as the ground above them is flooded again. The dry season here is usually the winter. *Lepidosiren* breeds early in the summer after the rain, thus shortly after leaving its burrow. The breeding nest is an almost horizontal burrow in the bottom mud into which dead leaves and grass are taken, and in which the eggs are laid. The male guards the eggs, remaining coiled around them; the suggestion that his elongated pelvics are used to keep up the oxygen content of the water of the nest needs further investigation according to Breder and Rosen (1966).

Seasonal rivers of Asia: the Mekong system

The Mekong, one of the ten great rivers of the world, arises in the snow-covered mountains of the Tibetan plateau and flows southwards through six countries on its way to the sea through a complex delta at 10° N in Vietnam (Fig. 2.7). In the Khmer Republic (formerly Cambodia) the Mekong floods back through the Tonlé Sap into the Grand Lac, a shallow seasonally fluctuating lake (11 000 km^2 in area at high water, shrinking to 2500 km^2 at low water and from 8 to 10 m to less than 1 m deep). In the wet season, about June to October, this lake used to flood back into the forest and to support one of the world's largest freshwater fisheries. The lakeside villages are on barges which move with the lakeshore as it advances and retreats. Much of the forest is now cleared, the lake is shallower, and fish catches have declined in recent years. The importance of the Mekong fisheries has stimulated research on how the planned Mekong control operations are likely to affect them (Pantulu, 1973). As part of this control plan, several large manmade lakes have already been created in Thailand (one of them near to Nam Phong).

The Mekong system has a fish fauna of about 500 species. Fish movements are controlled by water levels. Many fishes move into the Tonlé Sap Great Lake as it fills, then out into the flooded zone (formerly forest), returning to the lake and migrating down-river as the water level falls between October and February. Fishes are confined to the river bed in the dry season. Dry season conditions check fish growth, leaving rings on the scales which can be used for age determination (Chevey and Le Poulain, 1940). These provided evidence (*a*) that cyprinid growth is faster in the lake than in the river (two-year-old *Labeo* and *Hampala* being *c*. 32 cm in the lake compared with 17 cm in the Tonlé Sap channel), and faster in the flooded forest than in the open lake; and (*b*) that fishes in the delta show increased growth at the time when debris is brought down with the floods, marking the scales annually, in contrast with unmarked scales of fishes in the Indo-China Sea away from the river mouth.

The high fish production from the Grand Lac was attributed by Chevey and Le Poulain to the fish food in the flood forest; they predicted that should the forest be cleared the fishery would decline, as indeed it has. The feeding potentialities of flooded forest have direct relevance for forest clearance programmes in manmade lakes.

Some ripe fishes were found by them at all times of year except for a short period in April–May when the water was very low, the time of cessation of growth when rings were deposited on the scales. All reproductive stages were found in the population at one time, and it seemed that each fish had its own spawning rhythm. These were not synchronous. There was, however, a peak in spawning activity about June–July as the water was rising, and spawning diminished gradually in the following months though it continued until March.

The downstream movements between October and February, as the water falls, were studied at barrages on the river below the Tonlé Sap where over 100 fish species are caught (Blache and Goossens, 1954). The fishes move downstream in a definite order, and are caught during only part of each lunar month, mainly between the first quarter and the full moon from October to February. The largest fishes migrate down in the first lunar period (October), the siluroids travelling by night, the large cyprinids by day. The migration builds up to a maximum of species by the third lunar period (December). Studies on the migrations lower down the river were reviewed by Shiraishi (1970), and in the Mekong Delta, where there are very important fisheries, by Le-van-Dang (1970).

Many Mekong fishes, including the giant catfish *Pangasianodon gigas*, are believed to migrate many hundreds of kilometres up and down the river. Many catadromous marine fishes move into the estuaries and fresh-waters to feed in the wet season, returning to the sea to breed; and anadromous clupeids breed in the lower reaches. Local impoundments are made by the villagers to retain diadromous fishes and culture them in the delta region. Fishes living in the lower Mekong are classified broadly as 'white fishes', fluvial fishes feeding on plankton and small fish, and 'black fishes', bottom-dwellers feeding on benthic organisms; on the whole the white fishes including cyprinids (such as *Puntius*) migrate down by day, and the black fishes (which include many siluroids and *Channa*) by night.

A hydrobiological survey of some Southeast Asian inland waters and their fish faunas by Mizuno and Mori (1970) included a comparative study of foods eaten by some important fishes living in the rivers, lakes and reservoirs in relation to other trophic levels. The food habits differed from place to place and individual differences were shown.

5

Lacustrine Fish Communities – I. The Great Lakes of Eastern Africa

Lakes are formed when rivers are blocked or dammed; then they are colonised by riverine fishes. The lakes represent expanded feeding grounds comparable to permanent extensions of the lateral flooded areas of the great rivers; many of the lake fishes return to the rivers to spawn, and long after the lake has stabilized the lacustrine fish communities will include riverine as well as truly lacustrine species. Manmade lake studies (p. 175) have illuminated the way in which riverine faunas adjust to lacustrine conditions. The fishes are faced with two problems: adaptations to new sources of food, and spawning under greatly changed conditions. Riverine fishes are mostly euryphagous, and adjustments to new feeding conditions appear more easily made than those to changed breeding conditions. We have seen above that many riverine fishes make upstream migrations to spawn while others move out into the still water on flooded savannas. The former will continue to seek affluent streams in which to spawn, the latter may be able to spawn in the new lake and become truly lacustrine.

The Great Lakes of eastern Africa – Victoria, Tanganyika and Malawi – are all very large and very old lakes, with very diverse cichlid-dominated faunas. The history of these lakes was considered briefly in Chapter 2 (p. 37), and as Table 2.2 showed, differentiation has proceeded furthest in Lake Tanganyika and least in Lake Victoria where it is still mainly at the species level.

Tanganyika, the second deepest lake in the world (1600 m – over a mile deep) and Lake Malawi (722 m), are both long narrow, rift valley lakes; Tanganyika 640 km long by 64 km wide, Malawi 560 km long by 80 km wide. In contrast with these, Lake Victoria is a shallow saucer-shaped lake, 93 m deep though 68 635 km^2 in area, lying between the two East African rift valleys; drowned valleys form gulfs and bays along the very irregular coastline and the present lake probably resulted from the amalgamation of many smaller lakes and expansions on westward flowing rivers and their tributary streams.

The hydrological characteristics of these three lakes are summarised in Fig. 5.1. Although it straddles the equator, the open waters of Lake Victoria

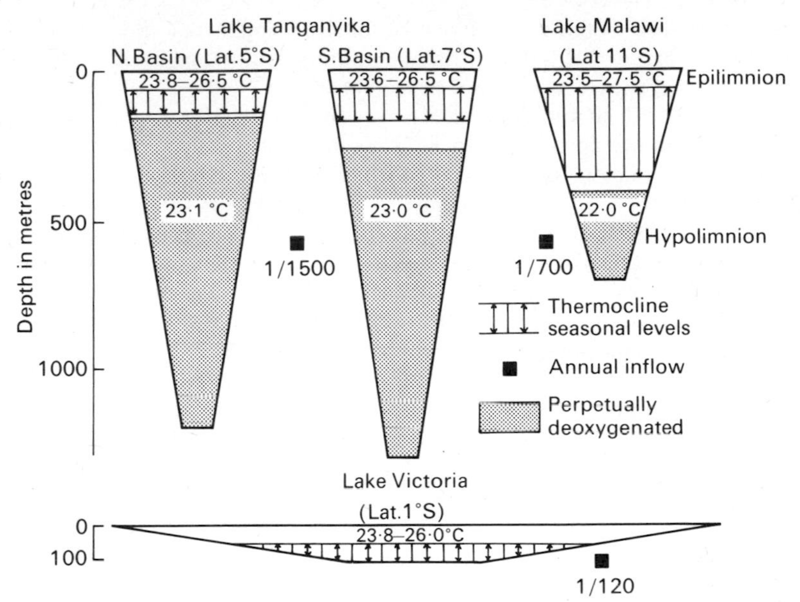

Fig. 5.1 Transverse sections of some African lakes (after Beauchamp, 1964).

have a regular annual stratification and 'overturn' as in a temperate lake, bringing the nutrient salts from the bottom water back into circulation, and internal water movements also spill hypolimnion water into the various gulfs and bays seasonally, which must affect the fishes.

The deep rift lakes Malawi and Tanganyika are more or less permanently stratified. Temperature differences between the surface and bottom waters (Fig. 5.1) are very small compared with those in temperate lakes (as mentioned on p. 10) but the difference in density per °C change of temperature at the prevailing high temperatures is enough to ensure that these lakes can remain stable for long periods. This stratification means both that nutrients are locked away in the hypolimnion water and that these bottom waters are permanently deoxygenated, and therefore out-of-bounds for the fish. Recent work in L. Malawi has emphasised the permanent nature of this stratification, except for some small-scale local upwellings. Although L. Malawi has a deeper epilimnion than L. Tanganyika, the open waters of Malawi are relatively less fertile, there are no regular cycles of plankton production, and this lake lacks the truly pelagic fish communities of L. Tanganyika. In L. Tanganyika the thermocline breaks down in certain years; the strong winds funnelling up the lake in the cool season, May to September, combined with Coriolis's force, lead to turbulent water conditions, with strong offshore drift, upwelling and mixing, especially at the southern end of the lake and in bays (Coulter, 1966). The nutrient salts thus brought into circulation cause local phytoplankton blooms (in July and again in November–December in some years). These in turn affect the abundance of the zooplankton on which the pelagic fish community depends. In L. Tanganyika the important fisheries are based on this pelagic fish community comprising small 'sardines' (clupeids) and their centropomid predators.

The annual inflow into these lakes is very small in relation to their volume, particularly in the deep lakes. In L. Tanganyika it is only 1 : 1500 (a great contrast with many manmade lakes in which annual inflows may far exceed the volume). For long periods of time L. Tanganyika has lacked any outlet, all water loss being due to evaporation. This has led to concentrations of certain salts in the lake water, particularly of sodium, magnesium and sulphate ions, instead of the more usual calcium, potassium and bicarbonate ions found in the river waters and most other lakes. This concentration of salts, and of unusual ions, may present barriers to certain fishes. No mormyrids live in L. Tanganyika, though the affluent rivers contain at least three species which have colonised L. Malawi (*Mormyrus longirostis*, *Mormyrops deliciosus* and *Hippopotamyrus discorhynchus*).

Lake Victoria

The lake and its major habitats

Lake Victoria, a squarish lake, 400 by 320 km, shared by Tanzania, Uganda and Kenya, lies across the equator (0° 21′ N to 3° 0′ S). At the north end equinoxial rains lead to biannual flooding of the inflowing rivers in March to May and between September–December, whereas at the south end of the lake the November–December rains are most marked. The present outflow is to the Nile system, through the turbines of the hydroelectric dam built at the Owen Falls, via the Victoria Nile into Lake Kyoga, a shallow waterlily-swamp lake, thence into the Murchison Nile and over the Murchison Falls into Lake Albert. These falls form a barrier to Nile fish ascending from Lake Albert. The present Lake Victoria has a modified Nile fauna, lacking *Hydrocynus*, *Polypterus*, citharinids and indigenous *Lates*. The non-cichlid fishes have nilotic affinities but endemic species of several occur: of the 38 non-cichlid species, 16 are endemic. The chief feature of the lake is its spectacularly large fauna of cichlid fishes, mainly of one genus *Haplochromis*, of which *c*. 150–170 species are known. Many discovered during trawling in deep water are still awaiting description. Two indigenous *Tilapia* formerly supported a large fishery.

Since 1957 the East African Freshwater Fisheries Research Organisation at Jinja, Uganda, has been investigating the ecology of the lake fishes. The major habitats appear to be few. The open lake water is mostly more than 50 m deep over mud, while nearer to the shore some of the channels between the islands have sandy-pebbly bottoms. Although on the equator, the open waters are mixed from top to bottom during June to August, between September and December stratification develops which results in a deep, well-marked thermal discontinuity from January to June (Talling, 1966).

Large vertical displacements of the thermocline can occur. Inshore areas, such as the Buvuma Channel near Jinja, stratify from August to December, with a thermocline around 10 to 15 m deep. Internal waves (seiches) slosh colder, richer less oxygenated water into the various gulfs and bays (Fish, 1957). Gulfs and sheltered bays in the indented (drowned river valley) coastline, and on the numerous large islands (former hilltops) which lie along the coast, have bottoms carpeted with a semi-liquid algal flock up to 2 metres thick. These form typical feeding grounds for *Tilapia esculenta*, formerly the mainstay of the commercial gillnet fishery.

The shorelines of many of the gulfs and bays are lined with papyrus (*Cyperus papyrus*), below which the water is deoxygenated and inimical to fish life. Open sandy beaches occur at intervals, and the western coast has a long stretch of sandy beach. There are also lateritic rock shores in exposed sites, and lateric cliffs on a few islands. Waterlily swamps with clear warm water lie in the estuaries of some affluents and sheltered bays. The mouths of some affluent streams are blocked with papyrus, through which the water seeps to the lake. Like all these African lakes, the lake level is subject to long-term rises and falls, and lagoons formed behind the papyrus fringe with the dramatic rise in lake level in 1962.

The affluent rivers range in size from large permanent rivers such as the Kagera on the Uganda/Tanzania border, the Sio River on the Kenya/Uganda border, and many smaller rivers of various widths, to flash flood streams, such as the well-studied Bugungu stream near Jinja.

The fish fauna and its distribution within the lake

The indigenous non-cichlid fishes of Victoria and Kyoga (into which Victoria flows) are indicated in Appendix 3. Of these the lungfish *Protopterus aethiopicus* frequents the swamps but is also caught far out in the lake where it feeds on snails and fishes. It can grow to over 2 m long, and it forms an important element of the commercial catch in gillnets. In the lake it does not aestivate. The seven species of mormyrid (two endemic) include the non-endemic *Mormyrus kannume*, here become a truly lacustrine species as it appears to breed around rocks in the lake itself; it is abundant on soft bottoms where it probes for insect larvae and can be caught in gillnets. Some of the smaller mormyrid species move up affluent rivers to spawn.

The characids are represented only by two small endemic *Alestes* species. The fifteen species of cyprinid include eight endemic ones, among them *Labeo victorianus* caught mainly when running up affluent rivers to spawn, and the small silvery *Engraulicypris argenteus* which has pelagic eggs and young and is one of the few species in the lake to feed on zooplankton throughout life. There are also several small species of *Barbus*, as well as the large *Barbus altianalis radcliffi* formerly caught in considerable numbers at the Ripon Falls where the Nile left the lake before the Owen Falls hydroelectric dam was constructed a few miles further downstream. The catfishes include the widely distributed *Bagrus docmac*, here one of the main predators in the lake, *Schilbe mystus* which moves into rivers to spawn, and two endemic *Synodontis* species of which *S. victoriae* is the most abundant in deep water in the open lake. The clariids include three *Clarias* species (*C. mossambicus*, *C. carsoni* and *C. alluaudi*), the endemic genus *Xenoclarias* (with one species) in which the accessory respiratory organs found in most other clariids have disappeared, and the anguilliform *Clariallabes petricola* which lives amongst rocks in the Nile and on wave-washed shores. The fauna also includes three small cyprinodonts (one endemic), a small anabantid *Ctenopoma muriei* living in swamps around the lake, and *Mastacembelus frenatus* an obligate insectivore living amongst rocks.

Experimental trawl fishing has contributed information on the distribution of the bottom-living fishes (Gee and Gilbert, 1967). *Bagrus docmac* is ubiquitous, caught at all depths down to 70 m, over all types of bottom, though it is possibly more abundant over mud than sand, and the very young stages are found on rocky shores. *Clarias mossambicus* is an important element of the trawl catch over mud, rarely over sand; in spite of the possession of accessory respiratory organs, in the trawl it is most abundant between 15 and 25 m, with no indication of decrease in abundance with depth, and it is taken down to 66 m; this species spawns in affluent streams where eggs and young develop very fast (Greenwood, 1955). The rather similar *Xenoclarias*, which lacks accessory respiratory organs, is common over mud, especially between 25 and 66 m, and never caught over sand. *Synodontis victoriae* is never caught over sand, and rarely over mud in less than 15 m of water; it is commonest from 25 to 66 m and below 33 m sometimes forms a great proportion of the catch; in deeper waters these fishes may shoal or congregate in particular areas for feeding or breeding. *Barbus altianalis*, which forms only a very small proportion of the trawl catch is only caught over sand. *Protopterus aethiopicus*, an obligate air breather, not caught in water more than 33 m deep, is commonest in shallow water especially over mud. Of the cichlids, three species of *Tilapia*, *T. zillii*, *T. variabilis* and *T. nilotica* are only caught when the trawl is fished over a sandy bottom. *T. esculenta* has been taken from all bottoms down to 25 m and very occasionally deeper. The distribution of this species appears to be correlated with the distribution of the phytoplankton rather than with the bottom type, and echo traces suggest that they are more abundant in midwater than on the bottom.

Haplochromis form the main bulk of the trawl catches (over 50 per cent by weight). These are taken from all habitats and at all depths, but are especially abundant on sand and mud in shallow waters where catches as high as 700 to 1800 kg/hour are reported (Bergstrand and Cordone, 1971). The species caught vary with the depth and type of bottom, and different species are more or less dominant over the same type of bottom in widely separated areas (Gee, 1969).

The differential distributions of small *Tilapia* (less than 6 cm long) and *Haplochromis* off Victoria beaches (Fig. 5.2) were studied by Welcomme (1964). Beaches were classified as 'gradient' or 'non-gradient' according to

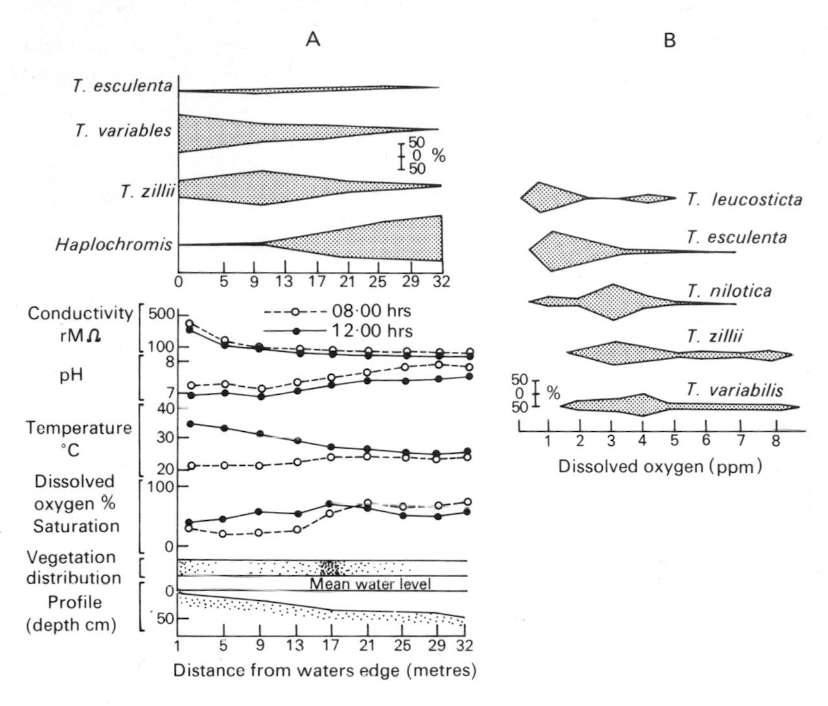

Fig. 5.2 The percentage representations of *Tilapia* species and *Haplochromis* on Lake Victoria beaches: A. at different distances from the shore on a semi-sheltered beach in relation to the prevailing ecological conditions; B. in relation to dissolved oxygen concentrations off various beaches (after Welcomme, 1964).

their physical and chemical conditions relative to those offshore (temperature, pH, conductivity and dissolved oxygen). On gradient beaches conditions fluctuated more, both diurnally and with the weather, becoming extreme on hot, calm days. Small *Tilapia* predominated here, graded in size according to the water depth, the smallest inshore in the shallowest water, away from any interference by larger fish. These fishes moved on and offshore with diurnal fluctuations in water temperature, reaching a maximum number inshore at midday. *Haplochromis* on the other hand came to gradient beaches mainly at night and on overcast cold days, living off non-gradient beaches at other times. Laboratory experiments showed that these *Tilapia* tolerate water temperatures up to 38° C which are lethal to *Haplochromis*. Juvenile *Tilapia* contrive to keep at the maximum temperature, and they are able to exploit epiphytic algae which grow in very shallow water, unavailable to *Haplochromis* young. The weedy shallows give some protection from predators, but at night these small fishes retreat offshore where predatory *Bagrus* and *Clarias* lie in wait for them; this suggests that exploitation of the algal food sources provides a more potent selection pressure for these movements into the shallows than does the avoidance of predators. Each

Tilapia species has its preferred conditions for a nursery environment: *T. variabilis* and *T. zillii* predominate over hard bottoms in well-aerated water, and *T. leucosticta* in the most deoxygenated water, while *T. nilotica* and *T. esculenta* occupy intermediate sites (Fig. 5.2B).

Such studies stress that in addition to physical barriers fish movements are affected by many physicochemical and biotic barriers of which we as yet know very little.

The foods of the non-cichlid fishes

A detailed study of the food of twenty-six species of non-cichlid fishes from Lake Victoria (Corbet 1961) included analyses of foods eaten over hard, soft and mixed bottom deposits, from lakeside swamps, affluent rivers up which the spawning fish run, and the effluent Victoria Nile. For the various food items, which fell into 35 categories, Corbet recorded occurrence of food item, expressed as percentage of stomachs containing recognisable food; and main contents, i.e. those occyping half the stomach volume (as large samples were examined, often in poor light), which were also expressed as percentage of stomachs containing food. Data were sorted according to species of fish, size of fish and habitat; changes with time of year could not be demonstrated, but for some species changes of food with phase of moon, with which insect emergences are associated, were shown. The food eaten changed with the size of fish in many cases.

Insects, their larvae and nymphs of many kinds, form by far the most important food of non-cichlids in the Victoria basin. There are hardly any fish species which do not include insects in their diet, and for many (especially Mormyridae and young fishes) they provide virtually the entire food. Insects from the surface are important for species such as *Alestes*, *Barbus*, *Schilbe*, one *Synodontis* and *Aplocheilichthys*, whereas mormyrids, *Clariallabes* and *Mastacembelus* feed almost exclusively on the bottom, and yet others search out insects from marginal vegetation. Insects are the most widespread of prey and require of their predators the least specialisation in feeding habits.

Molluscs form the principal food of adult *Protopterus*, *Synodontis victoriae* and *Barbus altianalis*. *Protopterus* can crush the shells of molluscs of any size; *Barbus altianalis* crush the shells, but only of the smaller ones; *Synodontis victoriae* is able to remove the flesh and opercula from gasteropods. Certain other species which eat gasteropods in small amounts, including *Clarias mossambicus* and *Synodontis afro-fischeri*, ingest the entire shells. Gastropods are eaten more than bivalves. None of the mollusc-eating fishes show particular lacustrine adaptations, but certain molluscs are very abundant in the bottom mud of the lake, which provides an extended feeding ground.

Fishes, particularly *Haplochromis*, are preyed on by three indigenous non-cichlids (as well as many cichlids). Of these *Bagrus docmac* is the most lacustrine and the main predator on *Haplochromis*, while *Clarias mossam-*

bicus eats relatively more large insects and arthropods, and *Schilbe mystus* feeds more at the surface taking *Engraulicypris* and surface insects. Damaged fishes (including those caught in gillnets) are scavenged by *Protopterus* and *Alestes jacksoni*. Small *Bagrus docmac* live among rocks and stones feeding on lithophilic insects, becoming piscivorous when about 15 cm long.

Zooplankton. The small cyprinid *Engraulicypris argenteus* appears to be

● ● • ○ · A B C D E MORMYRIDAE	Chironomid larvae	*Povilla* larvae	Anisoptera larvae	Trichoptera larvae	Chaoborid larvae	Ephemeroptera larvae	Ostracoda	Hydracarina	Gastropoda	*Caridina*	Fishes
Mormyrus macrocephalus	D	D	B		D	D			D	D	A
Mormyrus kannume	A	C	D	D	D	D	D	E	E	D	D
Pollimyrus nigricans	A	D	D	D	D	D	D	D		D	B
Hippopotamyrus grahami	A	D	E	C	D	D	D	D	C	E	
Gnathonemus longibarbis	A	A	B	D	D	D	D	D	D	D	E
Marcusenius victoriae	A	C	D	D	D	D	C	D	D	E	E

(a)

● ● • ○ · A B C D E SILUROIDEI	Insects	Chironomid larvae	*Povilla* larvae	Anisoptera larvae	Terrestrial insects	Ostracoda	*Caridina*	*Potamon*	Molluscs	Fishes	*Haplochromis*	*Tilapia*	Non-cichlids	*Engraulicypris*
Bagrus docmac	D	D	E	D	D		D	D	D	A	A	D	D	D
Clarias mossambicus	C			D	D		D	D	D	A	A	D	D	D
Schilbe mystus	B			D	C		D			A	B		B	B
Synodontis victoriae	C	D	D	D	D	D			A	D			D	D
Synodontis afro-fischeri	A	B	B		E				C					
Clarias alluaudi	A	D	E		D	D			D					

(b)

Fig. 5.3 Food preferences of Lake Victoria fishes. (a) Mormyridae. (b) Siluroidei. A = Main contents in 30 per cent or more; B = main contents in 10–29 per cent; C = main contents in 5–9 per cent; D = main contents in less than 5 per cent and/or occurrence in 10 per cent or more; E = occurrence in 5–9 per cent (after Corbet, 1961).

the only non-cichlid in the lake specialised as a pelagic feeder on zooplankton, though small surface feeders such as the cyprinodont *Aplocheilichthys pumilis* may ingest considerable amounts when taking insects from amongst marginal vegetation.

Plants and invertebrates are used as foods by the two endemic *Alestes* species, *A. jacksoni* and *A. sadleri*; *A. jacksoni* takes larger insects and some fishes. *Barbus altianalis* though primarily a mollusc feeder ingests some higher plant material, especially in rivers.

Most of these non-cichlids are facultative feeders, their diets varying according to the size of fish, its feeding grounds and even the lunar phase when this affects the emergence and movements of insect prey. For instance *Alestes jacksoni* feeds on the ephemeropteran *Povilla adusta* when these are emerging in the nights after full moon, and on chironomids (pupae, exuviae or adults) at other times. The size of an insect or other organism and its position in the aquatic environment is important in determining its value as prey.

Many *Haplochromis* species utilise these same foods, so the amount of interspecific competition for food cannot be assessed without also considering cichlid diets, and as Greenwood (1974) concludes, there is as yet too little precise information on the ecology of both cichlids and non-cichlids, and of the invertebrates on which so many of them feed, to discuss competition in any detail. The overlap in foods used by non-cichlids was well illustrated by food preferences amongst both the six species of mormyrid and amongst the six species of siluroid in the lake (Fig. 5.3). Most of these species are unspecialised feeders, but no two have exactly the same diet, except when food is locally abundant at some particular time and place (as when surface feeders are gorging on emerging *Povilla*). Corbet pointed out that greater knowledge of the taxonomy of prey organisms may reveal wider differences between prey used than is shown here; where two species do eat the same food they may collect it or utilise it in different ways (as do the mollusc-feeders), but on the whole these facultative feeders are able to range over feeding grounds of great variety and extent. Juveniles and adults of one species often live in different habitats and eat different foods.

These Victoria mormyrids provided unusually clear examples of how misleading food preference studies can be if based on few specimens of uncertain origin. In *Mormyrus kannume* the proportions of the main items in the diet varied with the size of fish, feeding ground (whether hard or soft bottom) and lunar phase. These fish feed mainly at night. Over mud the food consisted largely of chironomid and chaoborid larvae; over sand and rock it was more varied and included greater numbers of Trichoptera larvae, Ephemeroptera nymphs (especially *Povilla*) and *Caridina* shrimps. Over hard bottoms *M. kannume* eats larger kinds and larger individuals of prey species as its size increases. Over soft bottoms (characteristically lacustrine habitats) such a change is not possible, and chironomid (and to some extent chaoborid) larvae are eaten throughout life. In addition, the larger the fishes become, the more they feed over mud, supporting the contention that the *M. kannume* of riverine origin has become well adapted to the most extreme of lake environments, soft mud, where it can maintain itself on chironomid larvae. In this species the food becomes less varied as the fish becomes older.

In contrast with the great flexibility in trophic behaviour shown by the insectivorous mormyrids, *Mastacembelus* was found to be one of the very few stenophagous insectivores in the lake; such specialisation is possible as this species stays within one biotope, amongst rocks, throughout its life.

Corbet concluded that interspecific competition for food among these Lake Victoria non-cichlid fishes plays a very minor part in their ecology. The few species that share specialised feeding habits appear to have a superabundance of food, and the others cope with overlap by remaining mobile and facultative.

The foods of the smaller mormyrids (now known as *Marsusenius victoriae*; *Gnathonemus longibarbis*; *Hippopotamyrus grahami*; *Pollimyrus nigricans*; *Petrocephalus catostoma*) have been studied together with their fecundity and growth rates, both in the lake and in the Sio River where they migrate to spawn (Okedi, 1969–71). Their diets become more varied in the river, including large numbers of swamp-living oligochaete worms (*Alma*), fruits and dytiscid beetles.

The rivers here flood twice a year (April–May and September–December), and the fishes migrate up on both floods. The ripe mormyrids hang around the river mouth until the flood comes, then migrate up-river at night, with peak runs at dawn and dusk. They spawn in swamp pools 8 to 24 km up-river. After the eggs hatch the young fishes remain in river pools for three to seven months. Mormyrids are not very fecund fish, egg numbers ranging from a mean of less than 500 eggs in *P. nigricans* to a mean of 6300 in *M. victoriae* (with wide variations: Table 9.2, p. 219).

The fishes starve while breeding, but increased feeding after they have spawned leads to accumulations of abdominal fat, and the opercular bones show clear growth rings. The length frequencies of young fish in the swamps suggested to Okedi that individual mormyrids here spawn twice each year and lay down two growth rings a year on the bones. However, in 1965 when the September rains continued and merged with the first rains in 1966, three of these mormyrid species had an extended breeding season from October 1965 to May 1966.

In laboratory tanks these small mormyrids showed specific preference for special resting places: *G. longibarbis* chose to be among rocks, *M. victoriae* among smaller stones, *H. grahami* and *P. catostoma* over sand, and *P. nigricans* over sand or mud, rising to the surface at night to feed amongst the roots of floating vegetation. These mormyrids showed considerable agonistic behaviour for food and resting places (compare gymnotoids, p. 235), aggression increasing in ripe fish. In aquaria male and female *Hippopotamyrus grahami* dug nests in the bottom sand, and showed incipient courtship behaviour, as did *Gnathonemus longibarbis* and *Marcusenius victoriae*, but none of them spawned (Okedi, 1968).

The cichlid fishes: the *Haplochromis* species flock

The cichlid fishes have become so adapted to lacustrine life that well over 150 of them have evolved in this lake basin, the majority of them belonging to one genus *Haplochromis*. Other cichlids in the lake include several small genera evidently derived from *Haplochromis* but in which differentiation has proceeded to the generic level, and two endemic phytoplankton-feeding *Tilapia*.

The adaptive trends, feeding types and general ecology of the numerous endemic *Haplochromis* have been described by Greenwood in a series of papers (1956–73) and are brought together in a book (1974). These cichlids are small fishes, few more than 15 cm long. In those in which the breeding habits are known parental care is well developed, the female brooding eggs and young in her mouth for about three weeks. The males are polygamous, brightly coloured during the spawning periods, the breeding colour characteristic of the species. The male establishes a territory and may make a nest pit in the bottom sand; breeding behaviour is complex and is apparently based on the female's recognition of the colour and courtship display of a conspecific male. For each species at least some part of the population is always breeding (so breeding is continuous around the year), though one particular male may be sexually active for but a few weeks a year.

In Lake Victoria these *Haplochromis* have undergone explosive adaptive radiations to fill almost all niches, and they compete successfully and coexist with non-cichlids. The only habitats avoided are the dense marginal papyrus zone, where the water is deoxygenated, and the surface waters of the open lake; the recent exploratory trawl fishing has shown them to be abundant to almost all depths. *Haplochromis* show few external modifications associated with habitat, but some of the deeper water forms have large eyes and well-developed sensory canals on the head.

Despite the great size of Lake Victoria, the number of major habitats is small, and up to thirty species of *Haplochromis* may be found within a major habitat, such as in one of the extensive papyrus fringed bays, where the water is calm over a thick layer of mud, or along the exposed sandy shores, open to wind action and with little mud, or offshore over sand or mud bottoms. Their density appears greatest in inshore shallow waters, where up to 1800 kg/hour may be taken in the trawl (equivalent to about 10 g/m^2 of *Haplochromis*).

The *Haplochromis* adaptive radiations are concerned mainly with differences in feeding habit, involving adaptations in dentition, skull and jaw form and digestive physiology, to use all the varied food sources in the lake. In contrast with much older marine fish groups where evolution has advanced to the stage where the food eaten is relatively constant within a larger taxonomic unit, these *Haplochromis* show supralimital specialisations (see p. 54). Differences within this one genus are greater than between families of many marine groups. Furthermore in these *Haplochromis* the different feeding specialisations are repeated several times over, so that even within a single habitat two or more species may be tapping essentially the same type of food. Comparison of Greenwood's (1974) wheel diagrams of feeding habits (fig. 7) and tentative phylogenetic relationships (fig. 70) indicates that the most closely related species utilise the same types of food. This raises the question, so far largely unanswered, on how much interspecific competition there is, and how is it minimised or avoided. Greenwood found only a few examples of spatial isolation, and a few examples of ecological counterparts, for instance of the mollusc shell-crushers, *H. ishmaeli* is found inshore in less than 10 m of water over soft mud, while *H. pharyngomylus* occurs in slightly deeper water (less than 14 m) over hard bottoms with plant stands. There are far more species present than trophic groups among these *Haplochromis* (as we shall find again in Lake Malawi), and numerous species live together.

The least specialised feeders are those which feed on insect larvae (as among the non-cichlid fishes). These are anatomically and ecologically generalised species, the most like the small *Haplochromis* in the river systems, among which will have been the ancestors of the lacustrine species flock. Possibly 30 per cent of the *Haplochromis* species in Lake Victoria are insectivores and detritus feeders. Another group feeds on insects and molluscs. Other mollusc-eaters have specialised along two distinct lines, 'winkle-pickers' with strong jaw teeth for extracting molluscs from their shells and generalised pharyngeal teeth, and 'shell-crushers' with massive pharyngeal bones armoured with molariform teeth which crush the shells of their prey.

The herbivorous species include four species of algal grazers, and one which feeds on the leaves of higher plants. A surprisingly large number of species, estimated at around 30 per cent of the total number of species, are piscivorous, feeding mainly on other *Haplochromis* and other small fish. These are the largest species, elongated and slim in body form and with enlarged mouths. One particular group of about eight species of piscivores has specialised in feeding on the eggs and yolked young of other *Haplochromis*, which it must obtain from the mouth of a brooding fish; these 'paedophagous' fishes have a large maw and a reduced oral dentition, but how they make the parent fish disgorge its young is not yet known. This group is thought by Greenwood to be polyphyletic. These are the only known fishes to occupy such a niche, present in Lake Victoria as the continuous breeding of prey species ensures a supply of eggs and young throughout the year.

Greenwood considered that the piscivorous species probably evolved from one or two insectivorous species within the lake basin. There is no evidence that they came from an original fluviatile piscivorous stem species; the present day fluviatile predatory cichlids such as *Serranochromis* are more differentiated than generalised *Haplochromis. H. brownae* is named as a likely link between generalised insectivores and the least specialised predators. Convergence and parallel evolution obscure the phyletic lines amongst these predators, as the anatomical changes in their evolution are relatively simple: increase in adult size in relation to other trophic groups, changes in head and jaw shape, changes in body shape, the body becoming either elongate and slender, or deep; the development of unicuspid, curved and often strong teeth in the outer row of both jaws, which are used to hold prey fish, and the oropharyngeal dentition as a whole becoming adapted for gripping and macerating prey. Many predatory fishes merely grip and bolt prey, but in an aquarium *Haplochromis gowersii* was observed to rasp the tail of a small *Tilapia* prey for five minutes before making a frontal attack, and it took fifteen to twenty minutes to ingest this fish. *Tilapia* have never been identified from *Haplochromis* stomachs in nature, but fish prey are generally well mascerated in the guts (Greenwood, 1974).

The nature of the substrate has less effect on distribution of piscivorous species than on that of other trophic groups. These piscivorous species are found in all localities and the various species do not appear to be confined to a particular habitat. Most prey on other *Haplochromis*, some on *Engraulicypris*. Breeding data for many *Haplochromis* species are virtually non-existent, but the female mouth broods in all the cases for which there is any information.

Effects of food changes on cichlid dentition may be very rapid. Greenwood (1965*a*) found that in the mollusc feeder *Astatorheochromis alluaudi* the pharyngeal bones with their crushing teeth had become much less massive after less than ten generations in aquaria living on a mollusc-free diet. Greenwood (1973*b*) stressed that trophic specialisation in *Haplochromis*, and hence their ecological dominance, is founded on a relatively uncomplicated basis; skeletal changes are based on slight changes in differential growth, and the dental changes involved are principally modifications of a simple kind of tooth cusp. Compared with most other types of freshwater fish, the cichlids have reached a stage of anatomical differentiation that in terms of its potential for modification is neither too specialised nor too generalised for simple morphological changes to be effective. Also, continuous spawning within a cichlid population increases the rate of genetic reshuffling. As yet, nothing is known about the genetical basis for these changes, nor is anything known about the kinds or degrees of physiological differences involved in changing feeding habits.

The rivers of Uganda have only one or two *Haplochromis* species, which suggests that the early colonizers of the embryo Lake Victoria would have been mainly non-cichlid species, with which the initial cichlid colonisers would have had to compete for resources.

Lake Victoria food fishes

Lake Victoria has important commercial fisheries based mainly on *Tilapia* caught in gillnets. This fishery provides a classic example of a decline in catches following excessive fishing in inshore areas; then a reduction in gillnet mesh-size was permitted, leading to a further decline in catches (summarised by Fryer, 1972, 1973; Fryer and Iles, 1972). Non-cichlids in the catches include *Bagrus docmac*, *Clarias mossambicus*, *Protopterus aethiopicus*, *Labeo victorianus*, *Schilbe mystus* and the introduced *Lates niloticus*. The two endemic *Tilapia* were the mainstay of the fishery,

T. esculenta predominated in the sheltered gulfs, and *T. variabilis* on more exposed shores and in waterlily swamps. Both are phytoplankton-feeders and mouth brooders. As they grow these lake *Tilapia* move from swampy areas or open shores out into more open water, to bottom waters as they mature, to spawning grounds as gonads ripen, and the brooding females then move to swampy or rocky shores, according to the species, where they leave their young. There is also some evidence of seasonal movements, but also that populations in particular gulfs remain discrete. Tagging showed that *T. esculenta* may move considerable distances surprisingly rapidly, Kavirondo Gulf tagged fish being caught outside the gulf in the main lake 35 miles (56 km) away after twelve to forty days; one fish was caught 12 miles (20 km) away three days after release. But many were recaught near to where they were marked 228 and 700 days after release (Lowe-McConnell, 1956). Returns of tagged *T. variabilis* suggested that fishes tagged together stayed together for long periods, and that brooding females may return to the same nursery areas to leave their young (Fryer, 1961). It appears possible that the young might become imprinted on a certain area, which would tend to keep the populations discrete, but this suggestion needs investigation. The phytoplankton food supply appears to be superabundant, but much of the lake has a papyrus fringe where the water is deoxygenated and the extent of the suitable nursery areas, and of hard-bottomed areas suitable for spawning, may limit *Tilapia* numbers in this lake.

In 1951–3 four non-endemic *Tilapia* species were introduced to Victoria; it was thought that the herbivorous *T. zillii* from Lake Albert would fill a niche unfilled by the indigenous fishes, and *T. nilotica* and *T. leucosticta* fry must have been introduced at the same time, while *T. rendalli* (= *T. melanopleura*) escaped into the lake from fish ponds. The dramatic rise in lake level in 1962, following phenomenal rains, formed lagoons behind the papyrus fringe where *T. leucosticta* became very abundant (Welcomme, 1966, 1967*a*, 1970). The introduced *T. zillii* throve, and had an unexpected effect on *T. variabilis*, competing with this species for space in nursery areas (Fryer, 1961), which was followed by a decline in *T. variabilis* catches. *T. nilotica* colonised the open waters of gulfs and bays where it grows very large (in Lake Kyoga specimens of 4 to 7 kg were commonly caught by 1970; Okedi, 1971*c*). *Tilapia* catches in Victoria increased as the lake rose; the speed with which they did so was puzzling, as this occurred too soon for it to be explained merely by increased accessibility of nursery grounds.

The predatory *Lates niloticus* gained access to Victoria about 1960; it had been stocked into L. Kyoga, into which L. Victoria flows, in 1955. In both these lakes cichlids, particularly *Haplochromis*, became its commonest prey. Okedi (1971*c*) recorded 57 *Haplochromis* from the stomach of one *Lates* (110 cm long). Some mormyrids, *Engraulicypris*, *Alestes*, *Barbus*, *Clarias* and *Protopterus*, were also eaten (Gee, 1968). The introduction of *Lates* to L. Kyoga greatly increased commercial fish catches from this lake (though the catch statistics are disputed; Fryer, 1973), but the long-term effects of this predator on *Tilapia*, and on the *Haplochromis* species flocks which are of such outstanding scientific interest, are not easy to predict. Data on the food of *Lates* in other waters (p. 213) suggest that they take more pelagic species when these are available. The unexpected effects of the introduced *Tilapia zillii* on the indigenous *T. variabilis* in L. Victoria, where *T. variabilis* has now almost ceased to be a commercial species, show how difficult it is to make predictions, and stress the dangers of introducing exotic species.

Lake Malawi

Lake Malawi (formerly known as Lake Nyasa) is, like Lake Victoria, a lake in which cichlids dominate the fish fauna. Unlike Victoria it is a long, deep, rift valley lake. Lying about 500 m a.s.l. and well to the south of the equator (9° 29′ to 14° 25′ S) the climate is much more seasonal than that of Victoria, with one well-defined rainy season from December to March, and a relatively cool 'winter' season from May to September. During this cool season the southeast trade wind, known locally as the 'Mwera', often blows for days on end; its force is funnelled up the lake, with consequent effects on the hydrology. Before the rains sudden squalls come from the northeast. Livingstone who first described it considered calling it the lake of storms, had he not been assured that the winds were seasonal.

The surface temperature ranges between about 21·4 and 28·1° C, averaging around 24·9° C but dropping in the cool season. The lake appears to be permanently stratified, even though water temperatures are differentiated by less than 1° C in the top 200 m at certain periods of the year. The thermocline lies between 40 and 80 m in March, descending to around 150 m by August, after becoming very ill-defined in July. As the surface water starts to warm with the advent of hotter weather in September, a secondary thermocline forms at around 35 m, which sinks to between 50 and 100 m in October–December. The thermocline is an important barrier between the nutrient richer bottom waters and the surface waters where biological production occurs, and is the cause of the relative infertility of the lake. The main agent of mixing appears to be an internal wave (seiche) with a periodicity of sixteen to twenty-five days in summer and winter respectively; this is at its maximum in September, leading to a phytoplankton bloom in October/November in the relatively shallow waters at the south end of the lake (Jackson *et al.*, 1963). As in Lake Tanganyika the south end is the most productive part of the lake.

In most areas of Lake Malawi the water is much clearer than in Victoria, enabling the behaviour of the shore-living fishes to be observed. The pH is around 8·2 to 8·6. The lake level fluctuates just over a metre between wet and dry seasons, but also a metre or so with a wind-induced surface seiche. There are also long-term fluctuations in mean level which appear to have affected fish evolution.

Ecological studies of the fishes were initiated during a fisheries survey by Bertram, Borley and Trewavas (1942), continued by myself (Lowe, 1952) and then by members of the Joint Fisheries Research Organisation (JFRO) for Nyasaland and Northern Rhodesia (Jackson *et al.*, 1963), and at present by the Malawi Fishery Department. Many papers have been published on various aspects of fish ecology, and the evolutionary implications of the trophic studies of the 'Mbuna' group of cichlid rockfish by Fryer (1959) have stimulated an immense amount of discussion on mechanisms of evolution.

The lake shore has alternating stretches of open sandy beach and rocky coastline providing semi-isolated habitats. The two southern arms of the lake provide the largest relatively shallow areas. The southeast arm, base of the main *Tilapia* fishery, is fringed with sandy beaches from which shore seines are pulled. Open-water ringnets introduced by Greek fishermen are also fished in this area, nets 350 m long and 40 m deep reaching to the bottom. Some beaches are obscured by *Phragmites communis* reeds, and waterlily swamps occur in sheltered bays. The River Shiré flows out from the lake in the southeast arm, carrying the lake waters to the Zambezi River. The two southern arms of the lake are separated by hills and rocky shores. The shoreline in the southwest arm consists of sandy beaches or mudflats running underwater for considerable distances, where experimental trawling has recently brought to light a flock of cichlid *Lethrinops* species, many as yet undescribed. Much of the shoreline and the river mouths are here obstructed by dense growths of *Phragmites*. Sometimes the bays become choked with sudd islands of these reeds and other plants washed out of the river mouths during floods.

Where the mountains come close to the lake, on the west side from Nkata Bay northwards to Florence Bay, in the northeast and down much of the eastern side of the lake, the shores are mainly rocky, with sandy beaches only in small inlets and near inflowing streams. In the northwest there are more extensive beaches as there is here a comparatively wide plain, across which the Rukuru and Songwe Rivers enter the lake, large affluents up which the salmonlike *Barilius* migrate to spawn.

The fish fauna and its distribution within the lake

Lake Malawi has fewer fish families than Victoria and Tanganyika. Of the six mormyrid species, only one is endemic (*Marcusenius nyasensis*). *Mormyrus longirostris* is very common and an important food fish; it feeds on chironomid larvae from mud or sand bottoms and is caught in bottom-set gillnets down to the limit of dissolved oxygen (compare *M. kannume* in Lake Victoria). The piscivorous and widely distributed *Mormyrops deliciosus*, another food fish, also occurs in deep water but is commoner in sheltered lagoons. The smaller mormyrids live in the river estuaries and lagoons, feeding mainly on insects.

The family Characidae is represented by only one species, the widely distributed *Alestes imberi*, a small species living in small shoals in sheltered areas, feeding on insects, tiny fish and vegetable matter and preyed on by other fishes.

The well-represented Cyprinidae includes several large endemic species important as food fish:

(*a*) two species of piscivorous *Barilius*, the salmonlike mpasa *B. microlepis* and the smaller sanjika *B. microcephalus*, both of which run up the large permanent rivers at the north end of the lake to spawn.

(*b*) *Labeo mesops*, a mud sucker and one of the main food fishes of the lake which is caught in gillnets (the larger females predominating over the males in the larger mesh nets), in seines off sandy shores, and when ascending rivers to spawn, especially in the southern half of the lake. A non-endemic *Labeo*, *L. cylindricus*, haunts rocky shores and also lives in the lower reaches of rivers and streams. (Here again the lacustrine endemic species occurs on softer substrates while the non-endemic species continues to live around rocks.) Some *L. cylindricus* do, however, breed in the lake, eggs being laid among the rocks during a very short and well-marked breeding season around December.

(*c*) Several large *Barbus*, which are taken in gillnets; *Barbus eurystomus* which feeds mainly on molluscs, the predatory *B. rhoadesii* which feeds on fish and insects, and the rather omnivorous *B. johnstonii*. All these *Barbus* migrate up rivers to spawn, but not as far upstream as do the *Barilius* species. Another ten or eleven species of small *Barbus*, difficult to distinguish, are known from the lake and adjacent waters.

(*d*) An endemic *Varicorhinus*, *V. nyasensis*, which lives in small shoals on rocky shores grazing algae off rocks.

(*e*) The endemic *Engraulicypris sardella* 'Usipa', which though small (< 10 cm) is an important economic and bait fish, also preyed on by *Barilius* in their lacustrine phase and by many other open-water species. Truly pelagic with planktonic eggs and larvae, large shoals of Usipa appear inshore sporadically; its numbers appear to be limited by the abundance of its zooplankton food supply (Iles, 1960).

The Bagridae has only one species, the endemic *Bagrus meridionalis* widely distributed and of major economic importance, caught in gillnets set in deep water in the north of the lake, and from much shallower water further south. A piscivorous bottom-dwelling fish, the habitat preferences and depth distribution are determined by its food supply. In the south *Bagrus* frequent the *Tilapia* grounds in shallow water over sand, but in the north they live in deep rocky areas where they feed on *Haplochromis* and *Rhamphochromis*, or on *Engraulicypris sardella* when these are seasonally abundant. This ability to change distribution and habitat preference in relation to available food supply is typical of a piscivorous species, but atypical of the tightly knit ecological communities in Lake Malawi generally. The breeding season is October to March, when *Bagrus meriodionalis* migrates inshore to breed, making a circular nest in shallow water on a sandy substrate. The female returns to deep water after laying her eggs, leaving the smaller male to guard the nest. The young seek shelter among the rocks (Jackson *et al.*, 1963).

The Clariidae is represented by three non-endemic *Clarias* species. *C. mossambicus* which lives mainly in lagoons estuaries and rivers as an omnivorous scrounger over mud, is of considerable importance as a food fish away from the lake when it runs up into flooded 'dambos' (plains) to spawn during the rains. Another species *C. mellandi* feeds largely on molluscs, crushing the shells with its broad plate of vomerine teeth. A smaller species, *C. theodorae*, skulks amongst vegetation in stagnant lagoons and estuaries, where it eats mainly insects. There is also a distinctive species flock of large endemic clariids of the genus *Dinotopterus* (many originally described as belonging to a new endemic genus *Bathyclarias*, Jackson).* All closely related, these species have their accessory breathing organs much reduced (compare its loss in *Xenoclarias* from the open water of Lake Victoria), and lateral eyes. Some probably enter river estuaries and other flooded areas to spawn during the rains. Several species are important food fish, caught in gillnets on long lines and in special floating traps in open water. Some species have long, close-set gill rakers and feed on plankton and the pupae of 'nkungu' lakeflies (the chaoborid *Corethra edulis*) present in such vast numbers in the lake plankton; *D. lowae* is pelagic penetrating far into the open water and feeding on emerging nkungu flies. Another species *D. foveolatus* is piscivorous, a sluggish fish skulking among the rocks and mud at great depth. A smaller species, *D. worthingtoni*, is confined to rocks in the north of the lake where it feeds largely on the crab *Potamonautes*, found only in rocky habitats. Very little is yet known about the biology of some of these *Dinotopterus* species.

The Mochokidae is represented by only one species of *Synodontis*, *S. njassae*, an omnivorous scrounger widely distributed all over the lake off sandy and rocky shores and down to the limits of dissolved oxygen. Another mochokid, the little inconspicuous catfish *Chiloglanis neumanni* lives amongst stones on a sandy substrate in the lake and rivers.

A true eel *Anguilla nebulosa labiata* finds its way from the sea into L. Malawi where it feeds on fish and crabs. One indigenous mastacembelid, *Mastacembelus shiranus*, lives under stones and amongst weeds in the lower courses of the rivers where it feeds on insects and other small invertebrates.

The cyprinodonts *Nothobranchius orthonotus* and *Aplocheilichthys johnstoni* have been recorded here, also the anabantid *Ctenopoma ctenotis*, but these probably live in streams and marshes around the lake.

In addition to these forty-odd non-cichlid species, about half of them endemic, Lake Malawi has a rich and diversified fauna of cichlids, nearly all of which are endemic.

Among the twenty-three cichlid genera the genus *Haplochromis* has by far the most numerous species (120+), all endemic. Some are insect feeders, some predators, but for many the food habits are not yet known. Breeding males are frequently a striking bright blue. One group of about seventeen species of shoaling, zooplankton-feeding species, known as 'Utaka' by the local fishermen and studied as they form the basis of a fishery, are unique among cichlids in using zooplankton when adult. Although they

* Roberts (in press) disagrees that *Bathyclarias* is synonymous with *Dinotopterus*, attributing their similarities to convergent evolution.

are pelagic, at least some Utaka species have to move inshore to find a suitable substratum on which to spawn, making sandscrape nests in typically cichlid manner, the males guarding the nests and the females mouth-brooding the young in species in which the breeding habits are known. Length frequency studies suggest that these Utaka take three years to reach maturity, at about 10 to 16 cm according to the species (Iles, 1971). The feeding habits of all these Utaka species are very much alike, and in many cases apparently identical; the various species do not segregate for feeding; on the contrary they congregate in shoals of mixed species to feed in very definite areas well known to the fishermen as 'virundu' (Fryer and Iles, 1972, fig. 276).

In Lake Malawi, unlike Lake Victoria, several other cichlid genera also have numerous species living in the lake. The genus *Lethrinops* has 24 described species with many more discovered during exploratory fishing awaiting description (Eccles, personal communication). Small, rather deep-bodied, most are found off sandy shores, often associated with *Vallisneria* swards, but some live in quite deep water, the various species exhibiting zonation with depth. Invertebrate feeders, they dig in the bottom sand for Crustacea, chironomid larvae and molluscs. Fish of the genus *Rhamphochromis*, silvery slender elongate piscivorous species with large heads and mouths and spaced conical teeth, of which eight closely related species have been described, live in open water where they feed on small cichlids, especially Utaka, and on *Engraulicypris*. *Rhamphochromis* occur over a large depth range, some down to the limit of dissolved oxygen, and when *Engraulicypris* is scarce *Rhamphochromis* move inshore and feed on other species. Of the genus *Diplotaxodon* only two species have yet been described, both distinctive piscivores with large eyes taken from gillnets set in open and deepish water, but Iles reported that there are at least ten species which all live together between 30 and 40 m deep, all feeding on a single prey *Engraulicypris sardella* (Fryer and Iles, 1972). When not in breeding dress these are all almost uniformly silvery in colour and look alike.

Other smaller genera include *Corematodus* (two species) remarkable in that they mimic other cichlids and feed by scraping scales from the caudal fin or peduncle of the host fish. The vertically striped *C. shiranus*, which mimics *Tilapia*, swims with their shoals and feeds by rasping scales off the caudal fin with its broad bands of file-like teeth (Trewavas, 1947). The smaller *C. taeniatus* resembles and preys on *Lethrinops* and other cichlids which have an oblique black band from nape to base of caudal. The one species of *Docimodus*, *D. johnstonii*, has heavy powerful jaws and strong cutting teeth with which it takes pieces from the fins of other fishes; like so many of these Malawi cichlids, the breeding male is a rich blue, while the females and non-breeding fish are silvery with an oblique black band from nape to base of caudal fin.

Two of the most studied cichlid groups in this lake are the *Tilapia*, the basis of the commercial fishery, and the 'Mbuna' rockfish of such interest to the study of evolution, both considered in later sections.

Ecological zones

The broad ecological zones in Lake Malawi recognised by Jackson *et al.* (1963) include sheltered lake waters and estuaries, such as the southeast arm and lacustrine-like stretches in estuaries of affluent rivers. The *Tilapia* are most abundant in such waters, and the large cyprinids *Labeo mesops* and *Barbus eurystomus* are also important food fishes here. *Lethrinops* species are abundant on the shallow shelving sandy bottoms.

All the other zones are associated with the more open main lake. Where there are sandy or muddy shores many species found in the previous zone occur including many *Haplochromis* species. Rocky shores down to about 12 m have a very striking and distinct fauna of small endemic 'Mbuna' rockfish. Some are very brightly coloured and they can be seen easily in the clear water round the rocks. Recent marking experiments (p. 148) have shown them to be territorial. Another set of fishes tends to be restricted to the areas of shore intermediate between rock and sand.

The open-water fishes include the midwater fishes, not truly pelagic and seldom found far out in the lake but which feed in open water rather than on the bottom, such as certain *Haplochromis* species and certain non-cichlid predators. This lake also has zooplankton-feeding and piscivorous fishes living further out in the pelagic zone of which *Engraulicypris sardella* is the only truly pelagic species in the sense that it has planktonic eggs and larvae. The Utaka *Haplochromis* which live in shoals out in open water are not randomly distributed but found mainly near submerged rocks where there are upwelling currents at depths of 18 to 25 m, places where the zooplankton on which they feed is likely to be particularly abundant. Preying on these open water fishes are a number of *Rhamphochromis* species, the deep-living cichlid *Diplotaxodon*, and the widespread *Bagrus meridionalis*. Large catfishes such as *Dinotopterus lowae* are also found far out in open water.

The deep bottom waters harbour a little-known fauna of bathylimnetic fishes, down to about 100 m or the limits of dissolved oxygen. Fishes taken at great depth (in gillnets below about 70 m) include certain Utaka, *Rhamphochromis* species, and several members of the *Dinotopterus* clariid species flock, together with *Bagrus meridionalis*, *Mormyrus longirostris*, *Synodontis njassae* and *Haplochromis heterotaenia*, though the juveniles of some of these may be found in quite shallow water.

In the affluent rivers flowing into the lake, the middle and lower reaches often have associated lagoons or stagnant pools and quiet reedy stretches. A large fish fauna is found here, but mainly of non-endemic species. *Clarias* species are abundant, also *Tilapia* and certain *Haplochromis* living in the estuarine reaches. Other common species are *Alestes imberi* and various small mormyrids. In addition numerous cyprinids appear here seasonally on their way upstream to spawn. The upper reaches of the affluents, where the water is cold and highly oxygenated, carry few indigenous fishes, among them the catfishes *Amphilius platychir* and *Clarias carsonii* and a few small cyprinids. *Barilius microcephalus* were found in breeding condition at a very small size in small streams west of the lake (personal observation).

The Mbuna rockfish

The group of nine rock-frequenting cichlid genera recognised by the local fishermen under the name 'Mbuna', and more closely related to one another than to any other genus in the lake, have been studied intensively by Fryer (1959). Their adaptive modifications and trophic specialisations are discussed at length by Fryer and Iles (1972) so they are not considered in any detail here. Fryer contrasted the faunas of rocky and sandy shores at Nkata Bay on the western shore of northern Lake Malawi; the 300 m long rocky shore had thirty fish species, the sandy shore of equivalent length, twenty-three species. He also looked at the ecology of the fishes in an intermediate zone, and near a small inflowing stream.

These fishes show great trophic specialisation: body form, mouth shape and teeth being modified to use one type of food. Specialisations to use a particular food have occurred several times, and several species share the same resources within one community. In some cases competition is minimised by fishes of two species feeding at slightly different depths, or in slightly different ways. In other cases there appears to be a good deal of overlap. This is particularly marked among the aufwuchs feeders (those

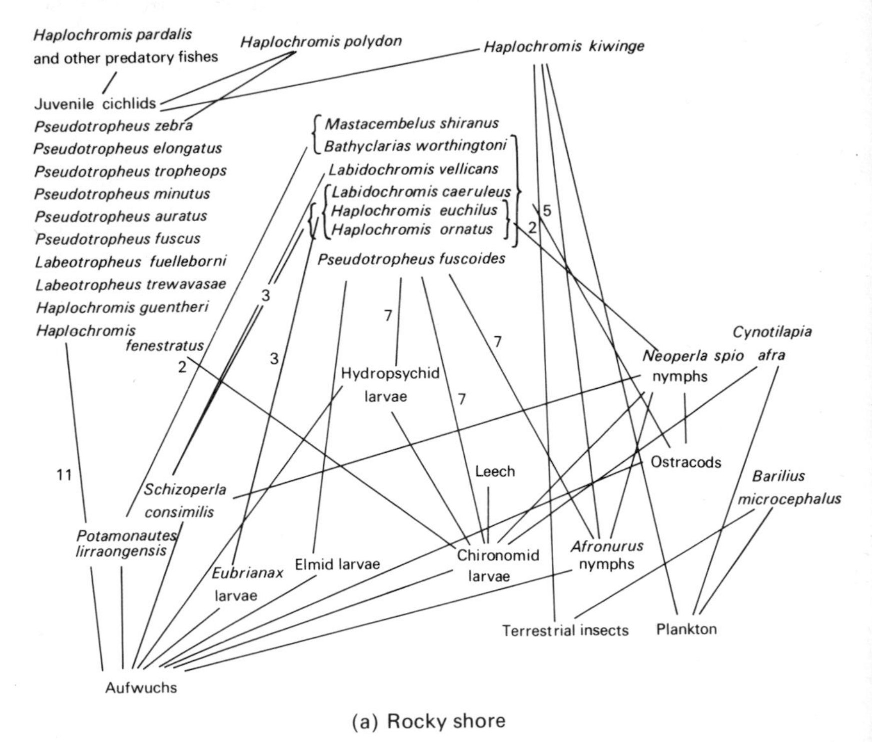

Fig. 5.4 Food webs on (a) rocky, and (b) sandy shores of Lake Malawi (after Fryer, 1959).

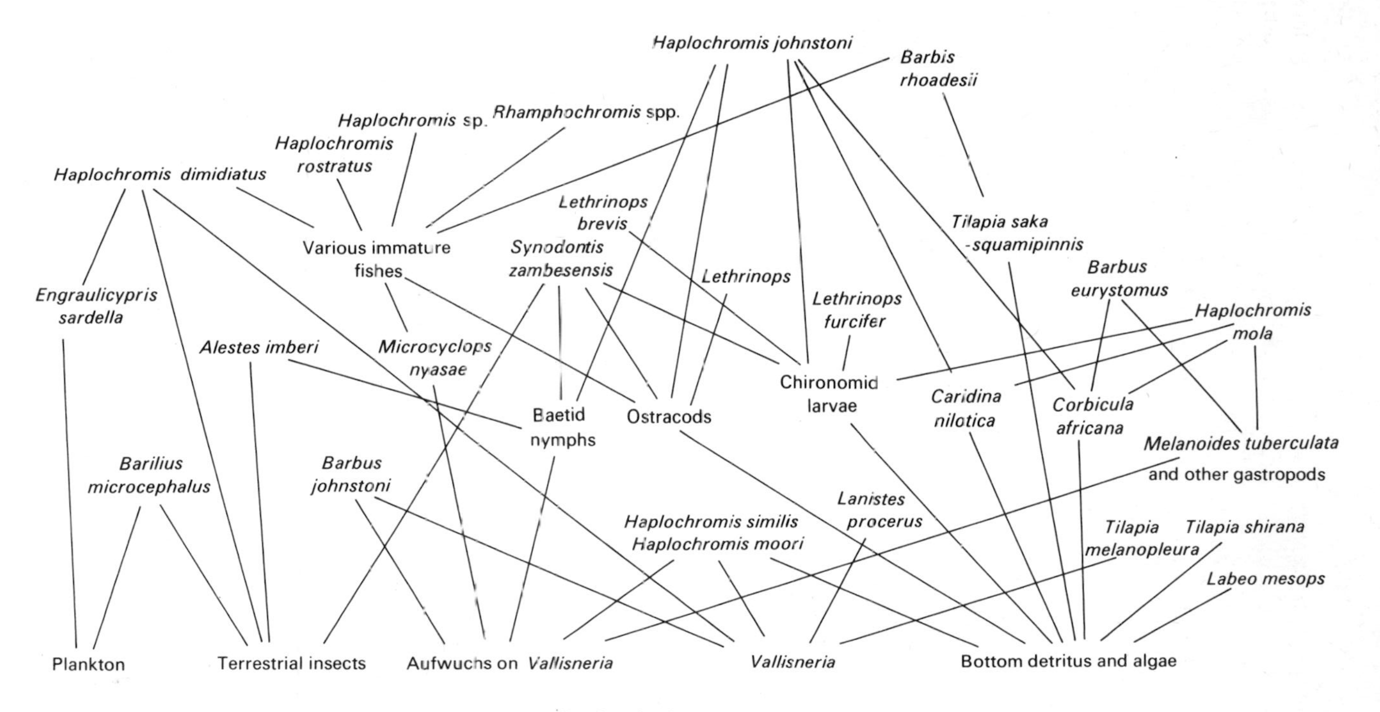

(b) Sandy shore

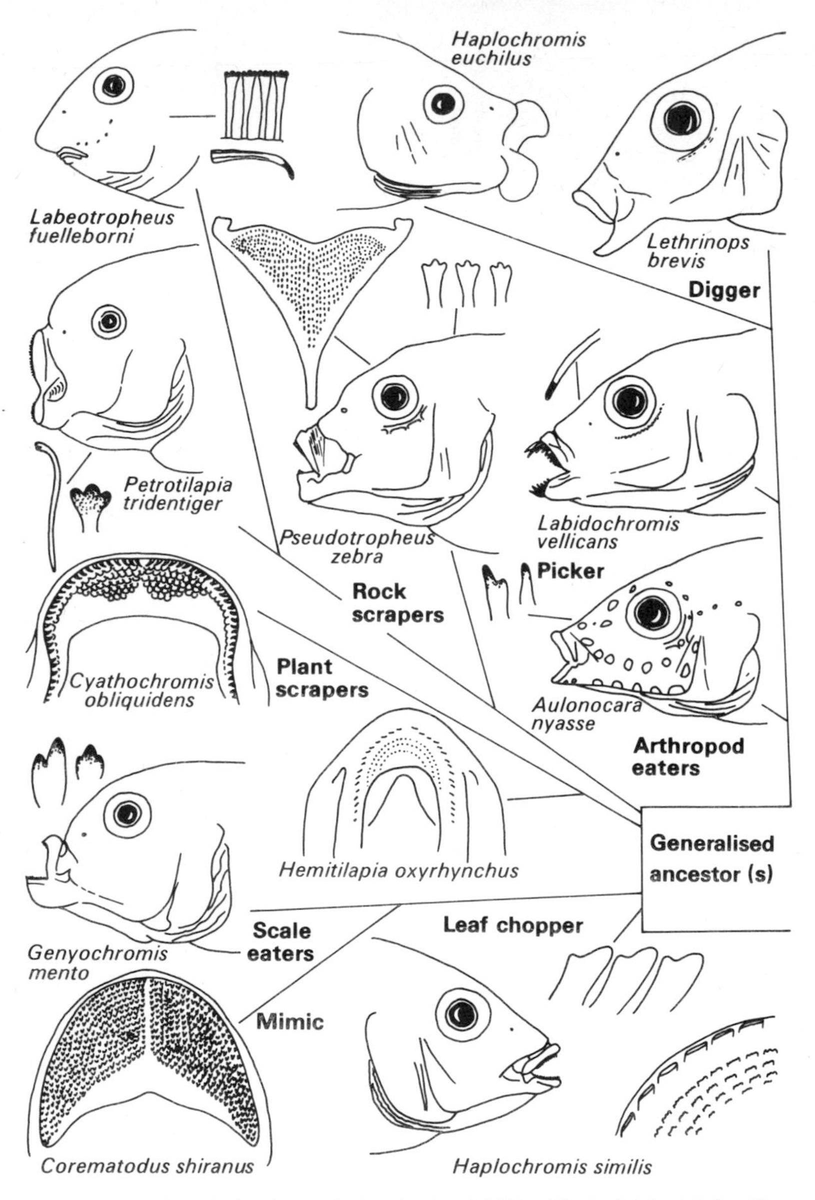

Fig. 5.5 Examples of adaptive radiation in the cichlids of Lake Malawi (after Fryer and Iles, 1972).

using the algal mat on the rocks with its enclosed micro-organisms), suggesting that this source of food is superabundant for these fishes. This has the corollary that factors other than food must be limiting the fish numbers.

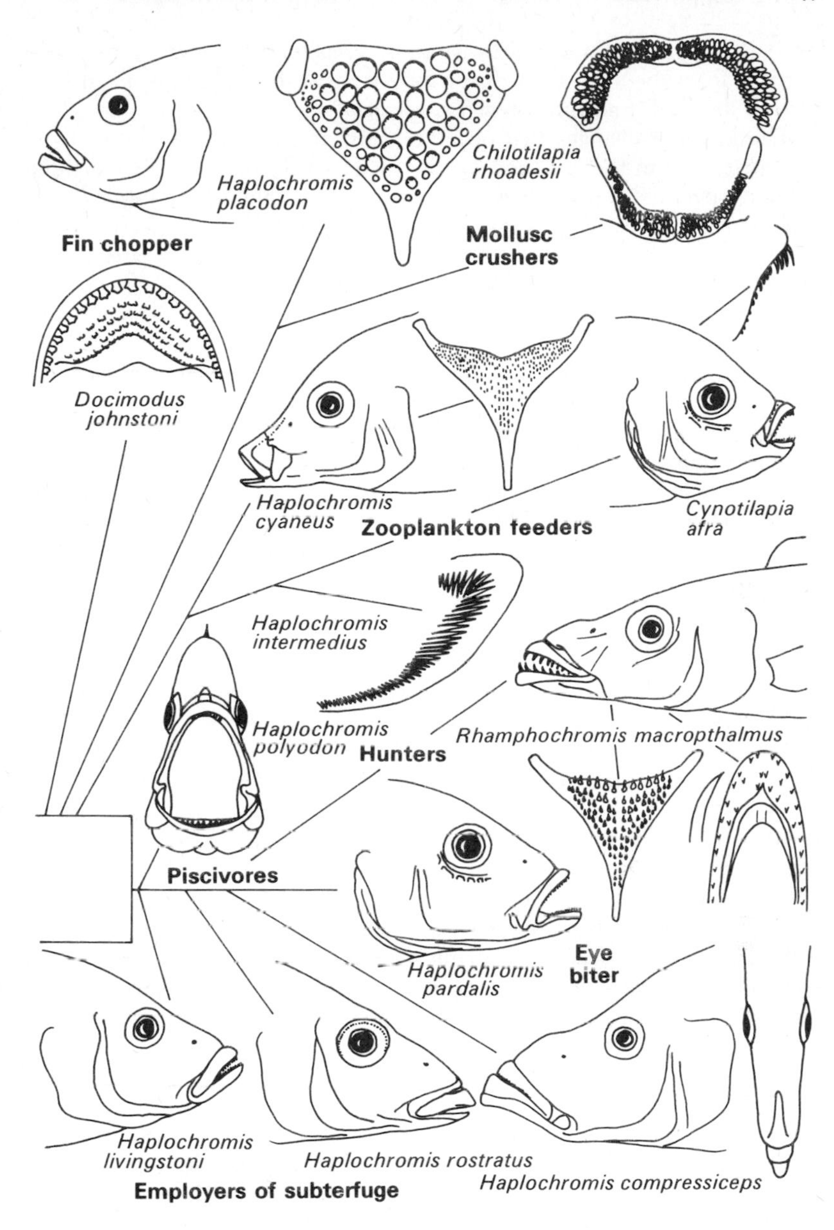

The food webs are based on very few items, particularly in the rocky habitat where aufwuchs forms the basis for about ten fish species (Fig. 5.4*a*). Though thin, this aufwuchs film is continually replenished throughout the year. On the sandy shore the basis of the food webs is broader (plankton, terrestrial insects, aufwuchs on *Vallisneria*, *Vallisneria*, bottom debris and algae (Fig. 5.4*b*). In the nearby swampy creek mouth, bottom algae and detritus form the main basis of the food webs, with higher plants and terrestrial insects supporting a few fish species.

The kinds of changes that occur to head and jaw shape, and to tooth structure both in the jaws and on the pharyngeal bones, as these cichlids become specialist feeders on various items, were studied by Fryer (1959) and are illustrated in Fig. 5.5. In this lake the generalised ancestors have diverged to become plant and rock scrapers, arthropod-eaters, zooplankton feeders, and piscivores which hunt their prey in different ways, even mimicking their prey to feed on their scales, or taking the eyes from living fish.

Mbuna remain in one biotope throughout life; the large yolked egg enables the young to hatch at a size large enough to use the same food as the parent, cutting out the need for a planktonic stage. They produce very few eggs at a time, throughout the year, so numbers remain very stable. Some Mbuna are known to be territorial; one *Pseudotropheus auratus* (a 64 mm long male) marked with a coloured bead was observed within one metre of its home crevice on a rock slope over five months, from May to October (Oliver, personal communication). Females mouth brood up to 30 days.

The *Tilapia* species flock

Unlike *Haplochromis*, few species of *Tilapia* occur together in one lake, and Lake Malawi is unique in having seven indigenous *Tilapia* species. These comprise five endemic species of the *Sarotherodon* group which have all evolved within the lake itself, and two non-endemic Zambezi–Zaïre species, *T. sparrmanii*, a small species living in lagoons around the lake, and *T. rendalli* (formerly known as *T. melanopleura*), a species which feeds on aquatic macrophytes in swamps around the lake. The endemic species belong to two groups: *T. shirana*, closely related to *T. mossambica* of southern Africa, feeds on higher vegetation and bottom detritus in shallow water close inshore, and four endemic species forming a species flock of very closely related forms which all feed mainly on planktonic algae, though they may take other algae if phytoplankton is scarce. Of these *T. karongae* appears to be restricted to the northern end of the lake. The other three, *T. saka*, *T. squamipinnis* and *T. lidole* are all most abundant at the southern end of the lake where they occupy increasingly offshore ones, *T. lidole* being best adapted for life in open water. They are, however, taken in shoals of mixed species at certain times when feeding on phytoplankton. The young, which are indistinguishable, live in a shoaling band along sandy shores; as the fish grow they move offshore and live in smaller shoals. Thus like the Lake Victoria *Tilapia*, and unlike the Mbuna, they change biotopes as they grow. In Malawi *Tilapia* breeding seasons are well defined, and as the season approaches the ripening males develop specific spawning colours, blue with a white head in *T. squamipinnis*, black with a white-edged dorsal fin in *T. saka* and *T. lidole*, and they develop long genital tassels. The males establish territories in the sandy bottom where each makes a sandscrape nest. *T. saka* spawns in the hot weather before the rains (August to November) in shallow water (2 to 4 m deep); *T. lidole* also spawns at this time (October and November), but off more open beaches in water about 8 m deep; *T. squamipinnis* spawn later in the year, during the rains (December to March) in deeper water (about 16 m). *T. saka* and *T. squamipinnis* look most alike, apart from the colour of the breeding males. The females visit the nests to lay, pick up eggs and sperm, then mouth-brood the eggs and young, taking them from the spawning grounds, which are in the clearest water of the species' range, to brooding grounds in richer greener water, generally closer to the shore, where the young are finally left (Lowe, 1953). Here the young live in a band until about 12 cm long, at which size they move further offshore. These Malawi *Tilapia* appear to have only one batch of young a year; there is no sign of the gonads ripening again in the brooding female as in *Tilapia* in equatorial waters and in pond-kept *Tilapia* of many species. In Malawi the young are brooded to a very large size, to over 50 mm TL in *T. lidole* (an adaptation to open-water life), and to 30 mm in *T. squamipinnis* and 24 mm in *T. saka* which live in more inshore waters. The young continue to return to the female's mouth for several weeks after they are first released. These *Tilapia* young are readily distinguished from those of other cichlids in the lake by the black '*Tilapia* spot' on the hind end of the dorsal fin in all species, a mark which may help the shoaling fish to orientate to one another.

This seasonality in spawning made it possible to trace length frequency groups among the young fish, which, combined with the analyses of growth rings on the opercular bones, enables growth rates to be estimated (Lowe, 1952). Most of these Malawi *Tilapia* do not breed until they are three years old, when they are between 240 and 285 mm in total length. Growth slows down considerably after maturity is reached.

These *Tilapia* support a valuable commercial fishery.

Lake Tanganyika

Set in mountainous country, the shore line of Lake Tanganyika is steep and rocky with some sandy beaches, but there are few areas of shallow swampy water. The aquatic vegetation is limited in extent and found only very close inshore. Water temperatures range between 23·5 and 27·5° C at 10 m and around 23° C below 1000 m. The water is beautifully clear, enabling the fishes to be observed, many of them brightly coloured. Underwater observations were described by Matthes (1962).

Biologically and chemically the water is divided into two layers: an epilimnion 100–200 m deep, and a hypolimnion below about 200 m, without oxygen and with little life apart from bacteria. Very strong southeast trade winds blow consistently between May and September which cause upwellings of deep water in inshore areas, particularly at the south end of the lake. The inflowing Ruzizi water at the north end of the lake is colder than the surface waters, sinking to below the thermocline (where it must take some oxygenated water, and with a loss of the nutrients taken down with it).

Although of great scientific interest, few of the L. Tanganyika cichlids are used as food, and consequently relatively little is known about the ecology of most of them, apart from initial observations on stomach contents and gonad states (Poll, 1956*b*). *Tilapia* are restricted to the few shallow areas and the estuaries of the inflowing rivers such as the Malagarasi. The endemic *Tilapia tanganicae* lives over sand: *T. karomo* is endemic in the Malagarasi river and not found in the lake. Ecological studies have been concentrated mainly on the economically important pelagic fish community of non-cichlids.

The fish fauna

The fish fauna is well known from the works of Poll (1953, 1956*a*) and a few of the distinctive species are shown in Fig. 5.6. Coulter has studied the influence of the hydrology on the pelagic and benthic communities at the south end of the lake (Coulter, 1963–70). The main lake has about 193 species representing 13 fish families (Table 2.2, Appendix 3). The cichlids, which make up 62 per cent of the fauna, are all endemic. The fauna is more fully differentiated than that of Victoria or Malawi, many more of the endemic fishes having achieved generic status, particularly among the cichlids.

The non-cichlid fishes include: *Protopterus aethiopicus* and two Zaïre basin species of *Polypterus*, *P. congicus* and *P. ornatipinnis*, which occur in the swampy muddy areas of the rivers and lagoons; *P. ornatipinnis* which lives in the Malagarasi delta on the eastside of the lake represents an interesting relic of the old fluviatile prelacustrine fauna (see p. 37). The two endemic species of Clupeidae have Zaïre affinities and the larger more inshore dwelling *Limnothrissa miodon* appears to be less specialised for open water life than is the smaller pelagic zooplankton-feeding *Stolothrissa tanganicae*. There are no mormyrids in the lake.

The lacustrine characids include two species of *Hydrocynus*, one of which *H. goliath* may be a recent immigrant from the Zaïre River, and two of *Alestes*, of which *A. rhodopleura* is endemic. These are all littoral species, taken over rock or sand. The citharinids are fluviatile, but *Distichodus* (of two species) are occasionally taken in bays and near rivers where vegetation is growing. The cyprinids in this lake are also littoral, rarely found far from a river; they include large endemic potamodromous *Barbus* and *Varicorhinus* which grow in the lake and reproduce in affluent rivers. Three large *Labeo* species (two apparently Zaïre species and one endemic) live mainly in the rivers. The very common potamodromous *Barilius moori*, originally endemic, has now entered Lake Kivu despite the rapids on the Ruzizi River flowing from Lake Kivu to Lake Tanganyika. The most lacustrine cyprinid in L. Tanganyika is a giant silvery blue–grey *Engraulicypris* which grows to 15 cm long but named *E. minutus* before the adult was discovered. The young live in bays and lagoons around the lake, but the adult is very specialised for life in the pelagic zone, where it is caught together with *Stolothrissa* and young *Luciolates* but feeds mainly on insects blown on to the water surface.

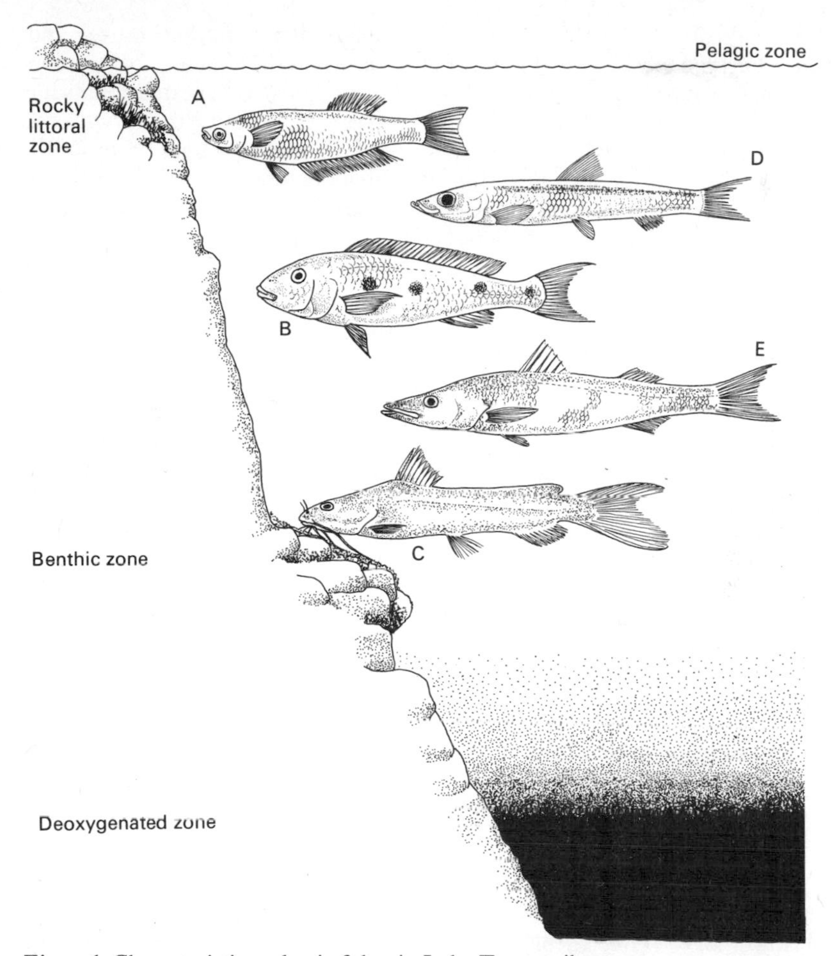

Fig. 5.6 Characteristic endemic fishes in Lake Tanganyika:
A. The large cyprinodont *Lamprichthys tanganicanus* (*c*. 10 cm) which lives over rocks in the littoral zone.
B. The large cichlid *Boulengerochromis microplepis* (*c*. 80 cm) which ranges widely in small schools.
C. The bagrid *Chrysichthys stappersii* (*c*. 46 cm) found down to the limit of dissolved oxygen.
D. The pelagic clupeid *Stolothrissa tanganicae* (*c*. 10 cm).
E. The pelagic predatory centropomid *Luciolates stappersii* (*c*. 35 cm).

Lake Tanganyika also has a very large endemic bright-blue cyprinodont *Lamprichthys tanganicanus*, growing to 13 cm long, which lives amongst the littoral rocks, where it feeds on insects, small crustacea and debris (Fig. 5.6).

In this lake it is the bagrid catfishes which have exploited the deep waters, and a species flock of seven endemic *Chrysichthys* and two endemic *Phyllo-*

nemus bagrids have evolved here. The non-endemic *Bagrus docmac* and *Auchenoglanis occidentalis* also occur in the lake and their young are found in the affluent rivers. The *Chrysichthys* species demonstrate specialisations for first littoral then demersal life. *C. cyclurus* lives exclusively on rocky bottoms, the others choose mud; the most specialised, *C. sianenna*, lives down to the oxygen limit at 120 m. The Clariidae includes one endemic species of *Dinotopterus* (contrast the species flock of clariids in Lake Malawi), and the monotypic endemic genus *Tanganikallabes*, an elongated clariid adapted for life in rock crevices in the littoral zone. The electric catfish *Malapterurus electricus*, which occurs in the lake over mud down to 50 m, is possibly a relatively recent addition to the fauna according to Poll.

Species flocks of centropomids and mastacembelids have also evolved within the lake. The centropomids have evidently evolved from the riverine *Lates niloticus* and they include the littoral *Lates microlepis*, the pelagic *L. angustifrons* and the deep-living macrophthalmic *L. mariae*, also two species of *Luciolates* (the only genus to have evolved from *Lates* in the whole of Africa). *Luciolates stappersii* is a pelagic fish living in shoals chasing *Stolothrissa*. The seven endemic species of *Mastacembelus* all live over hard bottoms; the most specialised of them *M. cunningtoni* lives down to 50 m deep.

The cichlid genera (40) in Lake Tanganyika and its affluents are far more numerous than in any other lake, and they contain 126 species all endemic. The genera mostly have very few species – only 5 of them have more than 4 species (contrast the huge *Haplochromis* species flocks in Victoria and Malawi): *Lamprologus* with 34 species, *Xenotilapia* with 12, *Limnochromis* with 11, *Trematocara* with 8, and *Bathybates* with 7. Of the other genera 23 are monotypic. Lake habitats frequented by cichlids are: rocky shores, sandy shores, benthic and bathypelagic regions. The rocky shores are full of hiding places, and most rock cichlids are small, but the fauna is rich and diverse (compare Mbuna in Lake Malawi); the fish are mostly carnivorous, but with very varied dentition related to their food: insect larvae, crabs, shrimps, algae (Poll, 1956*b*). Cichlids are less varied on sandy shores, all silvery in colour, and mostly microphagous or mollusc-feeders. Benthic cichlids penetrate down to the oxygen limit. Poll listed 23 cichlid species which are caught below 50 m, all bottom-living endemic species (e.g. of *Trematocara* and *Xenotilapia*), specialised for life at these depths. The giant cichlid *Boulengerochromis microlepis* is occasionally caught down to 100 m. Many of these deep-living fishes move up to the surface at night. There are no pelagic cichlids in the surface waters of this lake, but bathypelagic ones include a *Xenotilapia* which feeds on zooplankton, and *Plecodus* and *Perissodus* which feed on scales scraped from other fishes.

Many of the Tanganyika cichlids mouth-brood their young; this is known, or suspected with good reason, in species in twenty of the genera in the lake. However, species of four other genera, *Boulengerochromis*, *Lamprologus*, *Telmatochromis* and *Julidochromis*, are substratum-spawning guarders, not mouth-brooders; this was believed by Kosswig (1963) to have evolutionary implications (as discussed by Fryer and Iles, 1972, p. 572). For many species we have as yet no information on their breeding habits. The mouth-brooders include species of: *Aulonocranus*, *Bathybates*, *Callochromis*, *Cardiopharynx*, *Cyathopharynx*, *Ectodus*, *Grammatotria*, *Haplochromis*, *Hemibates*, *Lestradea*, *Limnochromis*, *Limnotilapia*, *Petrochromis*, *Simnochromis*, *Tanganicodus*, *Trematocara*, *Tylochromis*, *Tropheus*, *Tilapia*, *Xenotilapia* (Poll, 1956*a*; Coulter, 1968; Ladiges, 1968; Oppenheimer, 1970).

In both deep and shallow waters the numbers of species appear to far exceed the numbers of distinct niches in the various habitats. Poll (1956*b*) attributed this largely to the extraordinary diversity of habitats, with local variations in conditions, salinity, water level, depth and type of bottom. Poll also emphasised the probable importance of species appearing successively in time, in local conditions successively different, then confluence of habitats, or conditions becoming more uniform, permitting species to mix and their coexistence in the extraordinary polyspecific associations that we see today. That variations in conditions changing with time, together with the numbers of ecological niches at any one time, have allowed this type of evolution (compare the evolutionary effects of oscillating conditions in South American rivers).

The major habitats and their fish communities

Lake Tanganyika fishes include: (1) fluviatile species which breed in the affluent rivers and (2) truly lacustrine ones. Lacustrine habitats comprise three zones: the littoral, with rocky or sandy shores; the pelagic zone, and the benthic zone, each with distinct, but to some extent overlapping, fish communities.

Fluviatile habitats The affluent streams have waters of a different chemical composition from the lake, pH 7–8. Streams are cooler than the lake (20 to 23° C in fast, 25 to 28° C in slow stretches), and the water is much less clear than in the lake, especially in slow stretches.

In fast-flowing sections the fauna is poor; characteristic species are *Varicorhinus tanganicae*, *Barilius moori* and the catfish *Amphilius platychir*, of which the first two are found in the lake down to 10 m. The slow reaches with their lagoons, swamps and estuaries, and much vegetation and aquatic prairies, contain all the families of fishes common to the region. (The Malagarasi for instance harbours *Protopterus aethiopicus*, *Polypterus congicus* and *P. ornatipinnis, Mormyrus longirostris, Hippopotamyrus discorhynchus*, the characid *Alestes macrophthalmus*, citharinids *Distichodus maculatus* and *Citharinus gibbosus*, the small cyprinodont *Aplocheilichthys pumilis*, *Tilapia rendalli*, *T. upembae*, the endemic *T. karomo* and *Haplochromis burtoni*.) Few of the lake species penetrate the Malagarasi delta and most of the Malagarasi species are non-endemic species with Zaïre affinities; their presence east of the lake, which now forms an impenetrable barrier to them, demonstrates that the drainage of this area was westwards to the Zaïre before the lake was formed.

Amongst the fluviatile species (i.e. those which breed in the affluent rivers) both endemism and the proportion of cichlids is low, and they include many euryhaline species since the lake during its long isolation has increased in salinity and the lake water has considerable physicochemical differences from river water. This group includes three endemic cyprinids: *Barbus tropidolepis, Varicorhinus tanganicae, Barilius moori.* The characoids *Hydrocynus vittatus*, *Alestes macrophthalmus*, *Citharinus gibbosus* migrate up the affluent Lufubu River each year to spawn in the November to March rains (Badenhuizen, 1965).

Lacustrine habitats

1. **The littoral zone.** Here the physicochemical conditions are fairly homogeneous in the bays and down to 20 m deep and the water is poor in plankton, but the substrate may be rocky or sandy. The *rocky coasts* are abrupt and dissected, the shores wave-washed, boulder-strewn and bare of aquatic vegetation. Underwater rocks provide shady retreats for the fishes and cover from predators, carrying a very rich littoral fauna. The food sources are much more varied than on sandy beaches, with aufwuchs and aquatic insects, crabs and shrimps. The water is generally very clear, allowing the fish to be observed as they feed, generally on the bottom or among stones. The fauna here is dominated by cichlids, endemic species with very varied dentition according to the foods used; seventy cichlid species belonging to 16 genera live on rocky bottoms down to about 10 m, and others replace them at depth. The giant blue cyprinodont *Lamprichthys tanganicanus* also lives over these rocks, keeping at the surface close to the bank and in rocky bays, feeding on plankton and insects, whilst various *Mastacembelus* species live amongst the rocks.

The sandy beaches are less numerous than the rocky shores, and found mainly at the heads of bays or close to stream inflows. The fishes living here lack shelter from the sun, from predators, and from the waves which are quite violent in the dry season. Fishes here are characteristically uniform silvery grey and lie immobile on the greyish sand during the day, the cichlids mostly bottom-living, microphagous, or mollusc eaters such as *Tylochromis polylepis* with its large crushing pharyngeal teeth. *Barilius moori* and *Tilapia tanganicae* also live over sand, the *Tilapia* in shoals which skitter at the lake surface. The nocturnal fauna over the sand differs from the diurnal one; at night fishes such as *Bathybates* and *Trematocara* from mud-bottoms deeper in the lake come close to shore. Such diurnal lateral migrations amongst littoral and sublittoral fish populations lead to a large increase in the littoral fish fauna at night in this lake. By day the littoral fauna comprises only small rock-lurking cichlids, large active predators and occasional anadromous fish. Coulter considered that the presence of the piscivorous *Boulengerochromis microlepis*, *Lates angustifrons*, and to a less extent *Hydrocynus vittatus*, restrict the inshore habitat by day to the small rock-lurking fishes.

2. **The pelagic zone.** Lake Tanganyika, unlike these other lakes, has an

abundant pelagic fish community. In this lake the zooplankton descends to 60–120 m where it spends the day, then migrates through *c.* 40 m surfacewards at night, followed by the clupeids, which are in turn followed by their predators. All these pelagic fishes are endemic, and they fall into two groups: (1) those well integrated with the zooplankton and accompanying its vertical migrations: the two clupeids, *Engraulicypris minutus*, and their predators *Luciolates stappersii* and *Lates microlepis*; (2) species which range widely in the lake, such as some *Bathybates* and *Boulengerochromis microlepis*.

Information on the biology of the pelagic clupeids and their centropomid predators has been summarised by Coulter (1970).

(a) *The clupeids.* Both species of clupeid commonly occur together but in separate shoals. *Stolothrissa* is generally dominant offshore and *Limnothrissa* occupies mainly inshore areas. During the day they live at depth, but they migrate to the surface at night through distances of up to 150 m. *Stolothrissa* is believed to spawn in the pelagic zone, and *Limnothrissa* inshore. Both species probably release several batches of ova during their short lives, and spawning takes place through most of the year. The fry live inshore, moving offshore as they grow and into the pelagic community on maturity. *Stolothrissa* matures when about 70 mm long, *Limnothrissa* somewhat larger; few of either species survive larger than 95 mm (though *Stolothrissa* have been caught up to 100 mm and *Limnothrissa* up to 170 mm) and few *Stolothrissa* survive for more than one year. Both species feed on both phytoplankton and zooplankton when young. Adult *Stolothrissa* feed mainly on pelagic zooplankton (to a small extent on insect larvae, fish ova and diatoms), while *Limnothrissa* have a more unspecialised diet, including prawns, insects and their larvae and young clupeids.

The clupeid life cycles appear to be related to the annual cycles of hydrological change and plankton production. The strong winds in June to August are funnelled up the lake, causing surface offshore drift, upwelling and turbulence; the lake is most unstable at this time and offshore plankton increases during these months. September to December is the calmest period of the year, and plankton production in the open water is generally high in November–December. Inshore phytoplankton blooms occur in July and in November or December.

Stolothrissa, which depend on pelagic plankton as food, both in the larval and adult stages, is more affected by these seasonal changes, and responds with seasonal production of young. Adults are abundant and the production of young is at its greatest in November–December, the calm months when the water turbulence which might be damaging to the eggs and larvae has died down. Coulter suggested that the apparent failure of the 1964–5 and 1965–6 year classes may have been caused by shortage of planktonic food, or by unusual levels of larval mortality due to water movements.

Since both clupeid species feed on plankton and can occupy the same habitat at the same time, they may be in competition. *Limnothrissa* with its less specialised feeding habits appears to be better adapted to inshore life where the food is more varied, while *Stolothrissa* which specialises on pelagic plankton has the advantage in the pelagic zone, but the species can evidently replace one another in the pelagic zone. When *Stolothrissa* numbers are low (as they were in 1965 and 1966 and are in April–May most years) the *Limnothrissa* population can exceed that of the *Stolothrissa* offshore, which suggests that *Limnothrissa* tends to be confined inshore by competitive interaction. The continuity of clupeid abundance is shown by the largely dependent complex bottom fauna which has evolved in the depths of the lake.

(b) *The centropomid predators.* Young *Lates* of all three species (*L. mariae*, *L. microlepis* and *L. angustifrons*) up to about 3 cm long are common in the plankton. They then live amongst littoral macrophytes until about 35 cm TL, dispersing away from the shore as they grow. In these weed beds they feed mainly on prawns, small cichlids, insects and their larvae, and length frequency data suggest that they stay here for about one year, growing at about 1 cm/month. Soon after leaving the weed beds *L. microlepis* adopt a diet of clupeids; the others continue to take prawns and other invertebrates until maturity is reached. *L. mariae* is pelagic while *L. angustifrons* feeds on prawns and benthic fishes but migrates up to the surface at night to feed on clupeids in the months when these are most abundant. Maturity is at 44 and 49 cm for males and females respectively in *L. mariae*, at about 47 and 51 cm in *L. microlepis*, and at 50 and 57 cm in *L. angustifrons*. Spawning continues throughout the year with certain maxima.

Luciolates stappersii grows to *c.* 38 cm TL and seems to be completely pelagic all its life; it makes diurnal vertical migrations and sometimes occurs in huge concentrations. Both adults and young feed on clupeids. The main spawning period is probably between February and April.

The trophic niches of the predators are more clearly separated than are those of their clupeid prey. While all feed on clupeids, *L. mariae* and *L. angustifrons* do so mainly when these are most plentiful. Only *L. microlepis* and *Luciolates stappersii* appear to compete continually for the same food. None occupies the role of climax predator.

Purse seining for these predatory fishes started on a large commercial scale in 1962. The numbers of predators caught decreased from 1963 to 1966 and remained low. The clupeid catch rose in 1964 to 1967 and remained high in 1968. This suggested that predator pressure formerly kept the clupeid populations at a low level (Coulter, 1970).

3. The benthic zone. With increased pressure, decreased light and decreased temperature (27° C at the surface, 24° C at 100 m, 23·5° C at 200–400 m), the benthic habitat is the most specialised that Lake Tanganyika has to offer. As this lake is the second deepest in the world, and the deepest tropical lake, this is indeed a unique habitat. Below 60 m the dissolved oxygen falls rapidly, from 85 per cent at 60 m to only 20 per cent at 70 m, 10 per cent at 100 m, 4 per cent at 140 m, and 2 per cent at 170 m in the north basin. In the south basin the oxygen sometimes goes deeper, to 250 m (Coulter, 1966).

Below 20 m the bottom is generally of sand or mud and mollusc shells, and rocky areas are rare. Below 100 m it is mainly mud (with mud extending into shallower depths in the river estuaries). These muddy bottoms in deep water present very special conditions for freshwater fishes, and a remarkable fauna has evolved here. Cichlids predominate in this fauna, all endemic species (*Trematocara* the most numerous, *Xenotilapia* and *Limnochromis*), and the non-cichlid *Chrysichthys*. The species caught vary much with the depth and nature of the bottom. Gillnets set in deeper water take about 55 species of cichlid, 15 siluroids and 3 of *Mastacembelus*. Even at 120 m near the oxygen limit in the north basin 13 species were taken in gillnets, *Limnochromis*, *Xenotilapia* and *Trematocara* being most abundant. Many of these deep-living fishes move up to the surface at night.

Deep water fishes caught in bottom-set gillnets set at 120 m in the south end of the lake in July and August 1961 where there was no recordable oxygen included five cichlids (*Hemibates stenosoma*, *Bathybates fasciatus*, *Xenochromis hecqui*, *Limnochromis permaxillaris*), two *Chrysichthys* species (*C. stappersii* and *C. grandis*), *Dinotopterus cunningtoni* and *Lates mariae*. Coulter (1966, 1968) commented that these species appeared to be capable of some form of anaerobic respiration.

Not all the species found at these depths are restricted to the very deep water. *Hemibates stenosoma* is caught from 20 m to the oxygen limit, though most abundantly from 80–120 m. It feeds on cichlids (including its own young), clupeids and prawns, and is itself the main cichlid prey of *Lates mariae* and *L. angustifrons*. The female *H. stenosoma* is a mouth brooder. The six species of *Bathybates* were found to be widely distributed on the bottom, but most species were also found in the pelagic zone. Except for one species (*B. ferox* which lives in water less than 40 m deep), there appeared to be no marked depth preferences, nor of variations in size of fish with depth. Clupeids or cichlids are eaten. *B. fasciatus* and *B. vittatus* females were found with yolked young in the mouth (Coulter, 1968).

The six species of *Chrysichthys* are all benthic fishes. *C. stappersii*, the most numerous species at the south end of the lake, but not found in the north basin, was most abundant from 80 to 120 m. Its very generalised diet includes predominantly invertebrates: crabs, gastropods, insects, ostracods, lamellibranchs, and dead fish (cichlids) were scavenged. *C. graueri* was found down to 160 m but showed a preference for the sublittoral, eating invertebrates, prawns from rocky bottoms, and scavenging dead fish (cichlids from inshore). The other species were less abundant in gillnet catches. In spite of wide depth distributions the various species showed clear depth preferences, and pairs of species shared depth zones in which they were particularly abundant. *C. siannena* and *C. platycephalus*, though not common, were caught in the littoral zone (though *C. siannena* was found from 20 to 120 m); *C. brachynema* and *C. graueri* were most abundant in the sublittoral, but the size of fish increased with depth. *C. stappersii* and *C. grandis* lived mainly in the deep water, but in these species the size of fish decreased with depth. Food specialisation was greatest between members of a pair sharing preferred depth distributions; thus in the sublittoral *C. brachynema* took mainly crabs and *C. graueri* prawns and cichlids, and in the deep water *C. stappersii* fed mainly on crabs, while *C. grandis* took fish, especially cichlids, but also other *Chrysichthys* and crabs. Relatively large items were swallowed (the pieces of scavenged fish were often very large), full stomachs leading to distensions of the body wall (compare *Bathyclarias* in Malawi and deep-sea fishes in which the food supply may be rather erratic) (Coulter, 1968).

The large endemic cichlid *Boulengerochromis microlepis*, which grows to 80 cm long and 3·5 kg weight, is common and widespread in the lake. Streamlined in form (Fig. 5.6) *B. microlepis* is mainly a benthopelagic coastal predator which although piscivorous usually hunts in schools, chasing the large shoals of clupeids into bays and shallows. Matthes (1961*a*) found this species to have three breeding periods a year (the main one February to May, others from late July to early September, and October to January). The spawning peaks were distinct enough for him to estimate growth rates from length frequency data. Unlike most of the cichlids in the Great Lakes this species is not a mouth-brooder, but the parents guard the young.

B. microlepis changes its habitat in the lake according to its age, feeding behaviour and gonad state. The fry are microphagous bottom-feeders. The young live in shallower water than the adults. Omnivorous juveniles less than 15 cm long hunt in schools of 100 to 500 individuals in water 3 to 10 m deep. As they grow the school becomes smaller, the diet includes more fishes (clupeids and small cichlids), and they hunt deeper; juveniles over 15 cm long roam the lake at depths of 15 to 35 m (occasionally down to 100 m) in groups of several dozen individuals. The fishes make diurnal/nocturnal vertical movements, rising to the surface and coming inshore at night, and there are lateral movements of schools of hunting juveniles along the coast. The mature fish live in pairs amongst rocks in the littoral zone, where they revert to a more varied diet of crabs, molluscs, insect larvae and plant debris as well as fishes. They first mature when two and a half years old (about 33 cm and 500 g weight). The males are larger and more vividly coloured than the females. The pair defends a territory in the rocky littoral zone around 2·5 m deep; the nest is only a cleared space between the boulders. The olive eggs are very numerous (10 520 in a 35 cm female); they hatch rapidly and the young are guarded by the parents until they are 4 to 5 cm standard length. The young swim in a dense school, one parent leading, the other behind them, and when alarmed they huddle in dense groups between the stones. (This behaviour greatly resembles that in *Cichla ocellaris* in South America, Lowe-McConnell, 1969*c*.)

The effects of predation in Lake Tanganyika communities

In Lake Tanganyika the very marked increase in numbers of clupeids when their predators were reduced by fishing stressed the severity of predation pressure and the fine balance between numbers of predators and prey in unexploited pelagic populations. Coulter (1966) concluded that clupeid vertical migrations may have evolved in response to predation pressure (rather than just to following the movements of their zooplankton prey). The coexistence of clupeids and *Lates* involves a finely balanced compromise in which both have sufficient light for visual selection of food, but in which the clupeids also obtain an adequate degree of protection. The clupeids are attracted to light at night (which is used for their capture in scoop nets and seine nets). What mechanism sends them down by day? Gravity?

The general effect of both vertical and lateral migrations (as among the littoral fishes of Lake Tanganyika) is to decrease isolation in pelagic populations. In this lake it is only in the rocky littoral or sublittoral, and in the deep benthic zone, that confinement to restricted habitats occurs, and it is significant that most members of species flocks are of small cichlids confined to such areas. The most numerous cichlid genera, *Lamprologus* (34 species), *Xenotilapia* (12) and *Limnochromis* (11) have representatives in both environments. Other polyspecific genera are either littoral fishes (*Simnochromis*, *Petrochromis*, *Callochromis*, *Telmatochromis* or *Julidochromis*) or deep benthic fishes (such as *Trematocara*). Cover is given either by the rocks or by the dim light in the benthic zone.

In the sublittoral zone, the rocky bottoms have numerous cichlid species preyed on by siluroids and *Lates*, whereas the flat bottoms with little cover have far fewer species, and most of the cichlids living here are much larger than those found amongst rocks. The small fish on the flat bottoms are siluroids and stomach contents of *Lates*, *Boulengerochromis* and *Hydrocynus* examined by Coulter indicated that these are little used as food by these predators. The paucity of cichlids here may reflect the lack of microhabitats, but it seems probable that they are prevented from living here by lack of cover. Matthes (1962) found small *Lamprologus* sheltering in gasteropod shells.

The pelagic and benthic components of the deep-water community of Lake Tanganyika represent two levels of diversity (Coulter, 1966). The pelagic species are few in number with very specialised feeding requirements, whereas the benthic community, split into numerous semi-isolated populations, shows a very high diversity of species and of trophic links. This represents in microcosm the situation in the tropical oceans of the world, with their relatively simple pelagic clupeid populations and their very highly diverse coral reef communities.

The role of predators in speciation and maintaining diversity is considered later (Chapter 10). In Lake Tanganyika the presence of predators such as *Boulengerochromis* would appear to be both *inhibiting* speciation of open-water-living cichlids, and *promoting* speciation amongst the rock-dwelling cichlids by increasing isolation between the various populations.

Comparison of fish communities in the three Great Lakes

The following points emerge from a comparison of communities in these three lakes.

1. Although the faunas depend on the basic stocks of fish present in the river systems on which they lie, convergent evolution uses the faunal elements available to build up comparable communities in the three lakes, within the limits dictated by the hydrological conditions. Victoria in the Nile system has representatives of 11 fish families, Tanganyika in the Zaïre system of 13, and Malawi in the Zambezi system only about 8, but the total number of species is not dissimilar in the three lakes, and probably highest in Malawi (Victoria *c.* 200, Tanganyika 193, Malawi, 240+).

In the absence of clupeids in Malawi and Victoria, cichlids (Utaka) have exploited the zooplankton feeding niche in Malawi, as has the small cyprinid *Engraulicypris* in both these lakes. Even where the same basic stock is present, whether it speciates or not will depend on conditions: the large clariids is *Dinotopterus* and '*Bathyclarias*' have given rise to a species flock in Malawi but not in Tanganyika, where the deepwater scavenging niche is occupied by a bagrid *Chrysichthys* species flock.

2. The further evolution of the species probably reflects the *age* of the lake. The numbers of endemic genera are: Victoria 5, Malawi 21, Tanganyika 40. The faster evolution of cichlids under these lacustrine conditions (discussed by Greenwood, 1973*b*; p. 136) is shown by the relative numbers of endemic genera in cichlids and non-cichlids:

	Victoria	*Malawi*	*Tanganyika*
Cichlids	4	20	33
Non-cichlids	1	1	7

3. The effects of *seasonality* are modified by the shape of the lake. In distance from the equator, and so with increasing variation in day length and annual variation in air temperature, the series runs Victoria, Tanganyika, Malawi. But annual *mixing* is greatest in the shallow Victoria, making it limnologically more like a temperate lake than are the two deep permanently stratified ones. Mixing is local and mainly at the south end in these two deep lakes. Surface waters are enriched to a greater extent, and more regularly in Tanganyika than in Malawi, enabling Tanganyika to support a rich pelagic community, the only one of these lakes to do so. Its deep benthic fauna depends on the rain or organic matter from this pelagic community.

Tilapia breeding seasons reflect the increased seasonality in Malawi compared with Victoria. Victoria *Tilapia* produce a succession of broods, female gonads starting to ripen again while the female is mouth brooding young: this is not so in Malawi *Tilapia*. The possession of distinct breeding seasons appears to have been important in the evolution of a series of *Tilapia* species in Malawi. Bioenergetically it may not matter much to the lake communities whether two species produce a series of broods of young (as in the indigenous Victoria *Tilapia*), or four species produce only one brood a year (as in Malawi), but no one has yet studied any bioenergetic implications in these fish communities. In Malawi another group of cichlids, the Mbuna, appear to live aseasonal lives, producing few eggs at a time throughout the year, so what holds for one group of fishes does not necessarily hold for another (even within the same family and within the same lake).

Both the short lived clupeids in Tanganyika, and *Engraulicypris* in Malawi appear to respond to phytoplankton blooms, which may come at rather irregular intervals, by increased breeding, illustrating the effect of food on population density. But the increase in numbers of these pelagic clupeids after their predators were controlled by a new fishery, indicates that predation is also very important in controlling their numbers.

6

Lacustrine Fish Communities – II. Some other African lakes

The West Cameroon Crater Lake Barombi Mbo

The fishes of the small Cameroon crater lake Barombi Mbo studied by Trewavas *et al.* (1972) provide a splendid example of ecological separation to exploit the meagre resources of an oligotrophic lake, as described here from their work. The evolution of its endemic fishes also provides in miniature a picture of the kinds of changes that probably occurred in a lake such as Lake Tanganyika when it was first formed. Comparable ecological studies were also made in two other nearby crater lakes, Kotto and Mboandong, shallower, more eutrophic lakes considered to be less mature than Barombi Mbo (see p. 268), with fewer fish species, only one of which (a cichlid in Lake Kotto) is endemic (Corbet *et al.*, 1973).

Roughly circular in shape and only 2·5 km in diameter but over 110 m deep, Barombi Mbo lies in a small forested crater at 4° 38 N, 9° 22 E with an outflow to the Mungo River. With a surface temperature 29° to 30° C, not very productive of phyto- or zooplankton, it is a clear lake which enabled underwater observations to be made on fish behaviour. In this lake and its inflowing stream there are 17 species of fish, of which 12, including the 11 cichlids, appear to be endemic. The lake is structurally very uniform and has relatively few food sources: the main ones are phytoplankton, organic debris, aquatic invertebrates, fishes and adult insects. Most of the cichlids are clearly separated from one another in their distribution in space or time (feeding by day or night), or in their feeding habits. There is clear spatial separation between those that live and feed inshore and those that feed in the deeper water of the open lake, coming inshore only to breed. Among the inshore dwellers there is some overlap in diet, but each selects a 'main course' different from the others (Fig. 6.1). The importance of organic debris and bacteria in the diets of many of the fishes can be seen in Fig. 6.2.

Of the four *Sarotherodon* species (formerly called *Tilapia*), two live inshore, and two offshore when adult. The two inshore species both feed to a large extent on organic debris, but one (*S. lohbergeri*) collects it, together with aufwuchs, from the surfaces of rocks and plants, and the other (*S. steinbachi*) mainly from sandy areas. Young individuals of the offshore species (*S.*

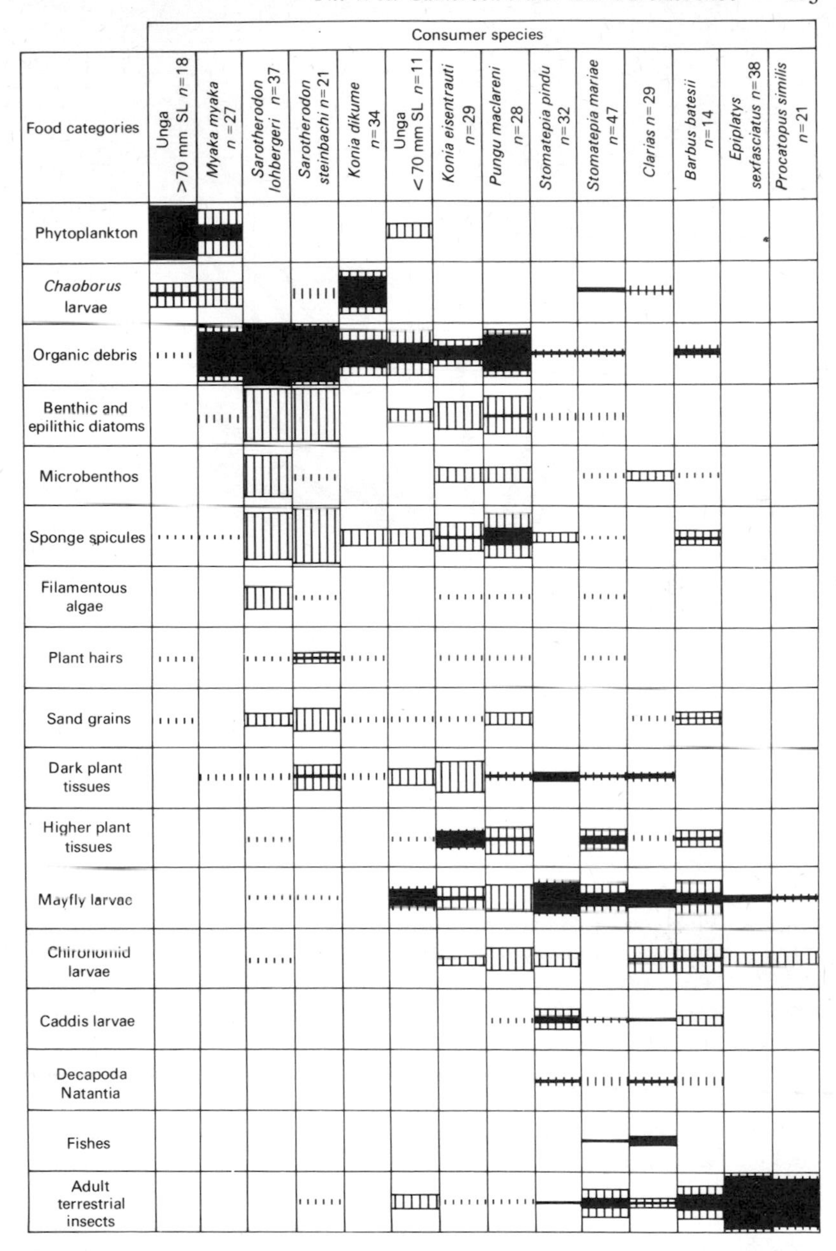

Fig. 6.1 Trophic spectrum illustrating the results of analyses of stomach contents of the fishes of Barombi Mbo. The depths of the black blocks show the percentages of stomachs with each food as the main contents, and the depths of the hatched blocks show the percentages of stomachs in which each food was present (after Trewavas, Green and Corbet, 1972).

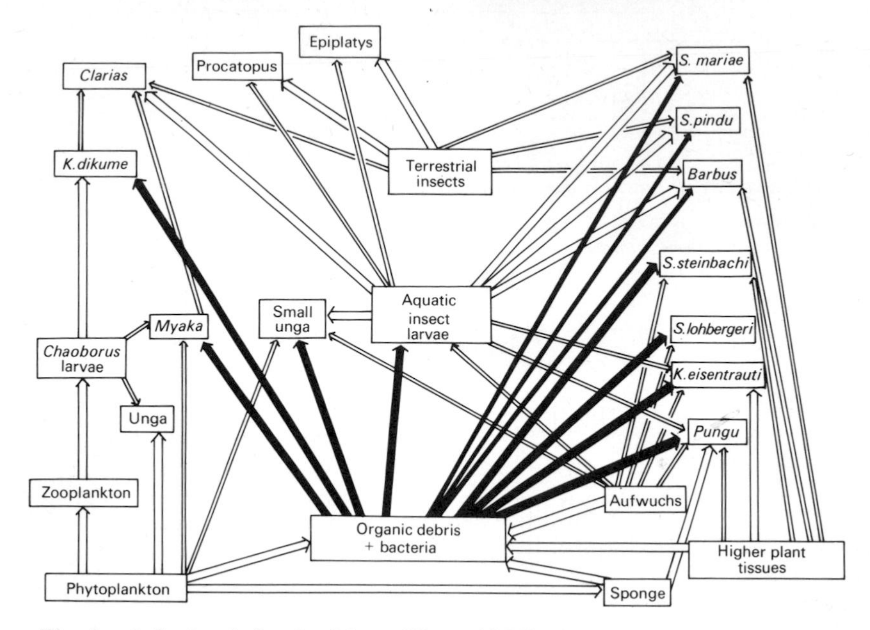

Fig. 6.2 A food web for the fishes of Barombi Mbo based on the examination of stomach contents. Wide arrows: more than 30 per cent of fishes have the food item as main contents; narrow arrows: fewer than 30 per cent have (after Trewavas, Green and Corbet, 1972).

linnellii and *S. caroli* both known locally as 'Unga') often feed very close inshore in water too shallow for other fishes, taking flotsam as well as bottom aufwuchs and insect larvae. Phytoplankton forms the sole food of both these offshore species and both of them swim a metre or so below the surface in midlake. Thus these two share the same food, which is not too plentiful, and if this resource were scarce severe competition might be expected. However, as in Lakes Malawi and Victoria, the limited space for spawning sites round the shore may be more limiting than food for these fishes. If so, competition between these sibling species would be reduced by a difference in breeding seasons, and there was some evidence that *S. linnellii* and *S. caroli* do breed asynchronously. *S. linnellii* is a mouth brooder, and the large and few ova ripening at a time.in many of these other cichlids suggested that these too are mouth brooders.

Of the other inshore species *Pungu maclareni*, a striking gold and black-blotched fish, feeds largely on chunks of living sponge, and its prominent teeth and thick lips may be an adaptation for this diet. Insect larvae support a group of predatory inshore fishes which differ from one another in the depths or times at which they feed, the size of their prey, and the relative importance of adult insects in their diets. *Konia eisentrauti* feeds in water 1–2 m deep, snapping up small invertebrates and sometimes taking the eggs of other fishes. *Stomatepia mariae* takes larger prey, including small fishes and adult insects from the water surface. *Stomatepia pindu* hunts like *K. eisentrauti* but seems to feed mainly at twilight or at night, so probably encounters different prey. The cyprinodont *Epiplatys sexfasciatus* feeds at the surface close inshore, where it makes use of a food source scarcely tapped by the cichlids. *Barbus batesii* also feeds inshore, singly or in groups, on small invertebrates.

Offshore, in addition to the phytoplankton-feeders already mentioned, *Konia dikume* feeds mainly on *Chaoborus* larvae, while *Myaka myaka* lives at considerable depths, where it probably feeds on dead phytoplankton and other organic debris raining down from above. No fishes seem to prey directly on the copepods and rotifers of the open water. (The lake lacks Cladocera.) The *Chaoborus* spend the day in deoxygenated water below 20 m, migrating upwards at night to feed on rotifers; their predator *Konia dikume* has physiological adaptations enabling its blood to store oxygen, permitting hunting forays into the hypolimnion, so extending the feeding period at twilight (Green *et al.*, 1973).

The cichlids in deeper water are silvery grey without markings, inshore species are blotched with black. Dead leaves form a thick covering on the sandy bottom at some places inshore, harbouring many types of invertebrate, Ephemeroptera and Odontata nymphs, chironomid larvae, ostracods, hydracharines, sponges, with the boring Ephemeroptera *Povilla* in dead wood. Fishes were more abundant where rocks and boulders lay along the shore. The submerged tree litter provides important habitats for invertebrates, and there were a few stands of aquatic plants supporting epibionts.

Man appears to be the chief predator. Cormorants, kingfishers, herons and two kinds of snake take some fish. The only piscivorous fishes found were large *Clarias* (which had eaten both the inshore dwelling *S. steinbachi* and the offshore *K. dikume* and *Myaka*), and *S. mariae* which included fish in its diet. Some *Barbus* may also take fish. On the whole, predation pressure does not appear very intense.

Barombi Mbo appears to have been colonised by three or four cichlid species feeding respectively on: (*a*) material sifted from sand, (*b*) phytoplankton, detritus and aufwuchs, and (*c*) – and (*d*)? – invertebrates. The sand sifter, a *Sarotherodon galilaeus*-like form, became more exclusively adapted to this habit (to become *S. steinbachi*); the second form (*b*) became divided in response to increased opportunity and competition (especially for limited aufwuchs) into a specialised aufwuchs feeder (*S. lohbergeri*) and two phytoplankton feeders (*S. linnelli* and *S. caroli*); the invertebrate-feeder (*c*) diverged to produce a bottom-feeder using invertebrates (*Konia eisentrauti*), and the species of *Stomatepia* which avoid competition by feeding at night (*S. pindu*) or in deeper water (*S. mongo*), or by including water-logged insects from the surface and small fishes in their diet (*S. mariae*). Driven from the crowded inshore rocks into deeper waters offshore, one species (*Konia dikume*) exploits the dense *Chaoborus* larvae populations, and another species *Myaka myaka* (possibly from group (*b*)) feeds on detritus near the bottom. Whether the sponge-feeding *Pungu* also diverged from group (*c*), or was highly modified from group (*d*) is not clear.

As the authors comment, this impressive ecological separation has clear adaptive advantages for a dense population of fishes exploiting the meagre resources of an oligotrophic lake, but the nature of the factors that initiated speciation within the lake, in the apparent absence of geographical barriers, remains open to speculation. Trewavas (personal communication) points out that even the same stream species invading the lake in floods at successive time intervals would find conditions in the lake different each time as niches were occupied by the earlier invaders.

The equatorial Lake George, Uganda

Lake George, bisected by the equator in western Uganda (0° 0′ N, 30° 10′ E), has been studied more intensively than any other tropical lake, as production processes were investigated here throughout a six-year International Biological Programme project (Fig. 2.4) (papers by Dunn *et al.*, 1969; Burgis *et al.*, 1973; Ganf and Viner, 1973; Greenwood and Lund, eds., 1973; Moriarty *et al.*, 1973). A shallow lake 250 km^2, mostly less than 2·5 m deep, the water is a peagreen soup of phytoplankton over a bottom of soft muddy ooze 3 m deep, with sandy patches in but a few places. The lake stratifies markedly by day (surface temperature up to 35° C, bottom 25° C), but mixes each night. Diurnal changes greatly exceed, and are biologically more important than, the seasonal changes, for day length, wind regime, and chemical conditions are very constant throughout the year. The lake has at least 29 fish species, including 16 *Haplochromis* species endemic to Lake George and the adjoining much larger Lake Edward (Greenwood, 1973*a*). Mostly less than 15 cm long when adult, these *Haplochromis* are not cropped commercially, but their biomass exceeds that of the other fish. A gillnet fishery removes up to 5000 tonnes of fish from the lake (equivalent to *c.* 2000 kg/ha/yr), 80 per cent *Tilapia nilotica* and 20 per cent of *Bagrus docmac*, *Clarias lazera* and *Protopterus aethiopicus*. Gwahaba (1973) discusses effects of 20 years fishing.

For this lake we now have a unique picture of biomasses at various trophic levels in a tropical lake and assessments of grazing rates. The midlake total standing crop biomass of *c.* 50 g C/m^2 is made up mainly of phytoplankton (46·8 g C/m^2), with zooplankton (0·5 g C/m^2), *Chaoborus* larvae (Diptera) predators on the zooplankton (0·2 g C/m^2), benthos of chironomid larvae, ostracods, oligochaetes, etc. (0·3 g C/m^2), herbivorous fish (0·9 g C/m^2), and carnivorous fish (0·5 g C/m^2). These biomasses remain very close to these levels throughout the year, in contrast with those in temperate zone waters which may equal those in Lake George at peak times, but drop far below these levels in winter.

The very abundant phytoplankton, mainly of *Microcystis* and other blue-green algae, is cropped by the zooplankton and three herbivorous fish species: *Haplochromis nigripinnis*, *Tilapia nilotica* and *T. leucosticta* (the latter also taking some detritus from the bottom). Zooplankton is cropped by *H.*

pappenheimi, the cyprinodont *Aplocheilichthys* and young fish including young *Tilapia*, and the benthos is utilised by *H. angustifrons* and other *Haplochromis* species. Piscivorous fishes include *Bagrus docmac*, *H. squamipinnis*, *Protopterus aethiopicus* and *Clarias lazera*; the latter two include invertebrates (particularly molluscs in *Protopterus*) and debris in their diet.

Extensive sampling of the open water with two purse seines (120 m long by 20 m deep, and 50 m by 8·5 m) indicated that the ichthyomasses ranged from 6 g/m^2 in the centre of the lake to 90 g/m^2 near one shore (with a mean ichthyomass of 22 g (fresh weight)/m^2). The relative ichthyomasses of the more important species distributed throughout the open waters of the lake were as follows (Burgis *et al.*, 1973):

herbivores: *H. nigripinnis* 6·4 g/m^2; *T. nilotica* 2·9 g/m^2; *T. leucosticta* 0·6 g/m^2;

benthos-feeder: *H. angustifrons* 2·5 g/m^2;

piscivores: *Protopterus* 1·4 g/m^2; *Clarias* 1·2 g/m^2; *Bagrus* 0·5 g/m^2; *H. squamipinnis* 0·4 g/m^2;

zooplankton-feeders: *Aplocheilichthys* 0·3 g/m^2; *H. pappenheimi* 0·02 g/m^2.

The general conclusion was reached that the herbivorous fishes are not limited by their food supply. Nor does predation appear very intense. What then does limit the fish populations? For some of the cichlids suitable areas for spawning may be limiting in this soft-bottomed lake. In aquaria in the Netherlands Lake George *Haplochromis* spawn in the usual manner of mouth-breeding cichlids, the males establishing territories (Barel, personal communication), though how the fishes communicate with one another in the soupy opaque water of Lake George is not yet known (a point discussed by Greenwood, 1973*a*).

In Lake George fishes in breeding condition were present throughout the year, comprising 20 per cent of the mature population in the case of *Tilapia nilotica*, with peaks of over 50 per cent in the two rainy seasons (C. M. Moriarty, 1973). *T. nilotica* living in cages of large-meshed netlon floating in the lake grew from 3 cm to 19·5 cm TL in 7½ months; in the cages some males started to attain breeding colours when 15 or 16 cm long and then became aggressive. The spawning peaks enabled the growth of a cohort of young *T. nilotica* to be traced from the progression of length frequency modes (Gwahaba, personal communication), and the growth rate so estimated agreed well with data from growth in the floating cages.

The Lake George phytoplankton is dominated by bluegreen algae, particularly *Microcystic* which Fish (1951) had stated were not digested by *Tilapia*, so the digestive physiology of these phytoplankton-feeding fishes and herbivorous zooplankters was studied in some detail (Moriarty and Moriarty, 1973). Both *T. nilotica* and *Haplochromis nigripinnis* were found to have a diurnal feeding cycle, starting to feed shortly before dawn and feeding continuously until about dusk. There was a linear increase in the average dry weights of stomach contents from dawn to dusk, and the quantities ingested were linearly related to the weight of the fish, all except the very small fish (less than 5 to 6 cm) ingesting mainly phytoplankton. The smaller fishes of both species were omnivorous. Digestion in *T. nilotica* occurs in the intestine, but only if the plankton cells have been lysed by acid in the stomach. Here secretion of acid also follows a diurnal cycle, commencing when the fish start to feed in the morning, but ceasing if the fish are in any way stressed. When acid secretion ceases, the food passes through the fish undigested and the faeces then turn from brown to green, a useful indication that stress has occurred. This also provided a marker for the rate of passage of food through the alimentary canal. The first algae ingested in the day (at *c.* 0500 hours) reach the anus around 1200 hours (taking about seven hours to pass through the gut in *T. nilotica* and about six hours in *H. nigripinnis*). The rate of passage is faster during feeding than after feeding has stopped. Using unialgal cultures labelled with ^{14}C it was shown that *T. nilotica* can assimilate 70 to 80 per cent of carbon from *Microcystis*, *Anabaena* and *Nitzchia*, compared with only about 50 per cent from the green alga *Chlorella*. Over the daily feeding cycle *T. nilotica* assimilate about 43 per cent per day of the ingested carbon from phytoplankton, and *H. nigripinnis* about 66 per cent. As not all the ingested phytoplankton is digested, undigested algae can be observed in the rectum especially in the late morning. A visual examination of the gut contents may thus lead to false conclusions about the value of food items, and it is necessary to study the feeding and digestion pattern through the twenty-four-hour cycle.

Quantitative studies were made of the grazing rates and ejection of faeces by the main herbivores in the lake (Moriarty *et al.*, 1973). Total daily ingestion rates of phytoplankton were found to be very similar in *Tilapia nilotica* and *Haplochromis nigripinnis*: 53 and 50 mg (dry weight)/m^2/day (equivalent to 17·5 and 16·5 mg C/m^2/d respectively, nearly thirty times less than the 504 mg C/m^2/d ingested by the dominant element of the zooplankton *Thermocyclops hyalinus*). Phytoplankton material was deposited as faeces at an equivalent rate of 6·5 mg C/m^2/d in both fish species (compared with 216 and 72 mg C/m^2/d in the raptorial and nauplii stages of *Thermocyclops*).

These calculated grazing rates showed that only a small proportion of the phytoplankton standing crop is eaten daily. The conclusion was reached that the net primary production seems adequate to maintain this cropping rate and to stand grazing and losses from other sources as well, and the authors suggested that food is not a limiting factor at least for the adult stages of the various vertebrate and invertebrate herbivores of Lake George.

Despite the abundance of phytoplankton-feeding fishes in this lake, the zooplankton has a more important role than these fishes in the turnover of nutrients, as zooplankter life cycles are so much shorter and their specific excretion and respiratory rates suggest that their metabolic rates are faster than those of the fishes.

Lake George has relatively few species in its flora and fauna compared with many other tropical waters. Burgis *et al.* (1973) attributed this partly to lack of seasonal succession, the same species being dominant throughout the year and from year to year. The biomass in this lake is dominated by phytoplankton to a remarkable extent (phytoplankton making up 95 per cent of the total biomass, and 99 per cent of the total plankton including the *Chaoborus*), and this provides a constant supply of food for herbivores able to use it. The remainder of the fauna is determined by the relatively limited types of food and uniformity of habitat across the lake. Greater variations in sources of food occur inshore, but the inshore zone is limited by the shape of the lake.

In Lake George it is clear that the majority of the photosynthetically fixed energy flow is through the primary producers and that proportionately little is transferred to higher trophic levels; the herbivorous fauna has been shown to be unlikely to be food limited, and the system as a whole appears to be inefficient in the transfer of solar energy from the primary to other trophic levels (Ganf and Viner, 1973).

In this lake occasional mass fish kills occur at infrequent intervals, probably under climatic conditions which lead to deoxygenation of the water column, as when sudden storms occur after long calm periods. Huge numbers of fishes, of species without accessory respiratory organs, were killed at one time during the six year study.* Such events, and calculations on the oxygen budget of the water, emphasize that the ecological stability of the lake depends on a delicately balanced equilibrium between climate and biota.

Lake Chad

Lake Chad presents an interesting contrast to the East African Great Lakes as it lacks endemic cichlids. This is perhaps not surprising, for, although a very large lake it is shallow and almost dries out at intervals. Once three times the size of the present Lake Victoria, in this century Chad has oscillated in size between 24 500 km^2 and considerably less than 8000 km^2. Lake Chad lies in very dry country, from 12° N to 14° 20′ N, just south of the Sahara, and is an inland drainage area with no outflowing river. The ecology of its fishes has been investigated as part of a comprehensive limnological study of the lake under the International Biological Programme by a French team (Carmouze *et al.*, 1972), and in the northwestern Nigerian waters of the lake the biology of *Lates niloticus*, *Alestes baremose* and some other fishes has also been studied in some detail (A. J. Hopson, 1972; J. Hopson, 1972) (Fig. 4.3).

Lake Chad is divided into two basins. The northern basin is more lacustrine, the southern basin greatly influenced by the seasonal inflows of the large rivers of the Chari/Logone system, which drain wetter regions far away to the south. During these studies, made from 1965 to 1972, the open water of the north basin was about 4000 km^2, the depth 4 to 7 m, while the open waters of the south were shallower (2 to 4 m); during this period the main lake level declined by over 2 m. Carmouze *et al.* (1972) commented that extensions of floating macrophytes might speed the separation of the basins by obstructing water flow, and the drought in 1973 divided the lake into three parts. The north basin is known to have dried out completely in 1907–8.

* Gwahaba (1973) reported *c.* 150,000 *T. nilotica* killed during one of three fish kills during this study.

The lake has three main ecological zones: open water; the archipelago of islands, flooded sand dunes colonised by vegetation, mainly along the east and southeast coasts; and the south coast which receives the inflowing rivers. Evaporation is very high, and conductivity increases very much towards the north, from where it appears to limit elements of the fauna, as oligochaetes, benthic snails, and mormyrid fishes are not found in the north. The fish fauna has many more species in the southeastern archipelago than in the northern basin.

Lake Chad is far enough north for a winter fall in temperature to affect fish growth in the northern basin. In the south the biology of the fishes is governed mainly by the seasonal inflows of the great rivers. Daget (1967)

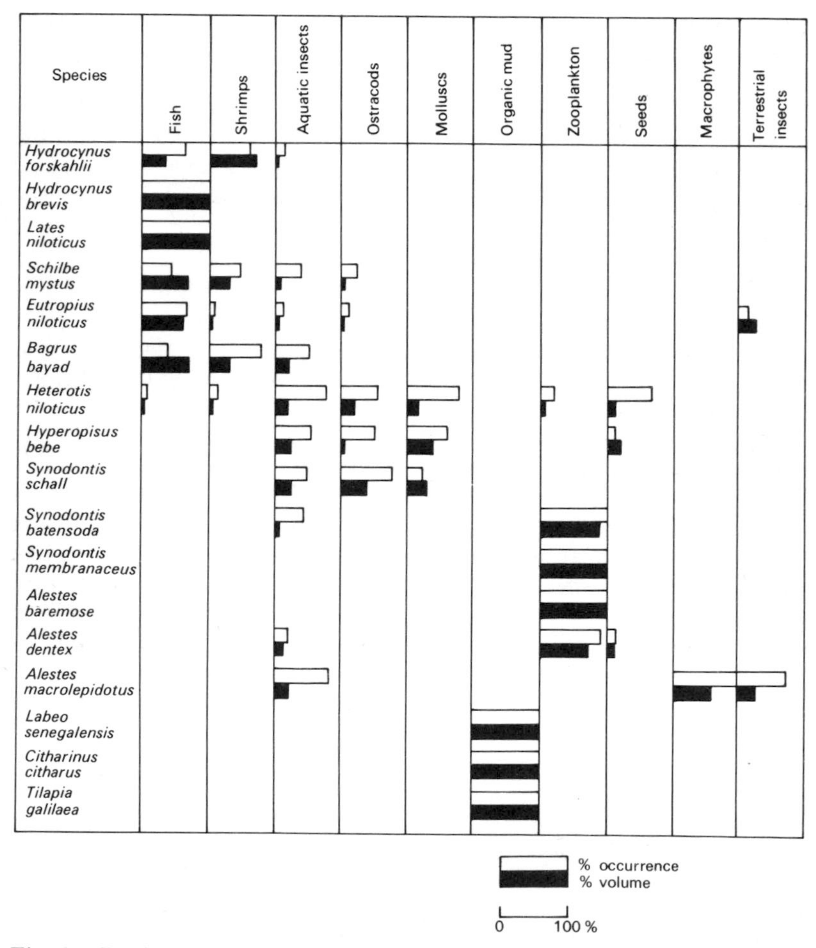

Fig. 6.3 Food habits of the principal fish species from the eastern archipelago of Lake Chad (after Lauzanne, 1972).

regarded Chad as an extension of these river systems in which fluviatile species had decreased in importance while stillwater species had flourished; this appears to be particularly true of the southern basin, while the northern one has a more truly lacustrine character.

The foods consumed by the seventeen principal fish species in the southeast archipelago were studied by Lauzanne (1972) (Fig. 6.3). Here the fishes fell into four main groups:

1. detritus-eaters (*Tilapia galilaea*, *Labeo senegalensis*, *Citharinus citharus*);
2. carnivores taking mainly zooplankton (*Alestes baremose*, *A. dentex*, *Synodontis membranaceous*, *S. batensoda*);
3. carnivores taking mainly benthic invertebrates (*Heterotis niloticus*, *Hyperopisus bebe*, *Synodontis schall*);
4. terminal carnivores taking mainly fishes, either (*a*) true predators feeding on live fish (*Hydrocynus forskahlii*, *H. brevis*, *Lates niloticus*), or (*b*) predators with a tendency to scavenge dead fish (*Bagrus bayad*, *Eutropius niloticus*, *Schilbe mystus*).

In this southeast archipelago zooplankton-feeders predominated, making 44 per cent of the total catch by weight, whereas benthic feeders comprised only 5 per cent, detritus feeders 17 per cent, and terminal carnivores 25 per cent (Lauzanne, 1972). However, elsewhere in the lake the feeding regimes were not necessarily the same, and the proportions of fishes in these various categories were probably different.

The lake has several macrophyte-feeders (such as *Distichodus rostratus*). Lauzanne found that phytoplankton-feeders were rare; phytoplankton was used mainly by young fishes of numerous species, and was also taken from the bottom by the numerous detritus feeders. Zooplankton was utilised by *Micralestes acutidens* and the endemic ubiquitous *Alestes dageti*, while some was ingested by the mormyrid *Pollimyrus isidori* which also eats insects. Oligochaetes were scarcely cropped, only *Mormyrus rume* took them occasionally. Molluscs did not appear to be an important food source in the southeast archipelago, though *Hyperopisus bebe* and *Synodontis schall* took them together with other items, and fishes less common here, such as *Synodontis clarias*, *Tetraodon fahaka* and *Chrysichthys auratus*, also take them, but in the open water of the southeast molluscs are the essential food of five species (*H. bebe*, *S. schall*, *S. frontosus*, *S. clarias* and *T. fahaka*).

Aquatic insects were found to be less important as food in the open water (where they were however important food for *Pollimyrus bane* and *P. isidori*) than in the southeast archipelago. Here they were found in stomachs of numerous species, but never formed the exclusive food of any one species. They were dominant food items for the mormyrids *H. bebe*, *M. rume*, *P. bane* (Hemiptera), and *Marcusenius cyprinoides* (chironomids), and a secondary source of food for *P. isidori*, and also found in *Heterotis niloticus*, *S. schall*, *S. frontosus*, *C. auratus*, *Auchenoglanis biscutatus* and *S. clarias*.

The terminal carnivores feed on different species and sizes of prey fish. In the southeast archipelago, *Lates* catch mainly *Labeo* and *Tilapia*, *H. brevis* smaller prey such as *S. batensoda* and *P. bane*, and *H. forskahlii* even smaller prey, *Micralestes*, *Barbus*, *Haplochromis* and especially prawns. However, in the open water *H. forskahlii*'s main prey were *Micralestes* and *Pollimyrus* and very few prawns.

The distribution of fish within the lake was examined in relation to the distribution of food organisms and physical and chemical factors. Among the predators *Lates niloticus* was common everywhere but *H. brevis* only in the southern basin; both take diverse prey and available foods could not apparently explain this difference in distribution. Among the detritus feeders *Tilapia galilaea* was found in sheltered waters and *Citharinus citharus* in open water. Of the benthic feeders the mormyrid distribution appeared to be governed by water conductivity as well as availability of insect prey; mollusc-feeders lived where molluscs were most abundant, but *Chrysichthys auratus* was absent from open water. The zooplankton-feeders showed variable distributions: *A. dageti* was ubiquitous, *S. membranaceous* and *S. batensoda* most abundant in the southern basin (the latter in sheltered water); *P. isidori* (like other mormyrids) was absent from the north basin, and *Alestes baremose* and *A. dentex* were absent from open waters. This latter case was particularly significant as although *A. baremose* distribution corresponded with zooplankton density in the southeast archipelago, in the north it was always restricted to sheltered zones although the density of zooplankton was higher in open water. (In Lake Volta *A. baremose* takes very different food, fish, higher plants and insects, Lawson *et al.*, 1969.)

The conclusion was reached by the French team that in Lake Chad the search for food does not seem to be a determining factor in the distribution of the fishes; there is a great variety of available foods, and the feeding regimes of most of the predatory fishes show great plasticity. But the team suggested that where there are large concentrations of predatory fishes these may limit the density of prey organisms, such as of certain benthic invertebrates.

Studies on the biology of the predatory *Lates niloticus* (Nile perch) in Lake Chad by A. J. Hopson (1972) showed that the food eaten varied very much with the size of the *Lates*, the biotope within the lake, and the time of year. Changes occurred with the abundance of food organisms, but there was also evidence of the selection of particular food items. The general pattern was of planktonic larval *Lates* (0·3 to 1·35 cm total length) selecting Cladocera (in preference to copepods), post larval fishes up to 20 cm TL feeding on larger invertebrates, including insects, prawns especially *Macrobrachium niloticum*, some molluscs with the mud-living gastropod *Melania tuberculata* predominating, and small fishes. These *Lates* up to 20 cm long live amongst aquatic plants along the shores for about one year; on open shores lacking weed cover cannabalism occurs amongst them. *Lates* longer than 30 cm may still be caught inshore, but the majority live offshore where they have a diet mainly of prawns and fish. When about 80 cm long the diet changes to one of large fishes, though even quite large *Lates* turn to prawns in the summer months. Fishes eaten include *Hydrocynus*, *Alestes* species (including the pelagic *A. dageti*) schilbeids especially *Eutropius niloticus*, and *Synodontis*, the latter two mostly in winter. The change in diet with increasing size in offshore *Lates* is shown in Fig. 6.4. Prey fish up to 50 per cent of the predator's length were taken (even by very small *Lates*), but spines reduced the size of

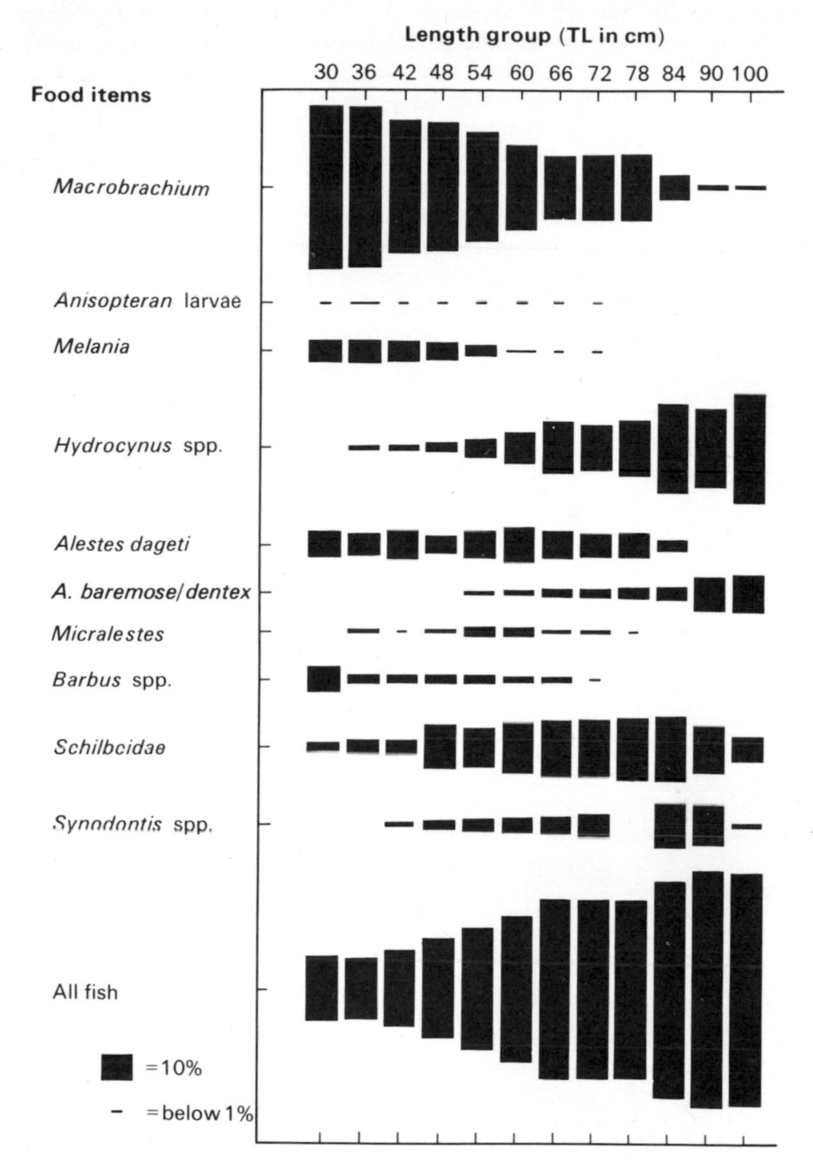

Fig. 6.4 Changes in the diet of 'offshore' *Lates niloticus* with size in Lake Chad. The number of points scored by each food item has been expressed as a percentage of the total points for each length group (after A. J. Hopson, 1972).

prey swallowed and the three-pronged *Synodontis* never exceeded 18 per cent of the predator's length (Fig. 10.1).

Lates niloticus is well adapted for lacustrine existence as it spawns in the lake and has pelagic eggs and larvae (A. J. Hopson, 1969, 1972). Winter checks in growth enabled ages and growth rates to be determined (Fig. 9.1B). The predatory *Lates* showed marked changes in diet with size (Fig. 6.4), season, and habitat (as discussed on p. 213). Prawns and small pelagic characids were generally the most important foods of *Lates* up to 80 cm TL, at which size they turned to a diet of larger fishes, a change reflected in the growth rate as described below (p. 203).

Scale studies of the growth of *Alestes baremose* in Lake Chad showed that there are two forms of this species in the lake, one which migrates up the inflowing rivers to spawn, and a lacustrine one which evidently spawns in the lake, a kind of incipient speciation; Lake Albert also has riverine and lacustrine forms of this species (J. Hopson, 1972).

7

Manmade Lakes

The significance of manmade lakes for fish community studies

The creation of a new lake behind a hydroelectric dam provides a natural experiment by which to study how riverine species become adapted for lacustrine life, and how faunas change and new lacustrine communities are formed. Within the tropics many very large lakes have been created in recent years, several of which have stimulated a great deal of ecological research. In Africa the largest of these are L. Kariba on the Zambezi, L. Volta on the Volta River in Ghana, L. Kainji on the River Niger in Nigeria and L. Nasser on the River Nile (Fig. 2.3). In Surinam (in northeastern South America) the changes in the new van Blommestein lake at Brokopondo have been studied in some detail. In Asia fish communities in the many large new lakes in the Mekong system are being investigated. Three symposia have brought together much information on these tropical lakes (Lowe-McConnell, 1966; Obeng, 1968; Ackermann *et al.*, 1973).

In temperate regions where the biology of fishes in manmade lakes has been studied over a much longer period, particularly in U.S.S.R. and U.S.A., the general sequence of events as the lake forms is now well known. The new lake will be colonised by riverine fishes (unless steps are taken to prevent this and to stock with other fish). Some of these will manage to adapt themselves to the new conditions, others will drop out of the fauna. New lakes, therefore, tend to have less complex faunas than their river systems. But after the new lake has stabilised, species from elsewhere in the river system may gain access to it, and the numbers of lacustrine species will then increase. As the lake level rises, it floods the surrounding land and the rotting vegetation liberates abundant nutrients. This leads to an explosive development of fish food. The fishes that can take advantage of the abundant new foods offered at this time, and those which can spawn under the new conditions, will become very abundant. As these nutrients are used up a 'trophic depression phase' sets in, the lake becoming much less productive. Eventually as organic matter accumulates the lake stabilises at a new level, with fish production generally slightly raised again, though not as high as in the initial stages. Fish spawning grounds may be reduced in area by fluctuations in lake level when the water is used for hydroelectric power.

In the U.S.S.R. this sequence of events has been studied in lakes at various latitudes, and it has been shown that lakes stabilize more rapidly at the higher temperatures in lower latitudes (6–10 years south of latitude 55° N, compared with 25–30 years north of this). In the tropics lakes may therefore be expected to stabilize even more quickly. Lake Kariba, the first large manmade lake in the tropics to be studied in detail, stabilized about 10 years after dam closure in 1958 (Balon and Coche, 1974, fig. 99).

The inevitable decline in catches after the initial outburst in a new lake has to be kept in mind when planning fishery development. In high-latitude lakes, where the fishes take several years to reach maturity, emphasis is rightly on protecting fishes in the initial years to allow the building up of breeding stocks. In tropical lakes where the fish life cycles are short and so many species are present, bumper catches can in many cases be made in the early years without, it seems, detriment to long-term fishery development. But these catches attract many fishermen to the new lake, and there is a temptation to overcapitalise on fishing gear at this stage, forgetting that catches will inevitably fall in later years. In Lake Volta fishermen found it increasingly difficult to repay loans for fishing gear as catches declined.

A new lake offers greatly expanded feeding grounds, but often of different types of food than those available in the river (such as increased plankton). Many riverine fishes feed on algae, insects and other invertebrates from rocky and stony bottoms, and as the new lake forms these bottoms often lie in deoxygenated water forcing the fishes to seek other foods. In the case of L. Volta described below, the epiphytic algae and insect fauna on the trees and bushes in the flooded riverine forest provided important replacement foods when bottom waters were deoxygenated.

Adaptations to spawn may be much more difficult. Many species will continue to attempt to reach affluent streams in which to spawn, and some of these may be lost to the fauna (as has happened in L. Volta). Finding their way to such streams through the still waters of the lake may present problems to the fish. Many species (characoids, cyprinids, catfishes) will continue to migrate up affluent rivers or streams to spawn and drop back to the lake to feed. On the other hand, populations of fishes able to spawn in still waters amongst flooded vegetation may build up very rapidly as the new lake forms. The cichlid fishes which spawn in still water are eminently pre-adapted to take advantage of the new lacustrine conditions.

On an evolutionary scale, Corbet (1960) recognised four hypothetical stages in the colonisation of lakes from rivers, fishes: (1) feeding and breeding only in rivers; (2) feeding in lakes and breeding in rivers; (3) feeding and breeding in both lakes and rivers; (4) feeding and breeding in lakes only (endemic species). He postulated that wave-washed rocky shores provide the nearest conditions in lakes to riverine spawning places, allowing riverine fishes to colonise lakes by this route, for the eggs and young are least well adapted to the new conditions. Manmade lake studies allow us to see these changes in action, for example, in L. Volta, *Leptotilapia irvinei*, previously known only from the Volta rapids, is now found in rocky places in the new lake. McLachlan (1974) discussed the development of new African lakes with special reference to the invertebrates, important sources of fish food.

Lake Kariba

Lake Kariba (Fig. 2.4) started to form in December 1958 when the dam across the Zambezi River was closed. It is now a 5364 km^2 lake 120 m deep, with a mean depth of 29 m and an annual drawdown of 9 m. Prior to its formation this area of the Middle Zambezi had a very seasonal flow and a fish fauna of only about 28 large species (Jackson, 1961*a*, and Table 8.2). After the dam was closed the water continued to rise for four and a half years before the lake reached its final level. During this period certain of these fish species increased their growth rates enormously, and became very abundant. This was particularly noticeable for the predatory characid *Hydrocynus vittatus*; in the Zambezi River this grew to 25 cm in two years, in the natal year of the lake it grew to 21 cm in one year, but by 1966 the growth rate had slowed to 26–30 cm in two years (Bowmaker, 1970). In addition to the riverine fishes the lake was stocked between 1959 and 1961 with some 26 tons of juveniles of two *Tilapia* species: *Tilapia macrochir* (66 per cent) and *Tilapia rendalli* (then called *Tilapia melanopleura*) (34 per cent), in an attempt to build up *Tilapia* stocks. *Tilapia macrochir* is an Upper Zambezi species, absent from the Middle Zambezi until it was stocked here as it was thought that it would thrive better than would the local species under the new conditions. *Tilapia rendalli* was already present in the Middle Zambezi but in small numbers. However, this stocking of *T. macrochir* failed completely, and in later years it was the indigenous *Tilapia mortimeri*, a Middle Zambezi species previously thought to be *Tilapia mossambica*, that became abundant in the new lake.

Once the lake was established ($4\frac{1}{2}$ yr) species new to the fauna started to appear. These were mainly Upper Zambezi or tributary dwelling species. The former may have dropped down over the Victoria Falls, the latter come from headwater streams elsewhere in the system.* Presumably occasional individuals did this in the past, but did not have the right conditions to get established until the new lake was formed. These new arrivals included *Labeo lunatus* and *L. cylindricus*, many small *Barbus* species, the ubiquitous catfish *Schilbe mystus*, the mormyrid *Marcusenius macrolepidotus*, the cichlids *Sargochromis giardi*, *Haplochromis carlottae*, *Tilapia andersonii*, *Serranochromis* species, *Pseudocrenilabris philander*, and the characid *Alestes lateralis*. The latter species appears to have more or less replaced *Brachyalestes imberi* in the new lake, and to have pushed out to exploit the pelagic zone until checked by the rapid expansion of the introduced *Limnothrissa miodon* in this niche (Balon, 1972). The catadromous eel *Anguilla*

* Discussed in Balon and Coche (1974, pp. 478–97).

nebulosa labiata worked its way up into the lake and became abundant at depths of 20 to 45 m.

This sudden replacement of *Brachyalestes imberi* by *Alestes lateralis* was probably explained by their different spawning biology and was not a matter of closely related species competing for food (Balon, 1971*b*). *B. imberi*, which is possibly better adapted to riverine conditions and to water without vegetation, spawns in the rainy season when the rising water level inundates grassy shores, conditions it found in Lake Kariba until 1963 when the operating level was reached. Thereafter the water level was artificially lowered in the rains (reservoir management), and this species lost its spawning grounds. *A. lateralis*, able to spawn on submerged flora, such as roots of the floating *Salvinia*, suddenly found exceptionally good spawning conditions in the new lake, and the population must then have built up from stray individuals possibly washed over the edge of the Victoria Falls.

Limnothrissa miodon from Lake Tanganyika was introduced in 1967 and 1968, and has since become abundant in the new lake.* Echo-sounder traces show that, as in Lake Tanganyika, small clupeids undergo diurnal vertical migrations in their new environment, but instead of rising right to the surface of Kariba at night they remain at about 8 m depth.

Lake Kariba is far enough south for fish scales and bones to show growth checks (Balon, 1972) enabling the growth rates and production of the twenty main commercial species to be estimated. The lake also offered especial opportunities for biomass determination, as an echo-sounder survey showed that the majority of the fishes live close to the shore and the many coves and bays made chemofishing feasible. Thus for Lake Kariba we have a picture of the biomass, production and yield of fish unique for a tropical or subtropical lake (Balon and Coche, 1974; Balon, 1974; information received too late for consideration here).

In Lake Kariba Balon (1972) noted a 'highly positive relationship' between nutrient contents and fish production (although attempts to relate fish production to primary production failed). The Zambezi River here had 26 p.p.m. TDS (total dissolved solids) before dam closure; after lake formation (prior to 1963) these rose to 65 p.p.m. TDS; after the lake had reached its final size in 1964–5 they then fell off rather suddenly to around 42 p.p.m. TDS and they stabilized around this level. Fish landings rose to a peak around 1963, although the diversity of species was then somewhat depressed, as several riverine species had dropped out of the fauna and the new immigrant species had not yet arrived (Balon and Coche, 1974, figure 99). These events demonstrated that fish yields depend on nutrient input rather than on species diversity.

The echo-sounding survey showed that Kariba fishes were concentrated inshore in water less than 30 m deep, living mainly in coves and bays, with a maximum in water 5 m deep by day and 10 m at night; at night some fish moved up to 2 km offshore. Around islands with steep shores fish were

* But failed to develop into a fishable stock (Balon and Coche, 1974, p. 541).

found only in coves and strips a few metres wide close to the shore. The fish were thus concentrated into an area estimated to be only 6·2 per cent of the whole lake area. The chemofishing was carried out in several coves, stream estuaries and on shorelines with three sides blocked by 8 mm mesh nets. Areas of from 0·5 to 5 ha were treated, using 5 per cent rotenone or 75 per cent toxaphene.

The Chikanka Island cove, 12 100 m^2 and mean depth 1·8 m, when treated produced 4149 fishes representing 28 species and equivalent to 3427 fishes/ha totalling 261 kg/ha. An inshore bay at Saivonga and a rocky island shore nearby produced fewer fishes (1139 fish/ha totalling 12 kg/ha and 1399 fish/ha totalling 34·48 kg/ha respectively). In the Chikanka Island cove *Alestes lateralis* was the most abundant species (1454 fish/ha, 42 per cent of the total number of fish), but its share of the ichthyomass was small (0·7 per cent, 1·87 kg/ha). The main ichthyomass here was of *Tilapia* species. Summarising catches from many inshore areas Balon (1973) found the highest mean standing crop to be of *Tilapia mortimeri* (97 kg/ha), followed closely by the mormyrids *Hippopotamyrus discorhynchus* (96 kg/ha) and *Mormyrops deliciosus* (92 kg/ha), *Tilapia rendalli* (56 kg/ha), *Clarias gariepinus* (52 kg/ha), and the completely unexpected electric catfish *Malapterurus electricus* (48 kg/ha), with smaller standing crops of *Hydrocynus vittatus*, *Alestes lateralis*, *Synodontis zambesensis*, *Mormyrus longirostris*, *Heterobranchus longifilis*, *Sargochromis codringtoni*, *Eutropius depressirostris*, *Labeo altivelis*, and *Haplochromis darlingi*. Balon noted, however, that the values held only for the years under study and were biased by sampling errors. The inshore areas of the lake inhabited by fish (33 422 ha representing 6·2 per cent of the lake area) were estimated to have a standing crop of 17 814 t, of which 64 per cent was of the 17 economically preferred species, 30 per cent of the 8 secondary species, and 6 per cent of 14 accompanying species. Preliminary estimates of production of preferred species were 686 kg/ha/yr, giving an available yield of 219 kg/ha/yr (7319 t/yr). Balon commented that the very rough estimates of catches from Lake Kariba for the year under study represented 56 kg/ha for the total lake area or 90 kg/ha for the fish inhabited area (compared with an annual harvest from the equatorial Lake George of *c.* 1850 kg/ha, of which 80 per cent is *Tilapia nilotica*). Balon and Coche (1974) should be consulted for full details and final estimates of production in Lake Kariba at this time.

The age, growth, and production of the predatory *Hydrocynus vittatus*, one of the most important fishes in the lake, was studied by Balon (1971*a*). Ages were determined from scale rings (II age group fish here included fish of I+ to II+, not fish that have achieved two complete years, see p. 202). In Kariba *H. vittatus* of O to IV age groups lived in the coves, and II to IV group fishes (over 38 cm long) were caught in gillnets. Fishes of each age group showed a large length variability. Back-calculated lengths (see p. 201) of juvenile marks and individual growth seasons increased with the age and size of the fish (contrary to 'Rosa Lee's paradox' well known for marine fish), which Balon interpreted to mean that faster-growing individuals of

H. vittatus survive better. Calculating fish production is a laborious process as it has to be calculated for each age group separately. The Kariba *H. vittatus* population was found by Balon to reach a maximum weight in age group III (i.e. II+ to III+ fish).

The fish preyed on by *H. vittatus* are mainly Cichlidae or Characidae, either of which will dominate in the diet according to its availability (Matthes, 1968). When characids were common in the diet, skin diving operations confirmed their abundance in large shoals, while the cichlids were then relatively scarce except for *Tilapia* fry and small *Haplochromis* hiding in weedy shallows where they were not easily available. When summer-born cichlids grow and move into deeper water seeking shelter among drowned trees they become more susceptible to predation. The percentage of foods eaten other than fish varied from almost none to over 34 per cent of the diet according to the area and conditions. Prey species (and their overall percentage occurrence in the diet) included the following: *Micralestes acutidens* (23 per cent); *Alestes lateralis* (18 per cent); *Haplochromis* (10 per cent); *Tilapia* species (15 per cent); *Aplocheilichthys johnstoni* (8 per cent); *Barbus* (5 per cent); mormyrids (2 per cent); *Synodontis* (2 per cent).

H. vittatus cease to feed on plankton when above 10 cm long; some individuals may include fish in their diet when less than 5 cm long, and individuals over 55 cm long continue to eat some insects (Matthes, 1968). Data on foods eaten by *H. vittatus* in other lakes and rivers summarised by Matthes show the same mixtures of fish of many species (including their own young), insects (aquatic insects, and termites and grasshoppers in the rainy season in South African rivers), shrimps, Entomostraca, water plants and even mud.

Volta Lake

The Volta Lake in Ghana, covering more than 8000 km^2 is one of the largest manmade lakes in the world. Less deep than Kariba (70 m as opposed to 120 m), it lies nearer to the equator (6° to 9° N), with a rainy season starting in May followed by floods until October, the outflow being about one quarter of its volume and the annual drawdown 3 m (see Fig. 4.3). The Volta dam was closed in May 1964, and as relatively little of the riverine forest and bush was cleared (owing to the expense of clearing), rapid deoxygenation led to fish deaths. In the more open waters oxygen extended to a greater depth, but at about 20 m there was an abrupt discontinuity and in the deeper waters there was virtually no oxygen (Lawson *et al.*, 1969). As the lake filled, which it did very gradually over a series of years until about 1971, there was more extensive mixing of the water, so that more oxygen became available in the deeper water (as also happened in Kariba). As a result, the duration of periods of deoxygenation when the lake was stratified in the dry season diminished and the lake became an increasingly attractive environment for fishes. The Volta River flows in at the northern end, where conditions remained more riverine than in the south where the lake is broader.

The Volta Lake is low in nutrients, with a low standing crop of phytoplankton, and the aufwuchs on the drowned trees formed the main basis of the food webs, supporting surprisingly high catches of fishes in the early years after impoundment. The fishes comprised potamodromous species (*Alestes*, *Citharinus*, *Distichodus*, *Labeo*) especially at the north end of the lake from where they moved into tributary rivers in the wet season, and species which spawned within the basin, either annually (*Lates niloticus*) or throughout the year (*Tilapia* species). The potamodromous species rely heavily on the flood-plains as feeding areas during the rainy season. Rotenone sampling of 150 m^2 areas of the littoral zone between September 1969 and March 1971 produced an ichthyomass of *c.* 155 kg/ha, the openshore line for some unexplained reason supporting a larger ichthyomass than the coves (Regier and Wright, 1972, summarising studies by Ryder and Loiselle).

Apart from a sudden fish kill just after dam closure, studies by Petr (1967–71) showed that most of the Volta river fish throve initially in the new lacustrine conditions. Exceptions were the mormyrids, which almost completely disappeared from the south end of the lake. Cichlids became very common in the south. The predominance of insectivorous fishes in the Volta River gave way to predominantly herbivorous and plankton-feeding fish. The mormyrids which are bottom-feeding may have vanished because their benthic insect food supply was submerged by deoxygenated water. After the first two years characid and cyprinid fishes (such as *Alestes* except for one species, and *Labeo*) also disappeared from the south. These may either have migrated up rivers to spawn and failed to return, or died out if they did not find suitable spawning grounds. Species common in Black Volta river samples became limited to the northern arm of the lake where the Black and White Volta Rivers flow into the lake.

Tilapia, on the other hand, flourished and fairly rapidly became the dominant fishes in most of the lake. Three species are present, *T. galilaea* which here feeds mainly on phytoplankton, *T. nilotica*, which takes periphytic algae, and *T. zillii* which feeds on submerged grass and detritus.

The bark of the flooded trees was found to develop a rich growth of periphyton, and the burrowing nymphs of the ephemeropteran *Povilla*

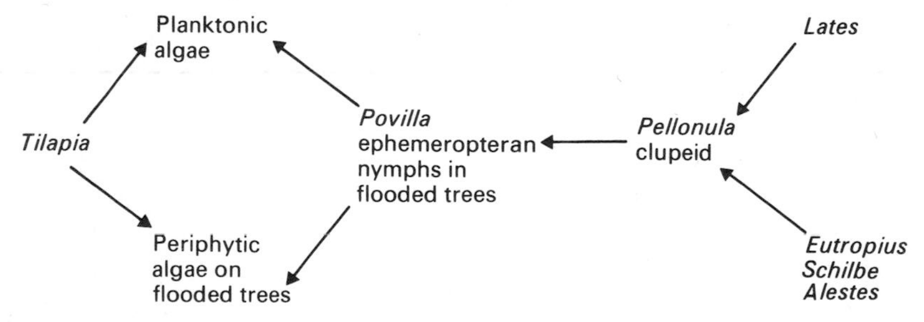

Fig. 7.1 Trophic relationships between the most important organisms in the Volta Lake in its first six years (after Petr, 1971).

adusta became exceedingly abundant in the dead trees. These were found to provide a source of food for species which had formerly been general feeders in the rivers, such as *Schilbe mystus* and *Eutropius niloticus*; providing a good example of a generalised feeder in the river taking to a more specialised source of food in a new environment. However, these same species also fed on the freshwater clupeid *Pellonula afzeliusi* which had become very numerous in the open waters of the lake and formed the major food item of both the Nile perch *Lates niloticus* and the smaller common predatory cichlid *Hemichromis fasciatus*.

In this new lake the flooded trees with their flora of periphyton and fauna of *Povilla*, have been a major element in the unexpectedly high production of fish, for this lake produced about ten times the weight of fish produced by Kariba in the early years after impoundment (Fig. 7.1). What will happen when the trees rot and this source of food disappears?

Ecological studies of the clupeids in Volta Lake appear to be the first of how pelagic fishes adapt to life in a new tropical lake (Reynolds, 1969–74). There are about 20 species of clupeids more or less adapted to freshwater life in tropical Africa, though many are restricted to estuaries and the lower courses of rivers: Lakes Tanganyika and Mweru have endemic species. The West African rivers from Senegal to the Niger harbour species of the *Pellonula* complex, to which the two Volta species, *Cynothrissa mento* and *Pellonula afzeliusi*, belong. The former species, which grows larger (to 170 mm total length) remained in the more riverine areas in the north of Volta Lake, and may undertake longitudinal migrations up-river to spawn, but the smaller *P. afzeliusi* (growing to 98 mm total length) became common and fairly evenly distributed throughout the new lake.

Both species undertake diurnal vertical migrations to and from the surface waters of the new lake. They appear in small compact shoals at the surface around 1730 hours. As the light fails groups become diffused and individuals disperse in surface waters where they feed actively on emerging insects. They remain close to the surface in bright moonlight, and are attracted to a light source. These feeding associations in Volta lake often contain other fish species, notably the transparent schilbeid catfish *Physailia pellucida* (up to 40 per cent of the feeding shoal) and *Barbus macrops* (up to 10 per cent), also the cyprinid *Barilius niloticus*, and the three predators *Eutropius niloticus*, *Schilbe mystus* and *Cynothrissa mento*. In inshore shallow areas two other predators, *Hemichromis fasciatus* and *Hepsetus odoe*, also join them. The clupeids reform their feeding shoals at dawn and vanish from the surface by 0730 hours. Thus these clupeids behave very much as do those in Lake Tanganyika (p. 155). *Pellonula* is, however, essentially a river fish, which can inhabit both fast-flowing and calm, muddy habitats: it is not known whether it carries out similar diurnal vertical migrations in rivers when conditions permit, and whether this is a legacy from a marine environment.

Pellonula is a facultative feeder taking mainly aquatic and terrestrial insects, the aerial forms being eaten in the evening soon after their emergence, and small crustacea (Ostracoda, Cladocera and Copeopoda) are also eaten. *Pellonula* are in their turn preyed on by a variety of fish, *Clarias*, *Hepsetus*, *Hydrocynus*, *Lates*, *Schilbe*, *Eutropius*, *Alestes* and *Synodontis*. *Cynothrissa* takes the young stages of many fish species, including *Pellonula* and its own young.

Pellonula, formerly a July to September spawner, has extended its breeding season in the new lake (Reynolds, 1974). The ova are relatively large and may be anchored to substrata in the lake, but the larvae are pelagic. In the Gambia rivers and swamps the larvae of *Pellonula afzeliusi* were present in great numbers in the rainy season, but Johnels (1954) thought that some spawning occurred throughout the year. In the Middle Niger the clupeid *Microthrissa* is almost alone among the fishes in not leaving the river for the floodplain to spawn, but they migrate upriver in small bands (Daget, (1957*a*). In Volta the *Cynothrissa* still appear to move into rivers to spawn, and are dry-season spawners. Both clupeids mature within one year. Reynolds commented that for these largely annual forms predation probably outweighs all other factors in determining population size each year, but the flexible and extended breeding season in *Pellonula* (and also in *Physailia*) is important in allowing rapid population growth and effective exploitation of the changed environment.

Lake Kainji

The dam across the River Niger at Kainji in northern Nigeria (Fig. 4.3), closed in 1968, led to the formation of a 1280 km^2 lake with a much higher throughflow of water than these other two lakes (outflow: storage ratio 4:1), and with a large, 10 m, annual drawdown. Preimpoundment studies here included the census of fishes in the stretch of river enclosed by coffer dams already described (p. 98 and Table 4.1).

About 90 fish species were found in the lake, the majority of them the same as in Volta Lake. The fish fauna started to change as soon as the dam was closed. Mormyrid fishes, very abundant in the river, almost disappeared from the shallow lentic parts of the lake (as in Volta). Cichlid fishes, though not numerous in the river, were expected to increase; surprisingly they did not become an important commercial species right away (as they did in Kariba and Volta). The delay in build-up of their populations in Kainji lake was perhaps related to the inhibiting effect of water level fluctuations in the littoral region where they make their nests. *Tilapia galilaea* populations did, however, build up in the flooded bush, where they were not fished, and by 1972 they were an important element of the fauna. In the first year *Citharinus* became the most important commercial fish, probably because of successful spawning as the lake filled. There was a boom in small clupeids and an increase in the predatory *Hydrocynus* and *Lates niloticus*.

The studies of young fishes after impoundment showed that there were two spawning patterns in the lake: one with an extended season which includes clupeids and *Tilapia* and the other with a restricted season, the fish spawning as the water level rises. Products of this restricted season predominated in the first year after impoundment; the young of these species are able to feed on detritus, they are not too affected by increased turbity, and are not so dependent on the formation of a littoral zone as are young *Tilapia*.

A comparison of the food eaten by fishes in different areas of the new lake showed that the greatest weight of fish from the northern (lotic) section and the deeper channels (over 15 m deep) were primarily zooplankton-feeding species, whereas in the shallow areas, both cleared and bush-covered, detritus-feeding species predominated, with some herbivorous and periphyton-feeding species. Predators were present in all zones.

Changes in the composition of the fish community between August 1969 and February 1971 were associated with a marked decline in catch per unit effort, both in numbers and weight. Species which declined significantly in the catch were *Citharinus* species, *Hemisynodontis membranaceous*, *Schilbe mystus*, and *Labeo pseudocoubie*, while there was a gradual increase in the catch of *Hydrocynus* spp., *Labeo senegalensis* and *Synodontis* species. The insignificance of *Tilapia* in catches was ascribed to the lack of rooted littoral vegetation and the few floodplain areas (Regier and Wright, 1972, summarising work by many others). Many people have contributed to our knowledge of these changes in ecology in the Kainji lake and much work is still in progress (Lelek and El-Zarka, 1973; Lewis, 1974).

8

The Production of Tropical Freshwater Fishes for Food

The main sources of tropical freshwater food fish

The estimated need for a fifteen to twenty-fold increase in world fish production (Holt, 1967) means that inland waters where factors governing production can be controlled will have to be made to produce more fish. Fish culture is best developed in Asia; in Africa and South America, which both lack traditions of fish culture, food fishes come mainly from natural lakes and rivers. Estimated areas of different types of cultivable inland waters in the Indo-Pacific region tabulated by Hora and Pillay (1962) indicated that of an estimated total of 38·5 million hectares (much of it still without fish culture) nearly half of this (46 per cent) was of wet rice fields, and another 45 per cent of brackish water. The $2\frac{1}{2}$ million hectares of freshwater comprised natural lakes (59 per cent), manmade lakes (19 per cent), and fish ponds (22 per cent).

The aim of fisheries management is to obtain the maximum sustained yield of fish from a water body; this involves removing fishes equivalent to the amount of fish flesh produced each year (the production) without making inroads into the capital stock (biomass). When assessing a fishery, it is necessary to know whether the population is underexploited, in which case the fishery can be developed, or overexploited, in which case measures must be sought to protect the fish. This involves finding out what kinds of fishes are present and understanding their population dynamics, how fast they grow and reproduce, the size and age at which they spawn, their mortality rates and its causes etc. Methods of investigation to determine such variables are described in Ricker, ed. (1971).

Fishing methods in tropical freshwaters include *gillnets* set generally overnight as walls of netting in which the fish become entangled, *seine nets* pulled into sandy shores or used as a *ringnet* to encircle the fishes and pull them into a boat, *barriers* across rivers fitted with non-return basket traps to catch migrating fishes, and a whole host of ingenious traps using indigenous materials and designed to catch locally abundant fishes. Such devices from the Lake Chad area are figured by Blache and Miton (1962). Tropical inland fisheries were described by Hickling (1961).

Table 8.1 Freshwater fishes used as food in the three tropical regions.

	AFRICA	SOUTH AMERICA	ASIA
MAIN SOURCES OF FOOD FISH	**Large lakes floodplain rivers**	**Rivers and small lateral lakes**	**Fish ponds and rivers**
Cichlidae	*Tilapia* *Haplochromis* (Great Lakes) other genera	*Cichla* *Astronotus* *Crenicichla* *Cichlasoma* *Aequidens* other genera	*Etroplus* (S. India and Ceylon)
Cyprinidae	*Labeo* *Barbus* (*Barilius*: L. Malawi)	—	Numerous genera, e.g. *Barbus (Puntius)* *Osteochilus* *Catla*, *Cirrhina*, *Labeo* } India (Chinese carps)
Characoids (numerous families)	*Citharinus* *Distichodus* *Alestes* *Hydrocynus*	*Colossoma* *Myletes* *Prochilodus* *Brycon* *Salminus* *Leporinus* etc, etc	—
Siluroids (numerous families)	*Bagrus* *Clarias* *Heterobranchus* *Schilbé* *Eutropius* *(Synodontis)* *(Chrysichthys)*	*Brachyplatystoma* *Pseudoplatystoma* *Pimelodus* *Rhamdia* *Hypophthalmus* *Hypostomus* numerous others	Numerous genera, e.g. *Pangasius* (Asia) *Mystus* (India) *Wallago* (India) *Clarias*
Mormyrids	*Gymnarchus* *Mormyrops* *Mormyrus* other genera	—	—
Anabantoids	—	—	*Osphronemus* *Helostoma* *Trichogaster*
Channidae	*Parophicephalus*	—	*Channa*
Notopteridae	—	—	*Notopterus*
Osteoglossidae	*Heterotis*	*Arapaima* *Osteoglossum*	—
Lepidosirenidae	*Protopterus*	—	—

Table 8.1 – *continued*

	AFRICA	SOUTH AMERICA	ASIA
MAIN SOURCES OF FOOD FISH	**Large lakes floodplain rivers**	**Rivers and small lateral lakes**	**Fish ponds and rivers**
Clupeidae	*Limnothrissa* (L. Tanganyika) *Stolothrissa* (L. Tanganyika)	*Rhinosardinia* *Neosteus*	*Hilsa* other genera
Chanidae	—	—	*Chanos* (brackish)
Sciaenidae	—	*Plagioscion*	—

Reliable statistics of fish catches are vital for fisheries research. Catch statistics from remote tropical regions are of very varying reliability, but those from African freshwaters co-ordinated by the Food and Agriculture Organisation (FAO) of the United Nations suggest that at least 1 400 000 tonnes of fresh fish a year pass through African fish markets, in addition to which unknown but considerable amounts are consumed by the fishermen and their families. Of this total about 40 per cent (*c.* 547 000 tonnes) comes from river fisheries, mostly from floodplains. (The ten major floodplains indicated in Fig. 4.1 produce about 17 per cent of the total freshwater fish catch.) In Africa the Great Lakes also support important fisheries. Lake Victoria alone produced nearly 100 000 tonnes in 1970, four times the total catch of 25 000 t/yr of marine fishes from the whole seaboard of East Africa (Mann, 1969). Comparable overall figures are not yet available for South American and Asian freshwater catches. In India the 1965 freshwater fish catch of over 507 000 tonnes live weight was estimated to be about 38 per cent of the total fish landings for the year (FAO Statistics).

Throughout the tropics nearly all the larger kinds of freshwater fishes are consumed by man, though those without too many bones are preferred, and there are sometimes local taboos or superstitions against certain species (some 'skinfish' naked catfish in Guyana, for example, were at one time erroneously believed to cause leprosy). In some cases women are not allowed to eat a particular fish (*Mormyrus kannume* in Uganda, for example, which has a local name suggesting that it can cause abortion). The main food fishes in the three continents are indicated in Table 8.1.

In Africa most of the lake fisheries are based primarily on cichlids, especially species of *Tilapia*. The exception to this is Lake Tanganyika, where the small clupeids and their predators (*Lates* and *Luciolates*) form the main catch. Predatory catfishes, such as *Bagrus*, *Clarias*, *Schilbe* and *Eutropius*, and fishes which migrate up the inflowing streams to spawn, the cyprinids *Labeo* and *Barbus* (and in Lake Malawi large *Barilius*), and charcoids *Hydrocynus* and *Alestes*, are also fished extensively, and in some

Table 8.2 Main fish species of economic importance in some seasonal rivers of Africa.
A. West Africa, L. Chad area (Blache and Miton, 1962).
B. Middle Zambezi, L. Kariba area (Jackson, 1961*c*, J.F.R.O., 1965).
Note that a few species are the same, others are geographical replacement species. West Africa has a richer fish fauna.

FAMILY	WEST AFRICA (Chad area)	MIDDLE ZAMBEZI (L. Kariba area)
Lepidosirenidae	*Protopterus annectens*	*Protopterus annectens*
	P. aethiopicus	
Polypteridae	*Polypterus senegalus*	
	P. bichir	
Osteoglossidae	*Heterotis niloticus*	
Mormyridae	*Mormyrus rume*	*Mormyrus longirostris*
	Mormyrops deliciosus	*Mormyrops deliciosus*
		Hippopotamyrus discorhynchus
Gymnarchidae	*Gymnarchus niloticus*	
Characidae	*Hydrocynus brevis*	*Hydrocynus vittatus*
	H. forskaklii	
	Alestes dentex	
	A. baremose	*A. imberi*
	A. nurse	*A. lateralis*
Distichodontidae	*Distichodus brevipinnis*	*Distichodus mossambicus*
	D. rostratus	*D. schenga*
Citharinidae	*Citharinus citharus*	
	C. latus	
	C. distichodoides	
Cyprinidae	*Labeo coubie*	*Labeo altivelis*
	L. senegalensis	*L. congoro*
		Barbus marequensis
Clariidae	*Clarias lazera*	*Clarias mossambicus*
	C. anguillaris	
	Heterobranchus longifilis	*Heterobranchus longifilis*
	H. bidorsalis	
Schilbeidae	*Schilbe mystus*	
	Eutropius niloticus	*Eutropius depressirostris*
Bagridae	*Bagrus docmac*	
	B. bayad	
	Clarotes laticeps	
	C. macrocephalus	
Mochokidae	*Synodontis membranaceous*	*Synodontis zambesensis*
	S. schall	
Malapteruridae	*Malapterurus electricus*	*Malapterurus electricus*
Centropomidae	*Lates niloticus*	
Cichlidae	*Tilapia galilaea*	*Tilapia macrochir*
	T. nilotica	*T. mortimeri*
		T. rendalli
		Sargochromis codringtoni

lakes certain mormyrid species, while *Protopterus* is also an important food fish in Lake Victoria. The seasonal rivers of Africa carry a very varied fauna of food fishes, particularly across the sudanian region from West Africa to the Nile. The rivers flowing into Lake Chad produce about thirty-six kinds of fish valued by the fishermen (Blache and Miton, 1962), mostly widely distributed species (representing fifteen fish families) as shown in Table 8.2. The seventeen principal species in the Lake Chad fishery are listed in Fig. 6.3, which shows their food habits. The Zambezi system has a few of the same species, and geographical replacements of others, a fauna representing fewer families (only eight) in which cichlids and cyprinids are correspondingly more important than in West Africa. Fish culture in ponds has not been very successful in Africa, though the possibilities are still being explored, especially in francophone territories (Bard, 1971). There is no long tradition of fish culture in Africa as there is in Asia. The species cultured in ponds in Africa are mainly *Tilapia*, but the osteoglossid *Heterotis niloticus* is considered a promising pond fish in Cameroun (Bard, 1973). This can grow fast (up to 3·5 kg/yr); breeding is delayed until it is twenty months old so it does not overpopulate the ponds and runt (as do many *Tilapia*, p. 205), and it can live in water with little oxygen. (See also Micha, 1974.)

In South America the food fishes come mainly from the rivers and their floodplains. In the forest zone the human population is so low that the rivers and their adjoining lakes are not yet heavily fished. Ecological studies have shown how dependent these fishes are on forest products for their food, and clearing the forest is bound to lead to diminishing fish stocks. As nutrients are low in forest rivers it would be very easy to overfish them once the human population of the area has increased. The long estuarine reaches of rivers such as the Amazon are among the most productive waters, the river water fertilised by salts from the sea. The numbers of species occurring in Amazon fish markets is very high (over 100); species most frequently occurring at Manaus (Table 3.2) included mainly characoids and siluroids, with the osteoglossids *Arapaima* and *Osteoglossum*, the cichlids *Cichla* and *Astronotus*, together with some species of marine families such as clupeids and sciaenids. Fishes cultured in ponds in the dry northeast of Brazil include *Arapaima*, *Astronotus*, *Cichla*, other cichlids and *Prochilodus* (e.g. papers by Azevedo, Fontenele, Braga). Brazilian biologists learnt how to induce river fishes to spawn by hormone injections way back in the 1940s, twenty years before this method came into general use in Asia and elsewhere (Fontenele *et al.*, 1946).

In peninsular India the monsoon-filled rivers are dammed at many points to hold the flood water through the dry season, and many of these impoundments are stocked with fry of the major Indian carps. The estuarine reaches have important fisheries based on anadromous clupeids (*Hilsa*). The Indian carps most commonly stocked, *Catla catla*, *Cirrhina mrigala*, *Labeo rohita* and *L. calbasu*, spawn in the June to September monsoon in the flooded shallows of rivers. They do not spawn in ponds, though they may do so in some large reservoirs, and since 1957 spawning has been induced by injections of pituitary hypophysis hormone. The fry are very hardy and transported long distances around the country to stock dams. These species differ in their eating habits, which makes them suitable complementary species, though they all take varying combinations of unicellular and filamentous algae, zooplankton, decomposing vegetable matter, detritus and organic waste. *L. calbasu* also takes some benthos. These carps grow fast: in one year to 35 cm (450 g) in *L. calbasu*, 45 cm (675 g) in *L. rohita*, 45 cm (900 g) in *Catla*, and 60 cm (up to 2 kg) in *C. mrigala*, and they can grow very large, *Catla catla* to 1·8 m. Catfishes such as *Mystus* species are also important food fish from Indian rivers.

The synopsis of biological data for the Indian carp *Catla catla* (Jhingran, 1968) indicates the immense amount of scattered information available on these Indian fishes. Catla is the fastest growing of the Indian carps. Annual scale rings attributed to spawning stress allow growth rate determinations, the first ring being laid down in the second year of life when the fish matures. Growth varies very much with conditions. In southern India Catla can reach 70 cm (*c*. 4 kg) in the first year of life, and 1 m (20+ kg) in three years. Growth of up to 10 cm a month for the first six months of life has been recorded. The proportions of vegetable matter, algae, and Crustacea in their diet varies with the locality and with the size of fish, juveniles taking more Crustacea and adults more algae. *Catla* are local migrants ascending rivers for short distances during the monsoon rains to find suitable spawning grounds and returning to the main stream after spawning. They breed in rivers, reservoirs and bundh-type tanks where fluviatile conditions prevail, but not in small confined waters. No single factor has been found to initiate spawning, but a rise in water level is important. The numbers of ova increase with size of female from about 230 000 in a three-year-old (78 cm long, 11 kg) fish, to over 3 million in a five-year-old (95 cm long, 18 kg) fish. Fingerlings and yearlings fall prey to many predators, notably the catfishes *Wallago atu* and *Mystus*, also to *Channa*, and *Notopterus*, as well as to crocodiles, many kinds of birds, otters and man.

The Mekong River with the Great Lake flooded by water backed up the Tonlé Sap (p. 122) and several new large manmade lakes in the Mekong system in Thailand all have very valuable fisheries. In the lower Mekong, below the Tonlé Sap, fishes are caught mainly when they are migrating downriver as the water falls in October to February (p. 123). Other species move from the sea into the estuary, where earth dams are constructed to retain these fishes in flooded areas for culture. Fish ponds, both brackish and freshwater, make a major contribution to food supplies in the densely populated parts of southeast Asia.

Pond culture has been practised for over 4000 years in Asia, and nearly seventy species of fish are cultured in ponds in the Indo-Pacific region. These are listed by Hora and Pillay (1962). Hickling (1971) and Huet (1972) give good general accounts of culture methods. Small shallow family ponds, manured with night soil and animal excreta, are common, and the fishes are fed on agricultural and domestic waste by the owners. Combinations of ecologically complementary species are grown, one carp feeding on the faeces of another, or on plankton in water fertilised by its excreta. Stocking is dense, and intermediate fishing is practised, that is, removing a few fishes at a time for food rather than cropping all the fish at once as in large commercial ponds. Brackish water ponds are also very important for fish production in parts of southeast Asia, such as the Philippines where the algal-feeding milkfish, *Chanos chanos*, gives very high yields, augmented by stock manipulation, stocking fishes of different sizes and stocking at frequent intervals (Rabanal, 1968).

Indonesian ponds are often stocked with combinations of carps and anabantoids. These latter can withstand deoxygenated water. They include the gouramy *Osphronemus goramy*, a herbivore feeding on plankton and leaves which grows slowly in its first year (though eventually reaching 60 cm), and does not reproduce very fast, a female producing only 3000 to 5000 fry a year which the male guards. The plankton-feeding kissing gouramy, *Helostoma temmincki*, grows faster (to 30 cm long); this is a surface-dweller which at one year old may start to reproduce every three months, producing 1000 to 4000 small floating eggs at a spawning. The still smaller (25 cm) *Trichogaster pectoralis* grows well in rice fields, where it spawns in a bubble nest when seven months old. Certain catfishes are also grown in ponds in southeast Asia, such as the omnivorous *Clarias* which is very tolerant of deoxygenated and heavily polluted water, and the schilbeid *Pangasius* which grows to 900 g in two years.

Chinese carp, the grass carp *Ctenopharyngodon idella*, the silver carp *Hypophthalmichthys molitrix* and the bighead *Aristichthys nobilis* are cultured as complementary species, the grass carp feeding on macrophytes and fertilising the water for the phyto- and zooplankton used by the other two species respectively. Sometimes the mollusc-eating black carp *Mylopharyngodon piceus* is also stocked with them. These Chinese carp all grow very fast at the high temperatures in the tropics. They spawn naturally in very few places, and hypophysis injections are now used to produce fry for stocking ponds.

The vast areas of land in tropical Asia flooded for rice cultivation has led to combined fish and rice culture in many areas (Coche, 1967; Huet, 1972). Wild fish may colonise the fields, such as *Trichogaster pectoralis*, and species of *Anabas*, *Clarias* and *Channa*, producing up to 135 kg/ha in six to ten months in Malaya, a bonus of protein. Elsewhere ricefields may be stocked with fingerlings, as in India and Indonesia. The fish improve rice growth by controlling the algae and weeds; they also control mosquitoes, and certain species may control molluscs. The culture of fish in rice fields does, however, limit the use of certain agricultural techniques, such as the use of chemical insecticides, and simultaneous culture is now being abandoned in favour of a rotation of fish and rice.

Biomass, production and yields of fishes from tropical freshwaters

These tropical waters carry many more fish species than comparable waters in the temperate zone, but is the biomass of fish higher? And is fish production per unit time greater than in the temperate zone?

Table 8.3 Estimates of fish biomass and production in tropical and temperate freshwaters. (Note: g/m^2 × 10 gives kg/ha.)

PLACE	TYPE OF WATER	BIOMASS g/m^2	PRODUCTION g/m^2/year	P/B RATIO per cent	AUTHORITY (Fishing methods)
AFRICA					
Nigeria	River pools				
Sokoto R.	Sandy bottom	69·1–100·7			Holden (1963)
	Muddy bottom	19·6–27·0			(dry season refuges)
	Intermediate	58·5–144·0			
Kafue Flats	Open lagoons:				
	high water	33·7			Lagler *et al* (1971)
	low water	59·2			
	Vegetated lagoons	268·2			
	Grass marsh	6·4			
	River channel	33·7			(chemofishing)
	River channel	51·1			(multiple seining)
R. Niger Kainji	Between coffer dams	5·9			Motwani and Kanwai (1970) (drained)
L. George	Openwater	22·7			Burgis *et al* (1973)
Uganda	Shallow lake	(range 6–90)			(openwater seine)
L. Chad	Lake	3–562			(Loubens (1969) (chemofishing)
L. Kariba	Cove (Chikanka I)	26·1			Balon (1971*a*)
	All samples	283·0	346·8	123%	Balon (1972) (chemofishing)
L. Volta	Littoral zone (150 m^2)	11·4			Regier and Wright (1972) (chemofishing)
Dahomey	Fish parks (acadjas)	100·0–150·0			Welcomme (1972*b*) (attracting traps)
Zaïre and Ruanda	Fish ponds:				
	unmanaged	10–100			
	managed	100–400			Huet (1957)

Table 8.3 – *continued*

PLACE	TYPE OF WATER	BIOMASS g/m^2	PRODUCTION $g/m^2/year$	P/B RATIO per cent	AUTHORITY (Fishing methods)
SOUTH AMERICA					
Venezuela	Lagoon	100·0			Mago (1970*a*) (chemofishing)
Argentina	Temporary lakes (8)	17·5–650·0			Bonetto *et al* (1969)
Middle Parana	Permanent lagoons (4)	55–128·7			Bonetto *et al* (1970)
CUBA					
	L. Sabanilla	32·1	22·0	70·8%	Holcík (1970)
	L. Luisa	32·5	27·6	85%	(chemofishing)
	Backwater	5·7			
ISRAEL	Ponds:				
	unfertilized	9–10			
	fertilized	30–40			
	fertilized + food	90–150			Hepher (1967)
	fertilized + food – mixed culture	250			
TEMPERATE WATERS					
New Zealand	Horokiwi trout stream	31·1	53·3	170%	Allen (1951)
England	R. Thames	65·9	42·6	65%	Mann (1964)
	Sewage lagoons (3)	18·2–38·3			White (personal communication)
Scotland	Loch Leven	13·0	17·0	130%	Morgan (1972)
	Loch Leven	—	7·3–71·3	—	Thorpe (1974)

The biomass (ichthyomass, standing crop or stock) is the amount of fish flesh present in a biotope at any one time. The biological production of fish is the amount of fish flesh produced per unit time whether or not all the fish survive to the end of that time; it is thus a rate. In fisheries literature the yield or catch, i.e. the proportion of the production cropped by man, is often loosely called the 'production'. Estimates of ichthyomasses from various tropical and temperate water are given in Table 8.3, based mainly on samples collected by chemofishing or some such method which catches all the fishes present. Data are as yet only fragmentary, and show that estimates of biomass vary very much with the conditions at the time of sampling. On the Kafue Flats, where nine 0·25 ha areas were chemofished, at highwater the ichthyomass was much higher in lagoons with vegetation, 268 g/m^2 (2682 kg/ha), than in open water lagoons 33·7 g/m^2 (337 kg/ha). In the open water lagoons the ichthyomass was higher (59·2 g/m^2, 592 kg/ha) at low water (Lagler *et al.*, 1971), though estimates for the whole vast area of the flats suggested that the low water ichthyomass was less (actually only about 60 per cent) than the high water ichthyomass (Welcomme, 1972). In Lake Chad, Loubens (1969) found ichthyomass estimates to vary from 3 to 562 g/m^2 (30–5620 kg/ha). Even in the relatively uniform open waters of Lake George (p. 167) ichthyomass estimates ranged from 6 to 90 g/m^2 (60–900 kg/ha) (Burgis *et al.*, 1973). Only small areas can be sampled comprehensively, and conclusions based on such data have to be regarded with caution as results are then often extrapolated for whole floodplains or lakes many thousands of hectares in extent, thus multiplying sampling differences or initial errors. Fishes move about a good deal and the presence of migrant fishes at times of sampling will greatly affect the results. Dry season pools are refuges for fishes from a very wide area, so the ichthyomass is not produced within the pool (as it would be in a fish pond); the flooded area which has contributed to the production of the fish is difficult to estimate and is likely to have varied considerably from year to year.

However, comparing biomasses from various tropical waters with those from some temperate waters (Table 8.3) makes it clear that in tropical areas ichthyomasses are not necessarily much higher. The River Thames in England, for example, has an ichthyomass of 65·9 g/m^2 (659 kg/ha), and New Zealand trout streams of 31·1 g/m^2 (311 kg/ha), although these waters have few fish species (twelve in the Thames, and trout only in the New Zealand stream), compared with the numerous species in the tropical waters, for example, 27–30 species in the Sokoto River pools.

Fisheries research in the tropics is complicated by (*a*) the large numbers of species present in a community, and (*b*) the difficulties of determining fish ages and growth rates. The true biological production, based on growth rates etc, in tropical waters is as yet known only for some Cuban lagoons (though data from Lake Kariba and Lake Chad may provide such information when investigations are completed). In these Cuban lagoons production based mainly on introduced North American species of fish (bluegill and largemouth bass, see p. 200) was 70 to 85 per cent of the biomass, higher than the Production/Biomass ratio for some lakes in Czechoslovakia with which Holčík (1970) compared them. Holčík attributed this to fast growth rates, early maturity and short life cycles in tropical waters. However, in some other temperate waters production may be as high in relation to biomass: in Loch Leven in Scotland fish production has been estimated as 130 per cent of the biomass, while in New Zealand Allen (1951) thought that trout production greatly exceeded biomass (though this production estimate was probably too high, according to Le Cren, 1972).

In the absence of true production data, the *yield* expressed as kg/ha is often used as an index of production. Yields tend to be greater in shallow than in deep lakes, partly for biological reasons – the higher temperatures and light in shallow water supporting higher production – and partly because the fish are easier to catch in shallow water, so a higher proportion of the production is cropped as yield. Data from African lakes summarised by Fryer and Iles (Fig. 8.1) show this relationship (with the exception of the

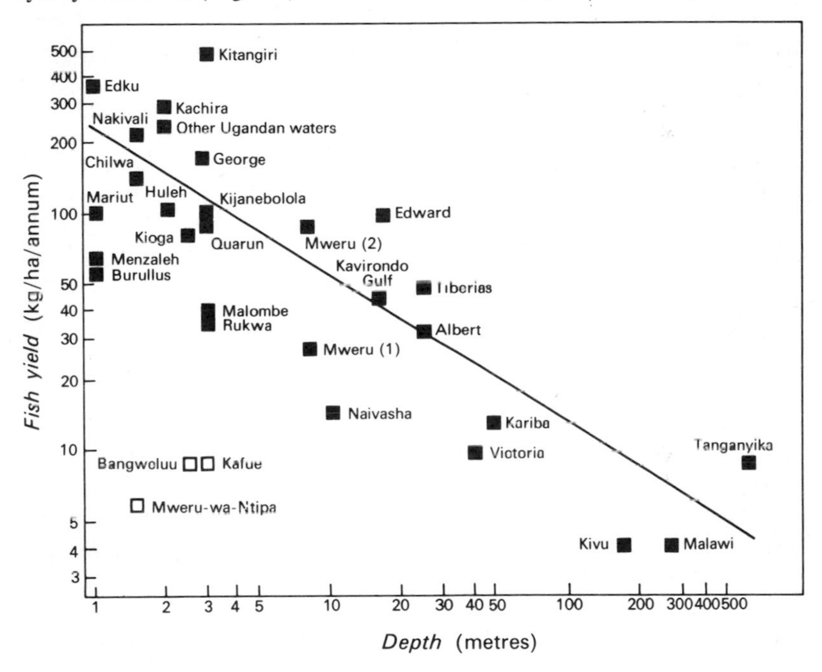

Fig. 8.1 Fish yields from African lakes of varying depths (after Fryer and Iles, 1972).

shallow Lake Bangweulu and Mweru-wa-Ntipa where the yields are low, probably for edaphic reasons). The reliability of some of the available catch statistics is questionable (see Fryer, 1973). In certain North American lakes Ryder (1965) found that the fish yields were proportional to a 'morphoedaphic index' of total dissolved solids divided by mean depth of lake, and attempts have been made to evaluate such an index for African lakes (Regier and Wright, 1972; Henderson and Welcomme, 1974). Methods for estimating fish production in tropical lakes are much needed, for example when planning fishery development in the new manmade lakes.

Yields (and in a few cases production) of fishes in various tropical and temperate waters are compared in Fig. 8.2. The yields from African lakes, proportional to lake depth, range from less than 10 kg/ha/yr in the deep lakes, Malawi, Kivu and Tanganyika, to 500 kg/ha/yr in the shallow Lake Kitangiri (a 1200 km^2 lake 5 m deep in Tanzania). The major flood plains of Africa (Fig. 4.1) have been estimated to yield about 40 to 60 kg/ha/yr (ranging from 3 kg/ha/yr from the Barotse floodplain to 100 kg/ha/yr from the Chari/Logone-Chad yaérés (Welcomme, 1973), while the fish parks in Dahomey described below are said to produce up to 8000 kg/ha/yr (Welcomme, 1971, 1972*b*).

The figures from Lake George, Uganda (p. 166) indicate that the yield of *c.* 2000 kg/ha/yr (all species) came from a biomass of 60 to 900 kg/ha; 80 per cent of the catch was on one species *Tilapia nilotica* which gave a yield equivalent to 910 to 1470 kg/ha/yr (Dunn, 1972) from an estimated biomass of 29 kg/ha.

In Dahomey fish yields from natural waters are greatly increased by the construction of 'fish parks' (known locally as 'acadjas'), clumps of floating vegetation introduced alongside rivers, and the planting of branches stuck into the bottom mud of shallow lakes and coastal lagoons. These attract fishes in search of food and refuge. Furthermore the branches provide a greatly increased surface area for the production of periphytic algae (aufwuchs) used as food by certain species. Some kinds of acadja act mainly as refuge traps and are fished within a few days of their construction, but others are left in for long periods and generally fished twice a year. In the latter the fish yields increased exponentially and the capture of breeding and brooding fish within them confirmed that biological production is actually increased in these areas by the planting of branches (compare the value of flood forest for fish production in the Mekong, p. 123). Coastal lagoon acadjas fished twice a year produced up to 8000 kg/ha/yr (Welcomme, 1972*b*), mainly of *Tilapia melanotheron* and *Chrysichthys nigrodigitatus*; these species formed 76 per cent and 24 per cent of the yield (by weight) from the acadjas respectively, compared with but 0·7 per cent and 1·4 per cent of the catches from the open waters of the lake. In the large riverine acadjas the proportions of fish species varied from year to year but included *Tilapia*, *Chrysichthys*, *Heterotis*, *Synodontis*, *Clarias*, *Distichodus*, *Alestes* and *Lates*.

In fish ponds the yield is almost equivalent to production since almost all the fish produced are cropped, but the amount produced depends very much

Fig. 8.2 Estimates of fish production or yield from various tropical and temperate waters. Such estimates range from 1·1 kg/ha/yr for fish from the open oceans of the world up to 1·5 kg/m^2 (equivalent to 150 000 kg/ha/yr) for fish fattened on agricultural products in running water tanks. (Latter extreme not shown on this log scale graph for reasons of page size.)

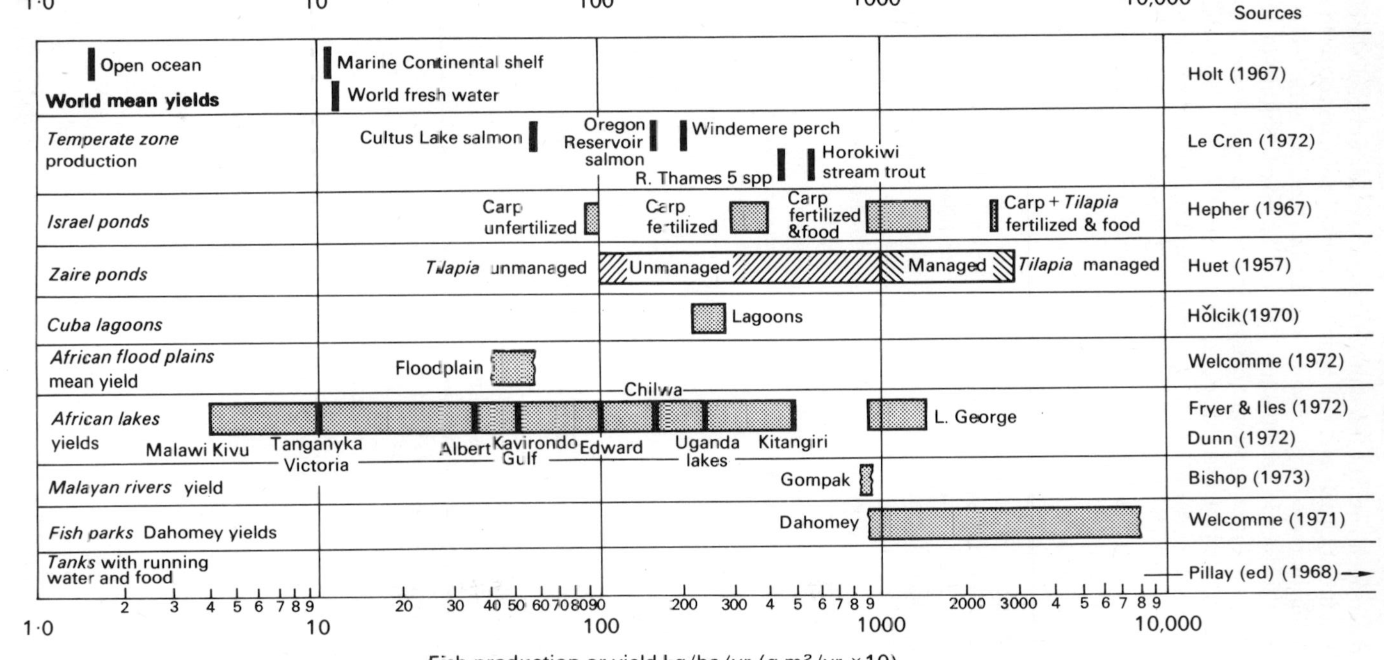
1·0
10
100
1000
10,000
Sources
Open ocean
Marine Continental shelf
Holt (1967)
World mean yields
World fresh water
Temperate zone production
Cultus Lake salmon
Oregon Reservoir salmon
R. Thames 5 spp
Windermere perch
Horokiwi stream trout
Le Cren (1972)
Israel ponds
Carp unfertilized
Carp fertilized
Carp fertilized &food
Carp + Tilapia fertilized & food
Hepher (1967)
Zaire ponds
Tilapia unmanaged
Unmanaged
Managed
Tilapia managed
Huet (1957)
Cuba lagoons
Lagoons
Hǒlcik(1970)
African flood plains mean yield
Floodplain
Welcomme (1972)
African lakes yields
Malawi Kivu
Tanganyika
Victoria
Albert
Kavirondo Gulf
Edward
Chilwa
Uganda lakes
Kitangiri
L. George
Fryer & Iles (1972)
Dunn (1972)
Malayan rivers yield
Gompak
Bishop (1973)
Fish parks Dahomey yields
Dahomey
Welcomme (1971)
Tanks with running water and food
Pillay (ed) (1968)
1·0 2 3 4 5 6 7 8 9 10 20 30 40 50 60 70 80 90 100 200 300 4 5 6 7 8 9 1000 2000 3000 4 5 6 7 8 9 10,000
Fish production or yield kg/ha/yr (g.m²/yr ×10)

on pond management. At a fish culture research station in Israel, the carrying capacity of unfed *Cyprinus carpio* in an unfertilised pond was 90 to 100 kg/ha. Fertilisation increased it to 300 to 400 kg/ha; feeding with cereal grains increased it further to 900 to 1500 kg/ha. The mixed culture of carp and *Tilapia aurea* of different weight classes, in a fertilised pond where food was added, augmented the carrying capacity to over 2500 kg/ha (Hepher, 1967). In Ruanda and the former Congo, ponds with little management produced 100 to 1000 kg/ha/yr (mainly *Tilapia*), while those with more intensive management, and in which the fish were fed, produced 1000 to 4000 kg/ha/yr (Huet, 1957). Capart and Kuffareth (1957) calculated from experiments on algal production that algal-feeding fish such as *Tilapia* in fertilised ponds at Congo temperatures should be able to produce up to a theoretical maximum of 100 000 kg/ha/yr, and questioned why in practice between 5000 and 9000 kg/ha/yr (using mill sweepings to fertilise the ponds and feed the fish) was the highest production ever achieved. Unfertilised ponds in the tropics rarely produce as much as 300 kg/ha/yr (depending on size of pond, mineralisation of soil, water supply, etc.). Java ponds fed by mineral hot springs have, however, been reported to produce between 2000 and 10 000 kg/ha/yr (Mortimer and Hickling, 1954). By feeding the fish very much higher yields can be obtained; the extraordinarily high yields (reportedly up to 1·5 kg/m^2) in the Far East from running water ponds, floatcages, and aquarium-type tanks with circulating water in Japan, are of fish fattened on artificial foods – agricultural products not produced within the water body (details in Hora and Pillay, 1962; Rabanal, 1968; Hickling, 1971; Huet, 1972). The removal of waste products by running water is an important part of these culture systems.

The culture of pond fish has demonstrated how much fish growth rates vary with the food supplied and conditions governing its utilisation. Pond production can be increased in many ways: by manuring the water to produce more natural food, by feeding the fishes (with vegetable debris, meal, offal, etc), by manipulating stocking densities and the sizes and combinations of species, the selection of faster growing strains and use of sterile hybrids to control breeding, elimination of fish parasites, etc. (Pillay, 1967–8).

If mature *Tilapia* are left in a pond they breed prolifically, the population density rises and as food becomes short they breed at a very small size and no further large fish are produced. For this reason *Tilapia* have ceased to be popular pond fish in many parts of the world, and much research effort has been devoted to finding ways to avoid this runting; for example, by monosex stocking with male fish, or by stocking predators with the *Tilapia* to control their numbers.

Higher yields in tropical than in most temperate ponds are possible because:

1. fishes grow faster at higher water temperatures, and life cycles are shorter, fishes maturing in less than one year;
2. the growing season extends over the whole year, and young fishes are available for stocking throughout the year;

3. herbivorous species can be grown, obviating losses in successive food chain links;
4. ecologically complementary species are available to increase yields;
5. many species can withstand poorly oxygenated water, so ponds can be very heavily fertilised.

The relationship between primary production and fish yield was studied in three upland lakes in Madras State by Sreenivasan (1964) who concluded that less than 0·2 per cent of the primary production was utilised by cropping the fish. In the equatorial Lake George (p. 167), soupy with bluegreen algae food of *Tilapia nilotica*, probably well over 90 per cent of the energy fixed by the planktonic algae is dissipated in respiration by the plankton community. Thus though the *gross* primary production is extremely high, the *net* primary production is less than 10 per cent of this. In this lake the system as a whole has been shown to be inefficient in the transfer of solar energy from primary to other trophic levels (Ganf and Viner, 1973). Nevertheless enough is passed on to support a fishery of some 5000 t/yr, equivalent to about 200 kg/ha/yr, more than in unfertilised fish ponds.

9

Reactions of Fishes to Conditions in Tropical Freshwaters

Fish growth in tropical freshwaters

Fishes are cold-blooded and growth rates vary very much with the environmental conditions, the available food, and factors such as temperature and crowding which affect its utilisation. This is shown clearly by the differences in growth rate in fish ponds just discussed, and in natural waters growth rates must also be influenced by many conditions interacting in their effects.

At the high temperatures prevailing in tropical waters growth rates are faster, the fish mature at a younger age, and the life span is shorter than in temperate waters. The culture of temperate fishes under tropical conditions demonstrates these effects: for example, the Chinese carp *Ctenopharyngodon idella* grows much faster (up to 10 g/day) in ponds at Malacca in Malaya compared with 3·5 g/day in south China, and at Malacca it matures in one year, compared with three to five years in south China (Hickling, 1967). Similarly the North American bluegill (*Lepomis macrochirus*) and large-mouth bass (*Micropterus salmoides*) acclimatised in Cuban lakes matured earlier (one year or less, compared with two to three years), grew faster, and had shorter life spans in Cuba than in the U.S.A. (Holcík, 1970). Conversely, tropical species such as *Tilapia* grow more slowly in temperate zone ponds, and at high altitudes where the temperatures are lower.

Tropical fishes show a wide range of sizes and growth rates. Some small cyprinodonts are annuals, completing their life cycles in less than one year (p. 226), and the Lake Tanganyika clupeids also rarely live longer than for one year. Larger species may live many years: in aquaria individual *Serrasalmus* have been kept up to twenty-two years (Lissmann, personal communication), and *Bagrus bayad*, *Clarias lazera*, *Barbus bynni*, and *Loricaria parva* have all survived for over sixteen years (Brown, 1957).

In Lake Kariba the majority of the 22 species studied had a life span of 7 to 9 years (including *Tilapia rendalli*, *Mormyrops deliciosus*, *Mormyrus longirostris*, *Hydrocynus vittatus*, *Labeo altivelis* and *Synodontis zambesensis*), or 4 to 6 years (as in *Tilapia mortimeri*, *Hippopotamyrus discorhynchus*, *Marcusenius macrolepidotus*, *Eutropius depressirostris*, *Schilbe mystus*, *Sargochromis codringtoni* and *Synodontis nebulosus*), but 4 species lived longer than 10 years

(*Heterobranchus longifilis*, *Clarias gariepinus*, *Malapterurus electricus* and *Anguilla nebulosa*), and 5 small species (including *Alestes lateralis*) did not exceed 3 years; most species reached maturity in their second growth season (Balon and Coche, 1974).

Many of the very large fishes (*Arapaima*, *Pseudoplatystoma*, *Lates*) are piscivores, but the giant catfish of the Mekong, *Pangasianodon gigas*, is a vegetarian. The microphagous African osteoglossid *Heterotis* grows very fast, as does the herbivorous grass carp *Ctenopharyngodon* under tropical conditions (up to 3 kg in one year). There are some adaptive advantages in growing fast and becoming very large (such as avoiding predation and being able to swim long distances), others in remaining very small (being able to exploit foods not used by other species, and also in avoiding predation). Small size may enable a species to move into an area which already has a well-differentiated fauna (as *Kneria* appears to have done from the Zambezi to the Zaïre system).

In more temporary communities, such as floodplain pools, the species as a whole may benefit from having most of its members reproducing at an early age and small size, and many fishes living in such environments generally mature within one year, or at the most two years for the larger ones, enabling the fish to spawn in the next, or next but one, flood season. In the Great Lakes, on the other hand, where fecundity is not at such a premium and efficiency is of greater advantage to the species, maturity may be delayed until the fishes are several years old.

Age and growth-rate determinations

The determination of fish ages and growth rates is often particularly difficult under tropical conditions, especially in equatorial regions. In temperate waters physiological changes lead to the suspension of growth during the winter, and this leaves growth checks as annual rings on skeletal structures such as scales and bones, fin rays and otoliths. A simple count of these rings will indicate the age of the fish, and by determining the proportionate growth of the scale or bone where the rings are laid down it is possible to 'back calculate' the length that the particular fish would have been at the end of each year of life. So fish scales can provide a complete history of the fish's life. In the tropics the lack of a well-defined winter means that scale and bone rings, if present, are difficult to interpret. They are often discernible to some extent, but unless they can be related to dated events in the life of the fish they are of little use for the determination of growth rates. When present they are generally related to (*a*) the effects of a 'physiological winter' which checks growth when food is short in the dry season (many floodplain fishes show particularly well-marked rings, in contrast with fishes in equatorial lakes); (*b*) the physiological changes associated with spawning (for example mobilisation of calcium as Garrod and Newell, 1958, concluded for *Tilapia esculenta* in Lake Victoria); or (*c*) seasonally lowered temperature in the waters at higher latitudes (as in *Lates* and *Alestes* in northern Lake Chad;

Hopson, 1972). Cichlid females which feed little while brooding young often show well-marked scale rings. But how many spawning periods a year do they have? And does this vary from year to year with the conditions? There is some evidence that it may do so.

Great care is therefore necessary in interpreting scale rings, and growth rates need to be checked by other means, though this too is often difficult. Where fish have a restricted spawning season, the progressions of the length frequency modes indicate growth through the year (Petersen's method). But in many tropical species an extended breeding season means that young fish continue to enter the population throughout much of the year, complicating this method. Furthermore, fishes such as *Tilapia* change their biotope according to the size of fish, so seine catches in inshore waters often catch fishes of the same restricted size ranges, even the same modal size, throughout much of the year if breeding is not very seasonal. Where males and females grow at different rates, length frequency data have of course to be treated separately for the two sexes. Growth in confined waters such as ponds and tanks is often very different from growth in lakes, so of little help in supporting data on growth rates in natural waters. However, direct measurements of growth in floating cages in the equatorial Lake George of the phytoplankton-feeding *T. nilotica* (p. 167) did agree quite well with growth estimates from length frequency analyses of a cohort of young, products of increased spawning during the rainy season. Returns of tagged fish can provide some growth rate data (provided the method of tagging used does not affect the growth), and the use of various mathematical devices (such as the von Bertalanffy growth equation and Walford plots) can assist the estimation of growth rates from incomplete data (e.g. Garrod, 1963; for details see Ricker, 1971).

Lengths are quicker and more accurate to measure than weights in large samples under field conditions. The weight of a fish increases with approximately the cube of the length (depending on the shape of the fish); a length/weight relationship curve for the particular species allows weights (biomass) to be calculated quickly. The 'condition' of the fish, i.e. its weight for length in relationship to the mean weight for length, reflects the conditions in its habitat at that particular time.

When comparing growth data from various sources it is necessary to check whether the total or fork length (including the caudal fin) has been used, as by most fishery biologists, or the standard length (without the caudal fin) as used by most systematists. When comparing length for age data from various sources it is also necessary to check the designation of the age groups; for instance, age group 'III' is generally taken to mean fish of three to four years old with three rings on the scales, but is used for 2+ to 3+ fish by some biologists (see discussion by Tesch, 1971). In the latter case the fish would appear to be growing more slowly if age for growth curves were compared without taking this into account. Because of this type of confusion marine fishery scientists have recently suggested a convention that the growth year starts on 1 January, but the implications of this for tropical species do not yet appear to have been considered. Age determinations present the same difficulties for tropical marine fish studies. In the red grouper *Epinephalus morio*, off Florida, Moe (1969) found that scale rings were laid down earlier in the year in young fish (March to May) than in mature fish (May to July), and that there were great overlaps of age for length, signifying changes in growth rate which he thought to be of adaptive significance.

Growth data for some tropical species

The most reliable growth data for tropical fishes come from waters where seasonal differences are greatest, as in Gambia (Johnels, 1952), Egypt (Jensen, 1957), the Middle Niger (Daget, 1952) and Lake Chad, though even here there may be different opinions over the interpretation of growth checks. In Lake Chad, J. Hopson (1972) has suggested that the scales of some *Alestes baremose* may show two rings a year, one due to the seasonal fall in temperature, the other to the seasonal floods, and if so, the fish would be growing faster than previously believed from estimates based on one ring a year by Durand and Loubens (1969) and more in line with her estimates for this species in the northern part of the lake (Fig. 9.1). In the Middle Niger, Daget (1952) found that *Alestes* of various species which fed on the floodplains at high water, then retired to the river in the low-water season, grew in length and weight and laid down fat stores only in the flood season, subsisting on their reserves and losing weight and fat content in the dry season. Here the small species *A. leuciscus* was never found more than two years old. Larger species lived longer, and in *Alestes baremose* and *A. dentex* the females grew faster than the males, a difference often found when fecundity is at a premium, as the egg number increases with the weight of the female.

In the large predatory *Lates niloticus* in Lake Chad scale studies suggested that males and females grow at comparable rates, but that the males mature at a somewhat smaller size (50 cm TL compared with 60 to 65 cm in females), and females survive longer (to fifteen years compared with twelve years in males). The length increased exponentially with age until the fish were seven to eight years old (75–90 cm TL). About this size the *Lates* switched from a mixed diet of invertebrates (especially prawns) and fish to one of larger fishes (Fig. 6.4), and growth in length then increased arithmetically with age (Fig. 9.1B) (A. J. Hopson, 1972). Such a change is known in temperate fishes (e.g. in *Perca fluviatilis*).

Tilapia growth has been much studied as these are such important food fishes. Several species of *Tilapia* grow large and delay maturity in large deep lakes, whereas in small water bodies, floodplain pools or fish ponds, they breed at a smaller size and younger age, even though they may grow quite fast to achieve this size (this is an unusual feature since many other fishes such as trout have slow growing populations which breed at a small size). *Tilapia* endemic to the Great Lakes show this well: *T. esculenta* and *T. variabilis* endemic to Lake Victoria do not breed in the lake until they are

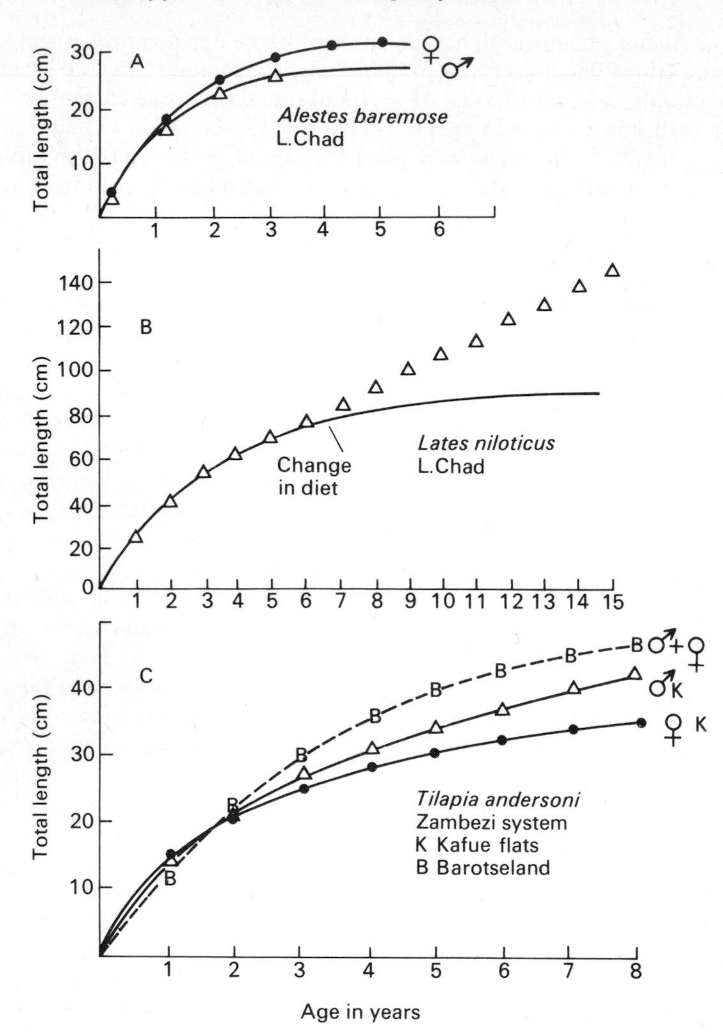

Fig. 9.1 Growth rates of representative freshwater fishes.

A. *Alestes baremose*, a lacustrine population from Lake Chad; as in many characids the females (●) grow larger than the males (△) (after Jane Hopson, 1972).

B. *Lates niloticus* from Lake Chad; data for sexes combined as these grow at comparable rates (after A. J. Hopson, 1972). Note change from geometric to arithmetic increase in length for age when the fishes are *c.* 75 cm long, the size at which they change to a diet of larger fish prey.

C. *Tilapia andersonii* from the Zambezi system; these cichlids grow to a larger size in Barotseland than on the Kafue Flats, where males (△) grow larger than females (●), as in many *Tilapia* (data from Duerre, 1969; Chapman *et al.*, 1971).

Curves are based on back calculated lengths from scale rings, supported by von Bertalanffy growth curves for the Lake Chad fishes.

two to three and three to four years old respectively (when about 23 cm and 20+ cm total length), but in ponds *T. esculenta* bred at 16 cm when less than seven months old and *T. variabilis* at less than 19 cm when under one year old. In aquaria growth was further reduced, *T. esculenta* maturing at 7 cm when only a few months old. Furthermore, these dwarfed fish produced eggs that were much smaller than usual (about one-third the weight of those from lake fish), many of them at a time, and the fish continued to produce batches of eggs every eight weeks or so (Cridland, 1961). In Lake Malawi the open-water species of tilapia, *T. saka*, *T. squamipinnis* and *T. lidole*, do not breed until they are three years old (and 27, 24 and 28 cm respectively); the more inshore-living *T. shirana* breeds when two to three years old in this lake (at 20 cm long), but its subspecies *T. s. chilwae* which lives in the shallow Lake Chilwa, subject to drying out, breeds when one year old (at 11 cm long).

Several, perhaps many, other *Tilapia* including *T. mossambica* which now has a circumtropical distribution in fish ponds, and the widely distributed *T. nilotica*, are able to breed when a few months old, instead of two years or more, when about 8 cm long instead of over 20 cm, even though the absolute growth rate is high. And they produce very small eggs, relatively more in relation to body weight than are produced by large individuals. A miniaturisation that Fryer and Iles (1969) considered to be unique in the animal world.

The adaptive advantage to the species of switching to a phase of rapid multiplication in environments where there is a danger of desiccation is very great, and this phenomenon may explain how *Tilapia* maintain themselves and make such rapid recoveries after drastic droughts, as they have been observed to do in Lake Rukwa in Tanzania and Lake Chilwa in Malawi after these lakes almost dried out. We do not yet know the mechanism for this switch, but in *T. nilotica*, which grows to over 64 cm total length in Lake Rudolf and dwarfs when trapped in lagoons and in ponds, it was found that populations with high weights for length matured late, whereas those with low weights for comparable lengths switched over to reproduction (Lowe-McConnell, 1959*a*).

In *T. nilotica* and *Tilapia* endemic to the Great Lakes (*T. esculenta* and *T. variabilis* in Lake Victoria and the open-water species in Lake Malawi) males and females grow at the same rate and to comparable sizes in the big lakes. But in dwarfed populations of *T. nilotica* the males are larger than the females, a difference that becomes enhanced as the females put so much more of their biomass into egg production, producing eggs at very frequent intervals under these conditions; also females almost cease to feed while mouth-brooding their eggs and young. *T. nilotica* in river pools in West Africa normally show this sexual dimorphism.

This type of sexual dimorphism appears to be different from the kind in the *T. mossambica* group of *Tilapia* (including *T. spilurus nigra* in Kenya) in which the male grows faster than the female throughout life, and in which the size difference can be used to select the larger male fingerlings for mono-sex culture in fish ponds. In this group of *Tilapia* the appearance of the two sexes also diverges as they grow older, males developing a concave profile and enlarged mouth. This form of sexual dimorphism is probably genetically controlled.

Other cichlids in the Great Lakes also take several years to attain maturity, for instance the Utaka *Haplochromis virginalis* in Lake Malawi, though much smaller than *Tilapia*, does not breed until three years old (at *c.* 10 cm TL) (Fryer and Iles, 1972). The large predatory *Boulengerochromis microplepis* in Lake Tanganyika grows much faster than either of these and breeds when two and a half years old (*c.* 40 cm long). The length at maturity constitutes a higher proportion of the maximum length in *Haplochromis* (0·86) than in *Boulengerochromis* (0·75) compared with values of 0·46–0·81 in various *Tilapia* species.

The growth of *Tilapia spilurus nigra* in Kenya ponds investigated by van Someren and Whitehead (1959–60) showed: (*a*) that growth can be surprisingly fast (over 4 cm/month) in isolated fish (compared with 1·6 cm/month for *T. nilotica* in Lake George); (*b*) that growth rates were not constant from month to month but fluctuated with environmental conditions, particularly water temperature (itself much affected by weather conditions, such as rainfall), which may operate on the fish through its effect on food utilisation. In these ponds, situated almost on the equator, there were two good growing periods and two poor growth periods every year. Factors limiting growth appear to be available food and the behaviour patterns of fishes in obtaining food. Fish growth proved very responsive to changed conditions; the transfer of mature and breeding fishes of various sizes from an overstocked pond in which growth had slowed down or ceased to another pond at a much reduced stocking rate resulted in renewed growth. As males in breeding colours were removed from a pond, other males developed breeding colours and took their place, suggesting that social hierarchies are important in the activities of these fishes. Under comparable conditions isolated *T. s. nigra* males grew faster than isolated females in these ponds.

Little is yet known about the growth rates of South American food fishes. In the Rupununi length frequencies and scale rings evidently caused mainly by dry season growth checks suggested that most of the cichlids matured in less than one year, ready to spawn by the next annual floods, but that the larger fishes such as *Osteoglossum* probably take two years to reach maturation size (Lowe-McConnell, 1964). In Brazil *Cichla ocellaris* matures in ponds when eleven to twelve months old (*c.* 28 cm TL) (Fontenele, 1950). In Brazilian ponds the giant *Arapaima gigas* matures when four to five years old (when the fish would be about 1·5 m long, for it grows up to 1·25 m in three years) and it can survive eighteen years (Fontenele, 1948; Allsopp, 1958).

The most complete information on growth in natural freshwaters of South America is for *Prochilodus*, *P. scrofa* in the Rio Mogi Guassu in Brazil (Godoy, 1959) and the very similar *P. platensis* in Argentina (Cordiviola, 1971) and in the Pilcomayo (Bayley, 1973). *P. scrofa* males mature when two years old and may live for nine years, whereas females mature at three years old, live longer (to thirteen years) and grow larger (to 68 cm,

5800 g). In Argentina and the Pilcomayo *P. platensis* grows to 58 cm in ten years. Argentine data on the growth of the salmonlike dorado *Salminus maxillosus* is somewhat conflicting (Ringuelet *et al.*, 1967, Cordiviola, 1966*a*), but the females grow larger than the males and may live up to fourteen years old. Preliminary studies using rings seen in the cross sections of vertebrae of the large catfish surubi *Pseudoplatystoma coruscans* suggested that fishes older than eight years are females (Cordiviola, 1966*b*); these fish grow to 1·5 m and 53 kg.

In Southeast Asia dry season growth checks were found to mark the scales of Mekong fishes (p. 122). In India numerous growth studies have been made but mainly of cyprinids and catfishes cultured for food and in which growth rates vary very much according to the conditions (p. 189).

Trophic relationships in tropical fish communities

The study of trophic relationships is so basic a part of ecology that we have already looked at the foods consumed by fishes in various waters: in rivers (Zaïre, Amazon, Borneo; Tables 3.1, 3.3, 3.4); in lakes (Victoria, Malawi, Barombi Mbo, Chad; Figs. 5.3, 5.4, 6.1, 6.2, 6.3). Competition for food and the impact of predation are treated in a later chapter in relation to their evolutionary consequences. This present section draws together material from the three continents and examines evidence on how much fishes change their food sources.

The various methods for assessing fish diets and rates of digestion were reviewed by Windell (1971), and for consumption rates related to growth by Davies and Warren (1971). Analyses of stomach contents are generally expressed either as occurrence or dominance (the number of fish in any one group containing a particular food item), or the numbers or volumes of items ingested. In rapid field studies it is helpful to distinguish between main contents and accessory items. The best method to use depends on the fish being investigated and type of food that it eats. Intestinal contents may differ from stomach contents, indicating the varied diet of an individual fish.

Although food webs are very complex, they may be based on relatively few sources (for example the numerous species depending on aufwuchs on the rocky shores of Lake Malawi, Fig. 5.4). As in any food chain, there are rarely more than four or five links; long chains are expensive bioenergetically as a large proportion of potential energy (80 to 90 per cent) is lost at each successive stage. In freshwaters alternative chains run (1) from bottom detritus, through micro-organisms, detritus-feeding invertebrates or fish, to several levels of piscivore; or (2) in the pelagic zone from phytoplankton to zooplankton, to zooplankton-feeders, then to one or more levels of piscivore. In river systems the detrital chain is more important, based largely on allochthonous materials in the headwater streams, while in the lower reaches detritus comes mainly from decomposition of the aquatic macrophytes. As a lake forms, the pelagic plankton chain becomes increasingly important, as is seen after the filling of manmade lakes, and also in lakes like Chad, populated with riverine fishes such as *Alestes baremose* which changes its riverine diet of insects and seeds to exploit the zooplankton in the lake.

In these tropical communities certain fishes have specialised on food at the lowest trophic levels: organic mud with its micro-organisms, aufwuchs, phytoplankton, and even forest debris, are all utilised directly by fishes able or specialised to do so, instead of these sources being converted into fish food by invertebrates, as is more often the case in temperate zone waters. This has important fishery implications, for food fishes can be cropped low in the trophic chain, avoiding losses in production inherent in moving from one trophic level to the next (generally about a 10 per cent loss of biomass for each successive link). There are also specialisations at all trophic levels, even such extreme ones as feeding on the fins or scales of other fishes. Despite these specialisations, however, most predatory fishes show a considerable amount of plasticity in the prey used.

Comparing diets of fishes in the three continents shows:

1. the importance of allochthonous vegetable material as direct food for many fish species;
2. the huge role that insects have as fish food, both aquatic stages of Odonata, Ephemeroptera and Diptera, and terrestrial insects stranded on the water surface;
3. the importance of mud and detritus as foods for fishes which have become specialised to strain large quantities of these for their contained micro-organisms;
4. the large numbers of individuals and kinds of piscivorous fishes present in the communities. The ecological effects of the widely distributed piscivorous *Hoplias* in South America greatly resemble those of *Hydrocynus* in Africa.

The studies considered in this book have shown clearly that there is a linear succession of dominant food sources in streams and rivers (Fig. 9.2). Fishes in headwater streams depend primarily on allochthonous foods (terrestrial insects and vegetable debris); fishes here are mostly eurytrophic, taking whatever food drops into the water and apparently not really using any feeding specialisations that they may possess. As the stream enlarges and deepens, predatory omnivores using benthic invertebrates become more important in the fauna, and laterally flooded areas with their adjacent pools etc. provide more niches. Feeding specialisations here appear to have a greater significance, though their importance may fluctuate seasonally. In the lower reaches, detritus and soft mud accumulate and support species specialised to use these foods (*Prochilodus* in South America, *Labeo*, *Citharinus* and some *Tilapia* in Africa, certain cyprinids in Asia). The extensive growth of macrophytes in the large swampy areas of tropical rivers leads

Fig. 9.2 The linear succession of dominant food sources for fishes in a tropical river system.

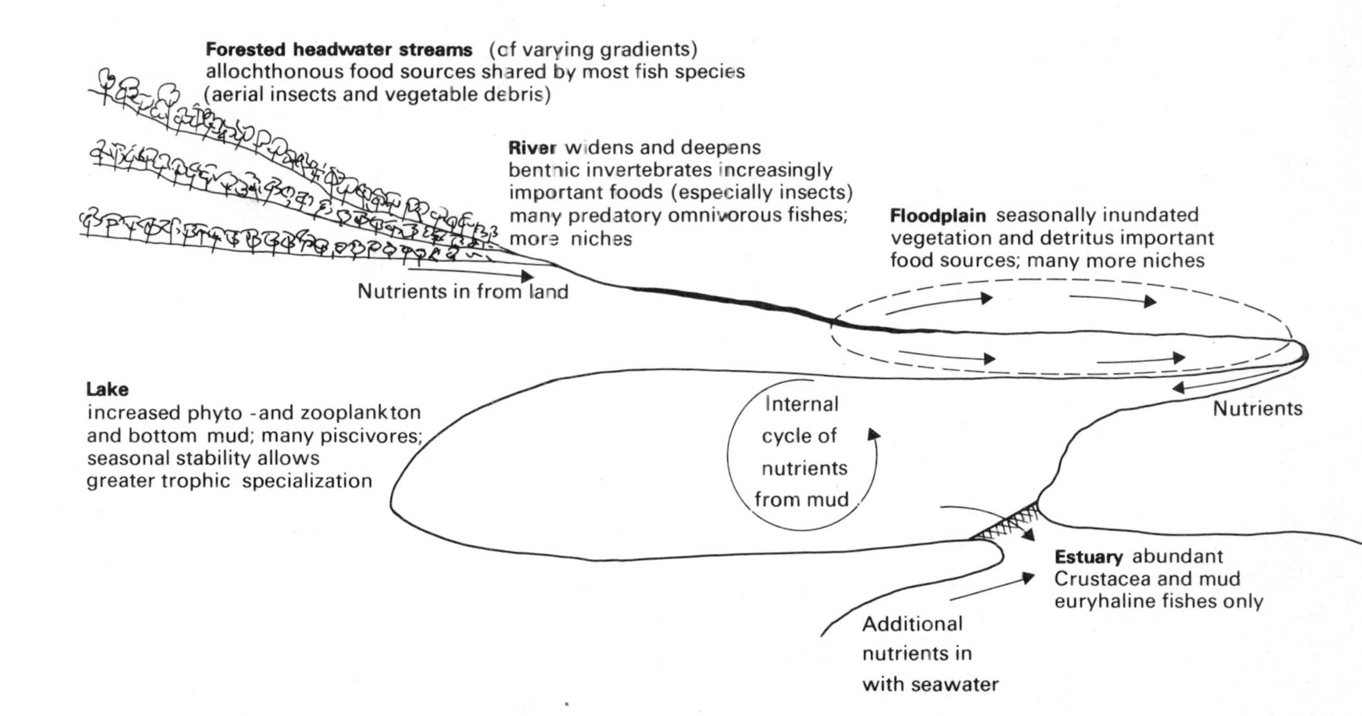
Forested headwater streams (cf varying gradients)
allochthonous food sources shared by most fish species
(aerial insects and vegetable debris)
River widens and deepens
benthic invertebrates increasingly
important foods (especially insects)
many predatory omnivorous fishes;
more niches
Floodplain seasonally inundated
vegetation and detritus important
food sources; many more niches
Nutrients in from land
Lake
increased phyto -and zooplankton
and bottom mud; many piscivores;
seasonal stability allows
greater trophic specialization
Internal
cycle of
nutrients
from mud
Nutrients
Estuary abundant
Crustacea and mud
euryhaline fishes only
Additional
nutrients in
with seawater

to very large accumulations of detrital mud and very large populations of mud-feeding fishes can be supported (e.g. *Prochilodus* in La Plata, p. 113), which may, however, have to move long distances to find suitable places in which to spawn.

Initial observations generally enable a fish species to be put into one of the following broad trophic categories: mud or detritus-feeders, herbivores using algae or macrophytes, plankton-feeders, omnivores using either primarily plant or animal food, carnivores using allochthonous surface insects or benthic insects $\pm$ other invertebrates, and piscivores. More detailed studies generally show that within several of these broad categories a species can change its food, and so its trophic niche and interrelationships with other species within the biotope. This is particularly so for predatory species (mud or aufwuchs feeders are more specialised for their particular diets).

Plasticity in fish diets

Most predatory fishes have great plasticity in their diets, using different prey as they grow and change their biotope, or with whatever foods are available seasonally or with the lunar cycle, or by active selection of preferred foods according to individual choice. This is particularly true of riverine fishes, many of which feed on benthic invertebrates or other fishes, and especially in the more seasonal rivers; also of lake fishes of riverine origin which still return to rivers to spawn, as do many non-cichlids. It is least true of the predators in the pelagic zone of lakes, and of the cichlids in the Great Lakes which are the most specialised in their diets; Malawi Mbuna use one type of food throughout the year and probably throughout life – their large eggs producing young big enough to use the same food source as the parent fish. Since the lake fishes have been much studied, their extreme specialisations have been regarded as normal, whereas they represent the end stage of a graded system of increasing specialisation. Specialisations lead to stenophagy, and the inability to change food habits should environmental conditions change, often leads to extinction. For this reason the Great Lakes have been regarded as 'evolutionary traps' (Briggs, 1966). However, if any of these fish with their 'supralimital specialisations' can survive in rivers when conditions change, they might as discussed later (p. 262) be the founders of new lines of evolution.

Widely distributed species such as *Schilbe mystus*, *Auchenoglanis occidentalis* and *Heterobranchus longifilis*, tend to be bottom insect feeders that can change easily to other diets. Euryphagy, the ability to use many different foods effectively, is an important characteristic of ubiquitous species, and omnivores have a better chance than specialists of becoming widely distributed. The food varies with what is available in each habitat, but it will also depend on interactions with the other fish species present. De Kimpe (1964), who examined data for widely distributed species that occurred in Mweru–Luapula and elsewhere (e.g. Verbeke, 1957, 1959), concluded that: (1) a large number of fish do not have a strict food regime; (2) a species may have different tendencies in different places (*Alestes macrophthalmus* for example eats plants in the Malagarasi swamps but is mainly carnivorous in Lake Mweru); (3) there are individual differences within a species, an individual selecting a particular food at one time. The food regime can vary with season, abundance of food organisms, activity of fish and change of biotope, and other species present.

Ivlev (1961) stressed the choice of food by a fish, comparing the composition of benthos in a fish diet with the composition of organisms in the benthos. This ratio, called by him the electivity (E), ranges from +1 to −1, an electivity of zero indicating complete lack of selection by the fish. In Lake George a study was made of the electivity of planktonic organisms and other items by *Haplochromis squamipinnis* (Moriarty *et al.*, 1973). Factors influencing the size of the food niche in *Clarias senegalensis* in Ghana were discussed by Thomas (1966), who stressed that intraspecific competition will tend to enlarge the food niche, while interspecific competition will restrict it.

Seasonal changes in diet and differences in food items taken by fishes of one species from three habitats within a lake are well shown by the analyses of foods eaten by *Clarias gariepinus* in Lake McIlwaine in Central Africa (Fig. 9.3, after Munro, 1967). In Lake Victoria (p. 132) diets of several fishes (mormyrids and *Alestes*) changed with the phase of moon, which affects the emergence of insect prey. In Lake George, Moriarty *et al.* (1973) found that the two main herbivorous species *Tilapia nilotica* and *Haplochromis nigripinnis* only adopt a phytoplankton diet after a period of carnivorous or omnivorous feeding as fry, and the piscivorous *Haplochromis squamipinnis* only changes to a fish diet after being an opportunist omnivore when young. In Lake Bangweulu in Zambia Bowmaker (1969) found that *Alestes macrophthalmus* fell into four groups entering different trophic relationships with other species in the lake, juveniles taking zooplankton, adults up to 14 cm (70 per cent of them males) living inshore eating insects, and larger adults (mainly females) preying on *Engraulicypris* offshore. These and numerous other cases all stress that it is impossible to base on small samples conclusions about overlaps in foods used by different species. Many marine fishes also show the same kinds of variations and individual differences in their diets.

The evolutionary effects of 'prey switching' have been much discussed and are considered in a later chapter (p. 251). Piscivorous fishes living in the pelagic zone may specialise, but most predatory fishes take a varied selection of prey. Data on foods eaten by *Hydrocynus vittatus* from various waters (p. 180), by the predatory fishes on the Kafue flats (p. 102) and by *Lates* in different lakes all show this clearly.

The most detailed study of food changes in a predatory tropical freshwater fish is that of *Lates niloticus* from Lake Chad based on 5070 fishes over the whole size range examined over six years (A. J. Hopson, 1972). This material revealed that the diet changes with the size of fish, the biotope frequented, the season, and may also vary from year to year (as shown in Fig. 6.4 and p. 172). Hopson concluded that it was impossible to assign the

Lates in Lake Chad to a particular niche because of the marked seasonal changes in size and type of prey used which result in fluctuations of the trophic level of food intake. During summer months when prawns were the

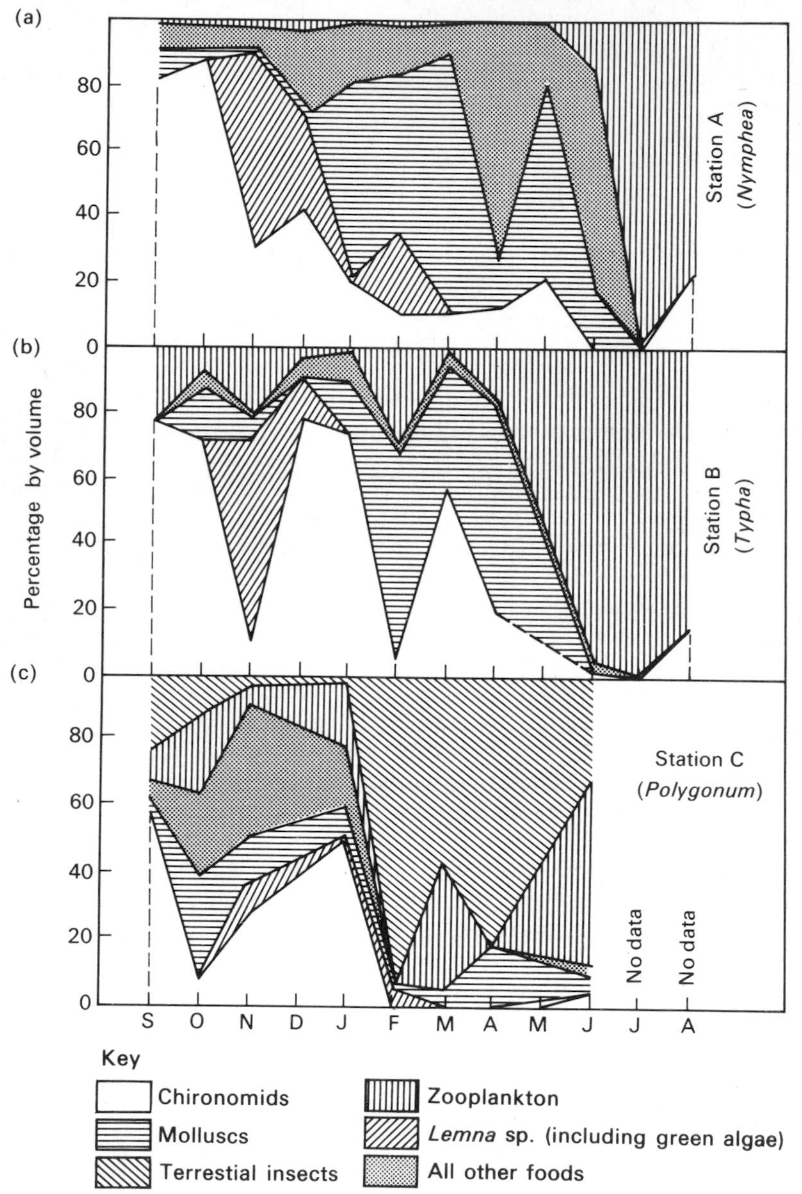

Fig. 9.3 The monthly percentage composition (by volume) of the diet of *Clarias gariepinus* in three habitats in Lake McIlwaine, Central Africa (after Munro, 1967).

dominant food of the offshore population the food chain was very short (adult *Lates* → *Macrobrachium* → bottom algae and detritus), but on other occasions there were three or even four links between *Lates* and the primary producers (adult *Lates* → *Hydrocynus* → small characins → Entomostraca → phytoplankton). Thus the relationship between *Lates* and smaller predators such as *Hydrocynus* and *Eutropius* alternated between the roles of competitor and predator. The composition of the diet probably depends on the relative abundance of various food categories modified by preferences for particular types of food by *Lates*.

A. J. Hopson also discussed data for food used by *Lates* in other waters. In Lake Albert *L. niloticus* is mainly piscivorous, almost entirely so above 30 cm TL (Holden, 1967); of 528 fish between 20 and 50 cm, 78 per cent had eaten fish, 8 per cent prawns (*Caridina*) and 7 per cent insects, almost half the fish eaten being *Tilapia*. In Lake Albert *L. niloticus* is the inshore form, restricted to shallow water, while a second endemic species, *L. macrophthalmus*, occurs offshore in the deep water of the open lake where it feeds primarily on the prawn *Caridina*. Whereas in Lake Chad *L. niloticus* is ubiquitous, exploiting a relatively broad food spectrum, in Lake Albert comparable niches are divided between two species. In Lake Rudolf separation of *L. niloticus* into inshore and offshore subspecies (or species) has also occurred (the offshore deepwater form having, as in Lake Albert, larger eyes; Worthington and Ricardo, 1936). Small pelagic fishes form a major part of the diet of *Lates* in various lakes: Petr (1967) reported that the clupeid *Pellonula afzeliusi* predominated in the stomachs of *Lates niloticus* in Volta Lake, the cyprinodont *Engraulicypris stellae* does so in stomachs of *Lates* in Lake Rudolf, and the two pelagic clupeids in *Lates mariae* in Lake Tanganyika. In Lakes Victoria and Kyoga, where *L. niloticus* have been introduced from Lake Albert, *Haplochromis* species were the commonest prey, but mormyrids, *Engraulicypris, Alestes, Barbus, Clarias* and *Protopterus* were also taken (p. 137). How *Lates* captures its prey has been investigated in the field and experimentally by Hamblyn (1966).

The sharing of food resources

Studies in Amazonian streams (p. 81) showed that the majority of the species present shared whatever food sources were available, much of it allochthonous vegetable matter and insects dropped in from the trees. This apparent lack of specialisation in foods eaten by many of the fishes was surprising in view of the adaptive radiations of the characoids. Why this apparent contradiction? Part of the answer would seem to be that only eurytrophic fishes can penetrate into the headwater streams. The species which do so are mostly widely distributed ones, and their feeding specialisations are probably of greater use elsewhere in their range, all the time or perhaps seasonally. Or they may have been of greater significance in the past as the fish communities were evolving, perhaps in the early stages of community development (as discussed later), or when conditions were different, as during the lacustrine episodes in the histories of Amazon and Zaïre. Today such specialisations appear to be of greater use in the middle and lower reaches of rivers, where so many species coexist. But is resource sharing greater at highwater when foods are abundant, or at low water when they are scarce? This appears to depend on the particular conditions.

In Lake Malawi several species of *Tilapia* shared the phytoplankton when this was abundant, but diverged in their feeding places when it was scarce (personal observation). In Lake Victoria, too, the food overlap in non-cichlids was greatest when they were exploiting a particularly abundant food source (as during an insect emergence). In a Central American stream in Costa Rica, Zaret and Rand (1971) found that among nine sympatric fish species food overlaps were at a minimum in the dry season, the time of least abundant food when competition might be expected to have increased; this they interpreted as being in accordance with Gause's competitive exclusion principle (p. 255). However, in the Rupununi (p. 105) the fishes were driven to sharing the only few food resources available in the dry season, and it was suggested that trophic specialisations would here come into play in the highwater season, the main feeding time. In Zaïre Matthes (1964) also found fishes reduced to sharing the same few foods in the dry season, mainly bottom debris as in the Rupununi. So in these two cases food overlaps appeared greatest in the dry season; feeding levels were however, reduced at this time in the Rupununi.

River studies show that there are great seasonal variations in pressure on resources. Throughout the tropics these appear to be greatest at the end of the rains and in the dry season. The highwater is the main feeding and growing time for most fish species, except for some zooplankton-feeders, and predators which may be able to catch prey more easily when they are less dispersed. As the water level falls, food supplies for most non-piscivorous fishes become restricted in a rapidly contracting environment. Most of these fish spawn early in the rains and the young grow fast, and the ichthyomass is at its greatest at the end of the rains before the enormous losses resulting from predation and stranding as the water falls. Hence pressures on food supplies are at a maximum at the time when resources are shrinking (Fig. 9.4). Is this the time when specialisations are of most benefit to their owners? As the dry season advances fish numbers are reduced and many species cease to feed; in some South American fishes parts of the alimentary canal are used as accessory respiratory organs at this time. Where fishes do not cease to feed in the dry season, this may be another time of intense competition for food in confined pools. Such fluctuations in pressure on food resources are likely to have greatly affected fish evolution. In equatorial waters where there are two floods a year, increased pressure on resources may occur twice a year instead of annually, thereby perhaps speeding the course of evolution.

Studies on fish-feeding behaviour are much needed, and on how social interference affects this in these polyspecific communities. For example teeth and mouth shape not only affect the type of food used, but also how

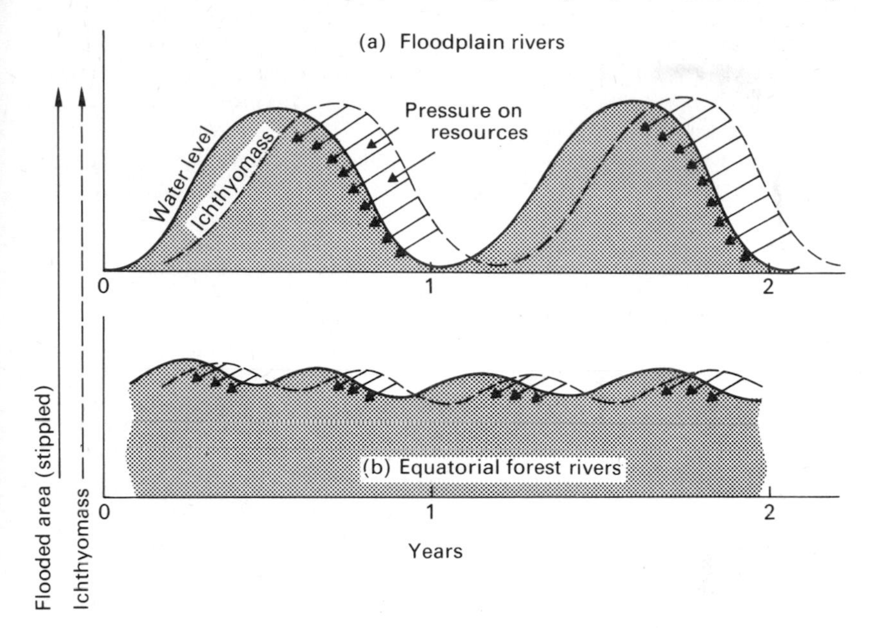

Fig. 9.4 The relationships between seasonal changes in size of aquatic environment (stippled area) and ichthyomass (fish numbers × size) in: (a) floodplain rivers; (b) equatorial forest rivers. In floodplain rivers the ichthyomass is greatest as the environment contracts, putting maximum pressure on resources at this time; in equatorial forest rivers fluctuations are biannual but not so extreme.

this is obtained and the attitude of the fish in the water while feeding. How much does it matter from a food gathering point of view whether a fish 'head stands' while grazing algae off rocks, and how much does this make the fish less accessible to being eaten by a passing predator as it does so? Observations in natural waters where other members of the community are present are needed to illuminate such interactions. Several good marine studies point the way – for example, those of Hobson, 1968, on predatory behaviour, and of Stevenson, 1972, on the regulation of feeding behaviour by environmental factors in reef-dwelling damselfish.

Not all the foods eaten are digested (see p. 167), and one fish species may ameliorate a food for others. In the Malagarasi swamps draining into Lake Tanganyika the characoid *Distichodus* feeding on macrophyte (waterlily) leaves ejected a flocculent material which became rich in micro-organisms and algae and was utilised as food by *Tilapia* and other fishes living in these clearwater swamps, thus increasing the carrying capacity of the swamps for fish. This is the principle on which polyspecific fish culture is based – for example, the macrophyte-eating grass carp, *Ctenopharyngodon idella*, fertilises the pond water for plankton-feeding species such as the silver carp *Hypophthalmichthys molitrix* and the bighead *Aristichthys nobilis*.

Few data are as yet available on quantitative or bioenergetic aspects of interrelationships between the various trophic levels in any tropical waters. The most complete picture that we have is that provided by the Lake George studies in Uganda (p. 166), where estimates of grazing rates showed that only a small proportion of the phytoplankton standing crop is eaten daily in this lake, and that the zooplankters have a more important role in the recycling of resources than do the herbivorous fishes.

Reproduction in tropical freshwater fishes

Seasonality of reproduction

A very few fishes spawn once in a lifetime and then die: 'big bang' spawners such as the catadromous *Anguilla* eels which feed and grow in freshwater then migrate back to sea to breed. The majority of fish spawn at repeated intervals. Amongst these the ova may either (1) ripen all at once so that the eggs are produced in one batch ('total spawners'), or (2) eggs may ripen in batches ('multiple spawners' of Bagenal, 1971), the eggs being laid either at intervals throughout a breeding season or aseasonally. Multiple spawners include a wide range of fishes from 'partial spawners' in which perhaps one third of the ova ripen and are released at one time, the other ova remaining in reserve for spawnings later in the season, to 'small-brood spawners' which produce small batches of eggs at frequent intervals. There is thus a whole range of breeding possibilities. How do these relate to seasonality of spawning and other ecological factors?

The total spawners are mostly very fecund fishes producing very large numbers of ova at a time. Many make long migrations, often up river, to spawning grounds, and spawning tends to be very seasonal. These fishes include the 'piracema' fishes of Brazil (p. 113), such as the large characoids *Prochilodus* and *Salminus* which tagging experiments have shown to make remarkably regular movements upriver. The large centropomid *Lates niloticus* in Lake Chad is also a total spawner, though here it has an extended breeding season and breeds in the lake; it is, however, very fecund producing very small pelagic eggs each buoyed up by an oil globule (Hopson, 1969). Okedi calculated that *L. niloticus* in Lake Victoria produce between one and eleven million eggs at a time. Many riverine characoids and siluroids produce demersal eggs which sink gradually as they descend with the current until they reach a quiet shore; other species lay adhesive eggs amongst water plants.

Tropical freshwaters include numerous multiple spawners. There must be an adaptive advantage in producing several batches of eggs where the first may be endangered by fluctuations in water level. Many of these fishes make only local movements to spawn. Many tropical fishes guard their eggs and young and tend to have smaller broods than amongst the fishes which leave their eggs unguarded. These guarding fishes often produce a batch in the low-water season before the floods come (this occurs in cichlids both in South America and in Africa and in some loricariid catfishes in South America which guard their eggs), and cichlids continue to produce batches through the early part of the highwater season. In equatorial waters in Africa and in ponds it is quite usual to find ovaries starting to ripen again in cichlid females which are mouth-brooding their young. These guarded eggs are relatively large.

Examples of these types of reproduction are indicated in Table 9.1, while Table 9.2 lists the fecundity of representative species defined as the number of ova ripening at one time in the ovaries. Gradations between categories exist, but on the whole the total spawners have more clearly defined spawning seasons, are more fecund, producing numerous small eggs, and many make long migrations to do so, whereas multiple spawners have less clearly defined breeding seasons, produce fewer eggs at a time, often very large ones, and may make only local movements to spawning areas. Multiple spawners (particularly small-brood spawners) generally establish a territory and often make a nest in which to spawn and guard the eggs, or the eggs may be attached to the body of one parent (male or female), or brooded in the mouth of one or other, or rarely both, parents; or the eggs may develop inside the female to be born as live young (or eggs almost ready to hatch in the poeciliid *Tomeurus*). Complex ritual breeding behaviour is important for synchronisation of spawning in these small brood fishes, whereas total spawners may be brought together by external factors such as floods.

Selection will determine that the young are produced at the time of year most favourable for their survival, when there is abundant food for rapid growth and cover from predators. Thus the majority of species spawn as the water level rises, at whatever time of year this occurs (with the exception of some small zooplankton feeders, such as clupeids, for zooplankton is more abundant in rivers when the current has slackened). Among the total spawners the start of the highwater season is the main spawning time for fishes in which the young feed in laterally flooded areas. Spawning may be stimulated either by the local rains, or by floods coming downriver from rain higher up in the drainage basin. Some species wait until they have moved out of the main riverbed before they spawn, moving out with the flood, i.e. travelling with the current, not against it as in the case of fishes pushing upstream to spawn. Some may spawn in the riverbed before they move out (as at Kainji, where numbers of young came from fishes trapped between the coffer dams, p. 98). Should the floods fail, the fish may not spawn that year as happened for *Labeo mesops* in Lake Malawi one year, and as Khanna reported for cyprinids in India (p. 53).

Some fishes which make long migrations upriver (in the Pilcomayo for example, p. 119) are trapped in feeding lagoons until the river level starts to rise, and only reach their spawning grounds upstream when the floods are no longer at their height. Certain large fishes such as *Arapaima* have to await floods to gain access to their spawning places and cannot make their

Table 9.1 Types of reproduction in representative tropical freshwater fishes.

TYPE AND FECUNDITY	SEASONALITY OF REPRODUCTION	EXAMPLES	MOVEMENTS AND PARENTAL CARE
1. **Big bang** ++++	— Once a lifetime	*Anguilla*	v. long migrations: catadromous no parental care
2. **Total spawners** +++	Very seasonal with floods: annual or biannual	Many characoids: e.g. *Prochilodus*, *Salminus*, *Hydrocynus*; Many cyprinids; Some siluroids	'Piracema' fishes, with very long migrations No parental care
	Extended season	*Lates* (L. Chad)	Local movements: pelagic eggs
3. **Partial spawners** ++	Throughout high water season(s)	Some cyprinids	Mainly local movements
		Some characoids:	
		e.g. *Serrasalmus*	Guard eggs on plants (♂; ♂+♀)
		Hoplias	Guard eggs on bottom (♂)
		Some siluroids:	
		e.g. *Mystus*	Guard eggs and young (♂)
Grades into		*Arapaima*	Guard eggs and young; bottom nest (♂+♀)
		Some anabantoids	Guard eggs, surface bubble nest (♂)
4. **Small-brood spawners** +	High water season; may start	*Hoplosternum*	Guard eggs surface nest (♂)
		Hypostomus	Guard eggs bank holes (sex?)
	*	*Loricaria parva*	Guards eggs under stone (♂)
	†	**Loricaria* spp.	Carries eggs on lower lip (♂)
		Aspredo sp.	Carries eggs on belly (♀)
		Osteoglossum	Mouth broods (sex?)
		Cichlids:	
		*Most S. American spp.	Guard eggs and young (♂+♀)
		*†Most African spp.	Mouth brood eggs and young (♀)
		†*Tilapia galilaea*	Mouth brood eggs and young (♂+♀)
		T. melanotheron	Mouth brood eggs and young (♂)
		Stingrays	Livebearing
		†Poeciliids	Live bearing
		Anableps	Live bearing
	End of rains	Cyprinodont annual spp.	Resting eggs in mud through dry season

* End of dry season.
† Or be aseasonal.

nest until the water is deep enough for them to do so; in West Africa *Gymnarchus* and *Heterotis* breed earlier downriver where the land is flooded earlier in the season. In the equatorial Lake George where seasonal changes are minimal, individuals of most cichlid species may be taken in breeding conditions in any month of the year; despite this, spawning peaks occur in the rains for *Tilapia nilotica* in certain years. Differences in time of spawning can help to keep sympatric species distinct, as they do between *Tilapia saka* and *T. squamipinnis* in Lake Malawi (p. 149). Differences in time of day at which the fish spawn (as in *Prochilodus platensis* and *P. scrofa*, p. 115) could have a similar role.

Table 9.2 The fecundity of representative tropical freshwater fishes.

SPECIES	NO. RIPE OVA IN OVARIES	FEMALES No.	FEMALES Length cm	AUTHORITY
Protopterus aethiopicus	1700–2300			Greenwood (1958)
Protopterus aethiopicus	468–58 422		68–91	Okedi (1971*b*)
Arapaima gigas	47 000			Allsopp (1958)
Osteoglossum bicirrhosum	180			Lowe-McConnell (1964)
Mormyrus kannume	1393–17 369	66	18–37	
Marcusenius victoriae	846–16 748	92	11–19	
Gnathonemus longibarbis	502–14 624	38	9–18	Okedi (1970)
Hippopotamyrus grahami	248–5229	32	7–13	
Pollimyrus nigricans	206–739	58	7–9	
Petrocephalus catostoma	116–1015	66	5–7	
			(*Age*)	
Alestes leuciscus	1000–1100		6–7(I)	
Alestes leuciscus	3500–4000		8(II)	
Alestes nurse	17 000		16(II)	Daget (1952)
Alestes dentex	24 800		22(II)	
Alestes dentex	27 800		23(IV)	
Alestes macrophthalmus	10 000			Bowmaker (1969)
Hoplias malabaricus	2500–3000			von Ihering *et al* (1928)
Salminus maxillosus	1 152 900–2 619 000		52–100	Ringuelet *et al* (1967)
Prochilodus scrofa	300 000			von Ihering (1930*a*)
Prochilodus argenteus	657 385		64	Fontenele (1953)
Labeo victorianus	40 133	1	18	Cadwalladr (1965)
Catla catla	230 830–4 202 250	8	78–95	Jhingran (1968)
Lates niloticus	1 104 700–11 790 000	8		Okedi (1971*c*)
**Mystus aor*	45 410–122 477	24	84–99	Saigal (1964)
Hypostomus plecostomus	115–118		12	von Ihering *et al* (1928)
Arius sp.	118			von Ihering *et al* (1928)
Loricaria sp.	*c.* 100			Lowe-McConnell (1964)
Tilapia leucosticta	56–498	9	7–16	Welcomme (1967*b*)
Tilapia esculenta	324–1672		17–36	Lowe (1955)
Pseudotropheus zebra	17–<30			Fryer and Iles (1972 p. 106)
Cichla ocellaris	10 203–12 559	2	56–78	Fontenele (1950)
Astronotus ocellatus	961–3452		27 29	Fontenele (1951)
Anableps anableps	6–13 embryos		21–23	Turner (1938)

* May spawn 5 times a season; most species above this in table (except *Arapaima* and *Osteoglossum*) are *total spawners*, those below it *multiple spawners*.

In equatorial areas where there are two rains and two floods each year, as in the rivers at the north end of Lake Victoria and elsewhere in Kenya and in the lower Zaïre, fishes are known to spawn in both floods, but it is not known if individual fishes spawn twice a year. In Lake Victoria gonad weights of *Labeo victorianus* increased to the level of sexual maturation about one month before the time of maximum rains twice each year, around March and September (Cadwalladr, 1965), but there appears to be no evidence that individual fish spawn twice each year. For the small mormyrids in Lake Victoria, Okedi (p. 133) concluded that the fattening and breeding cycles are biannual, leaving two rings a year on opercular bones. In East

Africa flooding regimes are often erratic and the relative importance of the second rains varies from year to year. In parts of the central Zaïre basin where there is one main spawning season and a second smaller one, the relative importance of the two seasons may vary from year to year. In Lake Tanganyika *Boulengerochromis microlepis* appears to have three breeding periods a year (p. 158).

At higher latitudes within the tropics, as in Lake Nasser on the River Nile, Lake Chad, and in southern Africa, fish spawning activity generally ceases when the water temperature is low in winter. In Lake Chad there appeared to be a virtual cessation of spawning activity in *Lates niloticus* from mid-December to late February (A. J. Hopson, 1972).

Spawning movements Most characoids and cyprinids leave adhesive demersal eggs unguarded among plants or on the bottom. The breeding habits of the potamadromous fishes are conditioned principally by the nature of their spawning grounds, their accessibility and suitability for the development of the eggs and larval fishes. The eggs of many stream fishes need to be kept free of silt and need water with a fairly high oxygen concentration. The spatial distribution of the spawning grounds determines both the distance travelled and the temporal opportunities existing for ascent. Streams tend to have short, compact migrations, whereas in large rivers the ascent is often long and entry into the river may continue for many weeks. For fishes ascending rivers from Lake Victoria Whitehead (1959) recognised four distinct patterns of migration:

1. **Long duration**, fishes such as the large cyprinid *Barbus altianalis radcliffi* entering the river over an extended period and ascending 50 miles (80 km) or more to breed in the swift rocky upper reaches.
2. **Medium duration**, exhibited by most of the potamadromous fishes, such as *Labeo victorianus* and *Schilbe mystus*, which enter the river in fairly compact shoals and run for 5 to 15 miles (8 to 25 km) upriver before moving laterally into the floodwater pools to spawn (as do the small mormyrids).
3. **Short duration**, species such as the small *Alestes* ascending streams in enormous numbers at certain times of year, and *Clarias mossambicus* and various *Barbus* which make very sudden ascents up short streams and take advantage of shortlived flood conditions (Welcomme, 1969).
4. **Riverine migrants**, purely riverine species or populations, which pass up or down stream in search of shallow flooded pools.

In Lake Malawi the large salmon-like *Barilius* migrated far up the large permanent rivers from the north end of the lake, *Labeo mesops* and certain other species moved up seasonal medium-sized rivers, and *Clarias* went short distances up spate streams (Lowe, 1952). Different species ascending the Mwenda River from Lake Kariba varied much in their behaviour (Bowmaker, 1973), *Clarias* moving up in a single massive early run, while more fragmented migrations were made by *Hydrocynus*, *Labeo* and *Mormyrus* according to the flow volume. *Clarias*, *Mormyrus* and *Hydrocynus* accumulated at the river mouth several months before the rains started; *Clarias* only then, but some *Hydrocynus* and *Mormyrus* moved to the river mouth continuously throughout the rains. *Labeo* concentrated at this river mouth only after the rains commenced and before the river started to flow, and then moved upstream at the earliest opportunity.

Thus many lake fishes retain the ancestral habit of moving into rivers to spawn, which they do seasonally. But amongst those which spawn in the lakes breeding may continue throughout the year, as it does in the cichlids in the equatorial lakes George and Victoria, and in the Mbuna, though not in the *Tilapia*, in Lake Malawi. Spawning may, however, be affected by hydrological events in the lake, as it is in the Lake Tanganyika clupeids (p. 155), or arrested during the colder months, as it is in *Lates* in Lake Chad.

Breeding behaviour adaptations

Parental care Oral incubation, the young being brooded in the mouth of one or other parent, has evolved independently in many fish groups in both freshwater and the sea (listed in Oppenheimer, 1970): in ariid catfishes, various anabantoids, *Osteoglossum* and *Scleropages*, and in the cichlids in which the mouth-brooding habit must have arisen several times independently from 'guarding' species. Bearing live young, as in stingrays, sharks, poeciliids and *Anableps* presents a further stage in the protection of the young.

Among the partial spawners and small-brood spawners there are variations within families as to whether eggs are guarded, by one or both parents, whether they continue to guard the young fishes after the eggs have hatched, and for how long they do so. Such differences between species are well illustrated in the anabantoids. In Asia many of these which live in deoxygenated water make floating bubble nests, generally guarded by the male (as in *Osphronemus goramy*) or by both sexes (as in some *Macropodus* species), though very small pelagic eggs are left unguarded in *Anabas testudineus* and *Helostoma temmincki*; in the African *Ctenopoma* there are two ethological groups, one which does not care for its brood, and another (which includes *C. muriei*) in which the male guards a surface foam nest (Berns and Peters, 1969), while the anabantoid *Sandelia capensis* produces adhesive eggs guarded by either sex (Breder and Rosen, 1966).

According to data on fish reproduction summarised by Breder and Rosen (1966), in the Channidae eggs and young are guarded by both parents in *Ophiocephalus striatus* in the Philippines and *O. punctatus* in the Punjab, but not by *Channa asiatica*. *O. striatus* produces 100 to 1000 eggs at a time, which take three days to hatch, in a clearing in the vegetation; breeding occurs in every month of the year and individuals may breed twice a year. *O. punctatus* in the Punjab spawns between April and July, and the 500-strong brood are guarded for over a month, until the fry are about 10 cm long. The male guards the eggs in *Notopterus chitila* in India and Thailand; the female is believed to spawn three times in the season, producing up to

10 000 small eggs which are attached to posts etc. The nandids all show some form of parental care. In the puffer fishes, the male of *Tetraodon fluviatilis* in Asia is reported to guard adhesive eggs, but there is no evidence of parental care in *T. schoutedeni* in Zaïre. The Indian *Mastacembelus pancalus* leaves 10 to 20 demersal eggs in algal masses and they are not guarded.

Among the characoids which guard nests (an unusual feature in this group of fishes) *Serrasalmus* species (*S. nattereri* and *S. rhombeus*) spawned in the main rains in Guyana, where they are reputed to guard eggs laid on tree roots trailing in the water. In Chicago aquarium (U.S.A.) a pair of *S. niger* (? = *S. rhombeus*) made a hollow depression in a thicket of plants, where they spawned, and both parents then guarded the site for three weeks, by which time young were found to be free-swimming on the bottom below the plants (Braker, 1963). *S. spilopleura* in aquaria laid adhesive eggs on water plants, the male then chased away the female and guarded them; they hatched in thirty-six hours and the fry were free-swimming in five days. *S. nattereri* which spawned in pools in the U.S.A., sprayed up to 5000 large golden eggs over plants; the eggs hatched in ninety-six hours and the adults were said to guard them and to spawn regularly once every two weeks (*Tropical Fish Hobbyist*, 1963). In South American streams the characoid *Hoplias malabaricus* produces batches of between 2500 and 3000

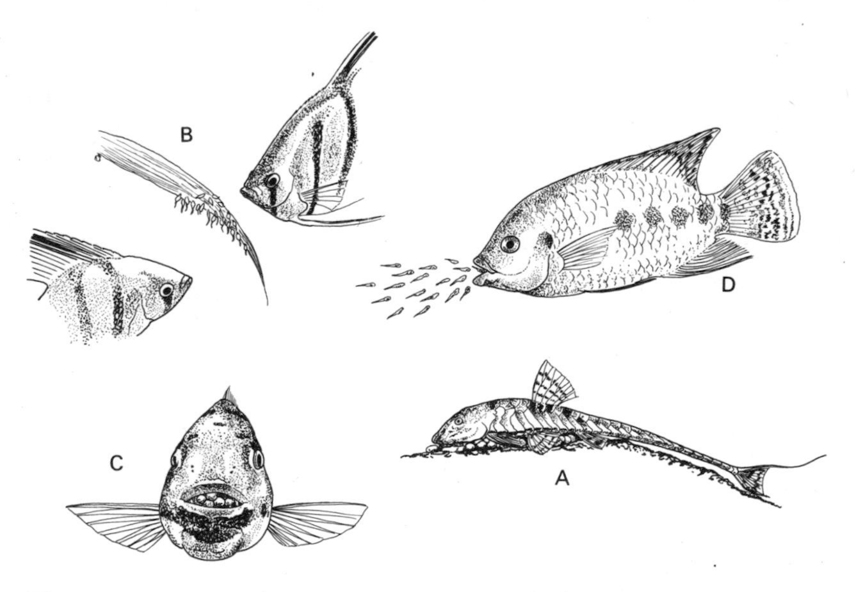

Fig. 9.5 Examples of parental care in freshwater fishes:
A. Male *Loricaria* guarding eggs (in some species these are attached to an elongation of his lower lip).
B. *Pterophyllum* pair guarding young attached to a water plant.
C. Oral incubation of eggs in *Tilapia*.
D. *Tilapia* young returning to mouth of female parent.

eggs at fifteen-day intervals; these are laid in a small depression in the bottom shallows where they are guarded by the male, and they hatch in four days to give 6 to 8 mm alevins which take about ten days to absorb the yolk sac (von Ihering *et al.*, 1928; Azevedo and Gomes, 1943).

In the small South American characoid *Copeina arnoldi* the eggs are actually deposited out of water on an overhanging leaf, where they are kept wet by the male splashing them with water every twenty or thirty minutes; they take two or three days to hatch. Fertilisation here is internal (see p. 225).

The nest-makers in South America include *Hoplosternum* armoured catfish in which the male makes a nest in the flooded trenches during the rains of grass or other vegetation buoyed up by air bubbles passed into it from his intestine (personal observation); the male guards the nest and several females may lay in one nest. In another callichthyid, eggs are laid under a large floating leaf buoyed up by bubbles. In Africa the mormyroid *Gymnarchus* also makes a floating nest (Svensson, 1933, Plate I), and the osteoglossid *Heterotis* a nest in the swamps. Eggs carried attached to the body include the groups of 100 to 200 eggs glued together and carried on the especially elongated lower lip of certain male *Loricaria*, as reported from aquaria in *L. vetula* and *L. anus* and observed for a Rupununi species before the rains (Fig. 9.5). In another South American catfish, *Aspredo*, the eggs are carried ahering to the belly of the female.

The young are guarded for a considerable period in *Arapaima*, some catfishes and many cichlids, for example, *Cichla ocellaris* and *Cichlasoma festivum* in South America, and in *Tilapia zillii* and *T. rendalli* in Africa. Also, surprisingly since most Great Lakes cichlids mouth-brood their young, in certain Tanganyika genera including *Boulengerochromis* (p. 158). Behaviour studies show that chemical and visual devices have evolved to keep the young near to the parent (p. 236). In certain *Haplochromis* the brooding female becomes territorial and the young learn her territory and stay within it. A pheromone is used in *Arapaima* and possibly some other species; chemical methods of binding the young to the parent may be much more general than is yet realised (p. 236).

In the majority of cases in which the young are guarded after they have become free-swimming both parents share duties, one leading the school of young the other following it (e.g. in *Cichlasoma festivum, Cichla ocellaris*, personal observation). Where eggs only are guarded, or where there is oral incubation, this is generally carried out by one or other sex (very rarely both as in *Tilapia galilaea*). The guarding parent can eat little. In some cases (in some anabantoids) the habit of the male being the guarder appears to be connected with the greater need for the female to recover after spawning, as more body weight is lost in egg production than in sperm production. In some cases the male appears more aggressive and thus a more effective defender of the next generation. Where the male alone guards the nest he may induce several females to lay in his nest in succession; he then rears a mixed batch of young, of different genetic constitution and of slightly different ages. There is evidence of this in such diverse groups as *Protopterus* (investigated by Greenwood, 1958) and in callichthyid catfishes in South America (Lowe-McConnell, 1969*c*).

The mouth brooders include most of the African cichlids but very few neotropical ones (some *Geophagus* and *Aequidens*, personal observation and Socolof, 1972). Within the genus *Tilapia* the male broods in a few West African species (such as *T. heudeloti*); *T. galilaea* is very unusual in that either sex may brood eggs and young (Iles and Holden, 1969). In most *Tilapia*, as in most other mouth-brooding cichlids of the Great Lakes in which breeding habits are known, it is the female which mouth broods (Lowe-McConnell, 1959*b*). In the L. Malawi *Tilapia* in which the males in spawning dress remain by their nests in spawning ground arenas and the females take the young to special brooding grounds (p. 149), there is segregation of the sexes immediately after spawning. The females eventually leave their young in nursery areas, generally inshore. The sequence of events differs in detail from species to species. Nest forms are often of specific pattern (for example domed, or with accessory pits around the central plaque), resulting from the movements used by the male to make the nest. Courtship displays are specific, using the specific colours of the breeding fish to full advantage. Some male *Tilapia* have long genital tassels with egg-simulating blobs of tissue on them which may enhance the chances of the female picking up sperm in her mouth together with the eggs (compare the function of egg dummy spots on the anal fin of *Haplochromis* (p. 231). Sperm and eggs carry adhesive filaments in some cases and their structure varies from species to species (Peters, 1963).

Predator pressure would appear to be an important factor in the evolution of some form of parental care for the eggs and young, and it is interesting that so few of the South American cichlids have evolved oral incubation, especially as predator pressure appears to be particularly intense in South American waters. Perhaps the presence of both parents to guard the young fishes when they are first free-swimming is of greater value to the fish here than oral incubation would be, as this is generally undertaken by one sex only.

Roberts (1972) considered that physicochemical factors may also have been important in the evolution of parental care, for this occurs in many fishes in which the adults spend at least part of the time in swamps or other oxygen-deficient habitats, and if they reproduce in such places they are obliged to take care of their young. He cites as examples the air breathers *Protopterus* and *Lepidosiren, Notopterus, Arapaima, Heterotis, Gymnarchus, Hoplosternum* and anabantoids, which all live in rather deoxygenated waters and care for their young. There are, however, other air-breathing fishes which lack parental care (such as *Polypterus* according to Arnoult, 1966), while all the cichlids provide examples of non-air-breathing fishes which guard their young. So it would seem that physicochemical factors may have been important in the evolution of parental care in many rather ancient fishes (and those that had it survived to tell the tale), while in some other groups, such as the cichlids (probably a young group) predator pressure has been more important. (It is perhaps significant in view of ideas about how communities evolve discussed in later chapters that physicochemical factors appear to have been important in the old families, and predator pressures in a young family.)

Producing live young appears to be the next stage in their protection from the exigencies of the environment, whether physicochemical or biotic. In tropical freshwaters this occurs in the elasmobranch stingrays, the freshwater hemirhamphids, and in many neotropical cyprinodontiform families: the Poeciliidae, Anablepidae, Goodeidae, Jenynsiidae. In these live-bearing cyprinodontoids the male is generally smaller than the female, unlike the males of the egg-laying cyprinodontids, which are generally larger than the females. In both poeciliids and cyprinodontids the males are much more colourful than the females. In *A. anableps* the larger female (which is the same colour as the male) grows up to 23 cm long and may contain up to thirteen live young all over 4 cm long (Turner, 1938, and personal observation). Internal fertilisation precedes live bearing. Superfetation (the production of several batches of young from one fertilisation) occurs in some poeciliid groups, though not in *Anableps*.

Internal fertilisation Internal fertilisation has been evolved many more times than live bearing, leading to the production of fertile eggs. Nelson (1964*a*) who discussed its adaptive significance, listed it in: *Pantodon*, the Glandulocaudine characids and *Creagrutus*, the siluroid *Trachycorystes*, the cyprinid *Barbus viviparus*, and in freshwater hemirhamphids, as well as in numerous cyprinodontoid groups and related Atherinomorph families. He pointed out that most of the fishes in which it occurs are small surface feeders, many of which leap out of water while mating, a habit evolved independently at least three times in the characids alone.

In the Glandulocaudine characids Nelson considered that the evolution of internal fertilisation was an adaptive response to a tropical habitat with well-marked wet and dry seasons, as it allows the temporal separation of mating and spawning. Mating can then occur when the fish are concentrated in small dry season pools, when a mate is easy to find. But such places, with their concentration of predators and shortage of food, are unpropitious places for the production of young, and the female delays egg laying until she can move out into flooded shallows, places rich in food for larval fishes and where predators cannot follow her (Fig. 9.6). She spawns there in the absence of the male. The spectacular radiation in sexual dimorphism in these glandulocaudine fishes appears to be related to the need to make the female receptive to mating when the eggs are not yet maturing inside her. Some of the males have enlarged fins, the *Corynopoma* male has greatly prolonged opercular extensions (Fig. 9.7D), others have grappling hooks; the caudal fin glands of the male direct a pheronome toward the female during courtship display, and male *Glandulocauda* croak.

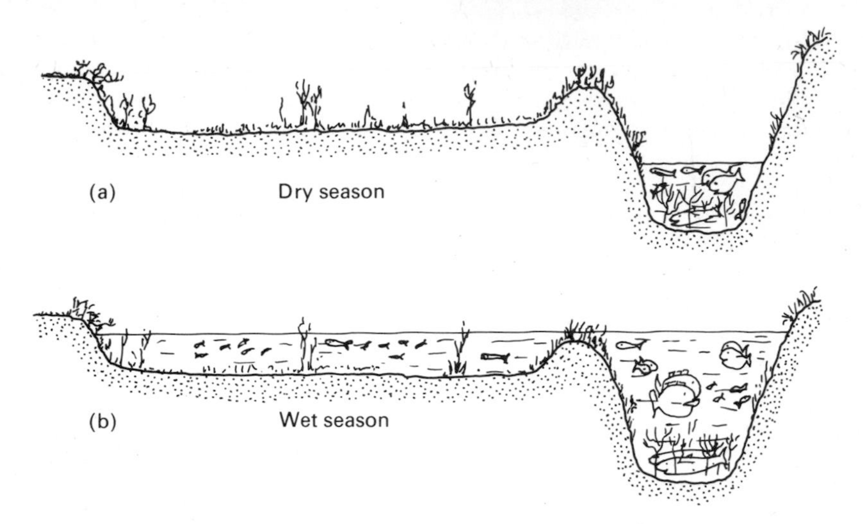

Fig. 9.6 The advantages of internal fertilization in a tropical habitat with well-marked wet and dry seasons (after Nelson, 1964). During the dry season (a) glandulocaudine fishes (small characids) are concentrated into pools where the probability of finding a mate is high, but survival prospects for young fish are low as predators and omnivores are also concentrated in the pools. With the annual floods (b) the adjacent areas are flooded and abundant food becomes available; the predators remain in deeper water but the top-living glandulocaudines move into flooded shallows where the females can spawn in the absence of males. (Originally published by the University of California Press; reprinted by permission of the Regents of the University of California.)

Annual fishes Certain cyprinodontids of the tribe Rivulini, *Cynolebias*, *Astrofundulus* and *Rivulus* in South America, and *Nothobranchius* and *Aphyosemion* in Africa, are 'annual fishes' which spend the dry season as resting eggs Myers (1952). These annual species are often readily recognisable by the large dorsal fin of the male by which he holds the female when spawning. The anterior parts of the anal fin of both sexes are folded into a tube to bury the eggs in the bottom mud and ensure proper fertilisation. South American annuals often dive deep into soft bottoms, African annuals generally place eggs less deeply in the mud. Air is brought down to the eggs by expansion and contraction with diurnal temperature fluctuations in the dry mud. Annual rivulins are generally very fertile and once mature spawn every day until they die. Some eggs remain transparent, while others develop and aestivate as 'resting embryos' (diapause II), while still others will develop ripe embryos and aestivate as 'resting fry'. There are generally three phases of diapause in the African rivulins. The adaptive advantages of this are obvious, for when rain falls and the oxygen supply is cut off from the eggs, those with ripe embryos have to hatch or die, but earlier diapause eggs remain if the pool should dry up again after the first showers. The eggs of the South American *Cynolebias nigripinnis* can remain viable even after three years under anaerobic conditions in soil below water (Scheel, 1968). The behaviour of the annual *Rivulus* which concentrates the breeding populations in drying pools in Peru was described above (p. 108).

Relative sizes and numbers of males and females and sex reversal

Male and female fishes may be of comparable sizes, but generally if the eggs are guarded by one sex the guarding sex (often the male) is the larger fish. Where fecundity is at a premium, as in most total spawners such as many characoids and cyprinids, the females are generally larger than the males; the egg number increases with the size of the female. Where breeding is very frequent, as in *Tilapia* when conditions are poor, the discrepancy in size between the sexes increases for bioenergetic reasons, more weight being lost with egg than with sperm production, retarding the growth of the female compared with that of the male. Furthermore the female feeds little while mouth-brooding young.

Attempts to produce sterile hybrid *Tilapia* for fish culture led to the unexpected discovery at Malacca in Malaya that crossing certain species produces all male offspring. This was first found when male *Tilapia hornorum* imported from Zanzibar were crossed with female *Tilapia mossambica* (a South African species) acclimatised in Malaya; the reciprocal cross produced about three males to one female. Since then skewed sex ratios have been found in a number of other *Tilapia* crosses (reviewed and discussed by Hickling, 1968).

These skewed sex ratios in *Tilapia* were not due to sex changes, but sex reversal is quite usual in some groups of fishes (reviewed by Atz, 1964; Reinboth, 1971). The change from female to male (protogyny) occurs in many reef fishes (e.g. serranids) which live in complex communities where efficiency rather than fecundity is at a premium (see p. 263). The change from male to female (protandry) appears to be less common in fishes (though commoner than protogyny in other vertebrate groups). In fresh and brackish waters protogynous hermaphrodites occur in all members of the Synbranchidae ('swamp-eels') that have been examined (e.g. *Synbranchus marmoratus, Monopterus albus*), and most synbranchids have two types of male, primary males born as males and secondary males evolved by sex reversal of functional females (Liem, 1963, 1968). Liem suggested that the precarious poise of sexual identity in synbranchids is a switch mechanism to compensate for the vicissitudes of the natural habitat, allowing reproduction in spite of severe population depletions by extreme droughts. Synchronous hermaphroditism occurs in some marine fishes (including deep sea fishes with sparce populations) and in the American fresh and brackish-water cyprinodont *Rivulus marmoratus*. In this species experiments have shown that environmental influences such as temperature, crowding and starvation can influence sex ratios (Harrington, 1967); its naturally occurring self-fertilisation, possibly an adaptation to unstable coastal conditions, probably assisted its island-hopping progress across the

Caribbean. The occurrence of natural sex reversal and hermaphroditism in radically different environments in such phylogenetically unrelated fishes as the Serranidae, Sparidae, Platycephalidae, Cyprinodontidae, Synbranchiformes and Myctophiformes (deep sea fish), all of which have evolved from different ancestors, indicates that it is due to convergence or chance evolution.

Fecundity and frequency of spawning Fecundity, defined by Bagenal (1971, p. 167) as the number of ripening eggs in the female prior to the next spawning period, varies very much in individuals of one species of the same weight, length and age. But in many species it increases in proportion to the weight of the fish, hence with the cube of the length. This occurs in the small mormyrids of L. Victoria (Okedi, 1970), and in the guarder *Tilapia zillii*. But in the mouth-brooding *Tilapia* Welcomme (1967*b*) found that fecundity generally increases with the square of the total length and that the number of young that can be brooded is limited by mouth size, which increases in linear relationship with body length, so brooding efficiency decreases as the parent increases in length. Welcomme made a special study of the effects of growth rate, maturation size, and spawning frequency on both fecundity (egg production) and fertility (the number of live young produced, equated by him with brood number) in the mouth-brooding *Tilapia leucosticta* in Lake Victoria. In *Alestes macrophthalmus* in L. Bangweulu, Bowmaker (1969) noted that lake fish appeared to be more fecund than swamp fish, and he thought that individual females bred twice a year.

Individual *Tilapia* (including *T. leucosticta, T. esculenta, T. variabilis, T. nilotica*) in equatorial lakes, and many other *Tilapia* (including *T. mossambica*) in ponds and dams throughout the tropics, may spawn three or more times in succession in one season. The number of eggs generally diminishes at each spawning. In aquaria individual *T. esculenta* spawned seven times in twenty-four months, with broods as close as thirty-nine days and at average intervals of two months. These small fishes in aquaria were as fecund as lake fish, producing as many, but smaller, eggs (Cridland, 1961). Peters (1963) also found egg number to be reciprocally related to egg weight, *Tilapia* producing many small or few large eggs. The maximum size to which *Tilapia* fry are brooded varies with the species and its normal habitat; in inshore-dwelling species it is smaller (to *c.* 12 mm long in *T. leucosticta*) than in the openwater-living species of Lake Malawi, where the most open water species, *T. lidole*, may continue to brood young that are 50 mm TL (Lowe, 1955).

Among the smaller cichlids of the Great Lakes, *Haplochromis* in Victoria and Mbuna in Malawi, small batches of young may be produced throughout the year, Mbuna including *Pseudotropheus zebra* (Table 9.2), producing less than fifty eggs per brood. But for many species we do not yet know the frequency or seasonality of spawning.

The South American *Cichla ocellaris* in ponds has a minimum of twenty-two days between spawnings; Fontenele (1950) recorded twenty-six spawnings in four and a half years. Females 56 to 78 cm total length contained between 10 000 and 12 500 ripe ova. The eggs hatch in seventy-eight hours and the young are guarded until they are *c.* 35 mm long by both parents.

Communications between fishes

In these complex communities, in which over fifty species may be found together in a 30 m diameter pool (p. 244), biotic interference is continual. Observations in the clear waters of Lakes Malawi and Tanganyika and in Rupununi pools showed how some fishes live and feed in small shoals, large solitary fishes wander through the pools at intervals, and other species remain hidden by day, packed away in crevices; at night another fauna is active. For each fish there is a conflict between the need to make itself known to its conspecifics, for successful breeding, for shoaling in gregarious species, or for territory maintenance in solitary species, while at the same time avoiding the attention of the numerous passing predators. Communications within and between species are of vital importance in these communities, providing a fascinating subject for future researches.

Significance of markings and colours in diurnal species

The diurnal cichlids and many characoids are mainly sight-orientated, their markings and colours being of prime importance in communication. These markings include permanent blotches or stripes, though the pattern may alter as the fishes grow and change their biotope and habits, for instance many young fishes living amongst plants have vertical stripes which are lost when the fish move out into open water. Patterns and colours may change at night, for example the diagonal black stripe in *Cichlasoma festivum* becomes a light one at night when seen in torchlight, but these changes have as yet been little investigated.

Fish colours are of various kinds: specific colours present all the time, and colours which vary with the emotional state of the fish (Baerends and Baerends van Roon, 1950). The former include the 'poster colours' used as display signals to demarcate territories, as Lorenz (1962, 1966) and Zumpe (1965) have shown for the gaudy coral reef-dwelling fishes; again these may change as the fish grow, as they do in the marine angel fish *Pomacanthus paru*. The vivid colours and stripes of some of the Mbuna rockfish of Lake Malawi are probably of significance in this way, for some species have now been shown to be territorial (p. 148). Permanent colours also include the brilliant shining 'neon' colours of small forest-water species (among them many aquarium species such as the tetras *Hyphessobrycon* species), which may have a role in enabling the fishes to build up viable populations after they have been scattered by the oscillating conditions in these forest waters

(p. 75). (These colours are not to be confused with the brass colours caused by parasitism (see below, p. 254) though this phenomenon demonstrates how such shining colours make the fishes more visible in these dark and humic acid stained waters.) On the whole black patterns surrounded or supported by white, yellow, orange or red, show most clearly in the dark waters. These are generally found as vertical, longitudinal or diagonal stripes on the body, in caudal and humeral spots or blotches, or on the caudal or adipose fin (Fig. 9.7), in contrast with brilliant spots on the head or opercular region of greater significance for close-up head to head encounters (as during sexual displays).

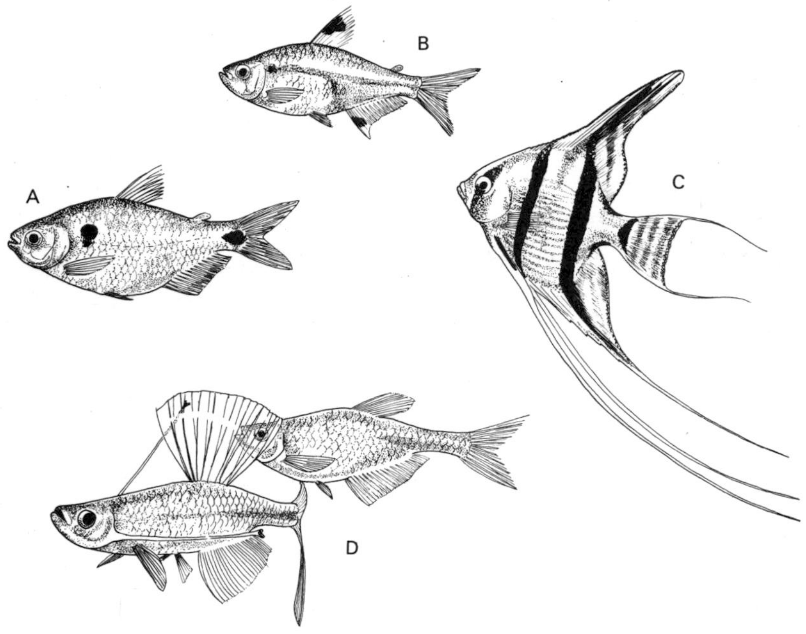

Fig. 9.7 Visual and chemical communication in freshwater fishes:

A. *Astyanax bimaculatus* which bears the humeral and caudal dark markings characteristically found in many midwater schooling fishes.

B. *Pristella riddlei* in which the black spot on the dorsal fin acts as a social releaser for schooling.

C. *Pterophyllum scalare* a cichlid in which the pelvic fins become conspicuously light in colour and are jerked to 'call' the guarded young.

D. *Corynopoma riisei* a glandulocaudine characid in which the male wafts a pheromone from the caudal gland to the following female, note extreme sexual dimorphism including opercular extension paddles of the male (after Nelson, 1964).

Colours which change with the emotional state include those figured by Baerends and Baerends van Roon (1950), and for *Hemichromis fasciatus* by Fryer and Iles (1972) to illustrate the language of the cichlids. In this species a neutral livery means 'I am quietly going about my business', vertical stripes and darkening colours (with reversed lateral spots in the very dark fish) show increasing readiness for combat to defend territory, the fright pattern is mottled with the development of a longitudinal stripe if there is nowhere to hide; brooding fish carry a series of lateral spots (rather like those when defending territory), but spawning fish lose their spots.

In *Tilapia*, breeding colours developed in the male fish advertise spawning ground areas. These colours are kept throughout the spawning season, which may last weeks or months, and they are best developed in species which have well-defined spawning seasons, as in Lake Malawi. In *Tilapia* species in which both parents guard young, there is less difference in colour between the sexes, and colours in both sexes change with fish mood, playing an important part in prespawning display which ensures the synchronous ejaculation of eggs and milt. Colour changes in relation to social behaviour have been analysed for *Tilapia mossambica* by Neil (1964).

Some (perhaps most) marks have quite specific functions, as is becoming clear from behaviour studies in aquaria, and certain movements may accentuate them. In the small characid *Pristella riddlei* the conspicuous black patch on the dorsal fin (Fig. 9.7), jerked more rapidly when the fish is alarmed, has been shown by experiment to be a 'social releaser' leading other *Pristella* to follow the shoal (Keenleyside, 1955). In certain mouth-brooding *Haplochromis* the male has 'egg-dummy' (egglike) orange spots on his anal fin, to which the female reacts by trying to take them into her mouth, thereby sucking up sperm with her eggs (Wickler, 1962). The pelvic fins become conspicuous in colour and are jerked in a characteristic fashion when 'calling' the young in many cichlids, as in *Pterophyllum*, *Cichlasoma festivum*, *Etroplus* (personal observation; Cole and Ward, 1969). The caudal ocellus developed in many cichlids which lead their young (e.g. in *Cichla ocellaris* and *Cichlasoma festivum*) appears to be important for the orientation of the young to the parent (Lowe-McConnell, 1969*c*). Changes in eye colour often have social significance, and their importance for dominance and the establishment of territory has been demonstrated in the marine fish *Pomacentrus* (Rasa, 1969); compare the importance of eye colour for isolation in gulls (N. G. Smith, 1967). Signals are being much studied in marine reef fish (Wickler, 1967). As we learn to decipher fish language we can guess a great deal about how a fish lives from its markings, guesses which call for field observations and experiment.

In Mato Grosso streams species schooling in midwater, in a band within two metres of the bank, mostly had a dark spot at the base of the caudal fin and often a second dark humeral spot. Mixed species (a dozen or so belonging to several genera) were found in these bands, the fishes all heading into the current. Selection here, as for shoaling species in lakes (p. 248), must be for uniformity in appearance, any individual differences making it easier for predators (of which there are many) to pick that one out. This must help to explain the many cases of mimicry, fishes in different genera being so similar in appearance. The small bottom-pecking fishes lacked the caudal blotch and were mainly uniformly sandy-grey in colour, making them very inconspicuous (compare fish on sandy bottoms in littoral regions of Lake Tanganyika, p. 154). Certain fishes living solitary lives carried very distinctive specific recognition marks. These included the small puffer fish *Colomesus asellus*, a fish capable of protecting itself by inflation when attacked and belonging to a family (Tetraodontidae) in which the fish are often poisonous. The various species of *Leporinus* also carry very distinctive stripes, lateral bands, or combinations of spots. The small ones may live in small shoals of two or three together, the large ones solitarily; the specific patterns change as the fish grow.

The hypostomines are among the few catfishes to have vivid specific markings, patterns of spots on contrasting backgrounds, white spots on black, or black spots on grey, even reds and yellows. Such bright colours are unusual in siluroids, most of which are drab grey-brown fishes like so many other nocturnal species. The hypostomines live under stones and in rock crevices in shallow water in South American streams. They are tied to this biotope by their algal-grazing habits (and are very unusual in being nocturnal algal-grazers). In their comparatively well-lit hiding places under rocks in shallow streams the distinctive iris peg of the eye expands in the light to cut down light to the eye. They live where there are many predators, birds, snakes and mammals as well as fish, and their survival depends on the protection of their crevice. Their specific colours, present in fish of all sizes, would appear to function as poster colours demarcating territory (as in coral reef fishes), unusual in a nocturnal fish and calling for experiment. The fish can survive with such striking colours as they remain under cover by day and are very difficult to remove from their crevices.

The roles of sound production

The Weberian apparatus, connecting the swim bladder with the inner ear in Ostariophysi, appears to be connected with the detection of sound, and possibly of locating the direction of the sound source. Mormyroids also have a special vibratory system connected with the inner ear, with which swim-bladder processes are in close contact (Poll, 1969). Ostariophysian fishes, and many others, transmit and receive sound, which travels very well under water (much faster than in air). Many fishes produce specific frequencies which may be used for communication between individuals, but this is still a little-explored field of research in tropical freshwaters, though the sounds of catfishes such as *Aspredo*, nicknamed the 'banjoman' in Guyana, and of many brackish and marine fishes, such as croakers (Sciaenidae) and grunts (Pomadaysidae) have long been known. The noises made by Rupununi fishes (p. 105) included those of:

1. *Prochilodus*, which sounded like an outboard engine coming up-river when they were on their spawning runs at the start of the rains, a time when underwater visibility was much reduced as the rapidly rising water swirled debris and mud into the river;

2. *Serrasalmus* of all sizes, which produced specific grunts when caught (perhaps with a warning function); it was possible to tell from the sounds which species had been netted before the nets were lifted;
3. the cichlid *Geophagus surinamensis*, which grated its pharyngeal teeth audibly when caught.

Spawning characoid *Curimata elegans* are said to sound like treefrogs (Azevedo, *et al.*, 1938), and *Glandulocauda* males also croak (Nelson, 1964*a*). In aquaria clicking sounds made by *Pterophyllum* are connected with aggression in the male (Myrberg *et al.*, 1965). In African waters *Synodontis* are known as 'squeakers' from the sounds they produce. There is here a huge field for research.

Fish sounds have been studied in the sea, but until very recently the ecological effects of sound production had been largely ignored (Breder, 1968). Bioacoustic studies of reef organisms have now related daily cycles of sound production to the activities of particular fish species, showing that sounds may be produced during aggressive behaviour, or escape, or be noises made when feeding, for example when crunching coral (Bright, 1972). The playback of sounds to reef fish by Myrberg (1972*a, b*) demonstrated the significance of sounds for courtship in the male damselfish *Eupomacentrus partitus*.

Electric signals

The gymnotoids of South America and mormyroids of Africa provide splendid examples of convergence in body shape, habits and ecology (Fig. 9.8). Mostly insectivorous, they all appear to be nocturnal fishes; some live in turbid water. They all emit and receive electric impulses (Lissmann, 1958, 1963). In both continents these fishes fall into two groups: (1) those emitting Type I 'tone' discharges of very regular sequences of continuously emitted monophasic impulses, which vary in frequency from species to species and within narrower limits from individual to individual; (2) those emitting Type II 'pulse' discharges which are less regular in frequency and with a much shorter pulse duration (0·2 sec in *Petrocephalus*). Type I tone discharges occur in *Gymnarchus niloticus* in Africa, *Hypopomus* and *Eigenmannia* in South America; frequencies range from 50 to 1600 pulses/sec according to the species and do not alter with the state of excitement of the fish, and the duration of the individual impulse is relatively long. Type II pulse discharges are found in mormyrids in Africa and *Gymnotus carapo* and *Steatogenys elegans* in South America; basic discharges are lower in these fishes, 1 to 6 pulses/sec in resting mormyrids but increasing up to 130/sec in excited fish, and they can be inhibited for long periods.

Field observations in South America showed that Type I tone discharge fishes live in fast-flowing streams and open water, those with the highest discharges (up to 1600/sec in *Porotergus*) living in the fastest-flowing water (Lissmann, 1961). Type II discharges are common among sluggish and

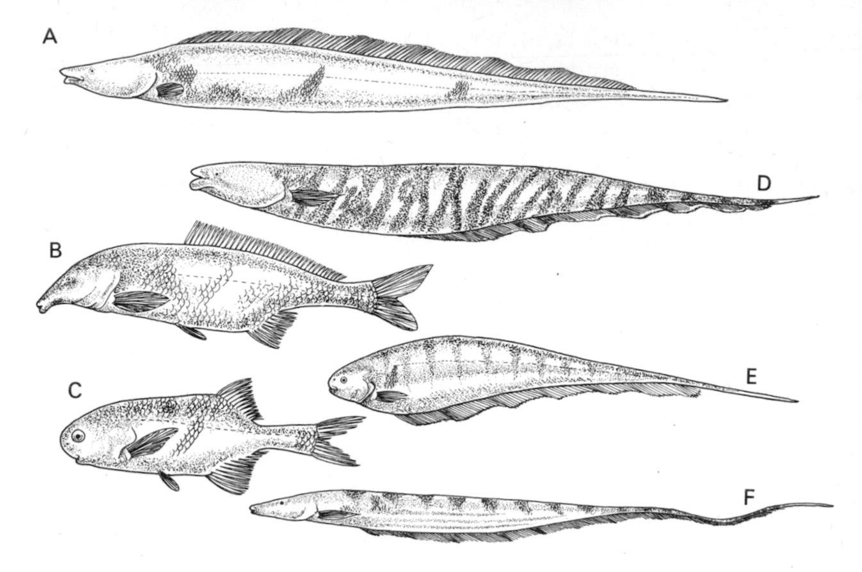

Fig. 9.8 Convergent evolution in two unrelated groups of electric fishes: the mormyroids of Africa (A, B, C) and gymnotoids of South America (D, E, F). Convergence occurs in types of electric discharge, ecology and body form; propulsion is by undulations of a long unpaired fin in many cases.
Mormyroids: A. *Gymnarchus niloticus* (100 cm); B. *Mormyrus kannume* (60 cm); C. *Petrocephalus catostoma* (9 cm). (See also Fig. 2.2a.) Gymnotoids: D. *Gymnotus carapo* (30 cm); E. *Eigenmannia virescens* (25 cm); F. *Gymnorhamphichthys hypostomus* (15 cm). (See also Fig. 2.5b.)

bottom-living forms, with basic discharges of 5 to 190 pulses/sec in undisturbed fish, but increasing when the fishes are excited. In Africa *Gymnarchus* (Type I) lives solitarily along the fringes of swamps and near the mouths of rivers.

Some of these gymnotoids (*Sternopygus macrurus, Gymnotus carapo, Apteronotus albifrons, Hypopomus species*) live solitary lives. Others, such as *Eigenmannia* species, live in small schools. Both solitary and gregarious species show homing tendencies. *Eigenmannia* hide away by day, under a bridge for example, then fan out to feed at dusk with clockwork precision (Lissmann, 1961). The individuals of the solitary *Apteronotus albifrons* observed in the Rupununi were belligerent in the defence of their daytime hiding places, crevices in the rocks. The young *Gymnorhamphthichthys hypostomus*, transparent elongated fishes *c.* 12 cm long, live buried in the bottom sand of the stream shallows during the day; the activity rhythms of this species have been studied by Lissmann and Schwassmann (1965) who found a sharp rise in frequency from 10 to 15 pulses/sec during the day when the fish is buried in the sand, to 65 to 100/sec at night when it is free-swimming.

Conditioned reflex experiments in tanks by Lissmann (1958) showed that

Gymnarchus niloticus and *Gymnotus carapo* (Type I and Type II discharge fishes respectively) use their weak electric fields to sense their environment. Their prey is not affected by their discharges, unlike the prey of *Electrophorus electricus* which in addition to an involuntary slow regular discharge has a voluntary one of up to 550 volts used to stun prey and deter enemies. These weak discharges provide a locating mechanism, an adaptation to nocturnal habits and life in turbid water, and they also have social significance. In Rupununi pools gymnotoids could be seen backing into crevices at great speed; in tanks it has been shown that they also use the electric field to detect food, and could use it to detect predators. Gymnotoids are palatable to other fishes (they make good bait for hooks); specimens with regenerating tails are not infrequently caught, and they have good powers of regeneration.

More recent work has stressed the social significance of these discharges. In tanks *Gymnotus carapo* form dominance hierarchies or become territorial according to the density of fish, and electrical displays are used agonistically in determining such hierarchies (Black-Cleworth, 1970). Sexual difference in electric signalling analogous to song in birds has been demonstrated for *Sternopygus macrurus* (a Type I tone discharge fish) in Rupununi streams (Hopkins, 1972). The Moco Moco Creek here had eleven species of gymnotoids all producing electric discharges (four of Type I (tone) and seven of Type II (pulse) discharge fish). Playback experiments in the field indicated that *Sternopygus* males are able to distinguish between their own species and other sympatric species that have tone discharges on the basis of the frequency alone. Males are also able to distinguish the sex of a conspecific fish, as they send out courtship signals to passing females but not to males.

Among the mormyrid species living in large schools over the mud banks out in the main current of the Zaïre river (p. 59) Poll (1959*b*) suggested that their electric signals may have a social use in keeping the schools together, and may also help to explain how so many sympatric species manage to coexist in the Pool. Poll found that the electric organs in the caudal peduncle were relatively longer in the species which lived in large schools out in the main stream than in the species living in quieter marginal waters (where they may not live in such large aggregations?) (ratio standard body length/length of electric organ less than 10 in open water species, much greater than 10 in marginal water species).

Chemical communication

The role of fish pheromones (i.e. chemical substances produced by the fish which have a signal function to other members of the species) have been reviewed by Bardach and Todd (1970). A complex world of chemical communication has been shown for rock pool blennies and among North American freshwater catfishes. Though as yet little work has been done on pheromones in tropical fishes, it seems likely that these will prove to be of vital importance in the social behaviour of many species, especially nocturnal ones such as the numerous catfishes, many of which produce mucus with a characteristic strong smell. An immense and exciting field is here just being opened to investigation.

Cyprinid fishes have long been known to produce 'alarm substances' when damaged, which warn other members of the school of danger, and fishes of the African families Kneriidae and Phractolaemidae also produce such alarm substances (Pfieffer, 1962).

In glandulocaudine characids (such as *Corynopoma*, Fig. 9.7D), the caudal glands of the males with their access tubes appear to direct a pheronome towards the female during courtship (Nelson, 1964*a*). In *Arapaima gigas* a pheromone exuded from the head of the parent attracts the young to stay near to the parent (p. 75). In the well-known aquarium cichlid *Symphysodon discus* the young feed on a secretion from the skin of the parent, but they are able to subsist in aquaria without this 'food', and perhaps the main function of this secretion is to keep the young near to the parent, a suggestion which calls for experimental investigation.

The role of chemoreception in the care of young by cichlid parents has been investigated experimentally by ethologists. The parents of certain cichlids respond to water in which their own young have been living (Kühme, 1963), and can distinguish this from water inhabited by conspecific broods of the same age, or of other species. Myrberg (1966), when reviewing the roles of vision and chemoreception in parental recognition of cichlid young, concluded that chemoreception is important when the young are at the wriggling stage, but vision is more important when the young have reached the free-swimming stage. But species vary very much in their behaviour, making generalisations dangerous in the present stage of knowledge.

The young of the Indian catfish *Mystus* are also said to feed on a secretion exuded by the guarding male (p. 53). Roberts (1973*b*) commenting on axillary glands opening near the pectoral fin base in many catfishes says that the function of the gland is unknown but in both the giant catfish *Pangasianodon* of the Mekong, and in *Brachyplatystoma* of the Amazon basin the local people claim that a secretion provides nourishment for the young. He adds that in *Brachyplatystoma* the glands are present in juveniles and adults of both sexes, producing a substance which varies from a clear liquid to a whitish cheesy cream, and that doradid glands produce a white liquid, whereas trichomyterid glands produce a copious mucous supply.

The North American bullhead catfishes (*Ictalurus nebulosus* and *I. natalis*), studied by Todd (1971), are a nocturnal, territorial, at times gregarious, species with poor vision and highly developed senses of taste and smell. The entire body is covered by hundreds of thousands of taste buds, and experiments have shown that it is the sense of taste that leads these fishes to their food. The very keen sense of smell, through olfactory receptors in the nose, is used for social communication. The formation and maintenance of a stable community depends entirely on its members' sense of smell. In an experimental community consisting of fish deprived of their nose tissues, the fishes behaved as if they were all strangers to one another, fighting viciously; only after their olfactory tissues had regenerated did they begin to act like members of a non-belligerent community. Through these pheromones a bullhead catfish can tell not only the species and sex of another bullhead, but also whether it is a dominant or subordinate individual in its community, and probably its age or size, and reproductive state. The clustering of bullheads appears to produce a concentration of pheromones which inhibit aggression. The effects of aggression are long lasting; after an aquarium battle the loser's growth was stunted.

In the Rupununi remarkable concentrations of catfishes (fifteen species with the auchenipterid *Tatia* and *Trachycorystes* predominating) were found packed into crevices in submerged logs in the dry season (p. 104). Such crevice-dwelling fishes call for studies on pheromones. Another interesting group to study would be the *Ancistrus* (loricariid) catfishes which live in rock crevices. The vivid colour patterns and large eyes of some of these suggest that vision may be important for territorial behaviour, but in *Ancistrus* the male develops remarkable dendritic structures on the nose (Fig. 2.5*b*). The function of these is not yet known. Are they pheromone or tactile receptors? Their presence in one sex only suggests that they may have a role in reproductive behaviour.

10

Community Development

High diversity at low latitudes: possible contributory causes

These multispecific tropical communities raise many problems:

1. Why and how have so many species evolved?
2. How are so many species packed into the community, and how do they manage to coexist?

Among freshwater fishes greater diversity is shown both within taxa and within communities at low than at high latitudes. In the preceding chapters we have seen that this diversity is highest in equatorial regions, but that diversity is very high compared with temperate zone waters both in the very stable environments of the Great Lakes, and in the seasonally fluctuating rivers.

Diversity in rivers does, however, become less (*a*) as the latitude increases and seasonal fluctuations in water level become more marked; (*b*) with increases in altitude, for example in Andean and Kenya highland streams where this is probably a temperature effect; and (*c*) towards the headwaters of streams, where physicochemical factors, such as obstructions causing water falls and high speeds of flow, and the size of and conditions in dry season refuges, may be more limiting than food resources. It is interesting that all these limiting conditions are physicochemical factors, not biotic ones.

Among the many reasons which have been put forward to help explain the more complex communities at low latitudes in both plant and animal communities are: time, climatic stability, spatial heterogeneity, competition, predation and productivity (Lowe-McConnell, 1969*a, b*). These aspects are re-examined here in relation to fish communities.

Dobzhansky (1950) suggested that the nature of selection differs in tropical regions from that in high latitudes. Where the physical environment is harsh, and indiscriminate, density-independent catastrophic mortalities are likely to occur, selection will be principally for increased fecundity (though there may also be some selection for physiological adaptations to the controlling factor such as cold or drought). But under tropical conditions, the individuals that survive and reproduce will be those most attuned to the complex interrelationships of the organic community, and the selecting agents will themselves be density- and diversity-dependent. Thus selection in the tropical environment is a more creative, moulding process, capable of producing subtleties such as concealment behaviour and mimicry, many fine examples of which are known in these tropical fishes. The studies of fish ecology considered here support this view. These fish communities are extremely dynamic, and in the complicated interaction of abiotic and biotic environmental factors affecting them, the biotic factors appear to be relatively more important, particularly in the equatorial regions.

Studies of Neotropical birds in response to the ecological opportunities offered to them convinced Keast (1972) that the most potent individual force affecting the direction in which a particular group will evolve is undoubtedly the associated fauna in the habitat, and this may also apply to many tropical fish groups.

New lines of research are continually being developed. Nikolsky has noticed from analyses of published data on fish chromosome numbers that there is a clear trend for numbers to decrease with latitude from the Arctic to the tropics: from a mean of 72 in 24 Arctic species, 57 in 155 Boreal species, 51 in 70 temperate species, to 46·8 in 155 tropical species (Nikolsky and Vasilev, 1973). This they suggested may be connected with increased trophic specialisation at lower latitudes. Chromosome numbers were also found to be lower in the more highly evolved percomorph fishes than in the Clupeiformes (taken to include herrings and salmonids), and amongst the latter in marine than in freshwater species.

Time

A community has been called a record of accumulations of species through geological time edited by extinctions. Many of these tropical ecosystems appear to be very old, the rivers in absolute terms, the Great Lakes younger than the river systems but still very old for lakes (a function of their size), allowing time for many species to accumulate. Conditions also appear very favourable for speciation, as discussed below, but the rate of total extinction seems to be low. This appears to be due partly to the nature of the environment, partly to the short life cycles of the fishes, and partly to the nature of selection under tropical conditions. In equatorial rivers most fishes are widely distributed through a vast system of anastomosing channels, and local variations in conditions are unlikely to affect the whole species. Such local variations, for instance of very heavy rainfall, are a feature of these equatorial regions. The short life cycles, in which maturity of most fishes is achieved in one or two years (or less) means that populations can build up very rapidly when conditions are good. Also fishes, being cold-blooded vertebrates, are able to survive adverse times by reducing their growth rates. The type of selection here, both in rivers and lakes, in which the agents of selection are principally biotic (predators, competing species and food organisms) and themselves density-dependent, probably means that it is more difficult for extinctions of the whole species to occur than when selection is principally abiotic. Local extinctions do occur, as witnessed by the loss of *Lates* from Lake Edward and from proto-Victoria. Although these tropical fish faunas contain large numbers of species, Roberts (p. 75) reported for Amazonian species collected by rotenone that only one third or less would be common, and a dozen or so very rare and in danger of local extinction. Among invertebrates of many kinds in neotropical rainforest Elton (1973) has suggested that adaptation to life at a very low population density may assist a species to escape the attentions of the numerous predators, that the low density is the end product of a very long evolutionary interaction between predators and their prey, and that historically this effect would have been assisted by local group extinctions.

Climatic stability

Compared with northern temperate regions where the Ice Ages decimated the faunas, conditions at low latitudes appear to have remained much more stable. There have been periods of large-scale expansion and contraction of the aquatic environments with pluvial and interpluvial periods, but these came after a long period of stability which would have allowed wide dispersal of many species, and their nature has been such that they may then have contributed to speciation, by dividing and recombining populations, rather than leading to the wholesale destruction of the faunas. The effects of dry epochs may, however, have been more drastic in Africa where the general level of the land is higher than in South America; the Kalahari sands advanced right into the Zaïre forest region in the Pleistocene. In South America contractions and expansions of the forest environment in dry and wet periods have been invoked to explain bird distributions, forest species being confined to certain forest refuges in periods of low rainfall (Haffner, 1967).

Diversity is not always very high; in the climatically very stable equatorial Lake George (p. 168) the relatively low diversity of flora and fauna for a tropical lake was attributed partly to lack of seasonal succession, and partly to the few types of food available and uniformity of habitat conditions over most of the lake.

There has been much discussion on diversity and stability in ecosystems (e.g. symposia, ed. Woodwell and Smith, 1969, van Dobben and Lowe-McConnell 1975; Regier and Cowell, 1972). The former view that diverse systems are more 'stable' than simpler ones is no longer held. May (1975) points out that a predictable ('stable') environment may permit a complex and delicately balanced ecosystem to persist, but that such complex systems are generally dynamically fragile (i.e. their stability is very easily upset, and local extinctions then occur). The fragility of the very complex aquatic systems in the Amazon basin has for a long time been stressed by Sioli, Marlier, Fittkau (see p. 84). Margalef (1969) commented that though it is often assumed that diversity and stability (in the sense of persistence) run together, he did not see any means of linking them logically, but he thought that if diversity is high then stability is more valuable. Slobodkin and Sanders (1969) have stressed the importance of *predictability* of the environment for high species diversity (and that low latitude environments tend to be high probability ones compared with those in higher latitudes); they discussed the selective effects of predictability, and concluded that the relative richness of species in a highly predictable environment is the steady state manifestation of a series of processes, which (*a*) increase the probability of speciation, (*b*) decrease the probability of extinction, (*c*) increase the rate of immigration, (*d*) decrease the rate of emigration, together with the ameliorative consequences of competitive interaction in predictable as opposed to unpredictable environments. When questioned about the role of factors controlling diversity in a fluctuating environment Sanders considered that rate of change or magnitude of fluctuations might be critical, but if oscillations are predictable and of long-term sequence high levels of diversity should be achieved. He added that it was difficult to think of examples of this, but among cases considered in this book tropical rivers with regular cycles of flooding would seem to provide one, while the Great Lakes provide examples of the most predictable of environments. In general it would seem much more difficult for fishes to adapt to *irregular* changes in the environment than to regular oscillations, but *Tilapia* have evidently evolved a mechanism to do so (Iles, 1973; see p. 205).

Spatial heterogeneity

Do more niches exist in low than in high latitude biotopes, allowing greater species diversity? Food sources that are only available seasonally in temperate waters are available throughout the year in many parts of the tropics. Plant life flourishes throughout the year allowing the evolution of specialist herbivores: phytoplankton-feeders, algal-grazers, macrophyte-feeders, which can remain in the community without migrating away from the area. Insects and other invertebrates are also available as food all though the year. The lack of well-defined breeding seasons ensures a continuous supply of small fish as food for piscivorous species – to the extent of permitting the evolution of specialist feeders on eggs and yolked young from brooding cichlids in Lake Victoria. Macrophytes and forest litter provide cover throughout the year, important for the survival of young fishes and for the development of a nocturnal fish fauna.

In many biotopes there are, however, many more fish species present than the seeming number of trophic niches available, and there is much overlap in foods used by closely related species living sympatrically (see p. 255). Conditions that are continually changing with time, particularly with fluctuating water levels, vastly augment the numbers of potential niches, as studies in Zaïre suggested (p. 65). Oscillating conditions are also thought to be important for the coexistence of the many species in South American rivers and here chance appears to play a large role in the distribution of species through the complex waterways (p. 75) and hence in the composition of the community at any one time and place. In long-established riverine and lacustrine communities there appear to be no 'empty niches' waiting to be filled, but the dynamic equilibrium is such that the system is elastic enough to continue to take in new species, as the success of the *Tilapia* introductions into Lake Victoria (p. 137) indicated.

The success of such introductions does, however, depend on conditions at the time. In Victoria the rise in lake level which happened to come soon after the *Tilapia* were introduced, helped the establishment of at least one species (*T. leucosticta*). *Tilapia* introduced into Lake Kariba as the lake filled failed to become established (p. 177), though this lake took in many new species when it became more stabilised. The zooplankton-feeding niche is often vacant in a new lake. In Kariba this was being taken over by *Alestes lateralis* until better-adapted clupeids from Lake Tanganyika were introduced.

In these equatorial rivers and among the Lake Malawi cichlids the presence of large numbers of sibling species living together and sharing the same food source (p. 255), suggests that there is no upper limit to the numbers of fish species that these communities can absorb. In this way fish communities resemble insect communities, in which there appears to be no discernible upper limit to the numbers of species in a biotope, though in bird communities the number of species appears to be fixed by the structure of the vegetation where they live (Whittaker and Woodwell, 1972).

The contributions that competition and predation make to diversity are considered in two later sections (p. 251, 255). Here we should note that these factors, and others such as climatic stability, may interact in their effects. Predation has a recognised effect in preventing species from monopolising a habitat by competitive superiority (as discussed by Paine, 1966; Janzen, 1970), but may become less efficient at doing this as habitats become more seasonal with increasing severity and unpredictability of the physical environment. We will therefore need to consider the relative roles of predation and competition in tropical fish communities in seasonally fluctuating rivers compared with those in the very stable conditions in the Great Lakes.

Productivity

Are productivity and biomass greater under tropical conditions, and if so does this allow greater diversity? Comparisons of biomass and productivity under tropical and temperate conditions have already been considered (p. 195 and Table 8.3). Despite popular belief to the contrary, the few data available suggest (*a*) that biomass is not necessarily greater than in temperate regions (such as the River Thames); (*b*) that productivity *may* be much higher in most tropical than most temperate waters, as the fishes have shorter life cycles, but that this is not necessarily associated with high diversity. As discussed later (p. 263), high productivity in relation to biomass is a characteristic of immature pioneer communities, and these have relatively few species in comparison with the mature communities generally found in the tropics. In these mature communities the efficiency of utilisation of nutrients is greater, and more nutrients are generally locked up in the biomass; efficiency appears to be increased by diversity, but the ratio of production to biomass is much lower than in pioneer and less diverse communities. As Margalef (1969) put it: in general diversity is negatively correlated with productivity, an increase in productivity means a decrease in diversity. Tropical marine environments show this particularly clearly, the upwelling areas of high productivity having but very few fish species, though huge numbers of them (pelagic clupeoids: Longhurst, 1971). And in tropical freshwaters the equatorial Lake George, one of the most productive of lakes, has relatively few species in its flora and fauna (p. 168), the fish fauna dominated by phytoplankton-feeding *Tilapia*. This appears to refute the suggestion of Connell and Orias (1964) that if more energy were available for production in the stable conditions of the tropics (as less would be needed for regulatory activities to counter environmental changes) this might result in larger populations, more genetic variation within populations and better opportunities for successful speciation. Slobodkin and Sanders (1969) commenting on this concluded that high productivity in itself will not result in greater species diversity but might be linked with it if linked with high probability (see p. 241) and if more energy is available for production in more predictable environments. However, in the aquatic systems considered here production is high both in the relatively unpredictable upwelling areas and in the highly predictable Lake George, and in both cases relatively few fish species are present (supporting Margalef's views of the inverse relationship between productivity and diversity).

In tropical waters it seems that the input of nutrients has a greater effect on the relative productivity of a biotope than has the efficiency with which all the various resources are used, as the major resources, such as plankton, are cropped very rapidly by the few species highly specialised to do so and able to use resources low in the trophic chain.

The role of diversity in efficiency for the utilisation of systems very poor in available nutrients has been stressed by Sioli for Amazonian waters, where the velocity of turnover of nutrients (i.e. their circulation through living matter, speeded by the prevailing high temperatures) may substitute for the poor quantity of nutrient ions. The importance of herbivores, and indeed of the biota generally in storing nutrients that would otherwise be lost to the effluents (a density-dependent process), and in speeding up mineralisation of allochthonous and littoral plant matter (a density- and diversity-dependent process), was discussed for Amazon waters by Marlier (p. 84), while Fittkau's observations on the effects of caiman removal

(p. 84) suggested that these impoverished systems cannot give up biomass or diversity without severe disturbance.

In the African Great Lakes herbivores have also been found to be important in maintaining productivity by speeding up mineralisation, because plant material is made available for renewed phytoplankton growth much more rapidly through the digestive systems of herbivores than when locked away in the bottom mud of the lake; hence the removal of large numbers of herbivores, such as *Tilapia*, from a lake will slow down its production of fish (Beauchamp, 1964). In the equatorial L. George (p. 168) grazing and recycling of nutrients by zooplankton was found to far exceed that by the herbivorous fishes.

Conditions in existing tropical freshwater fish communities

Packing and resource sharing

The fauna lists are very large for these immense bodies of water, but how many fish species actually share biotopes? The large total list could result from each section of the river and the innumerable tributary streams each having their own faunas. What is the distribution of species within the river system? We are concerned here with 'alpha diversity' or the number of species within a community (its richness) resulting from diversification into a variety of ecological niches, contrasted with 'beta diversity' of habitat-differentiated species added along environmental gradients (Whittaker and Woodwell, 1972).

The use of chemofishing, or some such method which takes all the fishes present, has shown that high numbers of fish species occur together in many tropical biotopes, though in some cases these are merely accumulations of fishes brought together by contracting environments in the dry season, when the fishes may feed little, rather than true communities. In Guyana, South America, Eigenmann (1912), using rotenone, collected (*a*) 60 fish species from a small brook on Gluck Island in the Essequibo River; (*b*) 54 species from a 30 m diameter pool at Konawaruk on the same river; (*c*) 29 species from under rocks at Warraputa cataract on the lower Potaro river; while (*d*) a trench in the Botanic Gardens, Georgetown (undisturbed for twenty years) produced 23 species. A Venezuelan lagoon only 1225 m^2 in area contained 25 fish species (p. 106); in Argentina the Don Felipe lagoon had 52 species (p. 109). In Amazonas the varzea Lac Redondo had 47 species, only six in common with the Prêto da Eva which had 49 species, even though these two lakes were part of the same river system and less than 100 km apart.

Examples from Africa include over 30 fish species (25 of them cichlids) from a 300 m stretch of rocky shore on Lake Malawi (p. 144) and 23 species

(15 of them cichlids and mostly different species) off a comparable and adjacent 300 m of sandy shore. Chemofishing in L. Chad produced 40 to 50 species in 0·5 ha (Loubens, 1969), and chemofishing in a 12 100 m^2 cove on Lake Kariba produced 28 species (Balon, 1971*a*), even though this was a new lake. The crater lake Barombi Mbo, only 2·5 km in diameter had 17 species (p. 162), though these did form more or less distinct inshore and off-shore communities. River Sokoto dry-season pools fished by Holden had up to 27 species in a pool. A headwater stream of the Zaïre carried 16 species (p. 62). Ninety species were taken from a stretch of river 1·7 km long between the coffer dams at Kainji (p. 98); these were, however, probably not fishes living permanently in this area, unlike the Lake Malawi rockfish most of which probably spent their entire lives in this restricted habitat, thus forming a true and very stable community. The same story holds true for Asia; for example, Vaas (1952) lists over 17 species from a deep pit in West Borneo.

Thus there is no doubt that alpha diversity is very high in many fish communities in the tropics. How do so many fish species manage to coexist? How do they share resources, and what controls the numbers of species and individuals in the communities? Food supplies? Living space? Predators? Parasites, disease?

Observations on fish behaviour where the water is clear, as in streams in the Rupununi and Borneo, and Lakes Tanganyika and Malawi, show how the three-dimensional world is fully utilised, certain species living always just below the surface, others in midwater, yet others on the bottom, their shape and colour fitting in with their way of life and position in the water column. (The individuals of the Amazonian stream fishes which Knöppel found taking food from all levels, p. 81, used much exogenous food, and Rupununi observations suggested that species using this all dash up to the surface to get it, no matter where they spend most of their lives in the stream.) The beautiful adaptations of body shape and colour for life near the surface (for example in the Gasteropelecidae), or in midwater, or for bottom-dwelling, as in so many of the catfish groups, are a striking feature of these faunas. Whether the fish live solitary lives, in pairs, or small shoals, is also quite characteristic. Many species live in shoals when small and vulnerable to predation, taking to solitary or paired existence later as they mature.

In these communities the time-sharing of resources, diurnally for feeding and seasonally by migrations is marked. In South American streams the cichlids and characoids are active by day, the gymnotoids and siluroids by night (p. 103). The presence of a nocturnal fauna appears to be dependent on cover where these fishes can hide by day; many of the nocturnal species are larger than the diurnal ones. In the forest waters of the Zaïre the mormyrids and siluroids are nocturnal, also using tree litter as a substitute for rocks in which to hide themselves by day. Of fishes migrating downstream at the end of the rains certain species were found to move down by day, others by night, in all three tropical areas (in the Rupununi p. 104, in rivers flowing into Lake Chad p. 97; and in the Mekong, p. 123). Diurnal changes in activity are also important for resource-sharing in the sea (Hobson, 1965; Collette and Talbot, 1972).

The headwater streams carry fewer species than the lower stretches; are these mainly endemic species, or ubiquitous river species, or both? The mere dozen species in the forested headwater streams in the Mato Grosso (p. 107) were nearly all ubiquitous species or their young stages, hardy fishes which could withstand poorly oxygenated acid waters and lowered temperatures, and which were able to utilise many kinds of allochthonous and autochthonous foods such as aerial and aquatic insects, vegetable debris, and small fishes. A similar situation was recorded by Knöppel from other Amazonian streams, and in Zaïre Gosse found small species and the young of widely-distributed large species in headwater streams. In both continents and in the Gombak river in Malaya (p. 88) the numbers of species increased very much in the lower stretches of the river where there are more biotopes. Some species may have evolved in the lower stretches, others probably evolved in the discrete tributaries, then dropped downstream and became more widely distributed. Species have thus accumulated in the lower stretches.

Flooding drastically alters the faunal composition in these rivers. The movements up and down river and out on to the floodplain mean that riverine communities are always changing their species composition with time and water level. In any one area the resident community may be augmented by immigrant fishes, which may join them for some time to feed or spawn, or just pass through. In this way these riverine communities are very unlike the stable communities of littoral fishes in the Great Lakes, where both the species composition and the number of individuals stay very constant throughout the year, and from year to year.

The richness of a community in any one place is affected by ecological conditions in adjacent areas, since fishes are so mobile. If the stream enters a lake or an estuary, fishes may move up into the area from these other types of water. One of the best studied examples of trophic displacement of resident fishes by migrants concerns the salmonid ayu, *Plecoglossis altivelis* in Japan. The fry of this small catadromous fish migrate upstream in large shoals in early spring, shoals which are gradually subdivided until each fish has a territory on the stony bottom where it feeds on algae. Their arrival displaces the resident cyprinid fishes; the chub *Zacco* is pushed into areas with no algae, and the free-swimming cyprinids take more surface food (terrestrial insects), and the diets of the gobies, loaches and carp vary according to the presence or absence of bottom-dwelling cyprinids. This interspecific social interference results in a hierarchical utilisation of the river bottom (Miyadi, 1960). Such changes in diet indicate competition for food; similarity in diet indicates that however else species are competing, they are not competing for food.

Experimental studies on social interference between the numerous species in tropical communities are much needed. 'Interactive segregation', i.e. the way in which ecological differences are magnified by interaction and species segregate into different niches under the influence of competition and predation, presupposes considerable plasticity in habits, and was thought by Nilsson (1967) to be typical of young faunas, but it still seems to be active in these old riverine communities as the fishes are so mobile.

The young stages of many fishes often live in different biotopes from the parent fish. Many species are potamodromous, moving up river to spawn, and the young often stay behind upstream, where they may be more likely to escape predation by large fish, or they remain in savanna pools, where many of them perish as the pools dry up or fall prey to birds and the predatory fishes which frequent these pools (such as *Hoplias malabaricus* in South America).

Many of the river-dwelling fishes appear to move about a good deal. The extensive migrations of the larger species such as *Prochilodus* have been discussed above (p. 115). The smaller, less strongly-swimming midwater-dwelling tetragonopterids would not be expected to move such long distances, but many of these are very widely distributed in South America, and many closely related species are found living together in any one biotope or stretch of river. Shorter movements over long periods of time and river captures could account for such distributions. Once such species are widely distributed, oscillations in conditions appear to help the continued coexistence of the species rather than lead to their total extinction.

Bottom-dwelling fishes living on stony or rocky bottoms, such as the hypostomine loricariid catfishes, appear to 'stay put', and their very distinctive specific colour patterns (p. 232) suggest that they have territorial habits. Types of fish which have localised distributions tend to have numerous species (provided there is some mechanism for intermittent dispersal to similar habitats in other areas, such as being washed down river by exceptional floods). There are, for example, over 400 loricariid species, but among the very large catfishes which make regular migrations up rivers, such as *Pseudoplatystoma* and *Brachyplatystoma*, relatively few species are known, and these few species are widely distributed throughout much of South America. The small trichomycterid catfishes are represented by large numbers of species, but some of these such as the parasitic candiru are widely distributed; their hitchhiking habit of living in the gill cavities of larger fishes will have extended their distribution.

Schooling and the role of cover

The advent of diving with self-contained underwater breathing apparatus (scuba) and underwater television, enabling fishes to be observed in their natural habitats, has led to greatly increased understanding of fish behaviour (for example studies by Hobson, Collette and Earle, Myrberg, Randall and others). Underwater studies, in both freshwater and the sea, indicate that in these old, long-established communities there is a very delicate balance between predator and prey, both represented by many fish species.

In general small prey fish cannot exist in open water unless they live in shoals (or schools).* Their protection in the school appears to derive from the difficulty that the predator has in focussing on any one target as it dashes at the school. There is thus very strong selection for prey fish to look alike, for uniformity. The surest way to get eaten is to look slightly different.† This leads to schools of similar sized fishes, and of mixed species all resembling one another, as among the Utaka or small *Tilapia* in Lake Malawi, and the similarities, including 'mimetic' resemblances in tetragonopterids and other characoid fishes in South American rivers. Such fishes may only develop specific colour differences if and when fish leave the school in preparation for spawning, when differences in appearance between species are important to achieve spawning success.

The open water predatory fishes feed visually. Prey fish may gain some protection by descending to dimmer lit zones during the day. This may have been one of the main selection factors leading to the evolution of the diurnal migrations that such fishes show. True they are following their prey, as the zooplankton also shows such diurnal migrations (perhaps evolved in the zooplankton for the same reason since the zooplankton-feeding fishes also select their food visually). Marine fish studies have shown how particular fish predators have special feeding times, often at dawn and dusk, times when predators may have the edge over the prey and the prey is in greatest danger (Hobson, 1968, 1972). The foods available to open water fishes, phytoplankton or zooplankton, are generally taken as a whole, making them rather uniform types of food; pelagic fishes have specialised to utilise one or other of these, for example, by developing long sievelike gill rakers, or to feed on the small fishes which do so.

Quite different types of communities live where there is cover. Cover permits diversity and appears to be a key factor in allowing it. This is true both in freshwaters, for example among the rock fishes of Lakes Malawi and Tanganyika, and in the sea, where the innumerable crevices in coral reefs have allowed this most diverse of aquatic communities to evolve.

Full advantage of cover can only be taken by fishes that have reached a certain stage of morphological evolution, so that they can 'back up' into crevices. The more primitive fishes, such as the clupeids, can only swim forwards through the water, which suffices for feeding on plankton or small fishes. But in some of the most highly evolved fishes, acanthopterygians, the pelvic fins have moved forward and the body has changed shape, enabling the fish to manoeuvre backwards into crevices (Alexander, 1970). These fishes also possess dorsal fin spines and other antipredator devices; such protection is important to them when they emerge from their crevices to

* The terms *shoals* and *schools* are almost interchangeable, the former being used in the United Kingdom literature (e.g. for clupeids), the latter in American and European literature (e.g. in behaviour studies). Thus the term shoals has generally been used for very large aggregations of pelagic fishes which all move as one unit, and schools for smaller groups of fishes which move in unison. Breder (1959) defines a school as a polarized group of fishes with little more than swimming distance between individuals.

† This applies to pelagic prey fish, predation may lead to aspect diversity in cryptic species in a featured environment (see Rand, 1967; Orians, 1975).

feed, for speed has generally been lost at the expense of manoeuvrability. These fishes have also evolved protrusible jaws, which enable them to exploit the very diverse foods offered by a biotope with cover. For the law that cover permits diversity holds for the invertebrate prey too.

Cover leads to territoriality, to solitary life, and to specialisation in the use of a particular food source if this is available throughout the year. Cover will probably lead to diversity through speciation faster in species which can stay in one area throughout life (as do the Mbuna rockfish, and mastacembelids in the Great Lakes, and hypostomine catfish in South American rivers), and might be expected to do so in any species which 'home' to certain areas to spawn. Some marine cover-dwelling fishes have planktonic larvae, and these species often have a wide, circumtropical distribution.

Cover may be provided in many ways: by crevices in rocks or tree litter, by beds of aquatic plants, even by gastropod shells, which are used by small cichlids in the Great Lakes (*Lamprologus* in Lake Tanganyika, *Pseudotropheus* in Malawi) and gobies in brackish water. Where plant growth is seasonal the great losses of young fish to predators when the plant cover dies down is very striking, for example, to *Hydrocynus* in African rivers and to *Hoplias* in South American pools. In the sea the construction of an artificial reef has been found to increase the local standing crop of fish (Randall, 1963).

Tree debris acts as an important substitute in providing hiding places for light-shy nocturnal fishes in streams without rocks, and where the bottom water is deoxygenated. Underwater observations on marine fishes has shown how fishes hiding in coral or rock reefs by day move out to feed on invertebrates over sandy bottoms under cover of darkness (Hobson, 1965, 1972), invertebrates which themselves seek cover by day by burrowing in the bottom sand. The hypostomine catfishes in South American rivers appear unusual in grazing algae by night; on marine reefs most of the algal grazers appear to be diurnal feeders.

Evolution in pelagic/open water and in littoral/benthic communities thus appears to lead to different ends. Pelagic fishes become uniform in genotype, specialised to use a particular food, and their numbers may be limited by that food source as well as by predation pressure. Fishes living with cover become diverse in genotype, undergoing adaptive radiations to use varied kinds of food, some of which (such as aufwuchs) may be in excess of requirements; for these fish predation pressure appears to be of great importance in restricting populations to small areas.

Predation pressures thus appear to have contrary effects in these two types of community. In pelagic and open water communities they appear to lead to uniformity (i.e. to control speciation), whereas predators patrolling areas with cover, off rocky shores and along coral reefs, help to split up the population of fishes utilising this cover, so promoting speciation and leading to diversity in littoral/benthic communities. The same would appear to hold in rivers and streams, though the distinctions between pelagic fishes and those using cover are not as marked as in lakes.

Selection pressures on tropical freshwater fishes

Selection pressures may operate at any point in the life history of an organism. Basically any organism has to obtain resources for maintenance and growth at all stages of its life history, and for reproduction, and to avoid destruction by predators, parasites or disease or other causes. Selection may operate on one, or very few, genes at a time, and different types of pressure will operate at different times in the life history. For example, amongst the small *Tilapia* living in shoals of mixed species near the shores of Lake Malawi, predation pressure would encourage similarity of appearance, whereas later in life selection pressures to mate with a conspecific mate, will overrule this and lead the fish to develop specific breeding colours. Agents of selection may be abiotic or biotic. We have already referred (p. 238) to Dobzhansky's suggestion that biotic selection is of especial importance in tropical communities, and more moulding in its effects than abiotic selection.

Among the fish communities considered in this book the main selection pressures appear to be *abiotic* effects of drought, desiccation and deoxygenation and *biotic* effects of competition for resources (food and living space) and predation. Selection pressures combine and interact in their effects; the very high fish mortalities on the Kafue flats (esimated to be over 35 per cent per annum, p. 102) result from the combined effects of drought and predation. The relative importance of different selection pressures is likely to change with time, as the environment changes and new species evolve, as well as with or without any seasonal or other short-term changes.

Food shortages were thought by Lack (1954) to be very important in regulating bird populations, and these often operate by bird parents failing to rear the usual number of young (as evolved by natural selection) in adverse times. Conditions are very different for fishes as the young have to feed themselves and in many cases use different foods from those eaten by the parents. General observations suggest that for many young fishes predation may be a more potent factor controlling their numbers than is food supply, but hard data are required. Possible exceptions to this occur in pelagic communities: there are indications in both the clupeids of Lake Tanganyika and *Engraulicypris sardella* of Lake Malawi that reproduction may be intensified following a phytoplankton bloom, leading to increased numbers of young after such blooms. Thus in these shortlived pelagic species the food supply does appear to have a direct influence on the numbers of fishes. As these blooms are of local occurrence and rather irregular in appearance in these lakes, this appears to be an adaptation to exploit such blooms whenever they occur. In Lake Tanganyika there is, however, also a delicate balance between the numbers of clupeids and numbers of their fish predators; the numbers of clupeids rose significantly after the fishery for predators was developed (p. 156), suggesting that predation is also important in controlling clupeid numbers.

In coastal pools in the Netherlands Antilles three small cyprinodontoid fishes (species of *Poecilia, Rivulus* and *Cyprinodon*) fill almost the same niche. In landlocked pools Kristensen (1970) found that their relative abundance was controlled by interspecific competition influenced by interacting environmental factors such as plant or algal growth, salinity, oxygen, or size of food available, rather than by predation. Amongst these fishes the maintenance of very small populations was helped by ovoviviparity (in *Poecilia*) and hermaphroditism (in *Rivulus*), and repopulation could also occur from the sea.

Predation and antipredation devices

High numbers of predatory species and individuals appear to be general features of tropical communities, and are certainly found in both lacustrine and riverine fish communities and in tropical groups such as the characoids (p. 82). Most of the piscivorous fishes, particularly those feeding on littoral and benthic prey, include fishes of many species in their diet (p. 211); those feeding on pelagic fishes often have fewer species on which to prey and may specialise on certain prey species. By taking as prey the more abundant species, and changing their prey as the numbers of prey fish are reduced, predators have an important role in permitting the coexistence of many prey species, keeping their numbers below the level at which they would compete with one another for food or space (Paine, 1966; Murdoch 1969; Janzen, 1970) as suggested for Lake Victoria *Haplochromis* (Greenwood, 1965*c*). It is obviously not in the interests of the predator to eliminate or endanger its prey species, and natural selection will ensure that this does not occur.

The role of predators in fish speciation has been hotly disputed (as reviewed at length by Fryer and Iles, 1972). The significance of schooling and cover discussed above, leads to the conclusion put forward here that predation has contrary effects on speciation in pelagic and in littoral/benthic communities.

Predation does appear to be one of the main factors in the maintenance of diversity in some tropical fish communities. The continual interplay between predator and prey, with the development of devices to avoid being preyed upon countered by adaptations by the predator, and recountered by further antipredation devices, is a feature of tropical insect communities particularly in South America (Kettlewell, 1959), and the same situation appears to hold for tropical fishes. The 'moulding' effect of selection in these tropical communities must be largely due to predation together with other forms of biotic interaction. (See also Rand, 1967; Orians, 1975.)

Piscivorous fishes such as *Hydrocynus, Lates, Cichla, Boulengerochromis*, generally take prey of less than about one-third of their own length. In *Lates niloticus* in Lake Chad Hopson (1972) showed that prey size bears a linear relationship with predator size. *Lates* of all lengths (including those only 3 or 4 cm TL) are capable of eating fish up to about half their own length, but the prey length is generally much less than this possible maximum. Once above the critical size prey species are relatively safe from predation, so predation must provide selection pressure for rapid growth of prey species.

Antipredation devices include stout spines on the pectoral and dorsal fins of many fishes. Many catfishes have locking mechanisms to keep these spines erect (described by Alexander, 1966). Crevice dwellers use their spines to jam themselves into crevices when any attempt is made to remove them, and the movable hooked spines on the cheek skin of *Ancistrus* (Loricariidae) are also used in this way (personal observation). The triangle of erect dorsal and pectoral spines also increases the size of the fish, making it more difficult to swallow and only available to the larger predators (Fig. 10.1). Hopson (1972) showed that *Synodontis* found in *Lates* stomachs in Lake Chad never exceeded 18 per cent of the predator's length (p. 174), compared with 30 to 40 per cent of its length in the relatively unarmed schilbeids also taken as prey, thereby demonstrating the effect of the three

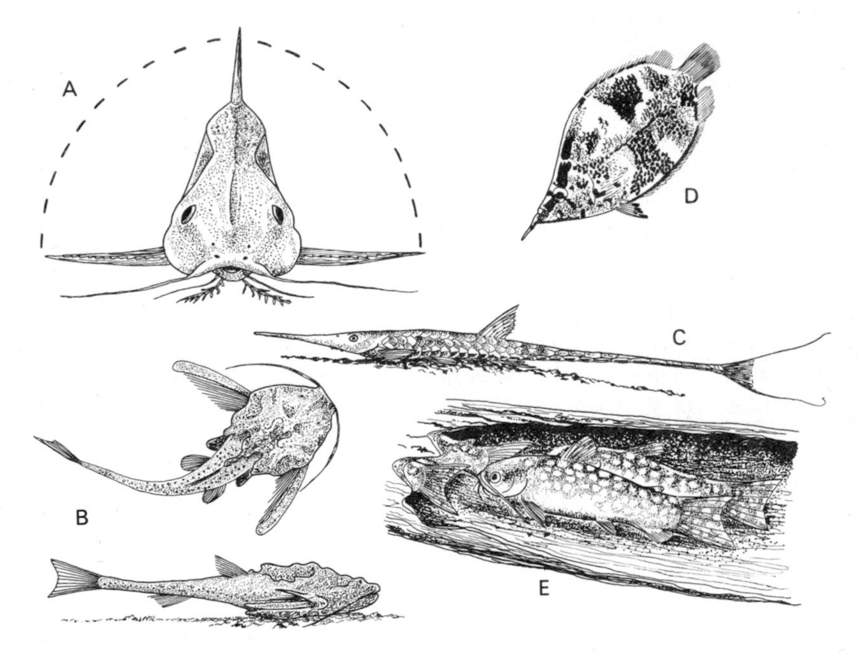

Fig. 10.1 Some antipredation devices in freshwater fishes:

A. The African catfish *Synodontis* (front view) demonstrating how the triangle of locked erect spines increases the effective size of the fish.

B. *Agmus lyriformis*, a little South American catfish with a remarkable protective resemblance to gnarled wood.

C. The twig-like *Farlowella*, a South American catfish.

D. The South American nandid *Monocirrhus*, in which protective resemblance to a leaf enables it to approach its prey.

E. The small South American catfish *Centromochlus* found packed into crevices in submerged logs by day.

Synodontis spines. These spines were sometimes found embedded in the gut wall of *Lates*, and the crocodile (*Crocodilus niloticus*) has been found dead with *Synodontis* jammed across its throat. Nevertheless, the cormorant *Phalacrocorax africanus* does manage to swallow *Synodontis*, taking numbers of *S. polystigma* from Lakes Bangweulu and Mweru and of *S. macrostigma* from the Kafue River (Tait, 1967), and *S. macrostigma* was also eaten by *Hepsetus* and *Schilbe* on the Kafue Flats (p. 102). In some South American catfishes the spines appear to be venomous. Freshwater stingrays, such as *Potamotrygon* in Guyana, have long venomous spines (Fig. 2.5*b*). In the gymnotoid electric eel *Electrophorus electricus* in South America (Fig. 2.5*b*) and the electric catfish *Malapterurus electricus* in Africa (Fig. 2.2*b*), the electric organs have developed a voluntary discharge which is a formidable defence weapon, as well as being used to stun prey fish by *Electrophorus*. Freshwater puffer fishes, Tetraodontidae, found in rivers of all three tropical areas, can inflate themselves to increase their size when attacked (Fig. 2.5*b*); these boldly striped fish may also be unpalatable, for many marine tetraodontids are poisonous. We know very little about the palatability of prey fish to predators. Observations in coral reef communities show that fish spines are much used to wedge their owners into crevices so that when sleeping they cannot be pulled out by predators, and that the inflation of puffer fishes may serve the same purpose. Concealment, in crevices or by burrowing in the sand, or by protective resemblance to some natural object, is most important for survival. Only fishes well protected in some way (by poisonous skin, spines, electric organs, etc), or which live in schools (as even the piscivorous barracuda *Sphyraena* do when young) are able to survive in open water.

Three families of South American catfishes, Doradidae, Callichthyidae and Loricariidae, all carry dermal armour. This forms an almost complete body cover in the latter two groups, and has formidable spines on it in the doradids. In Zaïre certain genera of amphiliid catfishes (*Phractura* and *Trachyglanis*) also carry dermal armour, as does the catfish *Sisor rhabdophorus* in India. The flesh of doradids and *Sisor* is palatable enough to be eaten by man and such armour must, it seems, deter predators in addition to the other uses suggested above (p. 16).

These tropical fishes present many fine examples of protective resemblances to natural objects, and of mimicry of one fish by another, both of which may be antipredator devices. For example the catfishes *Farlowella* and *Agmus* (p. 105) resembling twigs and dead wood, and the nandids *Monocirrhus* and *Polycentrus* which resemble dead leaves (Fig. 10.1). These nandids use their disguise to snap up unsuspecting fish prey, but it may also protect them from predators. The nocturnal behaviour of cichlids (p. 103) lying completely motionless amongst tree litter or against the bank, appears to be an adaptation to avoid giving away their presence to nocturnal predators such as large catfish which may detect prey chemically or by water vibrations. In the coastal brackish lagoons the young of a marine fish the tripletail *Lobotes surinamensis* greatly resembles a dead mangrove leaf, a resemblance enhanced by its behaviour as it drifts on its side to the bottom.

Among the characoids of South America associations of species and mimetic resemblances often occur between members of closely related fish genera (Myers, 1960*b*). The significance of this type of mimicry is not clear but it has characteristics of Müllerian rather than of Batesian mimicry (Gery, 1960). Possibly the way of life has led to convergence in appearance in these midwater-dwelling fishes which would be likely to gain protection from predators by all looking alike (p. 248). In Lake Malawi mimicry is used to obtain food by two species of *Corematodus* which scrape scales from the caudal fins of other cichlids; only when *C. shiranus* dons its breeding dress does it cease to resemble its *Tilapia* host fish.

Several cichlid species in Lakes Tanganyika and Victoria also specialise on a diet of fish scales; their dentition is not always similar, and convergence in these cichlids during the course of evolution is discussed by Fryer and Iles (1972). South America has several scale-eating characoids: about four genera and ten species are present in the Amazon (Roberts, 1970). Their teeth are specialised for removing scales and they generally attack fishes larger than themselves. The Zaïre lacks scale-eaters, but has a remarkable group of fin-eating characoids, all in the family Ichthyoboridae. In Lake Malawi the cichlid *Docimodus johnstoni* is a fin biter. Many Guyana fishes had caudal fin damage which was attributed to bites from *Serrasalmus*. The victims of these scale and fin eaters do not appear to be killed by these attacks.

The guarding of eggs and young, oral incubation, and live-bearing of young may all be considered antipredation devices, though Roberts (1972) pointed out that deoxygenated water may also have been a potent factor in the evolution of these habits (p. 224). Parent cichlids when leading their parties of young may be observed chasing off intruding fishes. These breeding devices have arisen independently in many fish groups.

Diseases and parasites

We know very little about diseases controlling fishes in the wild. Parasites are generally much in evidence in fishes from shallow water and when the fishes are in poor condition, as in lagoons where there is little food (lagoons off Lake Albert for instance), and in Mato Grosso streams at the end of the rains. The parasitism may have contributed to the poor condition of the fish. The intense silver or golden spots on the heads of certain small tetragonopterid characids, the 'Brass Tetras' of aquarists, have been found to be a response to a metacercarian stage of a parasitic trematode worm. This gives individuals of fishes such as *Hemigrammus armstrongi* a characteristic glitter (Gery and Delage, 1963). The infected fish is thereby made more conspicuous and the parasite thus has a better chance of reaching its definitive host which preys on the fish.

Certain chironomid larvae live as commensals on rather sedentary catfishes (astroblepids, and loricariids such as *Ancistrus* and *Hypostomus*), in South American streams (Freihofer and Neil, 1967, and personal observation).

Competition for food and living space

The struggle for existence is not only between predator and prey but also between species needing the same resources, in competition with one another for food and space. Examples given in previous chapters have shown that very complex food webs may be based on relatively few food sources, such as aufwuchs on the rocky shores of Lake Malawi (Fig. 5.4), or exogenous foods in forest headwater streams. In these circumstances many species share the same foods, not only omnivores and facultative feeders but also certain specialists. In Lake Malawi specialisations to use a particular food source have evolved many times and many species specialised to take this food may coexist in one habitat: 12 cichlid species share the aufwuchs from rock surfaces at Nkata Bay, *c.* 17 species of Utaka *Haplochromis* utilise zooplankton from the open lake, and according to Fryer and Iles (1972) *c.* 10 species of *Diplotaxodon* feed on the small cyprinid *Engraulicypris sardella*. In Lake Victoria many *Haplochromis* share the same foods (p. 135), in South American rivers many characoids do so, while hypostomine catfishes of several species share the algal grazing off rocks in small pools. These cases all indicate that factors other than food are likely to control the numbers of individuals in these species.

Many independent studies have suggested to their authors that competition for food is not the controlling factor governing numbers and distribution of fishes: among Malawi cichlids (Fryer and Iles, 1972), the non-cichlids of Lake Victoria (Corbet, 1961), in Lake Chad (Carmouze *et al.*, 1972), and among Amazon and Malayan stream fishes (Knöppel, 1970, Bishop, 1972). It is notable that these are all in places where conditions are fairly uniform around the year. This raises two questions: (1) if foods do not limit the numbers of the various species in these communities, then what does limit them? (The total food supply will, of course, put a ceiling on the fish biomass, but the allocation of food amongst diverse fish species is what concerns us here.) (2) Why and how have trophic specialisations evolved? A question already touched upon above (p. 213), and considered in a later section.

The sharing of food by several sympatric species appears to contradict the competitive exclusion principle (Gause's hypothesis) – the tendency for competition to bring about an ecological separation of closely related or otherwise similar species. Birds obey this principle well, but among insects many species may share a food source such as a host plant. Conditions under which competitive coexistence can occur were reviewed by Ayala (1970). In the case of the Malawi fishes Fryer and Iles (1972) suggested that the many species sharing the same food among the Mbuna, Utaka and *Diplotaxodon*, are in each case behaving as a 'condominium' in Wynne-Edwards's

(1962) sense that members of the association are not in competition with one another as a species, but only as individuals belonging to a mixed indivisible society.

Living space concerns protection from enemies and facilities for spawning as well as food. It is limited for littoral fishes, and obtaining a suitable territory may in many cases keep the numbers below the levels at which individuals would compete for food. In Lake Malawi tagging experiments have shown that the rock fish maintain territories for long periods. Fryer and Iles suggested that certain cichlid displays may enable the fishes to assess their own numbers and regulate their breeding accordingly (what Wynne-Edwards terms epideictic displays). This is still an open question, but the availability of suitable spawning grounds, and in some cases of nursery grounds for the young, does appear to limit populations of certain cichlids.

Territorial behaviour is undoubtedly important in limiting fish populations, especially of crevice-dwelling fishes such as the gymnotoids and catfishes in South America, and among littoral fishes in the lakes. In Lake Malawi this appears to keep numbers below the level of competition for food (as has also been found for algal-grazing fishes on the Great Barrier Reef in the sea).

Fishes demonstrate many kinds of territorial behaviour. Some species defend feeding territories, and this restricts the number of fishes than an area can support (as in small trout in streams, Backiel and Le Cren, 1967, Onodera, 1967, and in *Plecoglossus*, Miyadi, 1960). Territories may be established only for spawning, or for the protection of the family group. The males of the Lake Malawi mouth brooding *Tilapia* maintain nest territories in arenas for spawning only (p. 149), the females taking the eggs away from them to brooding areas. In the female mouth-brooder *Pseudocrenilabris multicolor* the young learn their mother's territory which keeps them near to her (Albrecht, 1963). Yet another pattern of territory holding is shown by the South American dwarf cichlid *Apistogramma trifasciatum* in which the male has a large territory wherein several smaller females each have their own nest (Burchard, 1965).

Aquarium observations on *Gymnotus carapo* indicated that dominance hierarchies, territories, or intermediate types of organisation are established according to the population density (p. 235) using electric displays to do so. Mormyrids also show agonistic behaviour for food and territory (p. 133). The lasting effects of dominance conflicts in catfishes have been noted above (p. 237). Rank order may also be established in some schooling fish, for instance in some chaetodontid marine fishes (Zumpe, 1965), a situation in which members of the group might be helped to find food by the more experienced fish. These chaetodontid and pomacanthid reef fish are territorial when young, their poster colours associated with intense intraspecific competitiion (p. 229). Aquarium experiments on the North American green sunfish, *Lepomis cyanellus*, suggested that social conditioning can modify agonistic behaviour, dominant fish becoming less dominant after being subjected to periods in the presence of larger fish (McDonald,

Heimstra and Damkot, 1968). Could the arrival of large migrant fish in an area have this kind of effect?

Thus we have glimpses of some of the devices that control the utilisation of space. Even for pelagic fishes the environment may be more structured than we at present comprehend; for the fishes may be kept within certain water strata by physical and chemical preferences (as studies in the Gulf of California seems to suggest, Robison, 1972), and by social interaction. These are exciting fields for observation and experiment and marine studies lead the way. The space-sharing mechanisms of coral reef fishes have been examined in some detail during sixty days of underwater living in the Virgin Islands (Collette and Earle, 1972), these mechanisms included diurnal/nocturnal activity cycles, separate feeding and hunting areas, shelter sites, territoriality, seasonal cycles and symbiotic relationships, leading to the conclusion that a combination of interspecific and intraspecific competition for space may play a major role, if not a decisive role, in maintaining numerical stability in coral reef communities (Smith and Tyler, 1972). Tagging experiments on Bermuda reef fishes have shown that some species stayed in the same area for long periods, and some homed to their reef when displaced (Bardach, 1958).

Marine communities have had much more time in which to evolve such interdependent complexity than have freshwater ones. In what are probably the oldest freshwater communities, those of the major equatorial rivers, fluctuations in water level have meant that territory cannot have so permanent a role in the lives of individual fishes. The Great Lakes, with their stable conditions the most resembling those on marine reefs, are not old enough for complexity to have evolved as far as in the sea, and their faunas are, of course, restricted to fishes which had access to the lake. Many of the same factors will operate here as in the sea, but symbiosis and commensalism for example do not seem so well developed in freshwater; certain groups such as large coelenterates and echinoderms with which fish have commensal relationships in the sea are absent from freshwater. Nor have we yet discovered in freshwater any cleaner-fish stations, which are such a feature of marine reef communities, leading to local concentrations of fishes waiting to have their parasites removed by specialist cleaner fishes.

A cleaning symbiosis has, however, recently been described for tropical freshwater fishes in tanks, the young of the cichlid *Etroplus maculatus* establishing cleaning territories wherein all age groups of *Etroplus suratensis* were cleaned, cleaning activity showing a daily circadian rhythm. These two species are sympatric in coastal estuaries and freshwater lakes in south-east India and Ceylon. The authors suggest that aspects of the breeding behaviour of these fishes may have helped the evolution of cleaning behaviour, intraspecific signals becoming important for interspecific behaviour (Wyman and Ward, 1972).

The kinds of changes in selection pressures that occur with changing environmental conditions, and with time as communities evolve, are indicated in Fig. 10.2 summarising events that occur after a new lake is

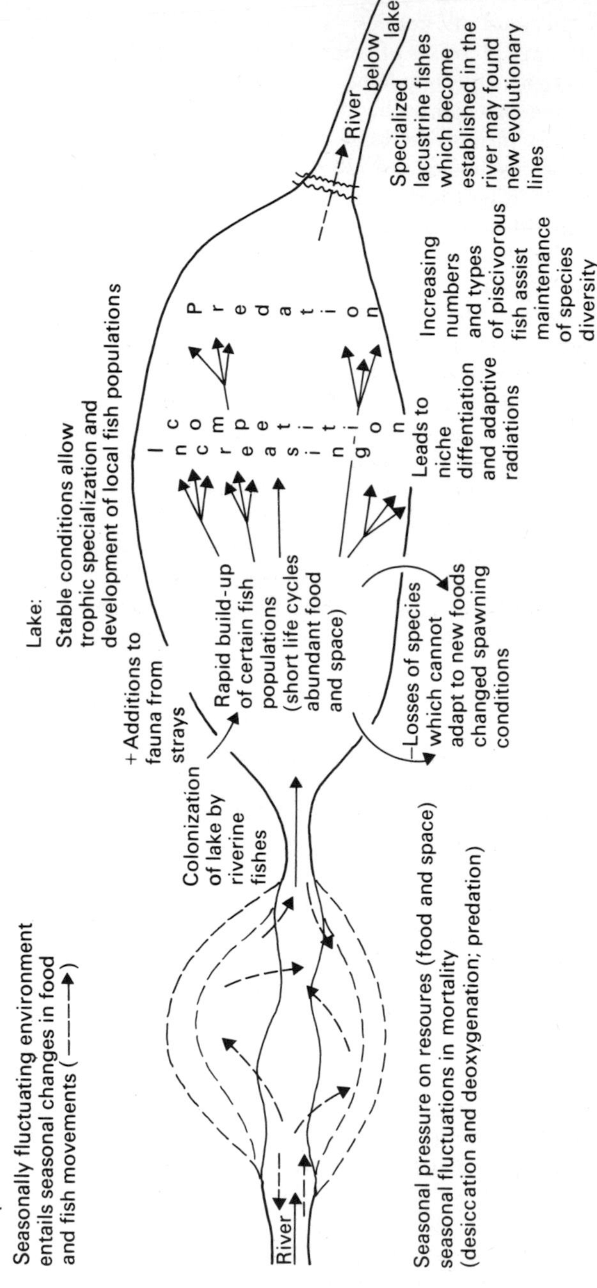
Floodplain:
Seasonally fluctuating environment entails seasonal changes in food and fish movements (----→)
River
Seasonal pressure on resoures (food and space) seasonal fluctuations in mortality (desiccation and deoxygenation; predation)
Colonization of lake by riverine fishes
+ Additions to fauna from strays
Lake:
Stable conditions allow trophic specialization and development of local fish populations
Rapid build-up of certain fish populations (short life cycles abundant food and space)
–Losses of species which cannot adapt to new foods changed spawning conditions
Competition
Leads to niche diffentiation and adaptive radiations
Predation
Increasing numbers and types of piscivorous fish assist maintenance of species diversity
River below lake
Specialized lacustrine fishes which become established in the river may found new evolutionary lines

colonised with riverine fishes. In the floodplain rivers abiotic selection, assisted by biotic selection, is of great importance seasonally (pressures being greatest as the water falls as indicated in Fig. 9.4). Of the riverine fishes which colonise lakes some will soon be lost to the fauna (as mormyrids were from Volta Lake), and others will be added at intervals (as *Alestes lateralis* and other species appeared in Lake Kariba). Fishes which thrive under the new lake conditions will multiply fast. Intraspecific competition will tend to push them to widen their food niches, but the presence of numerous species will lead to niche differentiation and specialisation. As the numbers and variety of predators increase, predation will play an increasing role in keeping the numbers of prey species below the levels at which they compete with one another for food and space, so preserving the diversity of the community.

Evolutionary aspects of community development

Speciation: the evolution of the constituent species

The most striking of the lacustrine adaptive radiations are those of the cichlid fishes of the African Great Lakes. The evolution of these fishes has been reviewed at length by Fryer and Iles (1972) and Greenwood (1974), so this is not considered in detail here. Since the review by Fryer and Iles Barombi Mbo studies (p. 162) have suggested how species divergence may have begun in these large lakes.

The numerous cichlids of Lake Malawi have almost all arisen within the lake, as is also the case for the cichlids in Lake Tanganyika. Fryer and Iles take the view that evolution is always basically allopatric, some form of microgeographical isolation being involved within the lake. This is relatively easy to visualise for the Mbuna rockfish of Lake Malawi on which Fryer worked, since the rocky stretches of coast alternate with sandy stretches, and are thus 'islands' more or less cut off from similar areas as these fishes rarely cross open water, providing semi-isolated small breeding populations, which geneticists maintain offer ideal conditions for rapid speciation. In Lake Victoria the sheer numbers of the *Haplochromis* species (nearly 200 of them) in a more uniform environment than that offered by Lake Malawi, suggest that other factors must have been operative. The finding of five endemic species of *Haplochromis* in a small lake (Lake Nabugabo) cut off from the west shore of Lake Victoria, has suggested that a series of such small lakes in the Victoria basin, probably along the drowned river courses, could have allowed allopatric speciation of some species groups (if not all the species). Greenwood (1973*a*) considered that the present-day *Haplochromis* flock of Lake Victoria could be interpreted as an amalgam of several different

Fig. 10.2 Summary of pressures and events which affect the development of tropical fish communities, as discussed in the text.

flocks, albeit of ultimate derivation from the same ancestral species or group of species.

Fryer also invoked allopatric speciation to account for evolution in the Lake Malawi *Tilapia* species flock which also quite certainly evolved within the lake. In these fishes personal observations suggested that the differences in breeding season, reinforced by depth at which the various *Tilapia* species spawn, and further reinforced by the colour of the breeding male, have undoubtedly been important in keeping the two most closely similar and related species, *T. squamipinnis* and *T. saka*, apart, species which may be caught in mixed shoals at other times of year (Lowe, 1952, 1953).

In the cichlids the ritual and often long courtship behaviour must help to keep species separate. Ethological isolating mechanisms are also important amongst sympatric poeciliids (Liley, 1966). We know a good deal about the visual aspects of behaviour from aquarium studies; we can as yet only guess at some other aspects. Experiments with young cichlids show that they react to water in which the parent has been living, so that smell or taste is evidently important for at least some of these fishes as well as sight. The young of a brood stay with the parent, and remain together in a small shoal for a considerable time. For *Tilapia variabilis* in Lake Victoria there was some evidence that tagged fish stay together while making long movements about the lake, and that females may 'home' to certain nursery areas to brood their young (p. 137). If the smaller cichlids remain near to one another, and stay in certain areas in this lake, this would be conducive to the formation of local breeding populations, and eventually to species formation. Albrecht (1963) has shown that the female mouth-brooding *Haplochromis wingatii* and *H. burtoni*, as well as *Pseudocrenilabris multicolor*, become territorial when the young reach the free-swimming stage. The young learn the mother's home territory and do not leave it; this compensates for the absence of one parent and makes leading them easier for the mother. *P. multicolor* young can probably distinguish the so-called mother-pattern only at a distance of about 10 cm. When the fish are about ten days old they migrate into shallow water and no longer live in an area defended by the female. The possible role of imprinting of environmental characteristics on young fishes needs study.

In Lake Malawi some rockfish remain in circumscribed areas for long periods and their big eggs have an evolutionary importance as the large yolk supply enables the small fish to cut out a plankton-feeding phase, which might lead to wider dispersal of the fish around the lake and reduce the effect of isolation on speciation. The same would appear to hold for hypostomine catfishes in South American streams; these algal-grazers living in rocky streams also produce few and very large eggs and young fishes are found in the same biotopes as the adults.

Divergences of niche can occur by differential selection among individuals whose genetic characteristics make them more closely or less closely competitive with other species in the community, as a larger proportion of the latter will survive and transmit their characters to future generations

(Whittaker and Woodwell, 1972). Whether this process can continue to the stage where a new species is formed will depend on some kind of isolating mechanism preventing the differentiating individuals from breeding out, and being swamped by other members of the population. Such differentiation will lead to trophic specialisation. (Specialisation can conceivably occur without competition, as when a species enters a new environment and is able to specialise on a preferred food, as *Schilbe mystus* apparently did on the ephemeropteran nymph *Povilla adusta* in the new Volta Lake, see p. 181.)

Many intriguing questions arise about the non-cichlid species flocks. Why for instance have clariids produced a species flock in Lake Malawi but not in Lake Tanganyika when they were present in both lakes? Did the presence of *Chrysichthys* which speciated in the latter lake prevent this? The *Mastacembelus* flock in Lake Tanganyika is easily understandable in terms of its rock dwelling habit and the microgeographical isolation which this confers. In the rivers of Africa the mormyrid species flock of the Zaïre basin is one of the most remarkable. In the Zaïre system the alternation of various types of water, rapids and pools for instance, suggests that microgeographical isolation within the river system has allowed allopatric speciation here too. The numerous small cyprinids, especially *Barbus*, in African rivers can also be accounted for by allopatric speciation in semi-isolated populations in the numerous tributary streams and associated water bodies.

In the rivers of South America the adaptive radiations of the characoids and various catfish groups are as remarkable as those of the cichlids in the African Great Lakes. Differentiation has proceeded much further in these groups, certain families or subfamilies now having particular feeding habits (approaching the condition in marine fishes). The semi-isolated conditions in tributary streams, varzea, oxbow and marginal lakes, would appear to offer ideal conditions for allopatric speciation. Oscillations in river levels, due to factors ranging in scale from sudden local downpours of rain to long-term climatic cycles, and geomorphological changes leading to river captures, give abundant opportunities for species evolved in semi-isolated communities to come together. Species from many areas then accumulate, as the overall extinction rate appears to be low.

Rates of evolution We know very little about rates of evolution, but they may be very rapid in new environments. The small Lake Nabugabo, cut off from Lake Victoria by a sandbar dated 4000 years old, has five endemic *Haplochromis* species (Greenwood, 1965*b*). Lake Lanao with its 20 endemic cyprinid species was thought to be 10 000 years old, but it now seems that it may be much older (p. 54). The incredibly rich species flocks in the African Great Lakes appear to have evolved in perhaps half to one million years for Lake Victoria, less than 2 m.y. for Lake Malawi and perhaps 6 m.y. for Lake Tanganyika (p. 37). In the river systems, evolution will have been in progress for very much longer. Certain characoid and catfish groups shared by Africa and South America indicate the scale of the differentiation which must have occurred before these two continents were finally separated in Cretaceous times. (Fish groups shared between Asia and Africa are less indicative since India was once part of Gondwanaland.)

The 'supralimital specialisations' acquired by many endemic fishes in Lake Lanao (p. 54) and in the Great Lakes of Africa include some so distinctive as to provide characters worthy of family or subfamily rank. Myers (1960*a*) suggested that such fish could become founders of groups at new adaptive levels should they escape from the lake and survive in other waters and that such events may account for the almost unbelievably rich fauna of characoid fishes in the Amazon. In its present form the Amazon is not a very old river; in its lower course it probably represents a reversed river, its Peruvian reaches formed a great lake in relatively recent geological times, and it still has immense fluctuating lakes lining its course. We mentioned (p. 73) the probable effects of changes in sea level associated with glacials and interglacials on conditions in the Amazon basin, as put forward by Myers (1972) who conceived that they would have led to great intermittent mixing of the fish populations. Roberts (1972) also suspected that the present Amazon fish fauna may be the product of only a few million years of evolution from an original stock of two- or three-hundred founder species, some of them representing groups of considerable antiquity; he also suggested that the Zaïre fauna is not necessarily ancient, as lakes do not necessarily present the only ecological situation in which explosive adaptive radiations have occurred. Such rapid ('tachytelic' or 'quantum') evolution could, according to Myers, only occur in biotopes where the invading species could overcome competition from resident species, or where there was little or no such competition; such evolution would be impossible where better balanced ecological conditions and a differentiated fauna held ecological divergence more tightly in check. Myers concluded that opportunity, the absence of well-adapted competing groups, is extremely important in the evolution of higher categories of fishes; geological changes, such as those leading to the formation of new lakes, provide such opportunities from time to time.

Evolution of fish communities

In the preceding chapters we have examined information concerning various riverine and lacustrine fish communities. Some attributes of their ecologies are summarised in the following Table 10.1, which brings out the different nature of the communities under the stable equilibrium conditions in the littoral and benthic communities in the Great Lakes, and of those in the disequilibrium conditions in the seasonally fluctuating rivers. Between these extremes communities of the pelagic zone in the Great Lakes and of the equatorial forest rivers have intermediate attributes.

There has been much discussion among ecologists as to the types of selection operating in 'initial' and 'mature' communities. Basically the problem is one of reproductive strategy. Any organism has only limited time and energy, and these resources have to be shared between non-reproductive activities (maintenance and growth) and reproduction. Communities evolve too, and are also subject to natural selection, and the proportion of resources put into reproduction by the organisms will generally be related to the needs of the community as a whole.

MacArthur and Wilson (1967) when considering island communities (which provide direct parallels with lakes) distinguished between selection in pioneer communities, in which maximum fecundity was at a premium, and that later in the more saturated communities when the emphasis was on increased efficiency for resource utilisation. They designated these two types of selection, each with characteristic attributes, '*r* selection' (since *r* is the term used for the intrinsic rate of growth in growth equations), and '*K* selection' (since *K* is used for equilibrium population size): '*r* selection' favours a higher population growth rate and higher productivity; this form of selection will come to the fore during colonising episodes, or in species which are frequently pioneer species, while '*K* selection' favours a more efficient utilisation of resources, such as closer cropping of the food supply, as achieved by species showing greater trophic specialisation.

The characteristics of species adapted to initial and mature stages of succession were also discussed by Margalef (1968) who defined success in terms of the replacement of one unit of the ecosystem by another doing the same work for less energy, or more work for the same energy, i.e. increased efficiency. He contrasted immature communities in which the keynote is opportunism, with mature communities in which the keynote is efficiency. In immature communities there is a fast turnover, the production is high in relation to biomass, and there is selection for high fecundity. Species tend to have a short life span but to leave numerous descendants; they have long-range dispersal mechanisms, and are very adaptable to changing conditions in time and space, and in these evolution is often very rapid.

In mature communities production is relatively low in relation to accumulated biomass; selection is for low fecundity with increased parental care, relationships between individuals become more important and trophic specialisation is much greater; species have a longer life span, and live isolated in small breeding communities, generally with poor possibilities for dispersal. In their behaviour and biochemically they are well integrated into the system and often territorial.

Changes during succession include increase in biomass, and generally also of primary production, though the ratio of primary production to total biomass drops. Diversity very often increases, also the presence of structures like burrows, paths, territory markers, etc., which may be considered as stores of information. Fluctuations are damped and rhythms change from reactions directly induced by external agents to indirect responses to stimuli associated with ecologically significant factors; the ultimate trend is for the development of endogenous rhythms.

Organisms of pioneer, initial, immature communities, do best (and

Table 10.1 Summary of ecological correlates of fish communities in different types of tropical freshwater.

	GREAT LAKES		RIVERS	
	Littoral and benthic	**Pelagic**	**Equatorial forest**	**Savanna floodplain**
Hydrological climate	Very stable	± seasonal; limited upwelling once/yr (Malawi), twice/yr Tanganyika)	Twice yearly variation. Rain all year but river level with 2 high, 2 low periods/yr	Very seasonal. Annual rains annual floods (± 2nd flood)
Environment size	Very stable	Very stable	Twice yearly variation lateral flooding into forest	Annual variation, lateral flooding over savanna and into swamp pools
Population size	Equilibrium. V. stable, small amount of reproduction throughout year No immigration Saturated community at carrying capacity	Variable following plankton blooms after upwelling and ceiling fixed by predation No immigration	Variable due to twice-yearly breeding and lateral movements	Disequilibrium. Great seasonal variation in breeding, mortality, and lateral movements Recolonization by migration
Food availability	Available throughout year	Available all year but some seasonal abundance	Seasonal variation, 2 peaks/yr at high water	Great seasonal variation, peak at high water
Use of food	Specialization ++ by adaptive radiation. Stenophagy	Specialization on few sources (plankton and small fish). Stenophagy	Specialization but facultative	Seasonal change of food. At low water maintenance only or migration to feeding areas
Predators	Many species. Most utilize varied prey Some specialize	Few species. May specialize on prey used	Many species, using many prey species	Many species using many prey species

Table 10.1 – *continued*

	GREAT LAKES		RIVERS	
	Littoral and benthic	**Pelagic**	**Equatorial forest**	**Savanna floodplain**
Competition for food	Not very keen, overlaps common	Overlaps common	Probably varies with 2 seasonal peaks	Varies seasonally, very keen at end of rains and early dry season
Competition for living space	Very keen. Territoriality of breeding sites may limit population	None for truly pelagic clupeids. Spawning or nursery areas may limit cichlids	Some groups territorial	Seasonally varying greatest at low water
Growth to maturity	Slow development 3+ years	1 year clupeids; several years predators	< 1 year small species, probably 2 year larger spp.	Mostly 1 or 2 years
Length of life	Many years?	1(+) year clupeids Many year predators and *Tilapia*	Many years?	Small cyprinodonts annual Many years some?
Reproduction	Cichlids: small batches at frequent intervals. River migrants: retain seasonality, total spawners	Clupeids follow plankton blooms	Mostly at high water, 2 peaks/yr	Seasonal. Total spawners breed as water rises; small-brood spawners at end of dry season and through rains
Predominant type of selection	K selection for efficient use of resources. Specialization	r and K?	? oscillating K and r?	r-selection for fecundity, great seasonal wastage, natural mortality high
Type of community	Very mature	—	—	Immature characteristics

therefore have survived to predominate in these situations) if they develop rapidly, reproduce early and have a high reproductive rate. They are often of small body size, short-lived (one or two years or less), and tend to spawn completely, laying all their eggs at one time. They tend to be generalist facultative feeders. In these unsaturated communities, often recolonised each year, competition is low in initial stages but may build up as the population builds up. The population varies greatly with time, but is generally well below the carrying capacity. These are the communities found where the climate is variable and unpredictable. Mortality is non-directed and density-independent.

In the mature communities, on the other hand, found where the climatic conditions are constant, stable and predictable, organisms are slower to develop and to mature; they live longer and may grow to a larger size. Reproduction is repeated, a few young being produced at a time and often guarded or brooded. The biota is generally at or near the carrying capacity of the environment; in these saturated communities no recolonisation is necessary (or possible) and population size is fairly constant in time (equilibrium situation). The keen competition has led to specialisation for exploitation of particular foods (and thus of adaptive radiations), and competition may be at generic level.

The fish communities of the Great Lakes where conditions are very stable, have all the hallmarks of mature *K*-selected communities. The population size remains very constant round the year, the fishes grow more slowly than in rivers and reproduction is delayed until they are several years old, and is repeated, the cichlids producing small batches of young at frequent intervals, with brood care. There is great specialisation for use of different foods, with which are associated the spectacular adaptive radiations and species flocks.

This applies primarily to the littoral and benthic fish populations. In Lake Tanganyika Coulter (p. 159) concluded that the benthic and pelagic components of the deep-water community represent two levels of diversity. There are many benthic fish species and their trophic interrelationships appear complex. The pelagic species, on the other hand, are relatively few (though each are numerically abundant) and their feeding requirements are highly specialised (for use of zooplankton or of fishes which feed on these zooplankton-feeding fish). The large and continuous populations found in pelagic species lead to constancy of character, in contrast with the small and divided populations of benthic fishes which lead to great genetic diversity. In the sea too, pelagic communities are composed of relatively few species, compared with the very diverse communities of a coral reef.

In the rivers the situation is more complex. As the rivers become increasingly seasonal away from the equator, so the *r*-selection appears to become increasingly more important (e.g. on the floodplains where the losses each year are enormous). Growth to maturity tends to be faster in these rivers than in the Great Lakes, and most fish species reach maturity in one or two years. Flooding and stranding puts a high premium on rapid development of eggs and young. Even in the very seasonal tropical rivers the numbers of fish species tend to be very high compared with temperate rivers, predators, including piscivorous fishes, are numerous, and there are intricate interactions between biotic and abiotic selection pressures. *Tilapia* have the ability to switch from a late-maturing form in the Great Lakes to an early-maturing phase in shallow pools, places where *r*-selection is predominant (p. 205).

The achievement of trophic specialisation by character divergence implies that there must have been competition for food or other resources at some stage during the evolution of the species.

As the communities become more complex different pressures build up which control numbers: for instance pressure for sheer living space, breeding grounds, nursery areas, and cover from predators, as well as feeding territories. Diversity begets diversity; the diversity of food organisms (invertebrates, etc.) also increases with time, thus enabling trophic specialisations in the fishes consuming them to proceed to a finer degree. Many behavioural devices have evolved to partition the living space. Visual means are used among diurnal fishes, electrical signals in the nocturnal gymnotoids and mormyrids, while chemical communication dictates social structure in the catfish world and sounds are used by many fishes. Experiments have shown how dominance, fighting, etc., can have lasting effects on the growth of the individual fish, and size in turn affects reproductive capacity. As the community becomes more complex, there are increasing numbers and kinds of predators, and their role in permitting diversity of prey species to persist is enhanced.

We also know from pond and field studies how one fish species can ameliorate the biotope for other species, and that cropping food speeds up the production of further fish food, which may be a diversity-dependent, as well as a density-dependent process. These fish communities illustrate very well theoretical ideas on how communities evolve.

The evolution of communities as a whole

The evolution of the fish communities is related to the evolution of the lake or river communities as a whole. Lakes are generally classified according to their primary productivity which depends on nutrients received from the regional drainage, the geological age and the depth of lake. Classical studies in temperate zones distinguished between oligotrophic ('few foods') lakes and eutrophic ('good foods') lakes. Typical oligotrophic lakes are deep, with hypolimnion larger than epilimnion, and low primary productivity; littoral plants are scarce and plankton density is low. Eutrophic lakes are generally shallower, with greater primary productivity; the littoral vegetation is more abundant (unless too shaded by plankton) and the phytoplankton is denser. These two types of lake carry different fish faunas. The natural succession is for lakes to fill, making them shallower, and in temperate regions landuse practices have led to greatly increased run-off of nutrients from the land, which enriches the lakes, a process known as eutrophication.

Margalef (1968) commenting on the assumption in most limnological literature that there is a natural succession in lakes from oligotrophic to eutrophic, a succession accelerated by human influence, pointed out that as nutrients become depleted in a system, eutrophy will give way to oligotrophy. The apparent conflict with classical ideas on succession is avoided if the nutrient input is kept in mind: as this increases, oligotrophy will give way to eutrophy, as it decreases, the reverse occurs. In eutrophic lakes compared with oligotrophic lakes the production/biomass ratio is higher, and the absolute production and absolute biomass are also usually higher, though their species diversity is lower. Margalef considered that oligotrophic lakes are more mature ecosystems than eutrophic ones, and that eutrophic lakes are kept in a state of low maturity because nutrients are continually forced into them (from farmland and pollution) without allowing time for them to become equilibrated. The West Cameroon crater lakes Barombi Mbo and Kotto provide examples of a more mature oligotrophic lake and a less mature eutrophic one with a much less diverse fauna (p. 162).

The terms eutrophic and oligotrophic were originally applied to lakes, which are closed ecosystems, not to rivers (which are classified on gradients). River systems antedate lakes, yet these large tropical lakes achieve a greater stability, a sign of maturity, than do any rivers. These tropical rivers are kept in a relatively low state of maturity by the throughput of nutrients which rejuvenate their systems, but this does not prevent them having very complex fish communities. In the laterally flooded areas of large tropical rivers lacustrine conditions prevail for much of the year, and some areas may be cut off and remain lacustrine for a series of years if rainfall is low or where a river course is changed.

Margalef (1963, 1968) also pointed out that many animals living in mature ecosystems as adults spend their juvenile life in a less mature one. The young stages of benthic lake fishes, for example, often live in the less mature systems of the plankton or upper reaches of affluent streams, places where the rapidly-growing young can take advantage of the excess energy in the less mature system. Mature systems thus exploit less mature ones.

11

Conclusions

Conclusions may be coloured by conditions in the relatively few areas of the tropics for which information is available. Nevertheless these data from ecological studies on tropical fishes have given us a picture of community development which supports theoretical ideas on how communities evolve. They also highlight certain points.

It is encouraging to find how well results of researches carried out quite independently in the various tropical regions, Africa, South America, tropical Asia, support one another, for instance concerning the linear succession of dominant food resources in streams (Fig. 9.2) and concerning the role of predators in maintaining diversity in mature communities. In all three regions fishes in headwater streams are primarily dependent on allochthonous foods, as the streams enlarge and deepen predatory omnivores using benthic invertebrates (especially insects) become more important in the fauna, and in the lower reaches detritus and soft mud accumulate supporting very large numbers of mud-feeding fishes, which may, however, have to move long distances to find suitable places in which to spawn.

In rivers the seasonal fluctuations in size of the environment, as they flood laterally into forest or over savanna, twice yearly or annually (Fig. 9.4), are followed by fluctuations in fish populations, since most fishes breed early in the rains and mortality is highest at the end of the rains. Thus pressures on food resources fluctuate seasonally, maximum pressures coming at the end of the highwater period, when the contracting environment reduces the resources and the fish population is at its highest, the well-grown young in many cases using the same food as the parent fish. These seasonal fluctuations in competition may have been very important in the evolution of trophic specialisation.

When a new lake forms, or is created by man, colonisation with riverine species may in some cases be of a highly differentiated river fauna (as probably occurred for Lakes Albert and Rudolf), or of just a few founder species (as may have occurred for Lakes Lanao, Victoria, Tanganyika, Malawi, and Barombi Mbo). The populations of founder species expand very fast as life cycles are short at tropical temperatures, and food is abundant as new land is flooded as the lake forms (Fig. 10.2). Some riverine species are lost to the fauna at this stage, either because they fail to change their diet from foods such as lithophilic insects which are no longer available, or because they fail to spawn successfully under the new conditions (as occurred in Volta Lake, p. 181). As the community stabilises new members continue to join it, originating from 'strays' which find the new conditions to their advantage (as occurred in Lake Kariba, p. 177).

As populations build up, intraspecific competition for the foods used by founder species will, in the absence or near absence of resistance from interspecific competition in adjacent niches, lead to trophic and character divergence and to explosive adaptive radiations to exploit the new sources of food available. Behaviour changes precede changes of structure, as observations underwater and in aquaria increasingly suggest. During this process of adaptive radiation predatory species evolve, as appears to be just starting in Barombi Mbo (p. 165). Predator pressure may then take over from, or become relatively more important than, competition for food or space as the main factor controlling the number of prey species. Predation is density-dependent and appears to have a major role in allowing the co-existence of prey species below the level at which they compete with each other for food and space.

As the community matures biotic relationships assume increasing importance. As populations build up and niches are filled fecundity is no longer at a premium and selection favours efficiency of resource utilisation instead of fecundity. The stable conditions around the year in the Great Lakes allow great trophic specialisation to develop in those fishes which can stay in one biotope throughout the year, as do many of the cichlids, free of the need to migrate up rivers to spawn.

There is, however, a divergence between evolution in pelagic communities and in littoral/benthic communities, the key factor being absence or presence of cover where prey fish can hide from predators. Predators can have contrary effects on speciation, inhibiting it in open water and promoting it where there is cover (see p. 249). In the pelagic communities selection is mainly for uniformity in appearance and genotype, and specialisation to use plankton, or plankton-feeding fish, as food; numbers may be controlled by an interaction of food supply (based on plankton blooms) and predators. Life cycles of prey fish are short (often annual), space is not limiting, and selection for fecundity will be important, as it is in less mature communities. In the littoral/benthic communities with cover, selection leads to great diversity of genotype, adaptive radiations to use the many kinds of food available, with stress on efficient use of resources; space is here limited, fish delay breeding and then produce small broods of guarded young. These communities show the characteristics of mature communities.

Brief mention has been made of the importance of these freshwater fishes as food in tropical countries (Chapter 8). This alone is a vast subject. River fishes provide local people with protein throughout all regions of the tropics, and the flood fisheries of the great plains, whether in Africa, South America or Asia, support fisheries from which food fishes are exported over very wide areas, and which are very important in the economies of the countries concerned. Pond fish culture, which has been developed over 4000 years in the Far East on an empirical basis, is now being investigated scientifically so that it can be more successfully transferred to other parts of the tropics. The advisability or otherwise of introducing exotic species for food raises problems that call for much careful research, for once introduced, fish may be possible to eradicate, and introductions often lead to extinctions of indigenous species.

Conservation is vitally necessary to safeguard future potentialities. These marvellous lake faunas are the most vulnerable and deserve active conservation. We now know that these complex tropical ecosystems with their many species and rich interaction structure, far from being stable, are dynamically very fragile. Although well adapted to persist in the very predictable environment in which they have evolved, they are likely to be far less resistant to any perturbations imposed by man than are the relatively simple and robust faunas of temperate systems (May, 1975).

There is so much that it has not been possible to consider within the limits of this book (for example adaptations of many fishes to withstand deoxygenation), and new lines of research are continually being developed. Studies such as those of Welcomme in Lake Victoria (p. 129 and Fig. 5.2) stress that in addition to physical barriers fish movements are affected by many physicochemical and biotic barriers of which we as yet know very little. Fishes provide very good material for experimental ecology. Experimental studies on their interrelationships, the effects of predation, etc., in nature and in ponds and tanks, should enable us to understand better how their behaviour is influenced by the environment and the other species present, and how this in turn affects their evolution. Recent marine studies point the way, such as those of Myrberg (1972*b*) in which results from field and laboratory studies are compared.

The problems are legion. So gentle reader, if you feel so disposed, go out and tackle them. You will find the work highly rewarding both aesthetically and scientifically, as well as contributing to protein supplies in a world becoming sadly overpopulated.

Quis, nisi vidisset, pisces habitare sub unda, crederet? (Linnaeus, 1758)

Appendix 1

Some sources of information

It is impossible, for reasons of space, to cite here all the work spread over three continents and published in five languages that has contributed to this picture of the ecology of tropical freshwater fishes. So many scientists have contributed, and often the same idea has cropped up quite independently in different parts of the world, which is reassuring. Some of the main centres of research are mentioned; papers published from these institutions, and in some cases annual reports, contain much ecological information.

Africa

In Africa the information on fish ecology comes from four main areas:

1. *West Africa.* French scientists have made a particularly large contribution (many papers by Daget, Blache, *et al.*, Carmouze *et al.*);
2. *Zaïre:* studied mainly by Belgian scientists (Poll, Marlier, Gosse, Matthes, *et al.*);
3. *East Africa.* Work mainly on the Great Lakes from the East African Fisheries Research Organisation (EAFFRO) based at Jinja, Uganda, following the pioneer fishery surveys by E. B. Worthington.
4. *Central Africa.* Studies from the Joint Fisheries Research Organisation (JFRO) in Zambia and Malawi, and later from their respective Fishery Departments.

   The creation of *man-made lakes*, particularly Kariba, Volta, Kainji, has stimulated much research by Fishery Departments, local Universities, and by special units set up by International Organisations (UNDP and FAO).

   The Committee for Inland Fisheries of Africa (CIFA) of the Food and Agriculture Organisation of the United Nations in Rome collates information from African waters (FAO, 1972, 1973, 1973*b*).

South America

In South America ecological information dates back to studies on fishes of the Mogi Guassu and other rivers in Sao Paulo State in the 1930s (von Ihering *et al.*), and studies made in connection with fish culture. Mogi

Guassu studies continue from the biological and fish culture station at Pirassununga (Godoy). In Amazonas the Instituto de Pesquisas de Amazonia (INPA) has a laboratory at Manaus. This has been used as a base by Dr H. Sioli's team from the Max-Planck-Institut für Limnologie, Plön, Germany (Sioli, Fittkau, *et al.*) over many years. Expeditions to the Upper Amazon to study fish ecology include those of Professor K. H. Lüling from Bonn, Germany. The Expedição Permanente da Amazonia has a research vessel on the Amazon from which fish ecology is being studied by a team from the Museu de Zoologia, University of Sao Paulo (directed by Dr P. E. Vanzolini). For Brazil there is a useful annotated bibliography of fish studies (Godinho and Britski, 1964). In Argentina the Instituto Nacional de Limnologia near Santa Fe, directed by Dr A. A. Bonetto, has made a big contribution. The book *Los Peces Argentinos de Agua Dulce* (Ringuelet *et al.*, 1967) includes ecological information.

India

In India the Central Inland Fisheries Research Institute with its headquarters at Barrackpore, Bengal and laboratories spread around the country is the main source of information on Indian fish studies (bibliography by Tripathi *et al.*). In Thailand manmade lake projects in the Mekong have stimulated research. Dussart (1974) has a useful bibliography.

Publications

Reviews of fish studies in South America and Asia are given in the proceedings of the International Biological Programme regional meetings of inland water biologists held in these two continents in 1968 and 1969 respectively: an African meeting was also held in 1968. Papers prepared for three symposia on manmade lakes, in London in 1965, Ghana in 1966 and Tennessee in 1971, also summarise ecological information. The International Biological Programme Handbook No. 3 (ed. Ricker, 2nd edn 1971) on *Methods for assessment of fish production in freshwaters* has useful bibliographies. Recent books which summarise much information and have extensive bibliographies include those cited in the Preface (p. vii).

Appendix 2

Fish Families Represented in Tropical Freshwaters

(Classification of Teleostean fishes according to Greenwood, *et al.*, 1966)

		South America	Africa	Asia
Class CHONDRICHTHYES				
Subclass Elasmobranchii				
Order Squaliformes				
Family Carcharhinidae	Requiem sharks	+	−	+
Order Rajiformes				
Family Pristidae	Sawfish	+	−	+
Dasyatidae	Stingrays (Estuarine)	+	+	+
Potamotrygonidae	Freshwater stingrays	+	+	−
Class OSTEICHTHYES				
Subclass Sarcopterygii				
Order Dipteriformes (Dipnoi)				
Family Ceratodontidae	Australian lungfish	−	−	−
Lepidosirenidae	Lungfish	+	+	−
Subclass Brachiopterygii				
Order Polypteriformes				
Family Polypteridae	Bichirs	−	+	−
Subclass Actinopterygii (Teleostean fishes)				
DIVISION I TELEOSTEAN FISHES				
Superorder ELOPOMORPHA				
Order Elopiformes				
Family Elopidae		+	+	+
Megalopidae	Tarpon	+	+	+
Order Anguilliformes	Eels	−	+	+
Superorder CLUPEOMORPHA				
Order Clupeiformes				
Suborder Denticipitoidei				
Family Denticipitidae	*Denticeps*	−	+	−
Suborder Clupeioidei				
Clupeidae (inclu: Congothrissidae)	Herrings	+	+	+
Engraulidae	Anchovies	+	−	+
DIVISION II				
Superorder OSTEOGLOSSOMORPHA				
Order Osteoglossiformes				
Suborder Osteoglossoidei				
Osteoglossidae	*Osteoglossum, Arapaima*	+	+	−

Appendix 2 Table—*Continued*

		South America	Africa	Asia
	Heterotis	–	+	–
Pantodontidae	*Pantodon*	–	+	–
Suborder Notopteroidei				
Notopteridae	Featherbacks	–	+	+
Order Mormyriformes:				
Mormyridae		–	+	–
Gymnarchidae		–	+	–
Superorder PROTACANTHOPTERYGII				
Order Salmoniformes:				
Salmonidae	Salmon (trout introduced)	(+)	(+)	+
Plecoglossidae	Ayu	–	–	+
Order Gonorynchiformes				
Suborder Chanoidei				
Chanidae	Milkfish	–	+	+
Kneriidae (incl:		–	+	–
Cromeridae, Grasseichthyidae)		–	+	–
Phractolaemidae		–	+	–
Superorder OSTARIOPHYSI				
Order Cypriniformes				
Suborder Characoidei				
Characidae (Characinidae incl: Crenuchidae, Acestrorhynchidae, Serrasalmidae, Tetragonopteridae, Creagrutidae, Glandulocaudidae)		+	+	–
Erythrinidae		+	–	–
Ctenolucidae		+	–	–
Hepsetidae		–	+	–
Cynodontidae		+	–	–
Lebiasinidae (incl: Nannostomidae)		+	–	–
Parodontidae		+	–	–
Gasteropelecidae		+	–	–
Prochilodontidae		+	–	–
Curimatidae (incl: Anodontidae)		+	–	–
Anostomidae		+	–	–
Hemiodontidae (incl: Bivibranchiidae)		+	–	–
Chilodontidae		+	–	–
Distichodontidae		–	+	–
Citharinidae		–	+	–
Ichthyoboridae		–	+	–
Suborder Gymnotoidei				
Gymnotidae		+	–	–
Electrophoridae	Electric eel	+	–	–
Apteronotidae (incl: Sternarchidae, Sternopygidae)		+	–	–
Rhamphichthyidae		+	–	–
Suborder Cyprinoidei				
Cyprinidae	Carps	–	+	+
Suborder Siluroidei (Nematognathi)	Catfishes			
Diplomystidae		(+)	–	–
Bagridae (incl: Porcidae, Mystidae)		–	+	+

Appendix 2 Table—*Continued*

		South America	Africa	Asia
Siluridae		–	–	+
Schilbeidae		–	+	+
Pangasiidae		–	–	+
Amblycipitidae		–	–	+
Amphiliidae		–	+	–
Akysidae		–	–	+
Sisoridae (Bagridae)		–	–	+
Clariidae		–	+	+
Heteropneustidae (Saccobranchidae)		–	–	+
Chacidae		–	–	+
Olyridae		–	–	+
Malapteruridae	Electric catfish	–	+	–
Mochokidae		–	+	–
Ariidae		+	+	+
Doradidae		+	–	–
Auchenipteridae (incl: Trachycorystidae)		+	–	–
Aspredinidae (Bunocephalidae)		+	–	–
Plotosidae		–	+	+
Pimelodidae (incl: Pseudopimelodidae)		+	–	–
Ageneiosidae		+	–	–
Hypophthalmidae		+	–	–
Helogeneidae		+	–	–
Cetopsidae		+	–	–
Trichomycteridae (Pygidiidae)		+	–	–
Callichthyidae		+	–	–
Loricariidae (incl: Hypostomidae)		+	–	–
Astroblepidae		+	–	–
Superorder ATHERINOMORPHA				
Order Atheriniformes				
Suborder Exocoetoidei				
Belonidae	Garfish	+	–	+
Suborder Cyprinodontoidei				
Cyprinodontidae (incl: Orestiidae)		+	+	+
Goodeidae		(+)	–	–
Jenynsiidae (Fitzroyidae)		+	–	–
Poeciliidae (incl: Tomeuridae)	Guppies	+	–	–
Anablepidae	Foureyes	+	–	–
Superorder ACANTHOPTERYGII				
Order Gasterosteiformes				
Syngnathidae	Pipefishes	+	+	+
Order Channiformes				
Channidae (Ophiocephalidae)		–	+	+
Order Synbranchiformes				
Synbranchidae (inclu: Flutidae Monopteridae)		+	+	+
Order Perciformes				
Suborder Percoidei	Perch			
Centropomidae	*Lates*	+	+	+
Lobotidae	Tripletails	+	+	+
Sciaenidae	Drums, Croakers	+	+	+

Appendix 2 Table—*Continued*

			South America	Africa	Asia
	Toxotidae	Archer fish	–	–	+
	Nandidae (incl: Polycentridae)		+	+	+
	Cichlidae		+	+	+
Suborder	Mugiloidei				
	Mugilidae	Grey mullet	+	+	+
Suborder	Gobioidei				
	Gobiidae (incl: Eleotridae)	Gobies	+	+	+
Suborder	Anabantoidei				
	Anabantidae		–	+	+
	Helostomatidae		–	–	+
	Osphronemidae		–	–	+
Suborder	Luciocephalidoidei				
	Luciocephalidae		–	–	+
Suborder	Mastacembelidoidei				
	Mastacembelidae (Rhynchobdellidae)		–	+	+
	Chaudhuriidae		–	–	+
Suborder	Soleoidei				
	Soleidae (incl: Achiridae, Synapturidae)	Flatfish, soles	+	+	+
	Cynoglossidae	Tongue soles	–	–	+
Order	Tetraodontiformes				
	Tetraodontidae	Puffer fish	+	+	+

Appendix 3

The Fish Faunas of Representative Rivers and Lakes of Africa

Data on numbers of species in each family from following sources: Middle Niger, Daget (1954); L. Chad (Blache *et al.*, 1964); Zaïre Central Basin (Poll and Gosse, 1965*b*); Luapula-Mweru (de Kimpe, 1963); Zambezi (Bell-Cross, 1965); L. Victoria, Greenwood (1966); L. Tanganyika (Poll, 1953); L. Malawi (Jackson *et al.*, 1963).

	Middle Niger	L. Chad	Zaïre Central basin	Luapula-Mweru	Zambezi	Upper Zambezi	Middle Zambezi	Kafue	Lake Victoria	Lake Tanganyika	Lake Malawi
Protopteridae	1	1	2	1	1	—	1	—	1	1	—
Polypteridae	4	3	7	—	—	—	—	—	—	1	—
Anguillidae	—	—	—	—	4	—	4	—	—	—	1
Denticipitidae	—	—	—	—	—	—	—	—	—	—	—
Clupeidae	1	1	9	3	—	—	—	—	—	2	—
Osteoglossidae	1	1	—	—	—	—	—	—	—	—	—
Pantodontidae	—	—	1	—	—	—	—	—	—	—	—
Notopteridae	1	2	2	—	—	—	—	—	—	—	—
Mormyridae	18	21	75	16	9	7	5	4	7	—	5
Gymnarchidae	1	1	—	—	—	—	—	—	—	—	—
Kneriidae	1	1	—	3	2	2	1	1	—	—	—
Phractolaemidae	—	—	1	—	—	—	—	—	—	—	—
Characidae	14	14	34	10	5	4	3	3	2	4	1
Hepsetidae	1	1	1	1	1	1	—	1	—	—	—
Distichodontidae	} 12	} 16	} 38	} 3		—	2	—	—	2	—
Citharinidae	}	}	}	}	4	2	—	2	—	1	—
Ichthyoboridae	—	—	} —	—	—	—	—	—	—	—	—
Cyprinidae	23	40	52	32	31	24	15	19	12	11	10
Ariidae	1	1	—	—	—	—	—	—	—	—	—
Bagridae	10	8	27	3	1	2	2	1	2	11	1
Schilbeidae	4	5	13	3	3	2	2	1	1	—	—
Amphiliidae	1	1	12	—	1	1	1	—	—	—	—
Clariidae	4	6	23	11	6	5	3	3	6	5	13
Malapteruridae	1	1	1	—	1	—	1	—	—	1	—
Mochokidae	18	18	36	9	4	3	3	2	2	5	1
Cyprinodontidae	8	12	11	5	6	5	2	3	3	2	(1)

Appendix 3 Table—*Continued*

	Middle Niger	L. Chad	Zaïre Central basin	Luapula-Mweru	Zambezi	Upper Zambezi	Middle Zambezi	Kafue	Lake Victoria	Lake Tanganyika	Lake Malawi
Ophiocephalidae	1	1	2	—	—	—	—	—	—	—	—
Centropomidae	1	1	1	—	—	—	—	—	—	5	—
Nandidae	—	—	—	—	—	—	—	—	—	—	—
Cichlidae	10	13	32	16	16	16	9	12	170+	126	200+
Gobiidae	1	1	1	—	—	—	—	—	—	—	—
Anabantidae	1	4	12	2	2	2	—	2	1	—	(1)
Mastacembalidae	1	2	11	2	1	1	—	1	1	7	—
Tetraodontidae	1	1	4	—	—	—	—	—	—	—	—
TOTALS	138	177	408	120	98	77	54	55	208+	184	234+

Appendix 4

Fish Faunas of Zaïre River Biotopes

	POOL MALEBO REGION					YANGAMBI				IKELA REGION							
	Total	Rapids	Pool	Streams & marginal waters	Protopterus nests (mud)	Totals	R. Zaïre	Streams	Swamps	Total	R. Tschuapa	Marginal waters	Little rivers	Streams	Inund. zone forest pools	Swamps	L. Tumba
Protopteridae	2	—	2	2	2	2	2	1	1	1	—	1	—	—	1	1	—
Polypteridae	5	—	2	4	1	6	3	4	2	3	1	1	—	—	1	2	2
Clupeidae	4	4	4	—	—	6	6	—	—	2	1	2	1	—	—	—	3
Osteoglossidae	—	—	—	—	—	—	—	—	—	—	—	—	—	—	—	—	—
Pantodontidae	1	—	—	1	—	1	1	1	1	1	—	1	—	—	1	1	—
Notopteridae	2	—	—	2	—	1	1	1	1	1	1	1	1	—	1	1	2
Mormyridae	38	1	35	7	—	43	38	14	6	13	9	3	3	1	—	2	21
Phractolaemidae	1	—	—	1	—	1	—	—	1	1	—	—	—	—	1	1	—
Characidae	13	4	8	6	—	25	16	12	—	20	8	13	13	3	4	—	13
Hepsetidae	1	—	1	—	—	1	1	1	1	—	1	1	—	—	—	—	1
Distichodontidae, Citharinidae, Ichthyoboridae	20	6	13	15	—	27	19	9	—	20	13	13	10	2	4	—	13
Cyprinidae	15	6	8	4	—	29	21	8	—	8	4	2	3	4	2	1	3
Ariidae	—	—	—	—	—	—	—	—	—	—	—	—	—	—	—	—	—
Bagridae	15	2	14	2	—	10	6	4	—	10	5	5	4	3	4	3	7

Appendix 4 Table—*Continued*

	POOL MALEBO REGION					YANGAMBI				IKELA REGION							
	Total	Rapids	Pool	Streams & marginal waters	Protopterus nests (mud)	Totals	R. Zaïre	Streams	Swamps	Total	R. Tschuapa	Marginal waters	Little rivers	Streams	Inund. zone forest pools	Swamps	L. Tumba
Schilbeidae	5	—	4	1	—	7	6	2	—	2	1	(1)	1	—	—	—	3
Amphilidae	3	1	1	3	—	5	2	4	—	4	—	(1)	4	4	2	—	—
Clariidae	7	1	1	4	5	15	7	14	7	10	—	(1)	2	6	10	[a]7	4
Malapteruridae	1	—	1	1	—	1	1	1	1	1	1	1	1	1	1	(1)	1
Mochokidae	21	5	13	6	—	20	16	5	—	7	4	4	3	1	1	—	2
Cyprinodontidae	6	1	—	4	—	5	—	5	—	6	—	1	5	4	3	1	1
Opiocephalidae	1	—	1	1	1	1	1	1	1	1	—	1	1	—	1	—	1
Centropomidae	—	—	—	—	—	1	1	—	—	—	—	—	—	—	—	—	1
Cichlidae	14	6	9	5	—	14	7	6	1	6	3	4	3	4	3	1	7
Gobiidae	1	1	—	1	—	1	—	1	—	1	—	—	—	1	1	1	—
Anabantidae	7	—	1	6	1	10	5	8	3	7	3	3	3	4	4	3	—
Mastacembalidae	6	4	2	3	—	5	3	2	—	1	—	—	1	1	1	—	1
Tetraodontidae	4	1	2	3	—	2	2	—	—	1	1	1	—	—	—	—	—
TOTAL	193	39	122	82	10	239	165	104	26	127	56	61	59	39	46	26	86

* Data from Pool Malebo (Stanley Pool) region Poll (1959*a*); from Yangambi region Gosse (1963); from Ikela region and L. Tumba Matthes (1964).

Appendix 5

Air-breathing in Tropical Freshwater Fishes

(Data from Carter, 1957, Johansen 1970)

	GENUS	DISTRIBUTION: S. America	DISTRIBUTION: Africa	DISTRIBUTION: Asia	AESTIVATES	AIR BREATHING: Obligatory	AIR BREATHING: Accessory	
Swim bladder functions as a lung	*Lepidosiren*	+	−	−	+	+	−	Aestivates without mucous cocoon
	Protopterus	−	+	−	+	+	−	Aestivates with mucous cocoon
	Neoceratodus	(Australia)						
	Polypterus	−	+	−	−	+		Aquatic respiration in well aerated water; air-breathing generally obligatory and increases activity of fish
	Arapaima	+	−	−	−	+		
	Hoploerythrinus	+	−	−	−	+		Moves 'overland'
	Gymnarchus	−	+	−	−			
Epithelia or Diverticular of Branchial Chamber	*Clarias*	−	+	+	+	−	+	Important when aqueous O_2 low. Migrates overland
	Anabas	−	−	+	−	−	+	Necessary when aqueous O_2 low. Migrates overland
	Heteropneustes	−	−	+	−			
	Osphronemus	−	−	+				
	Macropodus	−	−	+				
	Betta	−	−	+				
	Amphipnous	−	−	+				
Branchial chamber filled with air	*Hypopomus*	+	−	−	−	−	−	Gills capable of both aerial and aquatic respiration
	Synbranchus	+	+	+	+	+		Essential when aqueous O_2 low and during aestivation
Pharyngeal epithelia or diverticular	*Ophiocephalus*	−	+	+	+	+	−	
	Electrophorus	+	−	−	−	+	−	CO_2 elimination via vestigial gills and skin
	Monopterus	−	−	+	−	−	−	
	Periophthalmus	−	+	+	−	−	−	

Appendix 5 Table—*Continued*

		DISTRIBUTION			AESTIVATES	AIR BREATHING		
	GENUS	S. America	Africa	Asia		Obligatory	Accessory	
Stomach and Intestine	*Doras*	+	−	−	−			
	Callichthys	+	−	−	−			
	Hoplosternum	+	−	−	−	+		Intestine
	Hypostomus	+	−	−	−	−	+	Stomach
	Ancistrus	+	−	−	−	−	−	
	?*Cichlasoma*	+	−	−	−	−	+	?Stomach

(See also Beadle, 1974 chapter 18, Tropical swamps: adaptation to scarcity of oxygen.)

Bibliography

(References of most use to the general reader are marked with an asterisk)

*ACKERMANN, W. C., WHITE, G. F. and WORTHINGTON, E. B., ed. (1973) *Man-made lakes: their problems and environmental effects*, Geophysical Monogr., no. 17, American Geophysical Union, Washington, D.C.

ALBRECHT, H. (1963) 'Das Jungeführen bei *Haplochromis* (Pisces, Cichlidae)', *Z. Tierpsychol.*, **20**, 680–87.

ALBRECHT, H. (1966) 'Colour signals as dynamic means of demarcating territory', in *Signals in the Animal World*, ed. D. Burkhardt, W. Schleidt and H. Altner, trans. K. Morgan, Allen & Unwin (1967), pp. 115–16.

ALEXANDER, R. McN. (1962) 'The structure of the Weberian apparatus in the Cyprinid', *Proc. Zool. Soc. Lond.*, **139**, 451–73.

*ALEXANDER, R. McN. (1966) 'Structure and function in the catfish', *J. Zool. Lond.* (1965), **148**, 88–152.

ALEXANDER, R. McN. (1970) *Functional Design in Fishes*, Hutchinson.

ALLEN, K. R. (1951) 'The Horokiwi stream: a study of a trout population', *Fish. Bull. N.Z.*, **10**, 1-238.

ALLSOPP, W. H. L. (1958) 'Arapaima, the giant fish of South America'. *Timehri, J. r. agric. Comm. Soc. Br. Guiana*, **37**, 89–98.

ARNOULT, J. (1966) 'Behaviour and breeding in the aquarium of *Polypterus senegalus*', *Ichthyologia*, **37**, 135–40.

ATZ, J. (1964) 'Intersexuality in fishes' in *Intersexuality in vertebrates including man*, ed. C. N. Armstrong and A. J. Marshall, Academic Press, pp. 145–232.

*AXELROD, H. R. (1974) *African cichlids of Lakes Malawi and Tanganyika* (Second Edition), Tropical Fish Hobbyist Pubs Inc. (excellent photographs of lakes and fishes).

AYALA, F. J. (1970) 'Competition, coexistence and evolution', in *Essays in Evolution and Genetics in honour of Th. Dobzhansky*, ed. M. K. Hecht, and W. C. Steere, Amsterdam, North-Holland Pub. Co., pp. 121–58.

AZEVEDO, P. De and GOMES, A. L. (1943) 'Contribução ao estudo da biologia da Traira *Hoplias malabaricus* (Bloch, 1794)', *Bolm Ind. anim, S. Paulo*, n.s. **5**, 15–64.

AZEVEDO, P. De and VIEIRA, B. B. (1940) 'Realizações da Comissao Técnica de Piscicultura do Nordeste', *Archos Inst. Biol. S. Paulo*, **11**, 23–8.

AZEVEDO, P. De, DIAS, M. V. and VIEIRA, B. B. (1938) 'Biologia do saguirú *Curimatus elegans* Stdr. (Characidae)', *Mem. Inst. Oswaldo Crus, Rio de J.*, **33**, 481–553.

BACKIEL, T. and LE CREN, E. D. (1967) 'Some density relationships for fish population parameters', in *The Biological Basis of Freshwater Fish Production*, ed. S. D. Gerking, Oxford, Blackwell, pp. 261–93.

BADENHUIZEN, G. R. (1965) 'Lufuba River Research Notes', *Fish. Res. Bull. Zambia*, 1963–64, 11–41.

BAERENDS, G. P. and BAERENDS-VAN ROON, J. M. (1950) 'An introduction to the study of the ethology of cichlid fishes', *Behaviour*, Suppl. no. 1, 1–243.

BAGENAL, T. B. (1971) Eggs and early life history. Pt. I Fecundity. in: *Methods for Assessment of Fish Production in Freshwaters*, ed. W. E. Ricker, IBP Handbook no. 3, Oxford, Blackwell, 2nd edn, 167–79.

BAILEY, R. G. (1969) 'The non-cichlid fishes of the eastward-flowing rivers of Tanzania, East Africa', *Revue Zool. Bot. afr.*, **80**, 170–99.

BALON, E. K. (1971*a*) 'Age and growth of *Hydrocynus vittatus* Castelnau, 1861 in L. Kariba, Sinazongwe area', *Fish. Res. Bull. Zambia*, **5**, 89–118.

BALON, E. K. (1971*b*) 'Replacement of *Alestes imberi* Peters 1852 by *A. lateralis* Blgr. 1900, in L. Kariba, with ecological notes', *Fish. Res. Bull. Zambia*, **5**, 119–62.

BALON, E. K. (1972) 'L. Kariba ichthyological studies II. Technical Exhibit to American Fishery Society, 102nd annual meeting, 1972', *Fisheries in the age of ecology* (cyclostyled report of work in press).

BALON, E. K. (1973) 'Results of fish population size assessments in Lake Kariba coves (Zambia), a decade after their creation'. In *Man-made Lakes: their problems and environmental effects*, ed. W. C. Ackermann, G. F. White and E. B. Worthington, *Geophysical Monogr.*, no. 17, American Geophysical Union, Washington, D.C., pp. 149–58.

BALON, E. K. (1974) '*Fishes of Lake Kariba, Africa, length-weight relationship, a pictorial guide*', T.F.H. Publs. Inc. Ltd, p. 144.

*BALON, E. K. and COCHE, A. G. ed. (1974) '*Lake Kariba a man-made tropical ecosystem in Central Africa*', Monographiae Biologicae, **24**, Dr W. Junk, the Hague, p. 767.

BANISTER, K. E. (1973) 'A revision of the large *Barbus* (Pisces, Cyprinidae) of East and Central Africa', *Bull. Br. Mus. Nat. Hist.*, **26** (1), 1–148.

BARD, J. (1971) 'La production des eaux continentales en Afrique francophone au sud du Sahara et à Madagascar', *Bois Forêts Tropiques*, no. 140, pp. 3–12.

BARD, J. (1973) 'Les poissons de la famille des Osteoglossidae et la pisciculture', *Bois Forêts Tropiques*, no. 147, pp. 63–70.

BARDACH, J. E. (1958) 'On the movements of certain Bermuda reef fishes', *Ecology*, **39**, 139–46.

BARDACH, J. E. and TODD, J. H. (1970) 'Chemical communication in fish', in *Communications by chemical signals*, ed. J. W. Johnston, D. G. Moulton, A. Turk, New York, A.C.C. Meredith Corpn, pp. 205–40.

BAYLEY, P. B. (1973) 'Studies on the migratory characin *Prochilodus platensis* Holmberg, 1889', *J. Fish. Biol.*, **5**, 25–40.

*BEADLE, L. C. (1974) *The Inland Waters of Tropical Africa: an introduction to tropical limnology*. Longman, p. 365.

BEAUCHAMP, R. S. A. (1964) 'The rift valley lakes of Africa', *Verh. int. Verein Limnol.*, **15**, 91–9.

BELL-CROSS, G. (1960) Observations on the movements of fish in a fish ladder in Northern Rhodesia', in *CCTA/CSA 3rd Sympos. Hydrobiol. Inl. Fish., 'Problems of major lakes,' Lusaka, 1960, CCTA Publ. no. 63*, pp. 113–25.

BELL-CROSS, G. (1965*a*) 'Movement of fish across the Congo-Zambezi watershed in the Mwinilunga District of Northern Rhodesia', in *Proc. Centr. Afr. Med. Congr., Lusaka, 1963*, Oxford, Pergamon Press, pp. 415–24.

BELL-CROSS, G. (1965*b*) 'Additions and amendments to the check list of the fishes of Zambia', *The Puku, Occ. Papers, Dept. Game and Fish, Zambia*, no. 3, pp. 29–43.

BELL-CROSS, G. (1968) 'Preliminary observations on *Hydrocynus vittatus* in the Upper Zambezi River system', *Fish. Res. Bull. Zambia* (1965–66), **4**, 21–7.

BERGSTRAND, E. and CORDONE, A. J. (1971) 'Exploratory bottom trawling in L. Victoria', *Afr. J. Trop. Hydrobiol. Fish.*, **1**, 13–23.

BERNS, S. and PETERS, H. M. (1969) 'On the reproductive behaviour of *Ctenopoma muriei* and *Ctenopoma damasi* (Anabantidae)', in *Rep. Afr. Freshwat. Fish. Res. Org. 1968*, Appendix E, pp. 44–50.

BERTRAM, C. K. R., BORLEY, H. J. H. and TREWAVAS, E. T. (1942) *Report on the Fish and Fisheries of L. Nyasa*, London, Crown Agents.

BISHOP, J. E. (1973) 'Limnology of a small Malayan River Sungai Gombak', *Monographiae Biologicae*, vol. 22, The Hague, Dr W. Junk b.v.

BLACHE, J. and GOOSSENS, J. (1954) 'Monographie piscicole d'une zone de pêche au Cambodge', *Cybium*, **8**, 1–49.

BLACHE, J. and MITON, F. (1962) 'Première contribution à la connaissance de la pêche dans le bassin hydrographique Logone-Chari-Lac Tchad', *Mém. Off. Rech. Scient. Tech. Outre-Mer.*, Paris, 1–143.

BLACHE, J., MITON, F., STAUCH, A., ILTIS, A. and LOUBENS, G. (1964) 'Les poissons du bassin du Tchad et du bassin adjacent du Mayo Kebbi', *Mém. Off. Rech. Scient. Tech. Outre-Mer.*, Paris, pp. 1–483.

BLACK-CLEWORTH, P. (1970) 'The role of electrical discharges in the nonreproductive social behaviour of *Gymnotus carapo* (Gymnotidae, Pisces)', *Anim. Behav. Monogr.*, 3(1), 1-77.

BOESEMAN, M. (1960) 'The freshwater fishes of the island of Trinidad', *Stud. Fauna Curaçao Caribb. Is.*, The Hague, **48**, 73–153.

BONETTO, A. A. and DRAGO, E. (1968) 'Consideraciones faunisticas en torno a la delimitacion de los tramos superiores del Rio Parana', *Physis, B. Aires*, **27**, no. 75, 437–44.

BONETTO, A. and PIGNALBERI, C. (1964) 'Nuevos aportes al conocimiento de las migracion es de los peces en los Rios mesopotamicos de la Republica Argentina', *Com. Inst. nac. Limnol.*, Santo Tomé (S.Fé), 1, 1–14.

BONETTO, A., CORDIVIOLA, E., PIGNALBERI, C. and OLIVEROS, O. (1969) 'Ciclos hidrologicos del Rio Parana y los poblaciones de peces contebidas en las cuencas temporarais de su valle de inundacion', *Physis* (B. Aires), **29**, no. 78, 215–23 (Spanish with English summary).

BONETTO, A., CORDIVIOLA, E. and PIGNALBERI, C. (1970) 'Nuevos datos sôbre pobulaciones de peces en ambientes leniticos permamentes del Parana Medio', *Physis, B. Aires*, **30**, no. 80, 141–54.

BONETTO, A., DIONI, W. and PIGNALBERI, C. (1969) 'Limnological investigations on biotic communities in the Middle Parana River valley', *Verh. int. Verein. Limnol.*, **17**, 1035–50.

BONETTO, A. A., PIGNALBERI, C., CORDIVIOLA DE YUAN E. and OLIVEROS, O. (1971) 'Informaciones complementarias sôbre migraciones de peces en la Cuenca del Plata', *Physis, B. Aires*, **30**, no. 81, 505–20.

BOULENGER, G. A. (1915) *Catalogue of the Freshwater Fishes of Africa in the British Museum (Nat. Hist.)* 4 vols, London, B. M. Nat. Hist.

BOWMAKER, A. P. (1969) 'Contribution to knowledge of the biology of *Alestes macrophthalmus* Gnthr. (Pisces, Characidae)', *Hydrobiologia*, **33**, 302–41.

BOWMAKER, A. P. (1970) 'A prospect of L. Kariba', *Optima*, **20**(2), 68–74.

BOWMAKER, A. P. (1973) Potamodromesis in the Mwenda River, L. Kariba', in *Man-made lakes: their problems and environmental effects*, ed. Ackermann, et al; Geophysical Monogr., no. 17, Amer. Geophys. Union, Washington, D.C, pp. 159–64.

BRAGA, R. A. (1953) 'Crescimento do Tucunaré-pinima, *Cichla temensis* Humboldt, em cativeiro (Cichlidae)', *Dusenia*, **4**, 41–6.

BRAGA, R. A. (1953) 'Frequencia de desova de reprodutores de apaiari *Astronotus ocellatus* Spix (Cichlidae) mantidos em cativeiro', *Revta bras. Biol.*, **13**, 191–6.

BRAKER, W. P. (1963) 'Black piranhas spawned at Shedd aquarium', *Aquarium, Philad.*, **32**, no. 10, 12–14.

BREDER, C. M. (1959) 'Studies on social groupings in fishes', *Bull. Am. Mus. nat. Hist.*, **117**, no. 6, 397–486.

BREDER, C. M. (1967) 'On the survival value of fish schools', *Zoologia, N.Y.*, **52**, 25–40.

BREDER, C. M. (1968) 'Seasonal and diurnal occurrences of fish sounds in a small Florida Bay', *Bull. Am. Mus. nat. Hist.*, **138**, no. 6, 325–78.

BREDER, C. M. and ROSEN, D. E. (1966) *Modes of Reproduction in Fishes*, New York, *Am. Mus. nat. Hist.*

BRIEN, P., POLL, M. and BOUILLON, J. (1959) 'Ethologie de la reproduction de *Protopterus dolloi* Blgr', *Ann. Mus. r. Congo belge, Tervuren*, Ser. 8, Sci. Zool., **71**, 1–21.

BRIGGS, J. C. (1966) 'Zoogeography and evolution', *Evolution, Lancaster, Pa.*, **20**, 282–9.

BRIGHT, T. J. (1972) 'Bio-acoustic studies on reef organisms': Results of Tektite Program, *Bull. Nat. Hist. Mus., Los Angeles*, no. 14, pp. 45–69.

BROWN, M. E. (1957) 'Experimental studies on growth', in *Physiology of Fishes*, ed. M. E. Brown, Academic Press, vol. 1, 361–400.

BURCHARD, J. E. jr. (1965) 'Family structure in the dwarf cichlid *Apistogramma trifasciatum* Eig. & Kennedy', *Z. Tierpsychol.*, **22**, 150–62.

BURGIS, M. J., DARLINGTON, J. P. E. C., DUNN, I. G., GANF, G. G., GWAHABA, J. G. and McGOWAN, L. M. (1973) 'The biomass and distribution of organisms in L. George, Uganda', *Proc. roy. Soc. Lond., B.*, **184**, 271–98.

CADWALLADR, D. A. (1965) 'Notes of the breeding biology and ecology of *Labeo victorianus* Blgr (Cyprinidae) of L. Victoria', *Revta Zool. Bot. afr.*, **72**, 109–34.

CAPART, A. and KUFFERATH, J. (1957) 'Considerations biologiques sur la pisciculture au Congo Belge', *Bull. agric. Congo belge*, **48**, 1245–61.

CAREY, T. G. (1968) 'Feeding habits of some fishes in the Kafue River', *Fish. Res. Bull. Zambia*, **4**, 105–9.

CAREY, T. G. (1971) 'Hydrobiological survey of the Kafue flood plain', *Fish. Res. Bull. Zambia*, **5**, 245–95.

CARMOUZE, J. P., DEJOUX, C., DURAND, J. R., GRAS, R., ILTIS, A., LAUZANNE, L., LEMOALLE, J., LEVEQUE, C., LOUBENS, G. and SAINT-JEAN, L. (1972) 'Grandes zones écologiques du lac Tchad', *Cah. Off. Roch. Scient. Tech. Outre-Mer*, sér. Hydrobiol., **6**, no. 2, 103–69.

CARTER, G. S. (1934) 'Results of the Cambridge Expedition to British Guiana, 1933. The Freshwaters of the rain-forest areas of British Guiana', *J. Linn. Soc. (Zool.)*, **39**, 147–93.

CARTER, G. S. (1935) 'Respiratory adaptations of the fishes of the forest waters with descriptions of the accessory respiratory organs of *Electrophorus electricus* and *Plecostomus plecostomus*', *J. Linn. Soc. (Zool.)*, **39**, 219–33.

CARTER, G. S. (1957) 'Air breathing', in: *The Physiology of Fishes*, ed. M. E. Brown, Academic Press, vol. 1, 65–79.

CARTER, G. S. and BEADLE, L. C. (1930) 'Notes on the habits and development of *Lepidosiren paradoxa*', *J. Linn. Soc. Lond. (Zool.)*, **37**, 197–203.

CARTER, G. S. and BEADLE, L. C. (1931) 'The fauna of the swamps of the Paraguayan Chaco in relation to its environment II. Respiratory adaptations in the fishes', *J. Linn. Soc., Lond. (Zool.)*, **37**, 327–68.

CHAPMAN, D. W., MILLER, W. H., DUDLEY, R. G. and SCULLY, R. J. (1971) 'Ecology of fishes in the Kafue River', *Univ. Idaho, FAO FI:SF/ZAM 11 Tech. Rept. 2*, pp. 1–66.

CHEVEY, P. and LE POULAIN, LE F. (1940) 'La pêche dans les eaux douces du Cambodge', *Mém. Inst. océanogr. Indoch.*, **5**, 1–193.

COCHE, A. G. (1967) 'Fish culture in rice fields a world-wide synthesis', *Hydrobiologia*, **30**, 1–44.

COE, M. J. (1966) 'The biology of *Tilapia grahami* Blgr. in L. Magadi, Kenya', *Acta Tropica*, **23**, 146–77.

COHEN, D. M. (1970) 'How many recent fishes are there?' *Proc. Calif. Acad. Sci.* 4th ser., **38**, 341–6.

COLE, J. A. and WARD, J. A. (1969) 'The communicative function of pelvic fin-flickering in *Etroplus maculatus* (Cichlidae)', *Behaviour*, **35**, 179 99.

COLLETTE, B. B. and EARLE, S. A. eds (1972) 'Results of the Tektite program: ecology of coral reef fishes', *Bull. Nat. Hist. Mus. Los Angeles*, **14**, 1–180.

COLLETTE, B. B. and TALBOT, F. H. (1972) 'Activity patterns of coral reef fishes with emphasis on nocturnal-diurnal changeover. *Bull. Nat. Hist. Mus. Los Angeles*', **14**, 98–124.

CONNELL, J. H. and ORIAS, E. (1964) 'The ecological regulation of species diversity', *Am. Nat.*, **98**, 399–414.

CORBET, P. S. (1960) 'Breeding sites of non-cichlid fishes in L. Victoria', *Nature, Lond.*, **187**, 616–17.

CORBET, P. S. (1961) 'The food of non-cichlid fishes in the L. Victoria basin, with remarks on their evolution and adaptation to lacustrine conditions', *Proc. zool. Soc. Lond.*, **136**, 1–101.

CORBET, S. A., GREEN, J., GRIFFITH, J. and BETNEY, E. (1973) 'Ecological studies in crater lakes in West Cameroon Lakes Kotto and Mboandong', *J. Zool., Lond.*, **170**, 309–24.

CORDIVIOLA, E. (1966*a*) 'Edad y crecimento del dorado (*Salminus maxillosus* C & V) en el Parana medio', *Physis, B. Aires*, **26**, no. 72, 293–311.

CORDIVIOLA, E. (1966*b*) 'Nuevos aportes al conocimiento de la biologia pesquera del Surubi (*Pseudoplatystoma coruscans*) en el Parana medio', *Physis, B. Aires*, **26**, no. 71, 237–44.

CORDIVIOLA, E. (1971) 'Crecimiento de peces del Parana Medio. I. Sabalo (*Prochilodus platensis* Holmberg)', *Physis, B. Aires*, **30**, no. 81, 483–504.

CORDIVIOLA, E. and PIGNALBERI, C. (1962) 'Edad y crecimiento del Amarillo (*Pimelodus clarias*) y Moncholo (*Pimelodus albicans*)', *Ses. Cient. Asoc. Cienc. Nat. Litoral, An. Mus. F. Ameghino T.I.*, no. 3, S. Fé, pp. 67–76.

COULTER, G. W. (1963) 'Hydrobiological changes in relation to biological production in southern L. Tanganyika', *Limnol. Oceanogr.*, **8**, 463–77.

COULTER, G. W. (1965) 'Lake Tanganyika research report', *Fish. Res. Bull. Zambia*, **2** (1963–64), 4–10.

COULTER, G. W. (1966) 'Hydrobiological processes and the deepwater fish community in L. Tanganyika', Ph.D. thesis, Queens University, Belfast.

COULTER, G. W. (1968) 'The deep benthic fishes at the south of L. Tanganyika with special reference to distribution and feeding in *Bathybates* species, *Hemibates stenosoma* and *Chrysichthys* species', *Fish. Res. Bull. Zambia*, **4** (1965–66), 33–8.

COULTER, G. W. (1970) 'Population changes within a group of fish species in L. Tanganyika following their exploitation', *J. Fish. Biol.*, **2**, 329–53.

CRIDLAND, C. C. (1961) 'The reproduction of *Tilapia esculenta* under artificial conditions', *Hydrobiologia*, **18**, 177–84.

DAGET, J. (1952) 'Mémoire sur la biologie des poissons du Niger Moyen. I. Biologie et croissance des espèces du genre *Alestes*', *Bull. Inst. fr. Afr. noire*, **14**, 191–225.

DAGET, J. (1954) Les poissons du Niger Supérieur. *Mém. Inst. fr. Afr. noire*, no. 36, pp. 1–391.

DAGET, J. (1957*a*) 'Données récentes sur la biologie des poissons dans le delta central du Niger', *Hydrobiologia*, **9**, 321–47.

DAGET, J. (1957*b*) 'Réproduction et croissance d'*Heterotis niloticus* Ehrenberg', *Bull. Inst. fr. Afr. noire*, ser. A., no. 1, pp. 295–323.

DAGET, J. (1962) 'Le genre *Citharinus*', *Revue Zool. Bot. afr.*, **66**, 81–106.

DAGET, J. (1967) 'Introduction a l'etude hydrobiologique du Lac Tchad', *C.R. Soc. Biogeogr.*, **380**, 6–10.

DAGET, J. and ILTIS, A. (1965) 'Poissons de Côte d'Ivoire', *Mém. Inst. fr. Afr. noiré*, no. 74, pp. 1–385.

DAGET, J. and STAUCH, A. (1963) 'Poissons partie Camerounaise du bassin de la Benoué'. *(Mélanges Ichthyologiques)*, *Mém. Inst. fr. Afr. noiré*, no. 68, pp. 85–107.

DAGET, J., BAUCHOT, M. L. and ARNOULT, J. (1965) 'Etude de la croissance chex *Polypterus senegalus* Cuvier', *Acta Zool.*, Stockholm, **46**, 297–309.

DAHL, G. (1971) '*Los peces del norte de Colombia*', Inderena, Colombia Rep. Min. Agric., 391.

DAVID, A. (1959) 'Observations on some spawning grounds of the Gangetic major carps with a note on carp seed resources in India', *Indian J. Fish*, **6**, 327–41.

DAVIES, G. E. and WARREN, C. E. (1971) 'Estimation of food consumption rates', in *Methods for assessment of fish production in freshwaters*, ed. W. E. Ricker, 2nd edn, IBP Handbook no. 3, Oxford, Blackwell, pp. 227–48.

DIETZ, R. S. and HOLDEN, J. C. (1970) 'Reconstruction of Pangaea: break up and dispersion of continents, Permian to present. *J. Geophysical Res.*, **75**, no. 26, 4939–56 (reprinted in *Oceanography: Contemporary readings in Ocean Studies*, ed. R. G. Pirie, Oxford University Press, pp. 277–96.

DOBZHANSKY, T. (1950) 'Evolution in the tropics', *Am. Sci.*, **38**, 209–21.

DUERRE, D. C. (1969) 'Fishery developments in the Central Barotse flood plain (second phase, May 1967–April 1968)', *UNDP FAO. Rept.* no. TA 2638, pp. 1–80.

DUNN, I. G. (1972) 'The commercial fishery of L. George, Uganda (E. Africa)', *Afr. J. Trop. Hydrobiol. Fish.*, **2**, no. 2, 109–20.

DUNN, I. G., BURGIS, M. J., GANF, G. G., McGOWAN, L. M. and VINER, A. B. (1969) 'Lake George, Uganda; a limnological survey', *Verh. int. Verein. Limnol.*, **17**, 284–8.

DURAND, J. R. (1970) 'Les peuplements ichtyologiques de l'El Beid', *Cah. Off. Rech. Scient. Tech. Outre-Mer*, sér. Hydrobiol., **4**, 1–26.

DURAND, J. R. and LOUBENS, G. (1969) 'La croissance en longeur d'*Alestes baremose* (Joannis 1835) dans le bas Chari et le lac Tchad', *Cah. Off. Rech. Scient. Tech. Outre-Mer*, ser. Hydrobiol., **3**, 59–105.

DUSSART, B. H. (1974) 'Biology of inland waters in humid tropical Asia', pp. 331–353 in *Natural resources of humid tropical Asia*, Natural Resources Research, **12**, UNESCO, Paris, 456 pp.

EAST AFRICAN FRESHWATER FISHERIES RESEARCH ORGANIZATION, *Annual Reports*, Jinja, Uganda.

EIGENMANN, C. H. (1912) 'The freshwater fishes of British Guiana, including a study of the ecological grouping of species and the relation of the fauna of the plateau to that of the lowlands', *Mem. Carneg. Mus.*, 5, 1–578.

EIGENMANN, C. H. (1917) 'The American Characidae', *Mem. Mus. comp. Zool. Harv.*, 43, 1–558.

EIGENMANN, C. H. (1921) 'The origin and distribution of the genera of the fishes of S. America west of the Maracaibo, Orinoco, Amazon, and Titicaca basins', *Proc. Am. phil. Soc.*, **60**, 1–6.

EIGENMANN, C. H. and ALLEN, W. R. (1942) *Fishes of Western South America*, I and II, Lexington, University of Kentucky Press.

ELTON, C. S. (1973) 'The structure of invertebrate populations inside Neotropical rain forest', *J. anim. Ecol.*, **42**, no. 1, 55–104.

FAO (FOOD AND AGRICULTURE ORGANIZATION OF THE UNITED NATIONS) (1972) *A brief Review of the Current Status of the Inland Fisheries of Africa*, Committee for Inland Fisheries of Africa /72/8. FAO, Rome pamphlet.

FAO (1973) *Symposium of Evaluation of Fishery Resources in the Development and Management of Inland Fisheries, L. Chad, 1973*, CIFA /72/S.3. FAO, Rome.

FERNANDO, C. H. (1973) 'Man-made lakes of Ceylon: a biological resource' in *Man-made lakes: their problems and environmental effects*, ed. W. C. Ackermann, G. F. White and E. B. Worthington, Geophysical Monogr., no. 17, American Geophysical Union, Washington, D.C., pp. 664–71.

FISH, G. R. (1951) 'Digestion in *Tilapia esculenta*', *Nature, Lond.*, **167**, 900.

FISH, G. R. (1957) 'A seiche movement and its effect on the hydrology of L. Victoria', *Fishery Publs Colon. Off.*, no. 10, 1–68.

FITTKAU, E-J. (1967) 'On the ecology of Amazonian rain-forest streams', *Atas do Simposio sôbre a Biota Amazonica, Rio de J. vol. 3 (Limnology)*, pp. 97–108.

FITTKAU, E-J. (1969) 'The fauna of South America', in *Biogeography and Ecology in South America*, ed. Fittkau *et al.*, Monographiae Biologicae, **19**, Dr W. Junk, The Hague, vol. 2, pp. 624–58.

FITTKAU, E-J. (1970) 'Role of caimans in the nutrient regime of mouth-lakes of Amazon affluents (an hypothesis)', *Biotropica*, **2**, no. 2, 138–42.

FITTKAU, E-J. (1973) 'Crocodiles and the nutrient metabolism of Amazonian waters', *Amazoniana*, **4**, 103–33.

FLORES, G. (1970) 'Suggested origin of the Mozambique Channel, *Trans. Geol. Soc. S. Afr.*, 73, 1–16.

FONTENELE, O. (1948) 'Contribução al conocimiento de la biologie del Piraruca (*Arapaima gigas* Cuv.) en cautividad', *Revta bras. Biol.*, **8**, 445–59.

FONTENELE, O. (1950) 'Contribuçäo para o conhecimento de biologia des Tucunares (Cichlidae) em cativiero', *Revta. bras. Biol.*, **10**, 503–19.

FONTENELE, O. (1953) 'Contribução para o conhecimento da biologia do Apaiari *Astronotus ocellatus* (Spix) (Cichlidae) em cativiero', *Revta bras. Biol.*, **11**, 467–84.

FONTENELE, O. (1951) 'Contribuição para o conhecimento da biologia da Curimata pacu *Procholodus argenteus* (Spix)', *Revta bras. Biol.*, **13**, 87–102.

FONTENELE, O. (1959) 'Contribution to the biology of the Pirarucu *Arapaima gigas* in captivity', *Dep. Nac. Obras. Contr. Secas. Servico Pisciculture*, Publ. no. 177, Ser. 1-C., Fortaleza, Ceara.

FONTENELE, O., CAMACHO, E. C. and MENEZES, R. S. DE (1946) 'Obtenação de tres desovas anuais de Curimatá, *Prochilodus sp.* (Characidae, Prochilodinae), pelometodo de hipofisação', *Bolm Mus. nac. Rio de J. Zool.*, **53**, 1–9.

FOWLER, H. W. (1954) 'Os peixes de agua doce do Brasil', *Archos Zool. Est. S. Paulo*, **9**, 1–400.

FREIHOFER, W. C. and NEIL, E. H. (1967) 'Commensalism between midge larvae (Diptera: Chironomidae) and catfishes of the families Astroblepidae and Loricariidae', *Copeia*, no. 1, 39–45.

FREY, D. G. (1969) 'A limnological reconnaisance of L. Lanao', *Verh. int. Verein. Limnol.*, **17**, 1090–1102.

*FRYER, G. (1959) 'The trophic interrelationship and ecology of some littoral communities of L. Nyasa with especial reference to the fishes, and a discussion of the evolution of a group of rock-frequenting Cichlidae', *Proc. zool. Soc. Lond.*, **132**, 153–281.

FRYER, G. (1961) 'Observations on the biology of the cichlid fish *Tilapia variabilis* in the northern waters of L. Victoria (E. Africa)', *Revta. Zool. Bot. afr.*, **64**, 1–33.

FRYER, G. (1972) Conservation of the Great Lakes of East Africa: a lesson and a warning. *Biological Conservation*, 4, no. 4, 256–62.

FRYER, G. (1973) 'The L. Victoria Fisheries: some facts and fallacies', *Biolog. Conservation*, **5**, no. 4, 304–8.

FRYER, G. and ILES, T. D. (1969) 'Alternative routes to evolutionary success as exhibited by African cichlid fishes of the genus *Tilapia* and the species flocks of the Great Lakes', *Evolution* (Lancaster Pa.), **23**, 359–69.

*FRYER, G. and ILES, T. D. (1972) *The Cichlid Fishes of the Great Lakes of Africa*, Oliver & Boyd.

GANAPATI, S. V. (1973) 'Man-made lakes in South India', in *Man-made lakes: their problems and environmental effects*, ed. W. C. Ackermann, E. F. White and E. B. Worthington, Geophysical Monogr., no. 17, American Geophysical Union, Washington, D.C., pp. 65–73 (Fig. 1, map).

GANF, G. G. and VINER, A. B. (1973) 'Ecological stability in a shallow equatorial lake (L. George, Uganda)', *Proc. roy. Soc. Lond. B.*, **184**, 321–46.

GARROD, D. J. (1959) 'The growth of *Tilapia esculenta* Graham in L. Victoria', *Hydrobiologia*, **12**, no. 4, 268–98.

GARROD, D. J. (1963) 'The application of a method for estimation of growth parameters from tagging data at unequal time intervals', *Rapp. et Proc. Verb. Cons. Internat. Explor. de la Mer*, **370**, 258–61.

GARROD, D. J. and NEWELL, B. S. (1958) 'Ring formation in *Tilapia esculenta*', *Nature, Lond.*, **181**, 1411–12.

GASS, I. G. (1973) 'The Red Sea depression: causes and consequences' in *Implications of continental drift to the earth sciences*, vol. 2, ed. D. H. Tarling and S. K. Runcorn, Academic Press Inc., pp. 779–85.

GEE, J. M. (1968) 'A comparison of certain aspects of the biology of *Lates niloticus* (L) in endemic and introduced environments in East Africa, in *Man-made lakes: the Accra Symposium*, ed. L. E. Obeng, Ghana Univ. Press, pp. 251–9.

GEE, J. M. (1969) 'The establishment of a commercial fishery for *Haplochromis* in the Uganda waters of L. Victoria, Pt. III-1968', *E. Afr. Freshwat. Fish. Res. Org. Occas. Pap.*, no. 11.

GEE, J. M. and GILBERT, M. P. (1967) 'Experimental trawling operations in L. Victoria', in *E. Afr. Freshwat. Fish. Res. Org. Ann. Rep., 1966*, Jinja, Uganda.

GEISLER, R. (1969) 'Investigations about free oxygen, biological oxygen demand, and oxygen consumption of fishes in a tropical "blackwater" (Rio Negro, Amazonia, Brasil)', *Arch. Hydrobiol.*, **66**, 307–25 (in German, English summary).

GERY, J. (1960) 'New Cheirodontidae from French Guiana', *Senckenberg. biol'*, **41**, 15–39.

GERY, J. (1963) 'Systématique et évolution de quelques piranhas (*Serrasalmus*)', *Vie Milieu*, **14**, 597–617.

GERY, J. (1964) 'Poissons characoides nouveaux ou non signalés de l'Ilha do Bananal, Bresil', *Vie Milieu*, Suppl. no. 17, 447–71.

GERY, J. (1965) 'Poissons du bassin de l'Ivindo', *Biol. Gabonica*, 1, 375–93.

*GERY, J. (1969) 'The freshwater fishes of S. America', in *Biogeography and Ecology in S. America*, ed. Fittkau *et al.*, The Hague, vol. 2, 828–48.

GERY, J. and DELAGE, J. (1963) 'The pathological origin of the stratum argenteum in the "Brass Tetra"', *Trop. Fish. Hobbyist*, Dec. 1963, pp. 11–62 (translation of paper in *Vie Milieu*, 1963, **14**, 169–82).

GILSON, H. C. (1964) 'Lake Titicaca', *Verh. Internat, Verein Limnol.*, **15**, 112–27.

GODINHO, H. M. and BRITSKI, H. A. (1964) 'Peixes, in *Historia naturel de organismos aquaticos do Brasil, Bibliografia comentada*, ed. P. E. Vanzolini, Publ. Custeada pela Fundacaide Ampara a Pesquisa do Estado de S. Paulo, pp. 317–42.

GODOY, M. P. DE (1954) 'Locais de desovas de peixes num trecho do Rio Mogi Guassu,

Estado de Sao Paulo', *Revta bras. Biol.*, **14**, 375–96.

GODOY, M. P. DE (1959) 'Age, growth, sexual maturity, behaviour, migration, tagging and transplantation of the Curimbatá (*Prochilodus scrofa* Stdr, 1881) of the Mogi Guassu River, S. Paulo State, Brasil', *Anais Acad. bras. Cienc.*, **31**, 447–77.

GODOY, M. P. DE (1967) 'Dez anos de observações sôbre periodicidade migratoria de peixes do Rio Mogi Guassu', *Revta bras. Biol.*, **27**, 1–12.

GOSSE, J-P. (1963) 'Le milieu aquatique et l'écologie des poissons dans la région de Yangambi', *Annls. Mus. r. Afr. cent. Zool.*, ser. 8v, Sci. Zool., no. 116, pp. 113–270.

GREEN, J., CORBET, S. A. and BETNEY, E. (1973) 'Ecological studies on crater lakes in West Cameroon. The blood of endemic cichlids in Barombi Mbo in relations to stratification and their feeding habits', *J. Zool. Lond.*, **170**, 299–308.

GREENWOOD, P. H. (1955) 'Reproduction in the catfish *Clarias mossambicus* Peters', *Nature, Lond.*, **176**, 516.

GREENWOOD, P. H. (1956–67) 'A revision of the L. Victoria *Haplochromis* species (Pisces, Cichlidae)', pts i–vi, *Bull. Br. Mus. nat. Hist. (Zool.)*, vols. 3–15. **3**, 295–333; **4**, 233–44; **5**, 76–97, 179–218; **6**, 227–281; **9**, 139–214; **15**, 29–119.

GREENWOOD, P. H. (1958) 'Reproduction in the East African Lung-fish *Protopterus aethiopicus* Heckel', *Proc. zool. Soc. Lond.*, **130**, 547–67.

GREENWOOD, P. H. (1960) 'Fossil denticipitid fishes from E. Africa', *Bull. Br. Mus. nat. Hist.* (Geol.), **5**, 1–11.

GREENWOOD, P. H. (1965*a*) 'Environmental effects on the pharyngeal mill of a cichlid fish, *Astatoreochromis alluaudi*, and their taxonomic implications', *Proc. Linn. Soc. Lond.*, **176**, 1–10.

GREENWOOD, P. H. (1965*b*) 'On the cichlid fishes of L. Nabugabo, Uganda', *Bull. Br. Mus. nat. Hist. (Zool.)*, **12**, 313–57.

GREENWOOD, P. H. (1965*c*) 'Explosive speciation in African lakes', *Proc. roy. Instn Gt Br.*, **40**, 256–69.

*GREENWOOD, P. H. (1966) *The Fishes of Uganda*, 2nd rev. edn, Kampala, Uganda Society.

GREENWOOD, P. H. (1973*a*) 'A revision of the *Haplochromis* and related species (Pisces, Cichlidae) from L. George, Uganda', *Bull. Br. Mus. nat. Hist. (Zool.)*, **25**, no. 5, 141–242.

GREENWOOD, P. H. (1973*b*) 'Morphology, endemism and speciation in African cichlid fishes', *Verhandl. Deuts. Zool. Gesellsch. Jahresversamlung*, **66**, 115–24.

*GREENWOOD, P. H. (1974) 'The cichlid fishes of L. Victoria, East Africa: the biology and evolution of a species flock', *Bull. Brit. Mus. (Nat. Hist.), Lond., Zool. Suppl.*, **6**, 1–134.

GREENWOOD, P. H. and GEE, J. M. (1969) 'A revision of the L. Victoria *Haplochromis* species', pt vii, *Bull. Br. Mus. nat. Hist. (Zool.)*, **18**, 1–65.

GREENWOOD, P. H. and LUND, J., eds. (1973) 'A discussion on the biology of an equatorial lake: L. George, Uganda', *Proc. roy. Soc. Lond., B*, **184**, 299–319.

GREENWOOD, P. H. and PATTERSON, G. (1967) 'A fossil osteoglossoid from Tanzania', *J. Linn. Soc. (Zool.)*, **47**, 211–23.

GREENWOOD, P. H., ROSEN, D. E., WEITZMAN, S. H. and MYERS, G. S. (1966) 'Phyletic studies of Teleostean fishes, with a provisional classification of living forms', *Bull. Am. Mus. nat. Hist.*, **131**, 339–455.

HAFFNER, J. (1967) 'Speciation in Colombian forest birds west of the Andes', *Am. Mus. Novit.*, **2294**, 1–57.

HAMBLYN, E. L. (1966) 'The food and feeding habits of Nile Perch *Lates niloticus* (L) (Pisces: Centropomidae)', *Revue Zool. Bot. afr.*, **74**, 1–28.

HARRINGTON, R. W. Jr. (1967) 'Environmentally controlled induction of primary male gonochorists from eggs of the self-fertilising fish, *Rivulus marmoratus* Poey', *Biol. Bull. mar. biol. Lab. Woods Hole*, **132**, 174–99.

HENDERSON, H. F. and WELCOMME, R. L. (1974) 'The relationship of yield to morphoedaphic index and numbers of fishermen in African inland fisheries', *CIFA Occasional Paper* No. 1, FAO, Rome, 1–19.

HEPHER, B. (1967) 'Some biological aspects of warmwater fish pond management', in *The Biological Basis of Freshwater Fish Production*, ed. S. D. Gerking, Oxford, Blackwell Sci. Pubs.

*HICKLING, C. F. (1961) *Tropical Inland Fisheries*, Longmans.

HICKLING, C. F. (1967) 'On the biology of a herbivorous fish, the White Amur or Grass carp,

Ctenopharyngodon idella Val,', *Proc. roy. Soc. Edinburgh (Sect. b)*, **70** (1, no. 4), 62–81.

HICKLING, C. F. (1968) 'Fish hybridization', *Proc. World Sympos. Warm-water fish culture*, ed. T. V. R. Pillay, FAO, Rome, 1966, FR: IV/R-1:1-11.

*HICKLING, C. F. (1971) *Fish Culture*, rev. edn, Faber.

HOBSON, E. S. (1965) 'Diurnal-nocturnal activity of some inshore fishes in the Gulf of California', *Copeia*, **3**, 291–302.

HOBSON, E. S. (1968) 'Predatory behaviour of some shore fishes in the Gulf of California', *Res. Rep. U.S. Fish. Wildl. Serv.*, **73**, 1–92.

HOBSON, E. S. (1972) 'Activity of Hawaian reef fishes during the evening and morning transitions between daylight and darkness', *Fish. Bull. Fish. Wildl. Ser. U.S.*, **70**, 715–40.

HOLČIK, J. (1970) 'Standing crop, abundance, production and some ecological aspects of fish populations in some inland waters of Cuba', *Vestnik. Cs. spol. zool. (Acta soc. zool. Bohemoslov.)*, **34**, 184–201.

HOLDEN, M. J. (1963) 'The populations of fish in dry season pools of the R. Sokoto', *Fishery Publs Colon. Off.*, **19**, 1–58.

HOLDEN, M. J. (1967) 'The systematics of the genus *Lates* (Teleosti: Centropomidae) in L. Albert, East Africa', *J. Zool., Lond.*, **151**, 329–42.

HOLDEN, M. J. (1970) 'The feeding habits of *Alestes baremose* and *Hydrocynus forskali* (Pisces) in L. Albert, East Africa), *J. Zool. Lond.*, **161**, 137–44.

HOLLY, M. (1930) 'Synopsis der Süsswasserfische Kameruns', *Sber. Akad. Wiss. Wien*, **139**, 195–281.

*HOLT, S. J. (1967) 'The contribution of freshwater fish production to human nutrition and wellbeing', in *The Biological Basis of Freshwater Fish Production*, ed. S. D. Gerking, Oxford, Blackwell, pp. 455–67.

HOPKINS, C. D. (1972) 'Sex differences in electric signalling in an electric fish', *Science, N.Y.*, **176**, 1035–7.

HOPSON, A. J. (1969) 'A description of the pelagic embryos and larval stages of *Lates niloticus* (L). (Pisces, Centropomidae)', *Zool. J. Linn. Soc.*, **48**, 117–34.

*HOPSON, A. J. (1972) 'A study of the Nile Perch in L. Chad', *Overseas Res. Publ.*, no. 19, HMSO, London.

HOPSON, Jane (1972) 'Breeding and growth in two populations of *Alestes baremose* from the northern basin of Lake Chad', *Overseas Res. Publ.* no. 20, 1–50, HMSO.

*HORA, S. L. (1930) 'Ecology, bionomics and evolution of the torrential fauna, with special reference to the organs of attachment', *Phil. Trans. roy. Soc. Lond.*, **218**, 171–282.

HORA, S. L. (1937) 'Geographical distribution of Indian freshwater fishes and its bearing on the probable land connections between India and adjacent countries', *Curr. Sci. Bangalore*, **5**, 351–6.

HORA, S. L. (1949) 'Dating the period of migration of the so-called Malayan element in the fauna of Peninsular India', *Proc. natn. Inst. Sci. India*, **15**, 345–51.

HORA, S. L. (1950) 'Hora's Satpura hypothesis', *Curr. Sci.*, **19**, 364–70.

*HORA, S. L. *et al.* (1949) 'Symposium on Satpura hypothesis of the distribution of Malayan fauna and flora to Peninsular India', *Proc. natn. Inst. Sci. India*, **15**, 309–422.

HORA, S. L. and PILLAY, T. V. R. (1962) *Handbook of Fish Culture in the Indo-Pacific Region*, FAO Fish Biol. TP No. 14, 204.

HUET, M. (1957) 'Dix années de pisciculture au Congo Belge et au Ruanda-Urundi. Compte rendu de mision piscicolé, *Trav. Sta. Rech. Eaux Forêts, Groenendaal-Hoeilaart, Belgium*, ser. D, no. 22, 1–109.

HUET, M. (1972) *Textbook of Fish Culture: Breeding and cultivation of fish*, Fishing News (Books) Ltd. (translation by H. Kahn from 4th edition of *Traité de Pisculture*, Brussels, Ch. de Wyngaert (1970).

*HYNES, H. B. N. (1970) *The Ecology of Running Waters*, Liverpool University Press.

IHERING, R. VON (1929) *Da Vida dos Peixes*, S. Paulo, Comp. Melhoramentos.

IHERING, R. VON (1930*a*) 'Notas ecológicas referentes a peixes de água doce do estado de São Paulo e desciçao de 4 espécies novas', *Archos Inst. Biol. S. Paulo*, **3**, 93–103.

IHERING, R. VON (1930*b*) 'La piracema ou montée du poisson', *C. r. Seanc. Soc. Biol.*, **103**, 1336–8.

IHERING, R. VON, BARROS, J. DE and PLANET, N. (1928) 'Os ovulos e a desova dos peixes d'agua doce do Brasil', *Bolm biol. Bras, S. Paulo*, **14**, 97–109.
ILES, T. D. (1960) 'An opinion as to the advisability of introducing a non-indigenous zooplankton feeding fish into L. Nyasa', *CSA/CCTA 3rd Symp. Hydrobiol. Major Lakes*, p. 165.
ILES, T. D. (1971) 'Ecological aspects of growth in African cichlid fishes', *J. Cons. perm. int. Explor. Mer*, **33**, 362–84.
ILES, T. D. (1973) 'Dwarfing or stunting in the genus *Tilapia* (Cichlidae) a possibly unique recruitment mechanism', in *Fish Stocks and Recruitment*, ed. B. B. Parrish, *Rapp. Proc.-Verb. Réunions Cons. Int. Explor. Mer, Charlottenlund*, pp. 247–54.
ILES, T. D. and HOLDEN, M. J. (1969) 'Bi-parental brooding in *Tilapia galilaea* (Pisces, Cichlidae)', *J. Zool. Lond.*, **158**, 327–33.
INDRASENA, H. H. A. (1970) 'Limnological and freshwater fisheries development work in Ceylon', *Proc. International Biological Programme Regional meeting Inland water biol. SE Asia*, UNESCO, Djakarta: pp. 45–7.
INGER, R. F. (1955) 'Ecological notes on the fish fauna of a coastal drainage of North Borneo', *Fieldiana, Zool.*, **37**, 37–90.
INGER, R. F. and CHIN, P. K. (1962) 'The freshwater fishes of North Borneo', *Fieldiana, Zool.*, **45**, 1–268.
IVLEV, V. S. (1961) *Experimental Ecology of the Feeding of Fishes*, Yale University Press.
JACKSON, P. B. N. (1961*a*) 'Ichthyology: the fish of the Middle Zambezi', in *Kariba Studies*, Manchester University Press, pp. 1–36.
JACKSON, P. B. N. (1961*b*) 'The impact of predation especially by the Tiger fish (*Hydrocynus vittatus* Cast.) on African freshwater fishes', *Proc. zool. Soc. Lond.*, **136**, 603–22.
JACKSON, P. B. N. (1961*c*) *The fishes of Northern Rhodesia*, Govt. Printer, Lusaka.
JACKSON, P. B. N. (1963) 'Ecological factors affecting the distribution of freshwater fishes in tropical Africa', *Ann. Cape prov. Mus.*, **2**, 223–8.
JACKSON, P. B. N., ILES, T. D., HARDING, D. and FRYER, G. (1963) *Report on the Survey of Northern Lake Nyasa 1954–55*, Govt. Printer, Zomba.
JANZEN, D. H. (1970) 'Herbivores and the number of tree species in tropical forests', *Amer. Nat.*, **104**, 501–28.
JARDINE, N. and McKENZIE, D. (1972) 'Continental drift and dispersal and evolution of organisms', *Nature, Lond.*, **235**, 20–4.
JAYARAM, K. C. (1974) 'Ecology and distribution of freshwater fishes, amphibia and reptiles', pp. 517–84 in *Ecology and biogeography in India*, ed. M. S. Mani, *Monographiae Biologicae*, **23**, Dr W. Junk, The Hague, 773 pp.
JENSEN, K. W. (1957) 'Determination of age and growth of *Tilapia nilotica*, L, *T. galilaea* Art., *T. zillii* Gerv. and *Lates niloticus* C & V by means of their scales', *K. norske Vidensk. Selsk. Forh.*, **30**, 150–7.
JHINGRAN, V. G. (1968) 'Synopsis of biological data on Catla, *Catla catla* (Ham. 1822)', *FAO Fish. Synopsis* no. 32, Rev. 1 (FR/S 32 (Rev. 1)), Rome.
JOHANSEN, K. (1970) 'Air breathing in fishes', in *Fish Physiology* ed. Hoar and Randall, Academic Press, vol. 4, pp. 361–411.
JOHNELS, A. G. (1952) 'Notes on scale rings and growth of tropical fishes from the Gambia River', *Arkiv. Zool.* (ser. 2), 3 no. 28, 363–6.
JOHNELS, A. G. (1954) 'Notes on fishes from the Gambia River', *Ark. Zool.*, ser. 2, **6** no. 17, 327–411.
JOHNELS, A. G. and SVENSSON, G. S. O. (1954) 'On the biology of *Protopterus annectens*', *Ark. Zool.*, **7**, 131–64.
JOHNSON, D. S. (1967) 'Distributional patterns in Malayan freshwater fish', *Ecology*, **48**, 722–30.
JOINT FISHERIES RESEARCH ORGANIZATION (N. Rhodesia and Nyasaland) *Annual Reports*, Lusaka. (Discontinued and replaced by *Fish. Res. Bull. Zambia*.)
* JUBB, R. A. (1967) *Freshwater Fishes of Southern Africa*, Cape Town and Amsterdam, Balkema.
JUNK, W. J. (1973) 'Investigations on the ecology and production-biology of the "floating meadows" (Paspalo-Echinochloetum) on the Middle Amazon Pt II', *Amazoniana*, **4**, 9–102.
KAPETSKY, J. M. (1974) 'The Kafue River floodplain: an example of pre-impoundment

potential for fish production', in *Lake Kariba*, ed. E. K. Balon and A. G. Coche. Dr W. Junk, The Hague, pp. 497–523.

KEAST, A. (1972) 'Ecological opportunities and dominant families as illustrated by the Neotropical Tryannidae (Aves), pp. 229–77 in *Evolutionary Biology 5*, ed. Th. Dobzansky, M. K. Hecht and W. C. Steere, A. C. C. Meredith Corpn, pp. 229–77.

KEENLEYSIDE, H. A. (1955) 'Some aspects of the schooling behaviour of fish', *Behaviour*, **8**, 183–248.

KELLY, D. W. (1968) Fishery development in the Central Barotse flood plain. *UNDP Rept*, no. TA, 2554, FAO Rome, 1–83.

KETTLEWELL, H. B. D. (1959) 'Brazilian insect adaptations', *Endeavour*, **18**, no. 72, 200–10.

KHANNA, D. V. (1958) 'Observations on the spawning of major carps at a fish farm in the Punjab', *Indian J. Fish.*, **5**, 283–90.

KIENER, A. and MAUGE, M. (1966) 'Contributions à l'etude systematique et ecologique des poissons Cichlidae endemiques de Madagascar', *Mém. Mus. natn. Hist. nat., Paris, n.s.*, Ser. A. *Zool.*, **40**, 51–99.

KIENER, A. and RICHARD-VINDARD, G. (1972) 'Fishes of the continental waters of Madagascar', pp. 477–99 in *Biogeography and ecology in Madagascar*, eds. R. Battistini and G. Richard-Vindard, *Monographiae Biologicae*, **21**, Dr W. Junk, The Hague, 765 pp.

KIMPE, P. DE (1964) 'Contribution à l'étude hydrobiologique du Luapula-Moero', *Ann. Mus. r. Afr. Centr. 8vo, Sci. zool.*, **128**, 1–238.

KNÖPPEL, H-A. (1970) 'Food of Central Amazonian fishes', *Amazoniana*, **2**, no. 3, 257–352.

KNÖPPEL, H-A. (1972) 'Zur Nahrung tropischer Süsswasserfische aus Sudamerika', *Amazoniana*, **3**, 231–46.

KOSSWIG, W. (1963) 'Ways of speciation in fishes', *Copeia*, **2**, 238–44.

KOSSWIG, C. and VILLWOCK, W. (1965) 'Das problem der intralakustrischen Speziation im Titicaca- und Lanaosee', *Verh. dt. Zool. Ges., 1964*, pp. 95–102.

KRISTENSEN, I. (1970) 'Competition in three cyprinodont fish species in the Netherlands Antilles', *Uitg. natuurw. Stuckring. Suriname*, **32**, no. 119, 82–101.

KÜHME, W. (1963) 'Chemisch ausgelöste Brutflege- und Schwarm-reacktionen bei *Haplochromis bimaculatus* Peters', *Z. Tierpsychol.*, **20**, 688–704.

LACK, D. (1954) *The Natural Regulation of Animal Numbers*, Oxford, Clarendon Press.

LADIGES, W. (1968) 'Die Bedeutung ökologischen Faktoren für die Differenzierung der Cichlidae des Tanganyika- und der Njassa-Sees', *Int. Revue ges. Hydrobiol. Hydrogr.*, **53**, 339–52.

LAGLER, K. F., KAPETSKY, J. M. and STEWART, D. J. (1971) 'The fisheries of the Kafue flats, Zambia, in relation to the Kafue Gorge dam', *Univ. Michigan. Tech. Rept.*, FAO, Rome, no. FI:SF/ZAM 11 *Tech. Rept.*, **1**, 1–161.

LAUZANNE, L. (1972) 'Regimes alimentaires principales especes de poissons de l'archipel oriental du Lac Tchad', *Verh. int. Verein. Limnol.*, **18**, 636–46.

LAWSON, G. W., PETR, T., BISWAS, S., BISWAS, E. R. and REYNOLDS, J. (1969) 'Hydrobiological work of the Volta Basin Research Project', *Bull. Inst. fr. Afr. noire*, ser. A., **31**, 965–1005.

LE CREN, E. D. (1972) Fish production in freshwaters', *Symp. Zool. Soc. Lond.*, no. 29, pp. 115–33.

LE-VAN-DANG (1970) 'Contribution to a biological study of the Lower Mekong', *Proc. IBP Reg. Meeting Inland water biol. SE Asia*, UNESCO, Djakarta, pp. 65–90.

LELEK, A. and EL-ZARKA, S. (1973) 'Ecological comparison of the preimpoundment and postimpoundment fish faunas of the River Niger and Kainji Lake, Nigeria', in *Man-made lakes: their problems and environmental effects*, ed. W. C. Ackermann, G. F. White and E. B. Worthington, Geophysical Monogr., no. 17, American Geophysical Union, Washington, D.C., pp. 655–60.

LEWIS, D. S. C. (1974) 'The effects of the formation of L. Kainji (Nigeria) upon the indigenous fish population', *Hydrobiologia* **45**, 281–301.

LIEM, K. F. (1963) 'Sex reversal as a natural process in the Synbranchiform fish *Monopterus albus*', *Copeia*, No. 2, 303–12.

LIEM, K. F. (1968) 'Geographical and taxonomic variation in the pattern of natural sex reversal

in the teleost fish order Synbranchiformes', *J. Zool. Lond.*, **156**, 225–38.
LILEY, N. R. (1966) *Ethological Isolating Mechanisms in Four Sympatric Species of Poeciliid Fishes*, Leiden, E. J. Brill.
LISSMANN, H. W. (1958) 'On the function and evolution of electric organs in fish', *J. exp. Biol.*, **35**, 156–91.
LISSMANN, H. W. (1961) 'Ecological studies on gymnotids', in *Bioelectrogenesis*, ed. C. Chagas and A. Paes de Carvalho, Amsterdam, Elsevier, pp. 215–26.
*LISSMANN, H. W. (1963) 'Electric location by fishes', *Scient. Am.*, **208**, 50–9.
LISSMANN, H. W. and SCHWASSMANN, H. O. (1965) 'Activity rhythm of an electric fish, *Gymnorhamphichthys hypostomus* Ellis', *Z. vergl. Physiol.*, **51**, 153–71.
LONGHURST, A. R. (1971) 'The clupeid resources of tropical seas', *Oceanogr. Mar. Biol. Ann. Rev.*, **9**, 349–85.
LORENZ, K. (1962) 'The function of colour in coral reef fishes', *Proc. R. Instn. Gt. Britain*, **39**, 282–96.
*LORENZ, K. (1966) 'Coral fish in the laboratory', in *On Aggression*, Cox & Wyman, 1967, pp. 8–16.
LOUBENS, G. (1969) 'Etude de certains peuplements ichthyologiques par des peches au poison (lre note)', *Cah. Off. Rech. Scient. Tech. Outre-Mer Ser. Hydrobiol*, **3**, 45–73.
LOWE, R. H. (1952) 'Report on the *Tilapia* and other fish and fisheries of Lake Nyasa', *Fishery Publs Colon. Off.*, **1**, no. 2, 1–126, HMSO.
LOWE, R. H. (1953) 'Notes on the ecology and evolution of Nyasa fishes of the genus *Tilapia*, with a description of *T. saka* Lowe', *Proc. zool. Soc. Lond.*, **122**, 1035–41.
LOWE, R. H. (1955) 'The fecundity of *Tilapia* species', *E. Afr. agric. J.*, **11**, 45–52.
LOWE-McCONNELL, R. H. (1956) 'Observations on the biology of *Tilapia* (Pisces-Cichlidae) in L. Victoria, East Africa', *E. Afr. Fish. Res. Org., Suppl. Publ.* No. 1, pp. 1–72.
LOWE-McCONNELL, R. H. (1959*a*) 'Observations on the biology of *Tilapia nilotica* L. in East African waters', *Revue Zool. Bot. afr.*, **57**, 129–70.
LOWE-McCONNELL, R. H. (1959*b*) 'Breeding behaviour patterns and ecological differences between *Tilapia* species and their significance for evolution within the genus *Tilapia*', *Proc. zool. Soc. Lond.*, **132**, 1–30.
LOWE-McCONNELL, R. H. (1964) 'The fishes of the Rupununi savanna district of British Guiana. Pt. I. Groupings of fish species and effects of the seasonal cycles on the fish', *J. Linn. Soc. (Zool.)*, **45**, 103–44.
*LOWE-McCONNELL, R. H. ed. (1966) *Man-made Lakes*, Academic Press.
*LOWE-McCONNELL, R. H. ed. (1969*a*) *Speciation in Tropical Environments*, Academic Press.
LOWE-McCONNELL, R. H. (1969*b*) 'Speciation in Tropical freshwater fishes', *Biol. J. Linn. Soc.*, **1**, 51–75.
LOWE-McCONNELL, R. H. (1969*c*) 'The cichlid fishes of Guyana, S. America, with notes on their ecology and breeding behaviour', *Zool. J. Linn. Soc.*, **48**, 255–302.
LÜLING, K. H. (1963) 'Die Quisto Cocha und ihre häufigen Fische (Amazonia peruana)', *Beitr. Neotrop. Fauna*, **3**, no. 1, 34–56.
LÜLING, K. H. (1964) 'Zur biologie und ökologie von *Arapaima gigas* (Pisces: Osteoglossidae)', *Z. Morph. Ökol. Tiere*, **54**, 436–530.
LÜLING, K. H. (1970) 'Fishes of the Amazon headwaters', *Animals*, **13**, no. 2, 70–1.
LÜLING, K. H. (1971*a*) 'Ökologische Beobachtungen und Untersuchungen am Biotop des *Rivulus beniensis* (Cyprinodontidae)', *Neotropischen Fauna*, **6**, no. 3, 163–93.
LÜLING, K. H. (1971*b*) '*Aequidens vittata* (Heckel) und andere Fische des Rio Huallaga im Ubergangsbereich zur Hylaea', *Zool. Beitr.*, **17**, 193–226.
LÜLING, K. H. (1973) *Südamerikanische Fische und ihr Lebensraum*, Wuppertal/Elberfeld, Engelbert Pfriem.
MacARTHUR, R. H. and WILSON, E. O. (1967) *The Theory of Island Biogeography*, Princeton University Press.
McDONALD, A. L., HEIMSTRA, N. W. and DAMKOT, D. K. (1968) 'Social modification of agonistic behaviour in fish', *Anim. Behav.*, **16**, 437–41.
McKENZIE, D. P. and SCLATER, J. G. (1973) 'The evolution of the Indian Ocean', *Scient. Am.*, **228**, 62–72.

McLACHLAN, A. J. (1974) 'Development of some lake ecosystems in tropical Africa, with special reference to the invertebrates', *Biol. Rev.*, **49**, 365–97.

MAGO, F. M. L. (1970*a*) 'Estudios preliminares sobre la ecologia de los peces de los llanos de Venezuela', *Acta Biol. Venez.*, **7**, 71–102.

MAGO, F. M. L. (1970*b*) *Lista de los peces de Venezuela incluyendo un estudio preliminar sôbre la ictiogeografia del pais.* Ministerio de Agricultura y Cria Oficina Nacional de Pesda, Caracas, Venezuela.

MAGO, F. M. L. (1972) 'Consideraciones sôbre la sistematica de la familia Prochilodontidae con una sinopsis de las especies de Venezuela', *Acta Biol. Venez.*, **8**, 35–96.

MANI, M. S. (1974) 'Physical features' and 'Biogeographical evolution in India', pp. 11-58 and 698–722 in *Ecology and biogeography in India*, ed. M. S. Mani, *Monographiae Biologicae*, **23**, Dr W. Junk, The Hague, 733 pp.

MANN, K. (1964) 'The pattern of energy flow in the fish and invertebrate fauna of the R. Thames', *Verh. Int. Verein. Limnol.*, **15**, 485–95.

MANN, M. J. (1969) 'Freshwater fisheries', in *East Africa: its peoples and resources*, ed. W. T. W. Morgan, Oxford University Press, pp. 229–42.

MANTER, H. W. (1963) 'The zoological affinities of trematodes of South American freshwater fishes', *Syst. Zool.*, **12**, 45–70.

MARGALEF, R. (1963) 'On certain unifying principles in ecology', *Amer. Nat.* **97**, 357–74.

*MARGALEF, R. (1968) *Perspectives in Ecological Theory*, University of Chicago Press.

MARGALEF, R. (1969) 'Diversity, stability and productivity', in *Diversity and stability in ecological systems*, ed. G. M. Woodwell and H. H. Smith, Brookhaven Symposia Biology, no. 22.

MARLIER, G. (1960) 'Rapport sur le Lac Tumba', *CSA/CCTA 3rd Symp. Hydrobiol. Major Lakes*, pp. 75–80.

MARLIER, G. (1967) 'Ecological studies on some lakes of the Amazon valley', *Amazoniana*, **1**, 91–115.

MARLIER, G. (1968) 'Les poissons du lac Redondo et leur régime alimentaire; les chaînes trophiques du Lac Redondo; les poissons du Rio Prêto da Eva', *Cadernos Amazonia*, **11**, 21–57, Instituto Nacional de Pesquias da Amazonia, Manaus, Brazil.

MARLIER, G. (1969) 'Les eaux de l'Amazonie', *Nat. Belges*, **50**, 541–63.

MARLIER, G. (1973) 'Limnology of the Congo and Amazon rivers', in *Tropical Forest Ecosystems in Africa and South America: a comparative review*, ed. B. J. Meggers, E. S. Eyensu and W. D. Duckworth. Smithsonian Instn. Press, Washington, D.C., pp. 223–38.

MATTHES, H. (1961*a*) '*Boulengerochromis microlepis*, a L. Tanganyika fish of economical importance', *Bull. aquatic Biol.*, **3**, no. 24, 1–15.

MATTHES, H. (1961*b*) 'Feeding habits of some central African freshwater fishes', *Nature, Lond.*, **192**, 78–80.

MATTHES, H. (1962) 'L'exploration sous-lacustre du Lac Tanganyika', *Africa-Tervuren*, **8**, 1–11.

MATTHES, H. (1964) 'Les poissons du lac Tumba et de la region d'Ikela. Etude systematique et ecologique', *Annls Mus. r. Afr. cent. Sci. Zool.*, **126**, 1–204.

MATTHES, H. (1968) 'The food and feeding habits of the Tiger fish *Hydrocynus vittatus* (Cast. 1861) in L. Kariba', *Beaufortia*, **15** no. 201, 143–53.

MATTHES, H. (1973) *A Bibliography of African Freshwater Fish*, FAO, Rome.

MENEZES, N. A. (1969) 'The food of *Brycon* and three closely related genera of the tribe Acestrorhynchini', *Papéis Avulsos Zool. S. Paulo*, no. 20, 217–23.

MENON, A. G. K. (1951) 'Distribution of clariid fishes, and its significance in zoogeographical studies', *Proc. natn. Inst. Sci. India*, **17**, 291–9.

MENON, A. G. K. (1955) 'The external relationships of the Indian freshwater fishes, with special reference to the countries bordering on the Indian Ocean', *J. Asiatic Sci., Science*, **21**, 31–8.

MENON, A. G. K. (1973) 'Origin of the freshwater fish fauna of India', *Curr. Sci.*, **42**, no. 16, 553–6.

MESCHKAT, A. (1960) Report to the Government of Brazil on the fisheries of the Amazon region. BRA/TE/FI Rept. no. 1305, FAO, Rome.

MILES, C. (1947) *Los Peces del Rio Magdalena*, Min. Econ. Nac. Soc. Piscicultura, Bogota, Colombia.

MILES, C. W. (1973) 'Estudio económico y ecológico de los peces de agua dulce del Valle del Cauca', *Cespedesia*, **2**, no. 5, 9–63.

MILLER, R. R. (1966) 'Geographical distribution of Central American freshwater fishes', *Copeia*, **4**, 773–802.

MIYADI, D. (1960) 'Perspectives of experimental research on social interference among fishes', *Perspectives in Marine Biology*, ed. A. A. Buzzati-Traverso. University of California Press, pp. 469–79.

MIZUNO, T. and MORI, S. (1970) 'Preliminary hydrobiological survey of some Southeast Asian Inland waters', *Biol. J. Linn. Soc.*, **2**, 77–177.

MOE, M. A. jr. (1969) 'Biology of the Red Grouper *Epinephelus morio* (Val.) from the eastern Gulf of Mexico', *Florida State Bd Cons. Prof. Paper* no. 10, pp. 1–95.

MORGAN, N. C. (1972) 'Productivity studies at Loch Leven (a shallow nutrient-rich lowland lake)', *Proc. IBP-UNESCO Symp. on Productivity Problems of Freshwaters*, Kazimierz Dolny, pp. 183–205.

MORIARTY, C. M. (1973) 'Feeding of herbivorous fish in L. George, Uganda', Unpublished M.Sc. Thesis, University of Norringham.

MORIARTY, C. M. and MORIARTY, D. J. W. (1973) 'Quantitative estimation of the daily ingestion of phytoplankton by *Tilapia nilotica* and *Haplochromis nigripinnis* in Lake George, Uganda', *J. Zool., Lond.*, **171**, 15–23.

MORIARTY, D. J. W. (1973) 'The physiology of digestion of blue-green algae in the cichlid fish, *Tilapia nilotica*', *J. Zool., Lond.*, **171**, 25–39.

MORIARTY, D. J. W. and MORIARTY, C. M. (1973) 'The assimilation of carbon from phytoplankton by two herbivorous fishes: *Tilapia nilotica* and *Haplochromis nigripinnis*', *J. Zool., Lond.*, **171**, 41–55.

MORIARTY, D. J. W., DARLINGTON, J. P. E. C., DUNN, I. G., MORIARTY, C. M. and TEVLIN, M. P. (1973) 'Feeding and grazing in Lake George, Uganda', *Proc. roy. Soc. Lond.*, B, **184**, 299–319.

MORTIMER, C. F. and HICKLING, C. F. (1954) 'Fertilisers in fishponds', *Fishery Publs Colon. Off.*, **5**, 1–55.

MOTWANI, M. P. and KANWAI, Y. (1970) 'Fish and fisheries of the coffer-dammed right channel of the R. Niger at Kainji', in *Kainji Lake Studies*, vol. 1, *Ecology*, ed. S. A. Visser, *Nigerian Inst. Soc. Econ. Res.*, Ibadan University Press, pp. 27–48.

MUNRO, J. L. (1967) 'The food of a community of East African freshwater fishes', *Proc. zool. Soc. Lond.*, **151**, 389–415.

MURDOCH, W. W. (1969) 'Switching in general predators: experiments on predator specificity and stability of prey populations', *Ecol. Monogr.*, **39**, 335–54.

MYERS, G. S. (1947) 'The Amazon and its fishes', *Aquarium J.*, **18**, no. 3, pp. 4–9; **18**, no. 4, pp. 13–20; no. 5, pp. 6–13, 32; no. 7, pp. 8–19, 34.

MYERS, G. S. (1949) 'Salt tolerance of freshwater fish groups in relation to zoogeographical problems', *Bijdragen tot de Dierkunde*, **28**, 315–22.

MYERS, G. S. (1951) 'Freshwater fishes and East Indian zoogeography', *Stanford Ichthyol. Bull.*, **4**, 11–21.

MYERS, G. S. (1952) 'Annual Fishes', *Aquarium J.*, **23**, no. 7, 125–41.

MYERS, G. S. (1958) 'Trends in the evolution of Teleostean fishes', *Stanford Ichthyol. Bull.*, **7**, 27–30.

MYERS, G. S. (1960*a*) 'The endemic fauna of L. Lanao and the evolution of higher taxonomic categories', *Evolution, Lancaster, Pa.*, **14**, 323–33.

MYERS, G. S. (1960*b*) 'The South American characid genera *Exodon*, *Gnathopax* and *Roeboexodon*, with notes on the ecology and taxonomy of characid fishes', *Stanford ichthyol. Bull.*, **7**, 206–11.

MYERS, G. S. (1966) 'Derivations of the freshwater fish fauna of Central America', *Copeia*, **4**, 766–73.

MYERS, G. S. (1967) 'Zoogeographical evidence on the age of the South Atlantic Ocean', in *Studies in Tropical Oceanography, Miami*, **5**, 614–21.

MYERS, G. S. (1972) *The Piranha Book*, Trop. Fish. Hobby. Publs. Inc.

MYRBERG, A. A. (1964) 'An analysis of the preferential care of eggs and young by adult cichlid fishes', *Z. Tierpsychol.*, **21**, 53–98.

MYRBERG, A. A. (1966) 'Parental recognition of young in cichlid fishes', *Anim. Behav.*, **14**, 565–71.

MYRBERG, A. A. (1972*a*) 'Using sound to influence the behaviour of free-ranging marine animals' in *Behaviour of Marine Animals*, vol. 2, ed. Winn and Olla, Plenum Press, pp. 435–68.

MYRBERG, A. A. jr. (1972*b*) 'Ethology of the bicolor damselfish *Eupomacentrus partitus* (Pisces: Pomacentridae) a comparative analysis of laboratory and field behaviour', *Anim. Behav. Monogr.*, **5**, no. 3, 197–283.

MYRBERG, A. A., KRAMER, E. and HEINECKE, P. (1965) 'Sound production by cichlid fishes', *Science, N.Y.*, **149**, 555–8.

NEIL, E. H. (1964) 'An analysis of color changes and social behaviour of *Tilapia mossambica*', *Univ. Calif. Publs. Zool.*, **75**, 1–58.

NELSON, K. (1964*a*) 'Behaviour and morphology in Glandulocaudine fishes', *Univ. Calif. Publs Zool.*, **75**, 59–152.

NELSON, K. (1964*b*) 'Temporal patterning of courtship behaviour in the glandulocaudine fishes', *Behaviour*, **24**, 90–146.

NIKOLSKY, G. V. and VASILEV, B. P. (1973) 'O nekotorykh zakonomernostyakh v respredelenii chisla khromosoma u ryb', *Vop. Ikhtiol*, **13**(1), no. 78, 2–22.

NILSSON, N-A. (1967) 'Interactive segregation between fish species', in *The Biological Basis of Freshwater Fish Production*, ed. S. D. Gerking, Oxford, Blackwell, pp. 295–313.

OBENG, L. E. ed. (1968) *Man-made Lakes: the Accra symposium*, Ghana University Press.

OKEDI, J. (1968) 'Notes on the behaviour of the small mormyrid fishes of L. Victoria', *Rep. E. Afr. Freshwater. Fish. Res. Org. 1967*, Appendix E, pp. 42–8.

OKEDI, J. (1969) 'Observations on the breeding and growth of certain mormyrid fishes of the Lake Victoria basin', *Revue Zool. Bot. afr.*, **79**, 34–64.

OKEDI, J. (1970) 'A study of the fecundity of some mormyrid fishes from L. Victoria', *E. Afr. agric. For. J.*, **35**, 436–42.

OKEDI, J. (1971*a*) 'The food and feeding habits of the small mormyrid fishes of L. Victoria', *Afr. J. Trop. Hydrobiol. Fish.*, **1**, no. 1, 1–12.

OKEDI, J. (1971*b*) 'Maturity, sex ratio and fedundity of the lungfish (*Protopterus aethiopicus* Heckel) from Lake Victoria', *Repl. E. Afr. Freshwat. Fish. Res. Org. 1970*, pp. 17–20.

OKEDI, J. (1971*c*) 'Further observations on the ecology of the Nile Perch (*Lates niloticus*) in L. Victoria and L. Kyoga', *Rep. E. Afr. Freshw. Fish. Res. Org. 1970*, pp. 42–54.

ONODERA, K. (1967) 'Some aspects of behaviour influencing production', in *The Biological Basis of Fish Production*, ed. S. D. Gerking, Oxford, Blackwell, pp. 345–55.

OPPENHEIMER, J. R. (1970) 'Mouthbreeding in fishes', *Anim. Behav.*, **18**. 493–503.

PATRICK, R. (1964) 'A discussion of the results of the Catherwood Expedition to the Peruvian headwaters of the Amazon', *Verh. int. Verein. Limnol.*, **15**, 1084–90.

PAINE, R. T. (1966) 'Food web complexity and species diversity', *Am. Nat.*, **100**, 65–75.

PANTULU, V. R. (1973) 'Fishery problems and opportunities in the Mekong' in *Man-made lakes: their problems and environmental effects*, ed. W. C. Ackermann, G. F. White and E. B. Worthington, Geophysical Monogr., no. 17, American Geophysical Union, Washington, D.C., pp. 672–82.

PENNAK, R. W. (1971) 'Towards a classification of lotic habitats', *Hydrobiologia*, **38**, no. 2, 321–34.

PETERS, H. M. (1963) 'Eizahl, Eigewicht und Gelegeentwicklung in der Gattung *Tilapia* (Cichlidae)', *Int. Revue ges. Hydrobiol.*, **48**, no. 4, 547–76.

PETR, T. (1967) 'Fish population changes in the Volta Lake in Ghana during the first sixteen months', *Hydrobiologia*, **30**, 193–220.

PETR, T. (1968*a*) 'The establishment of lacustrine fish population in the Volta lake in Ghana during 1964–1966', *Bull. Inst. fr. Afr. noire*, **30**, ser. A, no. 1, 257–69.

PETR, T. (1968*b*) 'Distribution, abundance and food of commercial fish in the Black Volta and Volta man-made lake in Ghana during its first period of filling (1964–1966). I Mormyridae', *Hydrobiologia*, **32**, 417–48.

PETR, T. (1971) 'Lake Volta – a progress report', *New Scient.*, **49**, no. 736, 178–82.
PFIEFFER, W. (1962) 'The fright reaction of fishes', *Biol. Rev.*, **37**, 495–511.
PIANKA, E. R. (1970) 'On *r* and *K* selection', *Am. Nat.*, **100**, 593–7.
PILLAY, T. V. R. (1958) 'Biology of the Hilsa, *Hilsa ilisha* (Hamilton) of the R. Hooghly, *Indian J. Fish.*, **5**, 201–57.
PILLAY, T. V. R. ed. (1967–68) *Proceedings of the World Symposium on Warm-water pond fish culture*, Rome, May 1966. *FAO Fish Rep.*, no. 44, 5 vols, FAO, Rome.
POLL, M. (1950) 'Histoire du peuplement et origine des espèces de la faune ichthyologique du Lac Tanganyika', *Annls Soc. r. zool. Belg.*, **81**, 111–40.
POLL, M. (1953–6) *Résult, scient. Explor. hydrobiol. Lac Tanganika* (1946–7), 1953 Poissons non Cichlidae, **3** (5A), 1–251; 1956 Poissons Cichlidae, **3** (5B), 1–619.
POLL, M. (1956*b*) 'Ecologie des poissons du lac Tanganyika', *Proc. 14 Congr. Zool. Copenhagen, 1953*, pp. 465–8.
POLL, M. (1957) 'Les genres des poissons d'eau douce de l'Afrique', *Annls Mus. r. Congo Belge, Sci. Zool.*, **54**, 1–191.
POLL, M. (1959*a*) 'Recherches sur la faune ichthyologique de la region du Stanley Pool', *Annls Mus. r. Congo Belge, Sci. Zool.*, **71**, 75–174.
POLL, M. (1959*b*) 'Aspects nouveau de la fauna ichthyologique du Congo Belge', *Bull. Soc. Zool. France*, **84**, 259–71.
POLL, M. (1963) 'Zoogéographie ichthyologique du cours supérieur du Lualaba', *Publs Univ. Elizabethville*, **6**, 95–104.
POLL, M. (1966) 'Géographie ichthyologique de l'Angola', *Bull. Séanc. Acad. r. Sci. Outre-Mer, 1966–2*, pp. 355–65.
POLL, M. (1967) 'Revision des Characidae nains Africains', *Annls. Mus. r. Afr. cent.*, ser. 8, *Sci. Zool.*, **162**, 1–158.
POLL, M. (1969) 'Les poissons a appareil acoustique', *Africa-Tervuren*, 15–1969–3, 1–6.
POLL, M. (1971) 'Revision des *Synodontis* africains (family Mochocidae)', *Annls Mus. r. Afr. cent., Sci. Zool.*, **191**, 1–497.
POLL, M. (1973) 'Nombre et distribution géographique des poissons d'eau douce africains', *Bull. Mus. natn. Hist. nat., Paris*, 3 sér., no. 150, Ecologic généralc 6, 113–28.
POLL, M. and GOSSE, J. P. (1963) 'Contribution à l'étude systématique de la faune ichthyologique du Congo Central', *Annls Mus. r. Afr. centr., Sci. Zool.*, **116**, 43–110.
POLL, M. and GOSSE, J. P. (1969) 'Révision des Malapteruridae et description d'une deuxième espiece de silure éléctrique *Malapterurus microstoma* sp.n.', *Bull. Inst. r. Sci. nat. Belg.*, **45**, no. 38, 1–12.
POLL, M. and RENSON, H. (1948) 'Les poissons, leur milieu et leur peche au bief superieur du Lualaba', *Bull. Agric. Congo. Bclgc*, **39**, no. 2, 427 46.
PUYO, J. (1949) *Poissons de la Guyane française*, Paris, Off. Rech. Scient. Tech. Outre-Mer.
QASIM, S. Z. and QAYYUM, A. (1961) 'Spawning frequencies and breeding seasons of some freshwater fishes with especial reference to those occurring in the plains of northern India', *Indian J. Fish.*, **8**, 24–43.
RABANAL, H. R. (1968) 'Stock manipulation and other biological methods of increasing production of fish through pond culture in Asia and the Far East'. Proc. World Sympos. Warm-water pond fish culture, ed. Pillay, *FAO, Fish. Rept.*, no. 44, FAO, Rome, vol. 4, 274–88.
RANDALL, J. E. (1963) 'An analysis of the fish population of artificial and natural reefs in the Virgin Islands', *Caribb. J. Sci.*, **3** no. 1, 31–47.
RASA, O. A. E. (1969) 'Territoriality of the establishment of dominance by means of visual clues in *Pomacentrus jenkinsi* (Pomacentridae)', *Z. Tierpsychol.*, **26**, 825–45.
REGAN, C. T. (1929) 'Fishes', in *Encyclopedia Britannica*, 14th edn.
REGIER, H. A. and COWELL, E. B. (1972) 'Applications of ecosystem theory, succession, diversity, stability, stress and conservation', *Biological Conservation*, **4** (2), 83–8.
REGIER, H. A. and WRIGHT, R. (1972) 'Evaluation of fisheries resources in African freshwaters', *Sympos. eval. fish. res., Fort Lamy, Chad, 1972*, FAO, Rome CIFA/72/S.3, 1–14.
REINBOTH, R. (1971) 'Intersexuality in fishes' in *Hormones and the Environment*, ed. G. K. Benson and J. G. Phillips, Mem. Soc. Endocrinol., No. 18, CUP, pp. 515–41.
REYNOLDS, J. D. (1969) 'The biology of the clupeids in the new Volta Lake', in *Man-made*

lakes: the Accra symposium, ed. L. E. Obeng, Ghana University Press, pp. 195–203.
REYNOLDS, J. D. (1970) 'Biology of the small pelagic fishes in the new Volta Lake in Ghana. Pt. I, The lake and the fish: feeding habits', *Hydrobiologia*, **35**, 568–603.
REYNOLDS, J. D. (1971) 'Pt II, Schooling and migration', *ibid.*, **38**, 79–91.
*RICKER, W. E., ed. (1971) *Methods for Assessment of Fish Production in Freshwaters*, IBP Handbook no. 3, 2nd edn, Oxford, Blackwell.
RINGUELET, R. A., ARAMBURU, R. H. and ALONSO DE ARAMBURU, A. (1967) *Los Peces Argentinos de Agua Dulce*, Comision de Investigacion Cientifica, B.A., La Plata.
ROBERTS, T. R. (1969) 'Osteology and relationships of characoid fishes, particularly of the genera *Hepsetus*, *Salminus*, *Hoplias*, *Ctenolucius*, and *Acestrorhynchus*', *Proc. Calif. Acad. Sci.*, **36**, 391–500.
ROBERTS, T. R. (1970) 'Scale-eating American characoid fishes, with especial reference to *Prolodus heterostomus*', *Proc. Calif. Acad. Sci.*, 4th ser., **38**, no. 20, 383–90.
*ROBERTS, T. R. (1972) 'Ecology of fishes in the Amazon and Congo basins', *Bull. Mus. comp. Zool. Harv.*, **143**, no. 2, 117–47.
ROBERTS, T. R. (1973*a*) 'Osteology and relationships of the Prochilodontidae, a S. American family of characoid fishes', *Bull. Mus. Comp. Zool. Harv.*, **145**, 213–35.
ROBERTS, T. R. (1973*b*) 'Interrelationships of Ostariophysians', in *Interrelationships of fishes*, ed. P. H. Greenwood, R. S. Miles and C. Patterson, Zool. J. Linn. Soc. Lond., vol. 53, suppl. no. 1, pp. 372–95.
ROBISON, B. H. (1972) 'Distribution of the mid-water fishes in the Gulf of California', *Copeia*, 3, 448–61.
RYDER, A. (1965) 'A method for estimating the potential fish production of north-temperate lakes', *Trans. Am. Fish. Soc.*, **94**, 214–18.
RZOSKA, J. (1974) 'The Upper Nile swamps, a tropical wetland study', *Freshwater biol.*, 4, 1–30.
*RZOSKA, J. ed. (in preparation) 'The Nile, biological portrait of an ancient river', Monographiae Biologicae, Dr W. Junk, The Hague.
SAIGAL, B. N. (1964) 'Studies on the fishery and biology of the commercial catfishes of the Ganga R. system. II. Maturity, spawning and food of *Mystus (Osteobagrus) aor* (Hamilton)', *Indian J. Fish.*, 11, no. 1, sect. A, pp. 1–44.
SAIGAL, B. N. and MOTWANI, M. P. (1961) 'Studies on the fisheries and biology of the commercial catfishes of the Ganga R. system. I. Early life history, bionomies and breeding of *Mystus seenghala* (Sykes)', *Indian J. Fish.*, **8**, 60–74.
SCHEEL, J. (1968) *Rivulins of the Old World*, Trop. Fish. Hobby., New Jersey.
SCHUBART, O. (1943) 'A pesca na Cachoeira de Emas do Rio Mogi-Guacu durante a piracema de 1942–1943', *Bolm Ind. anim. N.S.*, **6**, 93–116.
SCHUBART, O. (1953) 'Ubereinem subtropischen Fluss Brasiliens, den Mogi-Guassu, insbesondered seine physikalischen Bedingungen wie Wasserstand, Temperatur und Sichttiefe', *Arch. Hydrobiol.*, **48**, 350–430.
SCHUBART, O. (1954) 'A piracema no Rio Mogi Guassu (Estado Sao Paulo)', *Dusenia*, **5**, no. 1, 49–59.
SCHWASSMANN, H. O. (1971) 'Biological rhythms', in *Fish Physiology VI*, ed. W. S. Hoar and Randall, Academic Press, pp. 371–428.
SHIRAISHI, Y. (1970) 'The migration of fishes in the Mekong River', *Proc. IBP Reg. Meeting Inland water. Biol. SE Asia*, UNESCO, Djakarta, pp. 135–40.
SIOLI, H. (1964) 'General features of the limnology of Amazonia', *Verh. int. Verein. Limnol.*, **15**, 1053–8.
SIOLI, H. (1967) 'Studies in Amazonian waters', in *Atas do Simposio sôbre a Biota Amazonica*, vol. 3, *Limnologia*, Conselho Nac. Pesquisas, Rio de J., pp. 8–50.
SIOLI, H. (1968) 'Principal biotopes of primary production in the waters of Amazonia', *Proc. Symp. Recent Adv. Trop. Ecol.*, pp. 591–600.
SLOBODKIN, L. B. and SANDERS, H. L. (1969) 'On the contribution of environmental predictability to species diversity', in *Brookhaven Symposia Biology* no. 22, ed. Woodwell and Smith, pp. 82–95.
SMITH, C. L. and TYLER, J. C. (1972) 'Space resource sharing in a coral reef community',

Bull. nat. Hist. Mus. Los Angeles, **14**, 125–78.

SMITH, H. M. (1945) 'The freshwater fishes of Siam, or Thailand', *Bull. U.S. natr. Mus.*, **188**, 1–622.

SMITH, N. G. (1967) 'Visual isolation in gulls', *Scient. Am.*, **217**, no. 4, 94–102.

SOCOLOF, R. (1972) *Aequidens paraguayensis*, a new mouthbrooding cichlid', *Advanced Aquarists Magazine*, Atlanta, Georgia, Sept. 1972, 6–7.

SREENIVASAN, A. (1964) 'Limnological studies and fish yields in three upland lakes of Madras State, India', *Limnol. Oceanogr.*, **9**, 564–75.

STAUCH, A. (1966) 'Le bassin Camérounais de la Benoué et sa pêche', *Mém. Off. Rech. Scient. Tech. Outre-Mer.*, Paris, 1–152.

STEVENSON, R. A. jr. (1972) 'Regulation of feeding behavior of the bicolor damsel fish (*Eupomacentrus partitus* Poey) by environmental factors', in *Behaviour of Marine Animals*, vol. 2, *Vertebrates*, ed. H. E. Winn and B. L. Olla, Plenum Press, pp. 278–302.

SVENSSON, G. S. O. (1933) 'Freshwater fishes from the Gambia River', *Kungl. Svenska Vetenskapsakad. Handl. Stockholm*, **12**, 1–102.

TAIT, C. C. (1967) 'A note on cormorant predation in the Kafue River', *Fish. Res. Bull. Zambia*, 3 (1964–65), p. 32.

TALLING, J. F. (1966) 'The annual cycle of stratification and phytoplankton growth in L. Victoria (E. Africa)', *Int. Revue ges. Hydrobiol.*, **51**, 545–621.

TARLING, D. H. (1972) 'Another Gondwanaland', *Nature, Lond.*, **238**, 92–3.

TARLING, D. H. and RUNCORN, S. K. (1973) '*Implications of continental drift to the earth sciences*', Academic Press. 2 vols.

TAVERNE, L. (1972) 'Considérations générales sur la systématique des poissons de l'ordre des Mormyriformes', *Annls Mus. r. Afr. centr., Sci. Zool.*, **200**, 1–194.

TESCH, F. W. (1971) 'Age and growth', in *Methods for Assessment of Fish Production in Freshwaters*, ed. W. E. Ricker, 2nd edn. IBP Handbook no. 3, Oxford, Blackwells, pp. 98–130.

THOMAS, J. D. (1966) 'On the biology of the catfish *Clarias senegalensis* in a man-made lake in the Ghanaian savanna with particular reference to its feeding habits', *J. Zool. Lond.*, **148**, 476–514.

THORPE, J. E. (1974) 'Trout and perch populations at Loch Leven, Kinross', *Proc. Roy. Soc. Edinb.* (B), 74, 295–313.

THORSON, T. B. (1972) 'The status of the Bull shark *Carcharinus leucas* in the Amazon River', *Copeia*, 3, 601–5.

THYS VAN DEN AUDENAERDE, D. F. E. (1968) 'An annotated bibliography of *Tilapia*', *Mus. r. Afr. Centr., Tervuren, Document. Zool.*, no. 14, 1–406.

*TODD, J. H. (1971) 'The chemical language of fishes', *Scient. Am.*, **224**, no. 5, 98–108.

TREWAVAS, E. (1933) 'Scientific results of the Cambridge expedition to the East African lakes, 1930–31: The cichlid fishes', *J. Linn. Soc. (Zool.)*, **38**, 309–41.

TREWAVAS, E. (1947) 'An example of mimicry in fishes', *Nature, Lond.*, **160**, 120.

TREWAVAS, E. (1973) 'On the cichlid fishes of the genus *Pelmatochromic* with proposal of a new genus for *P. congicus*; on the relationship between *Pelmatochromis* and *Tilapia* and the recognition of *Sarotherodon* as a distinct genus', *Bull. Br. Mus. Nat. Hist.*, **25**, 1–26.

TREWAVAS, E., GREEN, J. and CORBET, S. A. (1972) 'Ecological studies on crater lakes in West Cameroon: Fishes of Barombi Mbo', *J. Zool. Lond.*, **167**, 41–95.

TRIPATHI, S. D., CHAKROBORTI, P. K. and KHAN, R. R. (1962) *Bibliography of Indian Fisheries and Allied Subjects*, Central Inl. Fish. Res. Inst., Barrackpore, W. Bengal.

TURNER, C. L. (1938) 'Adaptations for viviparity in embryos and ovary of *Anableps anableps*', *J. Morphol. Philadelphia*, **62**, 323–49.

VAAS, K. F. (1952) 'Fisheries in the lake district along the R. Kapuas in West Borneo', *Proc. Indo-Pacific Fish. Council*, Sect. II(10), pp. 1–10.

VAAS, K. F. and SACHLAN, M. (1952) 'Notes on fisheries exploitation of the artificial lake Tjiburuj in West Java', *Contr. Agric. Res. Sta. Bogor*, no. 128, pp. 1–22.

VAAS, K. F. and SCHUURMAN, J. J. (1949) 'On the ecology and fisheries of some Javanese freshwaters', *Med. Alg. Proefst. Landb. Buitenzorg, Java*, no. 97, pp. 1–60.

VAAS, K. F., SACHLAN, M. and WIRAATMADJA, G. (1953) 'On the ecology and fisheries of some inland waters along the Rivers Ogan and Komering in S.E. Sumatra', *Contr. Inl. Fish.*

Res. Sta. Bogor, Indonesia, no. 3, pp. 1–32.

VAN DOBBEN, W. H. and LOWE-McCONNELL, R. H., ed. 1975 '*Unifying concepts in ecology*', Dr W. Junk, The Hague.

VAN SOMEREN, V. D. and WHITEHEAD, P. J. (1959–60) 'The culture of *Tilapia nigra* (Gunther) in ponds', *E. Afr. agric. J.*, **25**, no. 1, 42–6; **25**, no. 2, 66–72; **26**, no. 2, 79–86; **26**, no. 4, 202–9; **27**, no. 1, 11–12; **27**, no. 3, 176–84.

VERBEKE, J. (1957) 'Le régime alimentaire des poissons du lac Kivu (Congo Belge et Ruanda) et l'exploitation des ressources naturelles du lac', *Résult. scient. Explor. hydrobiol lacs Kivu, Edouard et Albert* (1952–1954), 3, no. 2, 1–24.

VERBEKE, J. (1959) 'Le régime alimentaire des poissons des lacs Edouard et Albert (Congo Belge)', *ibid.*, **3**, no. 3, 1–66.

VILLWOCK, W. (1972) 'Gefahren für die endemische Fischfauna durch Einbürgerungsversuche und Akklimatisation von Fremdfischen am Beispiel des Titicaca-Sees (Peru-Bolivien) und des Lanao-Sees (Mindanao/Philippinen)', *Verh. int. Verein. Limnol.*, **18**, 1227–34.

WEITZMAN, S. H. (1962) 'The osteology of *Brycon meeki*, a generalized characoid fish, with an osteological definition of the family', *Stanford Ichthyol. Bull.*, **8**, 1–77.

WELCOMME, R. L. (1964) 'The habitats and habitat preferences of the young of the L. Victoria *Tilapia* (Cichlidae)', *Revue Zool. Bot. afr.*, **70**, 1–28.

WELCOMME, R. L. (1966) 'Recent changes in the stocks of *Tilapia* in L. Victoria', *Nature, Lond.*, **212**, 52–4.

WELCOMME, R. L. (1967*a*) 'Observations on the biology of the introduced species of *Tilapia* in L. Victoria', *Revue Zool. Bot. afr.*, **76**, 249–79.

WELCOMME, R. L. (1967*b*) 'The relationship between fecundity and fertility in the mouth-brooding cichlid fish *Tilapia leucosticta*', *J. Zool. Lond.*, **151**, 453–68.

WELCOMME, R. L. (1969) 'The biology and ecology of the fishes of a small tropical stream', *J. Zool. Lond.*, **158**, 485–529.

WELCOMME, R. L. (1970) 'Studies of the effects of abnormally high water levels on the ecology of fish in certain shallow regions of L. Victoria', *J. Zool. Lond.*, **160**, 405–36.

WELCOMME, R. L. (1971) 'An evaluation of the acadja method of fishing as practised in the coastal lagoons of Dahomey (W. Africa)', *J. Fish. Biol.*, **4**, 39–55.

WELCOMME, R. L. (1972*a*) The inland waters of Africa (maps and data), CIFA/TI FAO, Rome.

WELCOMME, R. L. (1972*b*) 'A description of certain indigenous fishing methods from southern Dahomey', *Afr. J. Trop. Hydrobiol. Fish.*, **2**, no. 1, 129–40.

WELCOMME, R. L. (1973) 'A brief review of the floodplain fisheries of Africa', *Afr. J. Trop. Hydrobiol. Fish.* (Nairobi) Special Issue I, 67–76.

WHITEHEAD, P. J. (1959) 'The anadromous fishes of L. Victoria', *Revue Zool. Bot. afr.*, **59**, 329–63.

WHITEHEAD, P. J. (1962) 'A new species of *Synodontis* and notes on a mormyrid fish from the eastern rivers of Kenya', *Revue Zool. Bot. afr.*, **65**, 97–120.

WHITTAKER, R. H. and WOODWELL, G. M., ed. (1972) 'Evolution of natural communities', in *Ecosystem structure and function*, ed. J. A. Wiens, Oregon State University Press, pp. 137–56.

WICKLER, W. (1962) '"Egg Dummies" as natural releasers in mouth-breeding cichlids', *Nature, Lond.*, **194**, 1092–3.

WICKLER, W. (1967) 'Specialization of organs having a signal function in some marine fish', *Stud. Trop. Oceanogr., Miami*, **5**, 539–48.

WILLIAMS, R. (1971) 'Fish ecology of the Kafue River and flood plain environment', *Fish. Res. Bull. Zambia*, **5**, 305–30.

WINDELL, J. T. (1971) 'Food analysis and rate of digestion', in *Methods for Assessment of Fish Production in Freshwaters*, ed. W. E. Ricker, 2nd edn, IBP Handbook no. 3, Oxford, Blackwells, pp. 215–26.

WOODWELL, G. M. and Smith, H. H., ed. (1969) 'Diversity and stability in ecological systems', *Brookhaven Symposia Biology*, no. 22, pp. 1–264. Assoc. Univ. Inc. and U.S. Atomic Energy Commission (BNL 50175 (C-56).

WORTHINGTON, E. B. and RICARDO, C. K. (1936) 'Scientific results of the Cambridge Expedition to the East African lakes, 1930–31. The fish of L. Rudolf and L. Baringo', *J. Linn. Soc. (Zool.)*, **39**, 353–89.

WYMAN, R. K. and WARD, J. A. (1972) 'A cleaning symbiosis between the cichlid fishes *Etroplus maculatus* and *E. suratensis*. I. Description and possible evolution', *Copeia*, **4**, 834–8.

*WYNNE-EDWARDS, V. C. (1962) *Animal Dispersion in Relation to Social Behaviour*, Oliver & Boyd.

ZARET, T. M. and RAND, A. S. (1971) 'Competition in tropical stream fishes: support for the competitive exclusion principle', *Ecology*, **52**, 336–42.

ZUMPE, D. (1965) 'Laboratory observations on the aggressive behaviour of some Butterfly fishes (Chaetodontidae)', *Z. Tierpsychol*, **22**, 226–36.

Addendum

FAO (1973*b*) 'List of publications and documents 1948–1973', Fisheries Circular No. 100, Revision 2, FAO, Rome.

FLORES, R. F. (1974) 'Algumas espécies de interesse econômico da fauna ictiológica Amazônica', SUDEPE (Superintendência do Desenvolvimento da Pesca), Ministério da Agricultura, Rio de J. (cyclostyled report).

GWAHABA, J. J. (1973) 'Effects of fishing on the *Tilapia nilotica* (L) population of L. George, Uganda, over the past 20 years', *E.Afr. Wildl.J*, **11**, 317–28.

*HOEDEMAN, J. J. (1974) *'Naturalists' guide to fresh-water aquarium fish'*, Sterling Pub. Co. Inc., New York, pp. 1152.

JANZEN, D. H. (1974) 'Tropical blackwater rivers, animals, and mast fruiting by the Dipterocarpaceae', *Biotropica*, **6**, 69–103.

KAPETSKY, J. M. (1974) 'The Kafue River floodplain: an example of pre-impoundment potential for fish production', In *Lake Kariba: a man-made tropical ecosystem in Central Africa*, ed. E. K. Balon and A. G. Coche, Monographiae Biologicae, 24, Dr W. Junk, the Hague, pp. 497–523.

MARGALEF, R. (1963) 'On certain unifying principles in ecology', *Amer. Nat.* **97**, 357 74.

MAY, R. M. (1975) 'Stability in ecosystems: some comments', In *Unifying concepts in ecology*, ed. W. H. van Dobben and R. H. Lowe-McConnell, Dr W. Junk, The Hague.

MICHA, J. C. (1974) 'Fish populations study of Ubangui River; trying local wild species for fish culture', *Aquaculture*, **4**, 85–7.

ORIANS, G. H. (1975) Diversity, stability and maturity in natural ecosystems', In *Unifying concepts in ecology*, ed. W. H. van Dobben and R. H. Lowe-McConnell, Dr W. Junk, The Hague.

RAND, A. S. (1967) 'Predator-prey interactions and the evolution of aspect diversity', *Atas do Simpósio sôbre a Biota Amazonica, Rio de J. vol.* **5** (Zoologia), pp. 73–83.

REYNOLDS, J. D. (1974) 'Biology of small pelagic fishes in the new Volta lake in Ghana. Pt. III. Sex and reproduction', *Hydrobiologia* **45**, 489–508.

ROBERTS, T. (in press). 'Geographical distribution of African freshwater fishes', *Zool. J. Linn Soc.*

SREENIVASAN, A. (1970) 'Energy transformations through primary productivity and fish production in some freshwater impoundments and ponds', In *Productivity problems of freshwater*, ed. Z. Kajak and A. Hillbricht-Ilkowska, IBP-UNESCO Symposium Kazimierz Dolny, Poland, pp. 505–14.

WELCOMME, R. L. (1974) 'The freshwater ecology of African floodplains', FI:FPSZ/74/14, 1–40, FAO, Rome.

Index

Author Index

(For joint authors see entries under first-named author)

Index of Fish Names

(For family names see Appendix 2, pp. 274–7)

General Index